THE WORLD TO 1500

張 兩
九〇. 三. 清华

L. S. STAVRIANOS

The World to 1500
A GLOBAL HISTORY

Prentice-Hall, Inc.   *Englewood Cliffs, N.J.*

THE WORLD TO 1500:
A Global History

BY L. S. STAVRIANOS

13-968123-X

Library of Congress Catalog Card Number: 72-102096

Printed in the United States of America

Current printing (last digit):

10 9 8 7 6 5 4 3 2

PRENTICE-HALL INTERNATIONAL, INC., *London*
PRENTICE-HALL OF AUSTRALIA, PTY., LTD., *Sydney*
PRENTICE-HALL OF CANADA, LTD., *Toronto*
PRENTICE-HALL OF INDIA PRIVATE LTD., *New Delhi*
PRENTICE-HALL OF JAPAN, INC., *Tokyo*

Acknowledgments

While assuming full responsibility for all facts and interpretations in this book, I take pleasure in acknowledging the generous help of Speros Vryonis, Jr., of the University of California, Los Angeles, and of the following colleagues at Northwestern University who read and criticized individual chapters: Robert E. Lerner, John R. McLane, James E. Sheridan, and Stuart Struever.

I am also deeply appreciative of the patience and warm interest in the venture shown by Mr. Robert P. Fenyo, history editor of Prentice-Hall, Inc.

My son, Peter, has rendered invaluable research assistance to the point of virtual joint authorship of this volume, and I gratefully acknowledge his essential contribution.

Finally I should like to extend my thanks to the Carnegie Corporation of New York, which has contributed generously to the World History Project at Northwestern University, of which this study is a product. Another product is *A Global History of Man* (1962) in which I presented an abbreviated and simplified version of the approach to world history followed in this volume.

Grateful acknowledgment is made to the following authors and publishers for permission for quotation of the epigraphs:

On the page following the Contents—Étienne Gilson, *Les Meta-morphoses de la Cité de Dieu* (Paris: Publications Universitaires de

Louvain, 1942); Chapter 1—Geoffrey Barraclough, *History in a Changing World* (Oxford: Basil Blackwell & Mott, Ltd., 1955), p. 18; Chapter 2—Clyde Kluckhohn, *Mirror for Man* (New York: McGraw-Hill Book Company, 1949), p. 11; Chapter 3—R. J. Braidwood, "Near Eastern Prehistory," *Science*, Vol. 127 (June 20, 1958), 1419–30; Chapter 11—Robert Lopez, *The Birth of Europe*, © 1962 by Max Leclerc et Cie., Proprietors of Librairie Armand Colin and © 1966 translation by J. M. Dent & Sons, Ltd., and published in 1967 by M. Evans and Company Inc., New York, by arrangement with J. M. Dent & Sons, Ltd.; Chapter 12—Lynn White, Jr., "Tibet, India, and Malaya as Sources of Western Medieval Technology," *American Historical Review*, XLV (April, 1960), 515, 526; Chapter 15—William Carroll Bark, *Origins of the Medieval World* (Stanford: Stanford University Press, 1958), p. 66; Chapter 17—Lynn White, Jr., "Technology and Invention in the Middle Ages," *Speculum*, XV (1940), 156; Chapter 20 —Arnold J. Toynbee, *Civilization on Trial*, © 1948 by Oxford University Press, Inc.

The paragraphs from *The New York Times* quoted on pages 69–70 of the text are cited with permission (© 1957 by *The New York Times* Company). The quotation on page 209 of the text from *Everyday Life in Early Imperial China*, by Michael Loewe, is reprinted by permission of G. P. Putnam's Sons. Text © 1968 by Michael Loewe.

Illustrations appearing on the cover and on page ii are (*clockwise from top*): Shiva Nataraja (The Metropolitan Museum of Art, Purchase 1964—Harris Brisbane Dick Fund); ivory pendant mask, 16th century, Southern Nigeria (The Bettmann Archive); drawing of a seal of one of the early Caliphs; Aztec stone mask representing the god Xipe Totec (The Granger Collection); terracotta mounted figure from Central Asia, Hunnic period (Arborio Mella); detail from an ancestral tablet, from Elema, Papuan Gulf; Mycenean gold mask of Agamemnon (Gabriele Wunderlich); (*center*) Chinese mirror back showing Taoist deities (Museum of Fine Arts, Boston).

Cover design by Margaret Tsao.

This book is for
RAY ALLEN BILLINGTON
esteemed teacher and cherished friend

OTHER BOOKS BY L. S. STAVRIANOS:

The Balkans, 1815–1914

*Balkan Federation: A History of the Movement Toward
    Balkan Unity in Modern Times*

The Balkans Since 1453

The Epic of Modern Man: A Collection of Readings, editor

A Global History of Man (with others)

Greece: American Dilemma and Opportunity

The Ottoman Empire: Was It the Sick Man of Europe?

Readings in World History, editor (with others)

The World Since 1500: A Global History

Contents

MAPS BY THEODORE R. MILLER

*Past events make us pay particular
attention to the future, if we
really make thorough enquiry
in each case into the past.*

POLYBIUS

*. . . during this period history becomes,
so to speak, an organic whole.
What happens in Italy and in Libya is
bound up with what happened in Asia and in
Greece, all events culminating in a single
result. . . . Consequently separate
histories must be regarded as of very
little use in arriving at a realistic
conception of the total picture.
For it is only by exposing side by side
the threads that connect each event
with the whole complex, and also by
pointing out resemblances and
differences, that it becomes possible
to achieve this, and to be able to
derive profit as well as enjoyment
from the study of history.*

POLYBIUS

*The throes of the contemporary world are
those of a birth. And what is being born
with such great pain is a universal
human society. . . . What characterizes
the events we witness, what distinguishes
them from all preceding events
back to the origins of history is . . .
their global character.*

ETIENNE GILSON

MAN BEFORE
CIVILIZATION

Part I is concerned with man's two million years before civilization. The other parts of the book are devoted to man's history since he became civilized, less than six thousand years ago. Thus, by far the longest phase of man's evolution will receive by far the briefest consideration. The reason for the disproportionate emphasis on the story of civilized man is the constantly accelerating tempo of human history. Geologic time is measured in billions of years, and man's prehistory in millennia; but since the advent of civilization, the chronological unit has shrunk progressively to centuries and to decades, until fateful events now daily crowd us, unceasingly and inexorably. Indeed the pace of change has reached such proportions that it is a very real question whether the human species is capable of adjusting with sufficient dispatch to avoid obsolescence, or even extinction.

The disparity in the pace of events, and the corresponding disparity in emphasis in this study, should not lead us, however, to minimize the significance of what happened during prehistory. During those millennia, two developments provided the bedrock foundation for all later history. One was the gradual transition from primate to man—from hominid to Homo sapiens. The other was the transformation of the human newcomer from a food gatherer who was dependent on the bounty of nature to a food producer who became increasingly independent of nature—the master of his destiny. These two epochal events—the making of man and the advent of agriculture—are the subjects of the two chapters of Part I.

Although early man took those fateful first steps that were prerequisites for the future of his species, the fact remains that they were only first steps. In the process of becoming a thinking animal, man learned to use words and tools and fire; and in becoming a food producer, he learned to plant and to use the hoe and scythe. This technology placed him in an entirely different category from that of the animals about him, and yet it was a primitive technology compared to that which was to follow. The contrast is apparent if a stone hatchet or a flint-tipped scythe is placed beside a modern computer or space ship. Though the difference is self-evident, it needs to be underscored here because it explains the steady extension of the range of human activity, to be noted in the introduction to each part of this book.

The more primitive the technology, the more constricted its range of operation; conversely, the more advanced the technology, the more extensive its range. In prehistoric times, the food gatherer perforce was restricted to the few square miles of his hunting grounds; the early cultivator, to his village and the surrounding fields and pastures. Thus the range of prehistoric human communities may be defined as being "local." The later history of man, depicted in the following pages and in The World Since 1500, *was in large part the history of the extension of that range from local dimensions to regional, inter-regional, global, and planetary.*

. . . universal history is more than Chapter
the sum of its parts; it cannot be divided
and subdivided without being denaturalized,
much as water, separated into its chemical
components, ceases to be water and
becomes hydrogen and oxygen.

GEOFFREY BARRACLOUGH

Introduction:

Nature of World History

T he distinctive feature of this book is that it is a *world* history. It deals with the entire globe rather than with some one country or region. It is concerned not with Western man or non-Western man, but with all mankind. The viewpoint is that of an observer perched on the moon, surveying our planet as a whole, rather than that of one who is ensconced in London or Paris, or for that matter, in Peking or Delhi.

I. WHY WORLD HISTORY?

This global approach to history represents a new departure in modern historiography. Since the days of the Enlightenment in the eighteenth century the emphasis has been on the nation rather than on mankind. But in recent years, interest in world history has been growing largely as a reaction to the manifestly global sweep of contemporary events. With astronauts and cosmonauts encircling the entire planet in a few hours and even reaching the moon, and with newspaper headlines concerned fully as much with Asia and Africa as with Europe and the Americas, it is increasingly recognized that a wider angle of

3

vision is needed. World history is manifestly essential for the understanding of a world that has become "one" in reality as well as in rhetoric.

This utilitarian function, however, is not the only reason for turning to world history. Equally important is the fact that the story of man from its very beginnings has a basic unity that must be recognized and respected. Neither Western nor non-Western history may be properly comprehended without a global overview encompassing both. Only then is it possible to perceive the degree of interaction amongst all peoples at all times, and the primary role of that interaction in determining the course of human history.

It is true that the interaction was fitful and inconsiderable until Columbus and da Gama set forth on their overseas explorations. Within a few decades they and their successors brought all parts of the world into direct contact, and the intimacy of that contact has grown steadily to the present day. By contrast, the various human communities prior to 1500 had existed in varying degrees of isolation. Yet this isolation was never absolute. During the long millennia before the European discoveries, the various branches of the human race in fact had interacted one with the other, though the precise degree varied enormously according to time and location. The details of this interaction comprise essentially the subject of this book for the period to 1500. And following that date, the earth, in relation to man's growing communication and transportation facilities, has shrunk at such an accelerating tempo that it is now a "spaceship earth," and "global village."

II. STRUCTURE OF WORLD HISTORY

If the fact of a common world history shared by all mankind is accepted, then there arises the question of its pedagogical viability. Frequently it is stated that since world history, by definition, encompasses all civilizations, it is far too broad a subject for classroom purposes. Western civilization, it is pointed out, is barely manageable by itself; how can all the other civilizations—including the Chinese, the Indian, and Middle Eastern—also be encompassed? The answer, of course, is that they cannot, and that world history, *thus defined,* is obviously impracticable. But such a definition is inaccurate and misleading. World history is *not* the sum of histories of the civilizations of the world, in the same manner that Western history is *not* the sum of the histories of the countries of the West.

If the study of Western civilization involved successive surveys of British history, German history, French, Italian, Spanish, Balkan, and the rest, then this obviously would not be a feasible subject of study. Yet, in fact, it is feasible, and the reason is that the approach is not agglomerative. Rather it focuses on those historical forces or movements that affected the West as a whole, such as Christianity, Islam, the Crusades, the Renaissance, the Reformation, the French Revolution, the scientific and industrial revolutions, and so forth. So it is with world history, though the stage in this case is global rather than regional, and the emphasis consequently is on movements of worldwide influence.

In Paleolithic times, for example, there was the emergence in Africa of man himself and his gradual dispersal through Eurasia, Australia, and the

Americas. During the Neolithic period occurred the fateful breakthrough to agriculture, followed by metalworking and assorted other crafts, and leading to urban life and civilization—all of which diffused outward in all directions from their Middle East center of origin. This in turn led to the development of the great Eurasian civilizations—the Chinese, Indian, Middle Eastern, and European—which for millennia developed autonomously along parallel lines, though with varying degrees of interaction as a result of powerful interregional historical forces such as Hellenism, Christianity, Buddhism, and the recurring invasions from the Central Eurasian steppes. After 1500 this Eurasian balance gradually gave way to a global unity imposed by an emerging West and culminating in the nineteenth century in an unprecedented worldwide hegemony. Finally, the essence of twentieth-century world history is the growing reaction against this hegemony and the perilous groping toward a new world balance necessitated by the rapid diffusion of Western technology and ideology. Such, in capsule form, is the rationale and structure of world history.

III. GEOGRAPHY OF WORLD HISTORY

Just as the structure of world history is commonly assumed to be the sum of the histories of the world's civilizations, so the geography of world history is assumed to be the sum of the continents comprising the earth's surface. This latter assumption is as mechanical and misleading as the former. The traditional division of the globe into continents, useful though it may be for the student of geography, has little meaning for the student of world history. For the same reason that the structure of world history requires focusing on historical movements that have had major influence on man's development, so the geography of world history requires focusing on those regions that initiated those historical movements.

When this is done, one land unit stands out uniquely and unchallengeable: Eurasia, the veritable heartland of world history since Neolithic times. Eurasia encompasses two-fifths of the total land surface of the globe, and nine-tenths of the world's population. Within its confines developed the most advanced and most enduring civilizations. To an overwhelming degree, the history of man is the history of those Eurasian civilizations.

The distinguished anthropologist Franz Boas makes an observation that contains perhaps the chief reason for Eurasia's predominance:

> The history of mankind proves that advances of culture depend upon the opportunities presented to a social group to learn from the experience of their neighbors. The discoveries of the group spread to others and, the more varied the contacts, the greater the opportunities to learn. The tribes of simplest culture are on the whole those that have been isolated for very long periods and hence could not profit from the cultural achievements of their neighbors.[1]

In other words, *if other geographic factors were equal,* the key to human progress has been accessibility. Those with the most opportunity to interact with other people have been the most likely to forge ahead. Indeed they were driven to do so, for there was selective pressure as well as opportunity. Accessibility involved the constant threat of assimilation or elimination if opportunity was not grasped. By contrast, those who were isolated received neither stimulus nor threat, were free from selective pressure, and thus could remain relatively unchanged through the millennia without jeopardizing their existence.

The Eurasian peoples obviously were the prime beneficiaries of this principle of accessibility. All were accessible to each other. They stimulated and threatened each other at an increasing tempo through the ages, as technological advances facilitated communication amongst the regions of Eurasia.

These regions need to be defined, for Eurasia is too large a land mass to be viewed as a single unit. Nor may Eurasia be defined as the combination of Europe and Asia, for this definition is both geographically and historically misleading. Geographically, Europe obviously is not equivalent or comparable to Asia. A glance at the map shows that Europe is a peninsula of the Eurasian land mass, corresponding, for example, to the Indian Peninsula. Historically, also, Europe is comparable not to Asia but to another Eurasian center of civilization, of which again India provides a good example. Thus Europe and India are intelligible equivalents in territorial extent, size and variety of population, and complexity of culture and historical traditions. From the viewpoint of world history, therefore, Eurasia should be viewed as comprising not the two continents of Europe and Asia, but five historically meaningful regions: the Middle East, India, China, Europe, and the Central Eurasian steppes.

The fertile river valleys and plains of the first four regions gave rise to the great historical civilizations that together have been responsible for the vital role of Eurasia as the heartland of world history. More specifically, the innovative center or "core" of the Middle East comprised the Nile and Tigris-Euphrates valleys and the Iranian Plateau; in India, the center was the Indus and Ganges valleys; in China, the Yellow and Yangtze valleys; and in Europe, the northern shore of the Mediterranean, which was economically and culturally dominant from Minoan times to the late Middle Ages. It should be added that Europe as defined here includes North Africa, because this area historically has usually had closer ties with Europe and the Middle East than with the lands south of the great Sahara barrier. It follows that the term "Africa" henceforth refers to sub-Saharan Africa.

The Central Eurasian steppes comprise the endless grasslands stretching from Manchuria in the east to Hungary in the west and provide an overland channel of communication amongst the centers of civilization strung out in Eurasia's periphery. These steppes supported nomadic herdsmen who were ever on the move with their flocks and who were always ready, when opportunity presented itself, to grasp at the riches of Peking, Delhi, Baghdad, and Rome. Fertile valleys and plains created the ancient core civilizations of Eurasia, but the steppes facilitated contact amongst these civilizations, either by peaceful communication along overland trade routes or by the ceaseless nomadic raids from the arid interior to the provocatively affluent periphery. Thus the history of Eurasia was to a great extent molded by this interaction between nomadic tribes and sedentary civilizations. The continual raids, which periodically built up into elemental and wide ranging movements of peoples, were regenerative as well as destructive. They swept away fossilized dynasties, institutions, and practices, introduced new peoples, techniques, and ideas, and determined in large degree the course of Eurasian history. The ancient, the classical, and the medieval periods of pre-1500 Eurasian history—the three broad historical periods that will be studied in this volume—were heralded by major turning points primarily attributable to these nomadic invasions.

The non-Eurasian world was made up of the three remaining land masses: Africa, the Americas, and Australia. Viewed in the light of the principle of accessibility, their disadvantage compared to Eurasia is apparent. They had no contact whatsoever with each other.

Africa alone had a physical connection with Eurasia, yet even here the interaction was tenuous and intermittent because of formidable geographic barriers between Africa and Eurasia, and within Africa itself. Nevertheless the progress of the Africans did rest in large part on outside stimuli such as the introduction of agriculture, of ironworking, and of new plants and animals. Consequently, in the Sudanic lands immediately to the south of the Sahara, Africans were able to organize a succession of medieval empires that were comparable in certain respects to those of contemporary Europe.

The American Indians, by contrast, were relatively handicapped by virtue of their complete isolation after crossing over from northeast Asia over 15,000 years ago. Their general level of development was not equal to that of the Africans, though they did develop impressive civilizations in Mexico, Central America, and Peru.

Finally, the Australian aborigines were the most retarded, having been cut off on their remote island continent for some 30,000 years. They all remained at the food-gathering stage, in contrast to the Africans, who had large Sudanic empires in addition to Hottentot and Pygmy food gatherers, and the American Indians, who had the advanced Aztec, Inca, and Maya civilizations along with food gatherers in California and Tierra del Fuego. Indeed Australia's isolation in the South Pacific had led not only to the retardation of human culture but also to the survival of archaic forms of flora and fauna, such as the eucalyptus plant, the monotremes, and the marsupials.

Such, then, was the understandable diversity of human societies encountered by the Europeans when they set out on their explorations from the fifteenth century onward. The spectrum ranged from the ancient and sophisticated civilizations of Eurasia, through the mixture of imperial structures and food-gathering bands in Africa and the Americas, to the unrelieved Paleolithic level prevailing throughout Australia.

This global pattern determines the organization of this book. For the period to 1500, the emphasis is on the Eurasian civilizations, which were incomparably more advanced and consequently made correspondingly greater contributions to human development during those millennia. Thus Parts II, III, and IV are devoted to the evolution of the Eurasian civilizations, while Part V summarizes the developments in the non-Eurasian world.

SUGGESTED READING

The most recent overall treatment of world history has been provided by W. H. McNeill, *The Rise of the West: A History of the Human Community* (Chicago:

Univ. of Chicago, 1963) and the abbreviated version in *A World History* (New York: Oxford Univ., 1967). UNESCO's multivolume *History of Mankind: Cultural and Scientific Development* is now in preparation, with three volumes published thus far by Harper & Row: J. Hawkes and L. Woolley, *Prehistory and the Beginnings of Civilization* (1963); L. Pareti, *The Ancient World 1200 B.C. to A.D. 500* (1965); C. F. Ware, K. M. Panikkar and J. M. Romein, *The Twentieth Century* (1966). See also UNESCO's *Journal of World History* published since 1953. Standard studies of restricted periods of world history are R. Turner, *The Great Cultural Traditions: The Foundations of Civilization* (New York: McGraw-Hill, 1941), 2 vols., and V. Gordon Childe, *What Happened in History* (Baltimore: Penguin, 1942) for the period to the end of Rome; J. Bowle, *Man Through the Ages, from the Origins to the Eighteenth Century* (Boston: Little, Brown, 1962); L. S. Stavrianos, *The World Since 1500: A Global History* (Englewood Cliffs, N. J.: Prentice-Hall, 1966); G. Barraclough, *An Introduction to Contemporary History* (New York: Basic Books, 1964); and D. Thomson, *World History 1914–1961* (London: Oxford Univ., 1963, 2nd ed.).

Anthropology holds up a great mirror Chapter
to man and lets him look at himself
in his infinite variety.

2

CLYDE KLUCKHOHN

Man the Food Gatherer

One of the outstanding yet little-recognized achievements of modern man is his study and reconstruction of the past. The ancients had little comprehension of what had preceded them. Thucydides, the most objective of Greek historians, began his study of the Peloponnesian War by stating that nothing of great importance had happened before his time. His ignorance of history prevented him from recognizing the unique glory and contribution of Athens. By contrast, our age is more history minded than any other. We know more about the early history of the Egyptians, the Greeks, or the Chinese than they themselves knew. Furthermore, scientists in various fields—geology, archeology, anthropology, paleontology and biology—have extended our knowledge back before the beginning of civilization with its written records. This is of prime importance, for it was only about five thousand years ago that man learned to write, whereas his hominid beginnings have been traced back some two million years. We shall consider these long prehistoric millennia when man became man, yet at the same time contrived to sustain himself, as did the other animals about him, by collecting food wherever it was to be found, rather than by growing it as his agriculturist descendants were to learn to do.

I. Origins of Man

Our earth is a minor planet spinning in a minor galaxy. Compared to the entire universe it is inconceivably small—literally like a speck of dust on the Pacific Ocean. It took form about 4.5 billion years ago, and the first life appeared on it some 1.5 billion years later as single-celled creatures. This life traditionally has been viewed as qualitatively different from nonlife, but scientists no longer accept this assumed dichotomy between organic and inorganic. Rather they view living matter as having evolved naturally from nonliving matter. They classify all matter in a hierarchy of states of organization. At a certain level in this hierarchy the transition occurs from inorganic to organic. More specifically, electrons, protons, and neutrons combine to form atoms, the atoms form molecules, and the molecules become more or less well-organized aggregates, one class of which constitutes living matter.

Organic matter in turn underwent a comparable hierarchical evolution: from the original microorganisms to primitive plants such as seaweeds, to animals without backbones such as jellyfish and worms, and to backboned animals. These vertebrates, with some of their invertebrate and plant cousins, began their successful adaptation to life on land about 300 million years ago. First came the amphibians, then the great army of prehistoric reptiles, the birds, and finally the mammals; and for the past sixty million years, mammals have been the dominant form of life on earth.

Scientists accept without question the proposition that man belongs to the animal kingdom—more specifically to the order of the Primates, which he shares with the tree shrews, lemurs, tarsiers, monkeys, and apes. The evidence accumulated from several fields of study all lead to this conclusion. Anatomists have found basic similarities between men and the other higher animals in the general plan of their skeletal, muscular, and organic structures. Embryologists have noted that the human embryo displays, at different stages of its development, characteristics of some of the lower forms of life, such as gill arches at the end of one month and a rudimentary tail at two months. Anthropologists have shown that man's fossil remains demonstrate a consistent trend away from the general anthropoid type towards Homo sapiens. Other scientists have discovered many similar indications of man's ties to the other animals, including close resemblance between the chemical composition of the blood of apes and of man, possession of common parasites, and similarities in their ways of learning.

The differentiation of the human stock occurred during the Pleistocene epoch with its four glacial and three interglacial periods. These drastic environmental changes compelled all animals to adapt and readapt themselves continually to new conditions. Success in this crucial matter depended not upon brute strength nor upon the ability to resist cold, but rather upon the continuous growth of intelligence and the use of that intelligence to work out satisfactory adaptations. This, of course, is the secret of man's unchallenged primacy on earth. He has been, first and foremost, a generalist. He never adapted exclusively to one type of environment, as the gibbon did to the forest with his long lithe arms, or the polar bear to the arctic with his heavy white fur. Rather man adapted with his brain, which he then used to adapt to any environment.

At one time, it was assumed that man and the apes had developed from a common ancestor, and the task of anthropologists was to find the "missing link" between the two. Now it is agreed that Homo sapiens is the product of natural selection from a succession of manlike ancestors, or hominids, some of which were capable of using simple stone tools and weapons. The earliest of these hominids was Australopithecus, believed to have appeared first in the savannas of eastern and southern Africa some two and a half million years ago, though recent findings in southern Ethiopia indicate that the date may go as far back as four million years. The pelvis and leg of this hominid were strikingly similar to that of modern man, but his cranial capacity was only about one-third that of man, or hardly larger than that of living apes. Thus a manlike bipedal locomotive system was combined with an apelike brain. The low level of intelligence meant a correspondingly low level of speech and of toolmaking. The significance of this sequence is that the human brain did not appear first and then proceed to create human culture. Rather there was interaction back and forth. Speech and tool were both the causes and the effects of brain development.

The African savannas were ideal for primates at that level of development. The climate was warm enough to make the lack of clothing bearable, and the open grasslands, in contrast to dense forests and deserts, afforded both water and animal foods. Thus, despite their simple pebble tools with their single cutting edges, the australopithecines subsisted on an adequate diet including eggs, crabs, tortoises, birds, rodents, and young antelopes. The latter were easy prey because they "freeze" in the grass when faced with danger.

Australopithecus gave way about half a million years ago to man's immediate ancestor, the hominid Homo erectus. His brain was about twice as large as that of his australopithecine predecessor, or two-thirds that of modern man. His generalized stone tool, the fist hatchet, was more complex. It was the first overall designed tool, usually almond shaped, from six to eight inches long, several inches wide, and about one inch thick. The butt end was rounded for grasping in the palm of the hand, while the other end was pointed and sharpened on one side. It was used for all purposes—hand ax, knife, scraper, or awl. The huge quantities of skeletal remains of large slaughtered animals—deer, rhinos, pigs, elephants, buffalo, hippos, horses, antelopes and gazelles—demonstrate the effective use made of this tool. Such large-scale hunting of big game also reflects efficient group organization and action, including speech communication. Another indication of social life is the first evidence of reverence for the dead. Fossils of hominid bodies have been found that had been covered with earth upon which red ochre or hematite had been scattered. Almost certainly this represented some kind of ritual burial. Along the same lines there is evidence of the dawn of the decorative sense in the beads and perforated teeth and shells that have been found in association with the fossils. Finally there are the all-important telltale signs of fire making—circular dark discs in the soil, five to six inches in diameter.

The mastery of fire had fundamental and far-reaching repercussions. It freed man's ancestors from the bondage of the limited energy supply of their own bodies. It helped them to survive the advancing glaciers of the ice ages. It increased tremendously the available food supply by making possible the cooking of a great range of roots and seeds that hitherto had been inedible. Fire also made it possible for the hominids to break out of the warm savanna in which they had thus far been confined, to begin their dispersal throughout the globe, with repercussions being felt to the present day. (See Map I, "Tentative Global Distribution of Hominids and Homo Sapiens.")

II. MEANING OF MAN

The evolutionary process culminating in man was finally completed about 35,000 years ago with the appearance of Homo sapiens, or "thinking man." Viewed in broadest perspective, this represents the second major turning point in the course of events on this planet. The first occurred when life originated out of inorganic matter. After that momentous step, all living forms evolved by adapting to their environments through mutation and natural selection. That is, genes adapted to environment, as was evident during the climatic turmoil of the Pleistocene. But with the appearance of man, the evolutionary process was reversed. No longer did genes adapt to environment; instead, man adapted by changing the environment to suit his genes. Today, a third epochal turning point appears imminent, as man's growing knowledge of the structure and function of genes may soon enable him to modify his genes as well as his environment.

Man, and only man, has been able to create a made-to-order environment, or culture, as it is called. The reason is that only man can symbolize, or envision things and concepts divorced from here-and-now reality. Only he laughs, and only he knows that he will die. Only he has wondered about the universe and its origins, about his place in it and in the hereafter.

With these unique and revolutionizing abilities, man has been able to cope with his environment without mutations. His culture is the new non-biological way of having fur in the arctic, water storage in the desert, and fins in the water. More concretely, culture consists of tools, clothing, ornaments, institutions, language, art forms, and religious beliefs and practices. All these have served to adapt man to his physical environment and to his fellowman. Indeed, the story of man as related in the following chapters is simply the story of a succession of cultures that he has created, from his Paleolithic origins to the present day.

III. CULTURE OF THE FOOD GATHERERS

Just as Homo erectus had been able to fashion a more effective tool than his australopithecine predecessor, so now Homo sapiens with his superior intelligence developed the so-called "blade technique." He used the long, sharp flakes, or "blades," struck off the core of a stone to fashion a variety of new tools as well as "tools to make tools." The degree of technological progress is revealed by the estimate that whereas the australopithecines had produced only 5 centimeters of cutting edge per pound of flint, and Homo erectus, 100

Detail from American Museum of Natural History representation of a Neolithic village in Denmark, about 2700 B.C. (Courtesy of the American Museum of Natural History)

centimeters, man in the upper Paleolithic produced 300 to 1200 centimeters of cutting edge per pound.

Some of the new tools were composite, such as spears with hafted heads of bone, antler, or flint, and flint blades set in bone or wooden handles. Another departure was the construction of projectiles such as the bola, sling, spear thrower, and bow and arrow. The latter must have been relatively inefficient at first, but it was gradually improved until it became the most formidable weapon prior to modern firearms. Other inventions of the upper Paleolithic included bone and ivory bodkins, bone needles with eyes, belt fasteners, and even buttons—all of which indicate that the Magdalenian hunters wore sewn skin garments with fitting sleeves and trousers.

Although this technology of the late Paleolithic was advanced compared to that of the early Paleolithic half a million years earlier, it still was primitive in the sense that productivity was low. Food gatherers and hunters led a precarious hand-to-mouth existence. Normally they were able to support themselves and their dependents, but no surplus was left over for other purposes. This was profoundly significant, for it set inexorable limits to the evolution of the food gatherers' culture.

There was no possibility, for example, for an elaborate political structure for it simply could not be supported. Indeed, there was no formal political structure with full-time political leaders. Rather the hunters formed autonomous bands that usually numbered twenty to fifty persons, though larger groups were possible and did exist in areas that yielded plentiful food supplies, such as the American Northwest, with its inexhaustible salmon runs, and the Dordogne valley in southern France, with its great reindeer herds in Magdalenian times. Judging from contemporary hunting societies, authority in Paleolithic times was rigidly limited and lacking in established and recognized coercive power. Leaders arose naturally for specific purposes; an old man might be the accepted planner of ceremonies because of his ritual knowledge, while a younger person with proven skill in the chase might take the lead of hunting parties. But the important point is that all such leaders were more persons of influence than of authority, since there were no institutions for imposing one's will upon others.

Social organization necessarily was as simple as the political, if indeed the two can be distinguished at this stage. The basic unit was the family, consisting of the parents and their immature and unmarried children. Extra wives usually were permitted but in practice polygamy was rare. Intra- and inter-family relationships rested on kinship ties. Each one had duties towards the others and in turn enjoyed rights and privileges. They helped each other in the quest for food and in providing shelter from the elements and defense from their enemies. Some fighting between tribal groups arose from personal feuds and from competition for hunting and fishing grounds. But Paleolithic society lacked both the manpower and the resources essential for sustained large-scale warfare, which was not possible until the coming of agriculture with its greatly increased productivity and correspondingly increased population. In short, the essence of Paleolithic social organizations was cooperation. Families and bands were primarily mutual aid societies, working together in the harsh struggle for existence.

This cooperation was evident in economic matters as well as social. No specialization was needed amongst hunters, except on a sex basis. Every man and woman possessed all the knowledge and skills proper to their sex and functioned accordingly. During the early Paleolithic, women collected fruits, nuts, and grains and grubbed up roots and insects, while men caught small game and fish. At that level there was little to choose between the sexes as food gatherers. But as tools improved, the males were able to organize large-scale hunting parties and to kill large animals, while the women remained close to camp to cook, care for the children, and collect available edibles. This step enhanced man's importance as a food provider. It may be that this, combined with the extra strength, aggressiveness, and skill that went with it, led near the end of the Paleolithic era to the dominance of men over women, such as prevails today amongst the Australian aborigines.

Turning our discussion from social institutions and practices to general beliefs, we find that primitive man was basically ahistorical and nonevolutionary in his attitudes towards himself and his society. He assumed that the future would be identical to the present, as the present was to the past. Consequently there was no notion of change, and hence no inclination to criticize or to tamper with existing institutions and practices. Everything, including themselves, their culture, and their habitat, had appeared with the creation and was destined to continue unaltered into the future. The creation myths of hunting peoples are strikingly similar, involving heroes who fashioned the landscape, stocked it with game, brought forth the people, and taught them the arts and their customs.

The following origin myth of the Andaman islanders is fairly typical:

> The first man was *Jutpu*. He was born inside the joint of a big bamboo, just like a bird in an egg. The bamboo split and he came out. He was a little child. When it rained he made a small hut for himself and lived in it. He made little bows and arrows. One day he found a lump of quartz and with it he scarified himself. *Jutpu* was lonely, living all by himself. He took some clay (*kot*) from a nest of the white ants and moulded it into the shape of a woman. She became alive and became his wife. She was called *Kot*. They lived together at *Teraut-buliu*. Afterwards *Jutpu* made other people out of clay. These were the ancestors. *Jutpu* taught them how to make canoes and bows and arrows, and how to hunt and fish. His wife taught the women how to make baskets and nets and mats and belts, and how to use clay for making patterns on the body.[1]

Primitive man was very knowledgeable concerning nature. He had to be, for his very existence depended on it. Yet he had little explanatory knowledge; he could give no naturalistic explanation if there were floods or droughts, or if the hunting or fishing was poor. This meant that he did not know how to cope with nature by naturalistic means, so perforce he resorted to the supernatural. He turned to magic and spent much time in efforts to persuade or fool nature to yield a greater abundance. By making each useful animal or plant the totem of a particular group, and by using images, symbols, and imitative dances, primitive man believed that the animal or food could be encouraged to flourish and multiply. As long as the rules of the totems were strictly observed, the reproduction of the group and of its food supply could be assured.

All group members seem to have participated at first in the ritual ceremonies, but towards the end of the Paleolithic part-time specialists in the form of medicine men or shamans seem to have appeared. These people were thought to have peculiar relations with the forces deemed to control those parts of the universe or environment that mattered—primarily food and fertility, but also health and personal luck. They were, to an increasing degree, relieved from the full-time work of food and tool production, and in return they exercised their magical arts for the common good. Shamans are still found today in nearly every surviving food-gathering culture, including those of the Bushmen, the Eskimos, and the Australian aborigines. The earliest representation of these shamans is the "Sorceror" of the cave of Trois-Frères in France. This "terrible masterpiece," as it has been called, is a Paleolithic painting of a man clad in a deer skin, with the horns of a stag, the face of an owl, the ears of a wolf, the arms of a bear, and the tail of a horse. Other nearby paintings suggest that the cave was a place of assembly where a living sorcerer invoked the spirits of the animals for success in the hunt and aroused his audience to the emotional intensity necessary to face its dangers.

Paleolithic technology, however, was not sufficiently productive to support anything approaching a priestly hierarchy. This in turn meant that no cohesive theology could be elaborated. Conceptions of gods and spirits were hazy, and much emphasis was placed on individual visions. Religion was not used as a method of social control. Benefits were coerced from the supernatural rather than being dependent on the morality of the individual. This is apparent in the following statement made by an Eskimo to the Arctic explorer, Knud Rasmussen: "We believe our Angákut, our magicians, and we believe them because we wish to live long, and because we do not want to expose ourselves to the danger of famine and starvation. We believe, in order to make our lives and food secure. If we did not believe the magicians, the animals we hunt would make themselves invisible to us; if we did not follow their advice, we should fall ill and die." [2]

This fear of the inexplicable and this desire to bring the supernatural under human control found expression in art as well as religion. By far the outstanding example of Paleolithic art consists of the extraordinary cave paintings, the best examples of which are located in southern France and northwestern Spain. The subjects of the drawings are usually the larger game: bison, bear, horses, woolly rhinoceros, mammoth, and wild boar. The best of the drawings are in full color, remarkably alive, and charged with energy. Despite their extraordinary artistic quality, the cave drawings apparently were designed for utilitarian reasons. They were executed in the darkest and most dangerous parts of the caves, although only the openings were inhabited. Also the artists commonly painted one picture over another, with no apparent desire to preserve their works. Hence it appears that these Paleolithic artists made their way to the depths of the earth and created as realistic a reproduction as possible of the animals they hunted in the belief that thereby they gained some sort of magic power over them.

This association of image with a desired object prevails amongst contemporary primitives. A German anthropologist, Professor Leo Frobenius, witnessed a startling illustration of this during an expedition in 1905 in the Congo with a band of Pygmies.

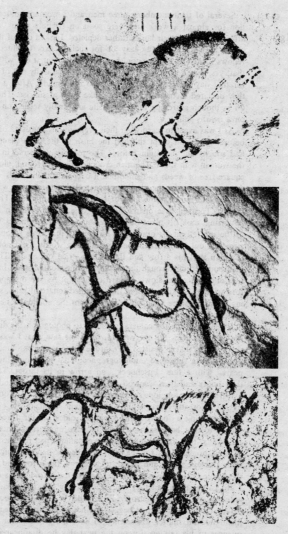

Three prehistoric cave paintings from France. The horse at top is from a cave at Lascaux, Dordogne; the other two were found at Ariège. (The Granger Collection)

Several of their members, three men and a woman, guided the expedition for almost a week and were soon on friendly terms with us. One afternoon, finding our larder rather depleted, I asked one of them to shoot me an antelope, surely an easy job for such an expert hunter. He and his fellows looked at me in astonishment and then burst out with the answer that, yes, they'd do it gladly, but that it was naturally out of the question for that day since no preparations had been made. After a long palaver they declared themselves ready to make these at sunrise. Then they went off as though searching for a good site and finally settled on a high place on a nearby hill.

As I was eager to learn what their preparations consisted of, I left camp before dawn and crept through the bush to the open place which they had sought out the night before. The pygmies appeared in the twilight, the woman with them. The men crouched on the ground, plucked a small square free of weeds and smoothed it over with their hands. One of them drew something in the cleared space with his forefinger, while his companions murmured some kind of formula or incantation. Then a waiting silence. The sun rose on the horizon. One of the men, an arrow on his bowstring, took his place beside the square. A few minutes later the rays of the sun fell on the drawing at his feet. In that same second the woman stretched out her arms to the sun, shouting words I did not understand, the man shot his arrow and the woman cried out again. Then the three men bounded off through the bush while the woman stood for a few minutes and then went slowly toward our camp. As she disappeared I came forward and, looking down at the smoothed square of sand, saw the drawing of an antelope four hands long. From the antelope's neck protruded the pygmy's arrow.

I went back for my camera intending to photograph the drawing before the men returned. But the woman, when she saw what I was up to, made such a fuss that I desisted. We broke camp and continued our march. The drawing remained unphotographed. That afternoon the hunters appeared with a fine "buschbock," an arrow in its throat. They delivered their booty and then went off to the hill we had left behind us, carrying a fistful of the antelope's hair and a gourd full of its blood. Two days passed before they caught up with us again. Then, in the evening, as we were drinking a foamy palm wine, the oldest of the three men—I had turned to him because he seemed to have more confidence in me than the others—told me that he and his companions had returned to the scene of their preparations for the hunt in order to daub the picture with the slain antelope's hair and blood, to withdraw the arrow and then to wipe the whole business away. The meaning of the formula was not clear, but I did gather that, had they not done as they did, the blood of the dead antelope would have destroyed them. The "wiping out," too, had to take place at sunrise. The man begged me not to tell the woman that he had mentioned the matter. He seemed to have the greatest fear of the consequences of his talking, for on the next day he disappeared, his fellows with him.[3]

In conclusion, Paleolithic culture was in many ways vastly appealing. It was thoroughly egalitarian, with warm bonds of kinship permeating and determining social relationships. It offered everyone specific and accepted obligations and rewards. There was no problem of alienation or of anxiety in the face of an uncertain or unpredictable future. To the present day, an Australian aborgine can take a piece of broken glass, fashion it skillfully into an arrow head or spear point, fit it to a spear thrower or to a bow that he has strung himself, set forth and kill his game, prepare his dinner with due attention to ceremonial, and after dinner, round out the day with storytelling in which he shares the adventures of the day with the stay-at-homes. In this manner the Paleolithic hunter was a complete man to a degree that has not been approached since the agricultural revolution.

But the bonds that held Paleolithic society together were also constricting as well as comforting. The individual was wholly subservient to the band or tribe, which was viewed as a timeless procession of the dead, the living, and the unborn, attended by all the unseen powers of the spirit world. To this procession of life the individual was completely subject. Doubtless the overwhelming majority of individuals felt themselves to be participants rather than captives. Yet the fact remains that the result was stagnation along with security. The Paleolithic way of life was psychically satisfying yet it was a dead-end street. Institutionalized authority did not exist among the Arunta of Australia, but the elders arranged with the enemy to kill those individuals who had not been living in accord with tribal tradition.

It was this tradition, this stultifying and constraining tradition, that was the historically all-important other side of Paleolithic society. Today it is customary to distinguish between two modes of life: the "progressive" of the modern industrialized West, and the "traditional" of the underdeveloped agrarian non-West. The latter is indeed "traditional" compared to the former, but it is anything but traditional compared to the primitive tribal society that it superseded following the agricultural revolution.

We shall see that this agricultural revolution set off a chain reaction of urbanization, class differentiation, and social cleavage that undermined the appealing egalitarianism of primitive society. But in doing so it also broke the constricting bonds of tribal traditionalism and thereby launched man, for good or ill, on the fateful course that was to lead from hunting ground to megalopolis, from human muscle to atomic power. Before turning to the agricultural revolution, however, it is necessary to consider the dispersal of Paleolithic man throughout the globe and the ensuing repercussions felt to the present day.

IV. DISPERSAL AND RACE DIFFERENTIATION

It is commonly assumed that population explosion is a phenomenon peculiar to our times, but this is not so. Spectacular population spurts have occurred with each major technological breakthrough, and for the obvious reason that an advance in technology leads to increased productivity, which can support a larger number of people. At this time the differential between early and late

Paleolithic technology did represent a major advance. This in turn led to a population jump from an estimated 125,000 hominids in the early Paleolithic to 5.32 million Homo sapiens on the eve of the agricultural revolution at the end of the Paleolithic ten thousand years ago. This increase of over forty-two times is thus comparable to the population explosions that, as we shall see, were to accompany each of the later technological revolutions. (See Map II, "World Population Growth.")

Another demographic pattern set at this time and repeated in the future was the disproportionate increase of any population that took the lead in technological innovation, and hence the spread of that population over larger areas. This pattern has prevailed since the first appearance of life on this planet, in accord with the Law of Cultural Dominance propounded as follows by the anthropologists M. D. Sahlins and E. R. Service: ". . . that cultural system which more effectively exploits the energy resources of a given environment will tend to spread in that environment at the expense of less effective systems. . . . Higher forms characteristically exploit more different kinds of resources more effectively than lower; hence in most environments they are more effective than lower; thus their greater range." [1]

At all times, the best adapted species, or that which is most efficiently exploiting the physical environment, is the species that has prevailed and extended its domain. Thus the australopithecines, with their primitive pebble tools and lack of clothing, were unable to extend their range beyond the warm savanna lands. Homo erectus, by contrast, with his superior tools and his clothing and control of fire, was able to expand north from Africa to the temperate zones of Eurasia—hence the discovery of his widely scattered fossil remains such as Java man, Peking man, and Heidelberg man. Finally Homo sapiens, with his still more complex technology and correspondingly more efficient adaptation, was able to push further north into the Siberian tundra, as well as south into the African and Southeast Asian tropical rain forests.

Under these circumstances, Homo sapiens occupied the remaining continents by crossing one land bridge to Australia and another to Alaska. Once in the New World he fanned out in all directions, though at varying rates of speed. He moved southward rapidly, covering the distance from Alaska to Tierra del Fuego during the period between roughly 15,000 and 8,000 B.C. The difficult environment of the Canadian Arctic, however, slowed down his eastward dispersal, so that he did not appear in Greenland until about 4000 B.C. Thus man occupied all the continents except Antarctica, thereby becoming, together with his inseparable dog, the most widespread animal in the world.

Hand in hand with the dispersal of Homo sapiens went race differentiation. A variety of so-called races appeared, with distinguishing characteristics in skin color, hair texture, and facial structure. These races are believed to have emerged because of the relative isolation of the various human populations and their adaptation to differing local environments. The significant point concerning this differentiation within the human species is that it occurred so late—well *after* the emergence of Homo sapiens. All modern races, then, stem from a common stock *after* it had attained its full human development. This explains why the Europeans were able to interbreed with all races in all the lands they discovered. It also explains why, as virtually all anthropologists agree, there are no significant differences in the innate mental capacity among the living races of mankind. Representatives of late Paleolithic man or of the contemporary Australian aborigines would stand as much chance of graduating from a university as would representatives of any other races.

The precise circumstances under which the races appeared in various regions are not known, and probably never will be. Suffice it to note that by the end of the latest Ice Age about ten thousand years ago, the global distribution of races had assumed a roughly recognizable delineation. The Caucasoids occupied Europe, North and East Africa, and the Middle East, extending into India and Central Asia. The Negroids were in the Sahara (better watered then) and a bit southward, while the Pygmies and Bushmen, in contrast to later times, occupied the remainder of Africa. Other Pygmies, the Negritos, lived in the forests of India and Southeast Asia, while in the open country of these regions and in Australia were the Australoids. Finally in East Asia and the Americas were the Mongoloids.

Although this racial configuration bears a vague resemblance to the one we know, Map III, "Global Race Distribution," shows that basic changes had occurred by A.D. 1000 and still more by today. These changes, as we shall note later, came as a direct result of later technological revolutions. It was the failure to keep up with these revolutions that explains the virtual disappearance of the Bushmen and Pygmies and Australoids, as well as the swamping of the American Indians in most of the New World. Put in other words, it explains why 10,000 years ago blonds probably were no more numerous than Bushmen, whereas today there are 100,000 blonds for every living Bushman.

As noted in the preceding chapter, the differential in technological leadership, and hence in numerical strength, did not reflect a corresponding differential in genetic endowment. Rather it stemmed from the fact that the Mongoloids and Caucasoids were located in the Eurasian heartland, and the Negroids in a region of Africa easily accessible to Eurasian stimuli, whereas the Bushmen and Pygmies were unfortunate enough to be isolated in remote areas of Africa, and the Australoids on their distant island continent. The resulting differences in tempos of development have determined the very composition of the human family today, as well as the status and interrelations of the various members of the family.

Suggested Reading

For the physical background of early man, see K. W. Butzer, *Environment and Archeology* (Chicago: Aldine, 1964), and I. W. Cornwall, *The World of Ancient Man* (New York: New American Library, 1964), Mentor Book. In the Foundations of Modern Anthropology Series (Englewood Cliffs, N.J., Prentice-Hall), edited by Marshall D. Sahlins, the relevant volumes for this chapter are by G. Loring Brace, *The Stages of Human Evolution* (1967), E. Goldschmidt, *The Evolutionary Basis of Race,* and E. R. Service, *The Hunters* (1966). Collective studies of Paleolithic man are by S. Tax, ed., *Horizons of Anthropology* (Chicago: Aldine, 1964); the September 1960 issue of *Scientific American* devoted exclusively to

"The Human Species," and C. Gabel, ed., *Man Before History* (Englewood Cliffs, N.J.: Prentice-Hall, 1964). Other recent studies that are noteworthy are by R. J. Braidwood, *Prehistoric Men*, 7th ed. (New York: Morrow, 1968); W. LeGros Clark, *Man Apes or Ape Men* (New York: Holt, 1967); and the well illustrated account by F. Clark Howell, *Early Man* (New York: Life Nature Library, 1965).

It is probably very difficult for us Chapter
now to conceptualize fully (or to exaggerate)
the consequences of the first appearance of 3
effective food production. The whole
range of human existence, from the
biological (including diet, demography,
disease, and so on) through the cultural
(social organization, politics, religion,
esthetics, and so forth) bands of the
spectrum took on completely new dimensions.

Robert J. Braidwood

Man the Food Producer

During Paleolithic times man became man by learning to speak, to make tools, and to use fire. This gave him an enormous advantage over the other animals about him, and yet in one fundamental respect he remained akin to them. He was still a hunter among other hunters. He was still a food gatherer as were countless other species that were completely dependent on the bounty of nature. And being dependent on nature, he was dominated by nature. He had to be constantly on the move in order to follow animals and to locate berry patches or fishing grounds. He had to live in small groups or bands because not many could find enough food to support themselves in a given area. It is estimated that even in fertile areas with mild winters, only one or two food collectors could support themselves per square mile. And as much as twenty or even thirty square miles were needed for each human soul in regions of cold climate, tropical jungle, or desert.

I. ORIGINS OF AGRICULTURE

Such subservience to nature left its imprint on all aspects of human society, as noted in the preceding chapter. But this subservience was greatly reduced when man made the epochal discovery that he could feed himself by growing his food as well as by gathering it. In doing so a new world with limitless horizons opened before him, as he left behind him the Paleolithic stage of his development and entered the Neolithic.

Neolithic man differed from his Paleolithic predecessor in two respects: he made his stone tools by grinding and polishing rather than by chipping and fracturing, and he obtained his food wholly or primarily from agriculture and/or stock raising rather than from hunting animals or gathering plants. Of these two changes, the latter is by far the more significant. This is not to minimize the importance of the new ground tools, which were much sharper and more durable than the earlier implements. Such highly important inventions as the plow and the wheel, which appeared towards the end of the Neolithic period, were facilitated by the availability of cutting tools made of ground stone. The fact still remains, however, that the trick of grinding a chipped or hewn ax to a smooth polished edge was a rather trivial matter compared to the transformation of man from a food collector to a food producer.

This transformation was not the result of sudden inspiration. It was not a case of some prehistoric Archimedes shouting eureka upon comprehending the idea of agriculture. Indeed the mechanics of plant growth were as widely known before the agricultural revolution as the fact that the earth was round was known before Columbus' voyage. It is well established that modern primitives who are wholly without agriculture nevertheless are thoroughly familiar with the nature and behavior of plants in their locales. They know that plants sprout from seeds, that they usually need water and sunshine to flourish, and that they grow better in one type of soil than in another. This type of knowledge is acquired naturally and unavoidably by modern primitives for the simple reason that their very existence depends upon such practical understanding of the surrounding flora and fauna. There is no reason for doubting, and plenty of evidence for believing, that prehistoric man acquired similar comprehension under comparable circumstances.

If the basic principles of plant life were known to man thousands of years before the agricultural revolution, then why did he delay so long in putting them into practice? One reason is that there was no incentive to do so. Contrary to what is commonly assumed, hunting peoples did not normally live on the brink of starvation. They did not increase in numbers to the limit that could be supported by the available food supply. Rather they resorted to practices such as infanticide, abortion, and lactation taboos in order to keep their numbers low enough to pull through the lean months of each year. Thus hunting societies continued to exist for millennia at a comfortable equilibrium and consequently lacked stimulus for radical change. Not only did the hunters under normal circumstances have plenty to eat, but they also had plenty of leisure. Once sufficient game had been killed or plant food collected, there was no particular incentive for working further. "There is abundant data," states one authority, "which suggests not only that hunter-gatherers have adequate supplies of food but also that they enjoy quantities of leisure time, much more in fact than do modern industrial or farm workers, or even professors of archeology." [1] Under these circumstances the natural question that arises is not why man remained a hunter for so long, but rather why he ever ceased to be one.

Another reason for man's delay in shifting to agriculture is the relative scarcity of domesticable plants and animals. Man has been able throughout history to domesticate only a few hundred plants and a few dozen animals that happen to possess certain essential characteristics. Plants must be potentially high-yielding and preferably should be adaptable to a variety of environments. If these requirements are not met, then plants will have little effect even though domesticated. Prehistoric Indians of present-day United States cultivated pigweed, marsh elder, lamb's quarter and sunflower, but none of these plants yielded enough to affect significantly the Indian way of life. Likewise animals, to be domesticable, must be capable of losing their instinctive flight-reaction before man, must breed under man's care, and must be willing to accept the diet provided by man. The peoples of the Old World were fortunate in having available a variety of such animals that provided them with meat, milk, wool, and beasts of burden. The American Indians, by contrast, were retarded by the lack of anything comparable; they had to do with a half-domesticated group of Andean cameloids; the llama, the alpaca, and the vicuña.

It follows from the above that no breakthrough to agriculture could be expected unless some change occurred which upset the comfortable equilibrium of the hunting societies, and even then, agriculture could occur only in areas where domesticable plants were available. This, in fact, is precisely what did happen. The end of the Pleistocene, as noted in the preceding chapter, was a period of drastic climatic fluctuations which upset the traditional balance between man and nature. And man, being Homo sapiens, adapted by using his knowledge of plant life to grow his own food.

This he had done innumerable times in various parts of the globe where he had experimented with a wide range of plants and animals. But now, in a few favored regions, he was able to increase the productivity of his domesticated plants and animals to the point where they provided such a high proportion of the diet that community life revolved primarily around the cultivation of the plants and the tending of the animals. This is what is meant by *agricultural revolution* as distinct from mere *domestication*. It was from the few centers of such agricultural revolution that food production as a new way of life gradually spread over large portions of the globe.

II. DIFFUSION OF AGRICULTURE

We know with certainty that the Middle East and Mesoamerica were independent centers of agricultural revolution, and recent research indicates that North China was also such a center. There is speculation, though no conclusive evidence, that other such centers may have evolved in Southeast Asia, West Africa, and the Andes. In the case of the Middle East and Mesoamerica, both regions had certain unique characteristics that seem to account for their pioneering role. Both enjoyed abundant variety of plants and/or animals.

In the Middle East were to be found the ancestors of modern wheat, oats, rye, and barley, as well as those of the modern goat, sheep, cattle, and pig. Likewise in Mesoamerica the two small republics of Costa Rica and Salvador, although comprising only one per cent of the area of the United States, yield as many plant species as do both the United States and Canada. This extraordinary diversity is the product of a corresponding diversity of habitats created by the wide range of altitude, temperature, and rainfall within a small area. Consequently, dozens of plants were successfully domesticated in Mesoamerica, the all-important ones being maize, amaranths, beans, and squashes.

Over a period of many centuries the various plants were adapted out of their particular local niches into a variety of environmental conditions, thereby culminating in a regional complex of multiple-species agriculture. This advanced type of agriculture had the great advantage of a high level of productivity and of "subsistence security." If one crop failed for climatic reasons, another with different requirements could survive, thus providing the dependable food supply essential for dense populations and for the civilizations that thereby were made possible.

It should be emphasized that the transition from the earliest domestication to agricultural revolution was very gradual and prolonged, and is known as the phase of "incipient agriculture." In the Middle East this phase spanned the period from roughly 9500 to 7500 B.C. In the New World it appears to have been even longer. One of the earliest centers of domestication in that area was the Mexican valley of Tehuacán, where incipient agriculture began approximately 7000 B.C. It is estimated that two thousand years later only 10 per cent of the diet of the local Indians was derived from their domesticated plants, primarily maize. By 3000 B.C., still only a third of the food came from this source. It was not until about 1500 B.C. that maize and other plants had been hybridized to the point where their yield was sufficiently high to provide most of the food, and thus to complete the transition from incipient agriculture to the agricultural revolution.

From these two original centers of full-fledged agriculture, and from others that might, and probably will, be identified in the future, the new mode of living spread to all parts of the globe. The diffusion process was sparked by two characteristics of this early agriculture. One was that it was an intermittent or shifting type of cultivation. The land was cleared and used for crop growing for a few years, whereupon it was abandoned to natural growth for eight or ten or more years in order to allow the fertility to be restored. This very extensive type of agriculture meant that the ratio of abandoned or recuperating land to that under cultivation at any one time was between five and ten to one. This, together with increasing population, necessitated constant extension of the limits of the tilled land into new regions. A closely related expansionist factor was overpopulation. Multiple-species agriculture yielded a greater and more reliable food supply, so that population increased correspondingly. When it reached the limit that could be supported by the prevailing level of agricultural productivity, the natural solution was emigration. Thus there was a continual "budding-off" or "hiving-off" from the agricultural settlements into the relatively sparsely populated lands of the food-gathering peoples. In this manner agriculture was diffused in all directions from the original centers.

This does not mean that agriculture eventually spread all over the globe. A great variety of local conditions determined where agriculture was to appear early, where late, and where not at all. In the Afro-Asian desert belt and in the arctic regions agriculture was precluded for obvious reasons. In parts of Africa and the Americas, as well as all of Australia, agriculture again was absent because of a combination of stultifying isolation and unfavorable physical environment. In other regions such as Central and Western Europe, agriculture was long delayed because the heavy forests were an almost insurmountable obstacle until the advent of the Iron Age with its cheap and effective implements. When the iron ax replaced the stone, the frontiers of cultivation were extended not only from the Mediterranean coastlands to the European interior, but also from the Indus River valley to the Ganges, from the Yellow River valley to the Yangtze, and from Africa's savannas to the tropical rain forests. Finally agriculture was delayed also by the superabundance in certain regions of natural animal and plant life that provided more food than could early agriculture. In southwest United States, for example, an extremely long period of selective breeding of the maize, beans, and squashes of Mesoamerican agriculture was necessary before the yield could equal that provided by the plentiful acorns and small game. This explains why the Indians of the Southwest remained food gatherers for so long, even though living adjacent to an early center of agriculture.

Very little is known concerning the precise details of the spread of agriculture from region to region. The least obscure is the radiation from the Middle East to Europe, which proceeded along several routes. One was north across Turkey to the Ukrainian plains and thence across Eastern Europe to the Baltic and Scandinavia. Another was west across the Straits to the Balkan Peninsula, up the Danube Valley into Central Europe, and eventually to the Atlantic. A third route was west across the Aegean Isles to Greece and thence to Italy, southern France, Spain, and up the Atlantic coast to the British Isles. There is general agreement also concerning the diffusion of agriculture from the Middle East eastward across the Iranian plateau to the Indus Valley, and northeastward along the shores of the Caspian into the plains of Central Asia.

Beyond these limits the archaeological evidence is so scanty that conjecture takes over. In China, wheat and barley were introduced from the Middle East about 1300 B.C., but the latest research demonstrates that native plants already had been domesticated and cultivated in that region for 3,000 years. This early and independent origin of agriculture had proven possible because the semiarid loess plains of North China with their relatively sparse cover of grass made cultivation possible even with early wooden digging sticks. Thus, native plants such as millets, sorghum, rice, soybeans, hemp, and mulberry had been grown from the fifth millennium B.C. as dry land crops. This explains why the wheat and barley that eventually appeared were also cultivated as dry land crops rather than in irrigated fields as had been the case in their place of origin in the Middle East.

The circumstances in which agriculture appeared in Africa remain obscure. Some maintain that it was developed independently about 5000 B.C. in West Africa around the headwaters of the Niger. Others accept this proposi-

tion but select a much later date—about 1500 B.C. The majority, however, believe that agriculture spread from the Middle East to the Nile Valley about 4000 B.C.; to the Sudan Negroes about 3000 B.C.; and then diffused through the savanna zone of sub-Saharan Africa, especially as the Negroes were driven south and west by the Berbers and Arabs.

For many centuries agriculture was confined to the open savanna lands and failed to penetrate southward into tropical rain forest. This was due partly to the fact that the millet and sorghum commonly grown in the savanna did not do well in the rain forest. About the beginning of the Christian era these obstacles were overcome by two important developments. One was the appearance of iron working, which reached Africa from its place of origin in the Middle East. The other was the arrival, apparently from Southeast Asia, of bananas and Asian yams. These flourished under forest conditions, so, together with iron tools, they were responsible for the rapid expansion of agriculture down to the southern part of the continent.

In the New World, the story is clearer thanks to the recent findings of American archaeologists. The initial domestication of maize occurred approximately 7000 B.C. in the semidesert valleys of the central highlands of Mexico. During the following millennia two major races of maize were developed by hybridization, one adapted to the semiarid Mexican plateau and the other to the humid tropical coastal lands. At the same time other plants were domesticated, including two species of squash, the bottle gourd, tepary bean, chili peppers, amaranths, and avocados. From this original Mesoamerican center, agriculture spread both north and south. Maize arrived in the American

Tempera copy of an Egyptian wall painting from the tomb of Menena, Scribe of the Fields of the Lord of Two Lands, about 1415 B.C. (The Metropolitan Museum of Art, Egyptian Expedition, Rogers Fund, 1930)

Southwest about 3000 B.C. but did not have much effect until A.D. 750 because the primitive nature of maize before that date left food collecting a more productive activity. Likewise, in eastern North America the Indians did not shift to predominant dependence on agriculture until about A.D. 800 when they developed field cropping based on several varieties of maize, beans, and squash. Meanwhile, agriculture had spread southward from Mesoamerica, reaching Peru about 750 B.C. On the other hand, the presence in Peru of non-Mesoamerican maize and bean varieties of considerable antiquity suggests the possibility of original plant domestication in the Andean as well as the Mexican plateaus.

III. Varieties of Agriculture

This world wide diffusion of agriculture required adaptation to a variety of local conditions and hence led to the domestication of a corresponding variety of plants suitable to those conditions. In the Middle East wheat and barley had been from the beginning the most common crops. But as the farmers moved northward they found that these crops did not do as well as rye, which originally had been a weed sown unintentionally with the wheat and barley. Hence there was a shift to rye in Central Europe and, under similar circumstances, another shift further north to oats.

Likewise, the extension of agriculture to sub-Saharan Africa led to the cultivation of native millets and of one type of rice, while around the shores of the Mediterranean the olive became one of the most important sources of edible oil. Across the Iranian plateau and in northwest India an essentially Middle Eastern type of agriculture was practiced. But a dividing line running north and south through central India marks the transition to an entirely different climatic zone with correspondingly different plants. This is the monsoon world, with heavy seasonal rainfall, constant heat, and dense jungles. Seed-bearing plants of the Middle Eastern variety, which require plenty of sun, cannot thrive here, so in their place are to be found yam, taro, banana, and above all, rice. Finally, in the Americas the staple everywhere was maize, supplemented by beans and squash in North America and by manioc and potatoes of both the sweet and "Irish" varieties in South America.

The net result of the agriculture diffusion described above was, very generally speaking, three great cereal areas: the rice area in East and Southeast Asia; the maize area in the Americas; and the wheat area in Europe, the Middle East, North Africa, and Central Asia to the Indus and Yellow River valleys. During the several millennia between the agricultural and industrial revolutions these three cereals were as fundamental for the history of man as coal and iron and copper were to become following the industrial revolution.

The diffusion of agriculture involved not only diversity in crops but also a corresponding diversity in cultivation techniques and consequently in ways of living. The original Neolithic agriculture in the Middle East was of the mixed variety, combining animal husbandry (cattle, sheep, goat and pig) with grain cultivation (wheat and barley). As domestication spread, adaptive variations in techniques were developed in the new environments, the two most important being "slash and burn" agriculture in forest areas, and pastoral nomadism in semiarid grasslands.

Slash and burn agriculture originally was practiced in temperate as well as tropical forests, but now is confined largely to the latter. Some 14 million square miles inhabited by 200 million people are still farmed by this time-tested method. Its essential feature is one or two seasons of staple cropping, followed by a long period of fallow to allow restoration of soil fertility. The area then may be cleared for another cycle of cultivation and fallow. A field may be planted principally to one crop such as rice or maize, but several other crops—legumes, squashes, tubers—are usually intercropped with the staple, so that the plot yields one or more foodstuffs throughout the year. This is labor intensive agriculture with correspondingly high productivity. In many regions two to three acres under cultivation suffice to feed a good-sized family for a year. The main disadvantage of this type of agriculture is the large amount of arable land needed, since each community must have much more land fallow at any one time than is under cultivation. This in turn means low population density, usually less than ten people per square mile, scattered in individual homesteads or in small villages of 100 to 150 people.

Pastoral nomadism, being an adaptation to open grasslands, represented the exact opposite of forest agriculture. It prevails today in the vast steppe and desert lands from the Sahara to Manchuria, as well as in the extensive savannas of sub-Saharan Africa. In these regions there is insufficient water for either rain-fed or irrigated agriculture, so that man was forced to depend on his domesticated animals rather than on plants. This pastoral nomadism was late in developing because it had to await the domestication of the horse and camel to provide suitable transport in open country. Once it got under way between 1500 and 1000 B.C., a variety of forms developed. Some pastoralists depended on a single animal—the camel in Arabia and cattle in Southwest Africa—while those of Central Asia had herds of horses, cattle, camels, sheep, and goats, which they adjusted to local climatic and grazing conditions. Regardless of the variety, nomadism required extensive grazing lands, so that the bands today rarely number more than 200 persons, and often less than 100. Population densities accordingly range mainly between 1 and 5 people per square mile.

These adaptive variations in the diffusion of agriculture and pastoralism were of profound significance for later history. Slash and burn agriculture and pastoral nomadism were not as productive per unit of land as the permanent irrigation type of agriculture that was developed later in the valleys of the Tigris-Euphrates, Nile, Indus, and Yellow rivers. Consequently it was these valleys, and certain other favored regions, that generated the material and human resources essential for the great civilizations that appeared later and were to dominate the globe to modern times. Also these opulent centers of civilization were to prove irresistible magnets to the comparatively poverty-stricken pastoral nomads of the Central Eurasian steppes, so that Eurasian history to modern times was in large part the history of the relations between the nomadic hordes of inner Eurasia and the surrounding river valley civilizations. Before turning to this history in the following chapters we will consider the manifold repercussions of the agricultural revolution on all aspects of human life.

IV. CULTURE OF THE FOOD PRODUCERS

The most obvious impact of the agricultural revolution was the new sedentary existence. Man now was able to settle down; in fact he had to in order to care for his newly domesticated plants and animals. Thus the Paleolithic nomadic band now gave way to the Neolithic village as the basic economic and cultural unit of mankind. Indeed it remained the basis for a pattern of life that was to prevail until the late eighteenth century and that persists to the present day in the vast underdeveloped regions of the world.

It is easy to romanticize Neolithic village life, but to do so would be grossly misleading. Everyone—men, women and children—had to work, and work hard, to produce food and a few handicraft articles. Productivity was low since man learned slowly and painfully about soils, seeds, fertilizers, and crop rotation. Despite the hard labor, famine was a common visitation, following upon too much or too little rain, or a plague of pests. Epidemics swept the villages repeatedly as sedentary life introduced the problem of the disposal of human excreta and other garbage. While dogs helped with sanitation and the cultural habits of personal modesty presumably demanded that stools be deposited at some distance from habitation, neither of these were sufficient to prevent the various diseases that follow the route from the bowel to the mouth. Also malnutrition was the rule because of inadequate food supply or unbalanced diet. Life expectancy under these circumstances was exceedingly low, but the high birth rate tended to increase village populations everywhere until famine, epidemic, or emigration restored the balance between food and mouths.

Yet Neolithic village life was not all misery and suffering. This was a time when man made technological progress at an infinitely more rapid rate than in the preceding millennia of the Paleolithic. The basic reason probably was not so much that he had more leisure time than the hunters, a common assumption that is now questioned, but rather that sedentism made a richer material existence physically possible. The living standards of the nomadic hunter were limited to what he could carry, whereas the Neolithic villager could indulge in substantial housing together with furnishings, utensils, implements, and assorted knickknacks. Thus he learned to make pottery out of raw clay, at first imitating, naturally enough, the baskets, gourds, and other containers of preagrarian times. Gradually he grasped the potentialities of pottery materials and techniques and fashioned objects that no longer resembled the earlier containers. By the end of the Neolithic period man in the Near East was building kilns or ovens, which permitted a higher temperature when firing and thereby made glazing possible. The glazed surface sealed the pottery and prevented seepage or evaporation. Thus the agriculturist had vessels that could be used not only for storing grain but also for cooking and for keeping liquids such as oil and beer.

Similar progress was made with textiles. Late Paleolithic peoples may have twisted or spun wild mountain sheep, goat, dog, or other animal fibers into coarse threads, and may have woven them to make belts, head bands, or even rough blankets. Indeed they probably also had modelled clay into crude containers. But it was during the Neolithic that man was able to develop the textile art as he did that of pottery. He used fibers of the newly domesticated flax, cotton, and hemp plants, and he spun and wove the fibers on spindles and looms that he gradually evolved. Neolithic man also learned to build dwellings that were relatively substantial and commodious. The materials varied with the locality. The Iroquois of northern New York were known as the people of the long house because they lived in huge bark and wood structures that accommodated ten or more families. In the Middle East adobe was used for the walls, while in Europe the most common material was split saplings plastered with clay and dung. The roofs were probably usually of thatch. These dwellings were furnished with fixed beds that might be covered with canopies. Also there were modern-looking dressers with at least two tiers of shelves, and various wall-cupboards or keeping places. Light and warmth were provided by an open fire, generally placed near the center of the room. There was no chimney to let out the smoke—only a hole in the roof or a gap under the eaves.

Sedentism also made possible a tribal political structure in place of the individual bands of the hunting peoples. The inhabitants of the villages of a given region comprised the tribe, which was identified and distinguished from others by distinctive characteristics of speech and custom. Some tribes, usually those with primitive economies, were so amorphous and underdeveloped that they were almost at the hunting band level. Others boasted powerful chiefs and primitive nobilities as against the commoners, though the lines were blurred and never reached the class exclusiveness characteristic of the later civilizations.

The basic social unit of the Neolithic village customarily was the household consisting of two or more married couples and their children. This extended family was more common than the independent nuclear family because it was better suited for coping with the problems of wresting a livelihood. It could

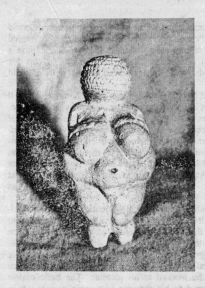

Venus of Willendorf, a stone figure dating from between 15,000 and 10,000 B.C. Because of the proportions of this figure, it can be considered a manifestation of early man's fertility cults. (Museum of Natural History, Vienna)

Remains of a Neolithic temple discovered on Malta. (Arborio Mella)

absorb the temporary or permanent loss of an individual producer. It could function more efficiently during "choke" periods when many hands were needed for clearing forest, harvesting, or pasturing livestock. It could also exploit a large area effectively by dispatching members for long periods to care for distant gardens or grazing herds, while others tended nearby plots and did household chores.

The distinctive feature of the Neolithic village was social homogeneity. All families had the necessary skills and tools to produce what they needed, and, equally important, all had access to the basic natural resources essential for livelihood. This was assured because every family automatically was a component part of the village community, which had proprietary rights to farmlands, pastures, and other resources of nature. Hence there was no division between landed proprietors and landless cultivators in tribal society. "Hunger and destitution," reports an American anthropologist, "could not exist at one end of an Indian village . . . while plenty prevailed elsewhere in the same village. . . ." [2]

Precisely because of this egalitarianism, tribal societies, whether of Neolithic times or today, have a built-in brake on productivity. Output is geared to the limited traditional needs of the family, so there is no incentive to produce a surplus. This in turn means that labor is episodic, diversified, and correspondingly limited. The daily grind—the eight-hour day, five-day week—is conspicuously absent. The typical tribesman worked fewer hours per year than modern man and furthermore he worked at his pleasure. The basic reason was that he labored and produced in his capacity as a social person—as a husband or father or brother or village member. Work was not a necessary evil tolerated for the sake of making a living; rather it was a concomitant of kin and community relations. One helped one's brother in the field because of kinship ties, and not because one might be given a basket of yams.

The new life of the soil tillers also meant new gods—new religions. The spirits and the magic that had been used by the hunters were no longer appropriate. Now the agriculturists needed, and conceived, spirits who watched over their fields and flocks and hearths. Behind all these spirits stood a creator, usually vaguely conceived. But most important, almost everywhere was a goddess of the earth, or the goddess of fertility—the earth mother. She was the source of productivity of plants and animals, and of the fecundity of women. Life and well-being, the annual cycle of death and rebirth, ultimately depended upon her. Hence the proliferation of fertility goddess cults. This is manifested in the numerous clay figurines with exaggerated female characteristics—pendulous breasts and heavy thighs. Reflecting the spread of agriculture from the Middle East, these have been found throughout Europe and as far east as India.

Myths arose, of course, to explain the origins of the staple crops upon which various peoples depended. An example is the following "Legend of Indian Corn" from the Wabanaki of Maine.

A long time ago, when Indians were first made, there lived one alone, far, far from any others. He knew not of fire, and subsisted on roots, bark, and nuts. This Indian became very lonesome for company. He grew tired of digging roots, lost his appetite, and for several days lay dreaming in the sunshine; when he awoke he saw something standing near, at which, at first, he was very much frightened. But when it spoke, his heart was glad, for it was a beautiful woman with long *light* hair, very unlike any Indian. He asked her to come to him, but she would not, and if he tried to approach her she seemed to go farther away; he sang to her of his loneliness and besought her not to leave him; at last she told him, if he would do just as she should say, he would always have her with him. He promised that he would. She led him to where there was some very dry grass, told him to get two very dry sticks, rub them together quickly, holding them in the grass. Soon a spark flew out; the grass caught it, and quick as an arrow the ground was burned over. Then she said, "When the sun sets, take me by the hair and drag me over the burned ground." He did not like to do this, but she told him that wherever he dragged her something like grass would spring up, and he would see her hair coming from between the leaves; then the seeds would be ready for his use. He did as she said, and to this day, when they see silk (hair) on the cornstalk, the Indians know she has not forgotten them.[3]

As important as Neolithic man's religion was his world view—his general attitude towards life and his conception of what ought to be and of what is. In this regard he remained static, primarily because of the isolation of village life. He viewed the future as a reproduction of the immediate past. It never occurred to him to change society in accordance with some principle, or to educate his children "for a changing world"—as our schools today proudly claim to be doing. His world, so far as he could see, had not changed in the past and would not do so in the future. Accordingly he trained his children to do as he had done, and as his father and grandfather had done before him. On this point we have suggestive testimony from an American Indian, a Winnebago named Crashing Thunder. Though he lived in our times, he came from a Neolithic tribal environment. In his autobiography he states, "My father used to keep the old habit of teaching us the customs of the Winnebago. He would wake us up early in the morning and, seated around the fireplace, speak to us. . . . The girls would be taught separately. Now this is what my father told me. . . ." After describing specifically how he was trained according to tradition in this manner, Crashing Thunder concludes:

These are the things of which the old people spoke and this also is the advice I give you. I myself never asked for these things, but my father did. Your grandfather did. He asked for the information relating to the manner in which people are to behave. Never, when you are older, should you allow yourself to get in the predicament of not knowing what is the right thing to do. Ask for this instruction my son. It is not a matter requiring a few moments; it is something that must be thoroughly learned. You, too, must learn it.[4]

V. DEMOGRAPHIC AND RACIAL REPERCUSSIONS

The agricultural revolution generated another population explosion comparable to that accompanying the advent of man. Improved tools developed by evolving man during the Paleolithic led to increased productivity and to a corresponding increase in population. Hence there was the jump from 125,000 man-apes one million years ago to 5.32 million Homo sapien hunters 10,000 years ago, a 42-fold increase. (See Chapter 2, section IV.) Now, with the agricultural revolution, a given area yielded a larger and more dependable food supply, so that population figures rose even more dramatically than before. Between 10,000 and 2,000 years ago, the human population soared from 5.32 to 133 million, a 25-fold increase within 8,000 years as against the million year spread during the Paleolithic. (See Map II, "World Population Growth.")

This population increase was selective rather than generalized. As noted earlier, peoples that have led in technological innovation also have led in numerical growth. Consequently just as Homo sapiens earlier had outstripped and displaced his hominid predecessors, so now the agriculturists outstripped and displaced the hunters. The precise manner in which this "outstripping" and "displacing" functioned was probably somewhat as follows. Because of the extensive type of agriculture that was practiced, population pressure soon built up in the villages. The surplus population would "bud-off" to adjacent fresh lands, till the soil, and establish a new village. The relations with the native population varied according to local conditions. If there were marginal lands nearby that could not be used profitably by the agricultural immigrants, then the natives could find sanctuary there and thus preserve their identity. This happened in Africa, where the once widespread Pygmies and Bushmen were crowded into dense jungles and barren deserts respectively. Likewise, in North America the once widespread Shoshone-speaking Indian food gatherers were displaced by the Pueblo agriculturists. (See Map IV, "Recession of the Hunters" and Map V, "Expansion of the Agriculturists.")

Another type of relationship was of the symbiotic variety. An example of this prevails to the present day in the Congo forest, where Pygmy hunters provide Negro cultivators with meat, honey, and other forest products and receive in return cereals and iron weapons. Thus both peoples have been able to coexist and to preserve their identities.

The most common relationship between agricultural immigrants and local food gatherers has been intermarriage and gradual biological fusion. Then as population pressure built up again, the new hybrid population would "bud-off" in turn into fresh lands, where further interbreeding would take place with native peoples. In this way agricultural techniques and crops were transmitted long distances, and the people who emerged at the end of the line were of an entirely different racial type from the original initiators. Thus the immigrants who brought wheat, cattle, the wheel, and the plow into North China were thoroughly Mongoloid, even though these materials originated in the Middle East. Similar migrating and interbreeding occurred with the diffusion of agriculture westward from the Middle East to Europe, and from the savanna lands to southern Africa. Evidence of the latter is the presence today in southern Zambia of Negro-Bushman hybrids.

The net result of these migrations by which agriculture spread over the globe was that by A.D. 1000 the hunters, who 10,000 years ago comprised 100 per cent of the human race, had shrunk to little more than one per cent of the population. This occupational shift led in turn to a racial shift. Ten thousand years ago the race map of the globe showed a rough balance amongst six races—the Caucasoid, Mongoloid, Negroid, Bushman, Pygmy, and Australoid. (See Map III, "Global Race Distribution.") By A.D. 1000 this balance was drastically changed in favor of the agriculturist Mongoloids, Caucasoids and Negroids, and against the Bushmen-Pygmies who had remained food gatherers. The only reason the Australoids held their own was that their isolated island home had not yet been discovered by any agriculturists. This had to wait for the European explorers of the eighteenth century, and when the discovery did take place belatedly, the consequences were all the more catastrophic for the hapless aborigines.

The most striking racial repercussions of the agricultural revolution were in sub-Saharan Africa and East Asia. In the latter region the Mongoloids expanded in all directions at the expense of scattered Pygmy-Australoid peoples, thereby laying the basis for their present numerical superiority over all other races. Likewise, in Africa the Negroes enjoying the advantage of agriculture and iron working broke out of their original savanna homeland and worked their way through the rain forests to southern Africa. Thus, whereas there had been a fairly equitable racial balance in Africa as late as 4000 B.C. amongst Negroes, Bushmen, and Pygmies, by A.D. 1000 this balance had been completely upset in favor of the Negroes. Considering the globe as a whole, then, the racial effect of the agricultural revolution was to end the millennia-old racial equilibrium and to establish the Mongoloid-Caucasoid-Negroid predominance that persists to the present.

SUGGESTED READING

Theories concerning the origins and nature of the agricultural revolution are now in constant revision because of the continuing field work and its theoretical implications. The latest thinking is presented in L. R. Binford and S. R. Binford, eds., *New Perspectives in Archeology* (Chicago: Aldine, 1968), especially the article by Frank Hole on the shift to agriculture in Iran. Also see the relevant chapters in R. J. Braidwood, *Prehistoric Men*, 7th ed. (Chicago: Scott Foresman, 1967); in S. Tax, ed., *Horizons of Anthropology* (Chicago: Aldine, 1964); and in the September 1960 issue of *Scientific American*. Finally there are important comparative studies of agricultural revolutions in various parts of the world in R. J. Braidwood and G. R. Willey, eds., *Courses Toward Urban Life* (Chicago: Aldine, 1962). Important new material demonstrating the autonomous origin of Chinese agriculture is presented in Ping-ti Ho, "The Loess and the Origin of Chinese Agriculture," *American Historical Review*, LXXV (October, 1969), 1–36.

ANCIENT CIVILIZATIONS
OF EURASIA,
3500–1000 B.C.

*We have seen in Part I that after man became man, his first major achieve-
ment was the agricultural revolution. If an observer in outer space had kept
planet earth under surveillance and reported periodically on the developments
he noted, his description of the advent of agriculture might have been somewhat
as follows:*

> *The bipedal species that hitherto has sustained itself by collecting plants
> and hunting animals is now beginning to produce its own food by delib-
> erately nurturing the growth of certain plants and by raising certain an-
> imals. The groups living in this new fashion are increasing disproportion-
> ately in numbers and are settling down in certain localities where they are
> constructing durable shelters. A few dozen of these shelters normally are
> clustered together in locations particularly suitable for the growing of
> plants and the raising of animals.*

*Several millennia later our mythical observer would have noted a radically
new development amongst the enterprising earthlings—the advent of civilization—which he might have reported as follows:*

> *The great majority of the bipedal species still hunt and collect their food,
> but the percentage that grow crops or raise livestock is now increasing*

rapidly. *Also a new development is noticeable in several regions, where members of the species are living permanently in very large settlements that are protected by high walls. Some of the individuals in these settlements do not produce their own food or work in any crafts. Rather they have persuaded or compelled their fellow residents to yield their surplus foodstuffs and handicrafts in return for certain services. This small minority, although freed of all manual labor, is living in far greater luxury than any members of the species have in the past.*

If these reports on the doings of man were continued through the millennia they would have described not only a basic change in the nature of his activities but also in their scale. For the attainment of civilization involved an advance in technology, and this in turn, as noted in the introduction to Part I, led to a corresponding increase in the range of human activity. Whereas the food gatherer was restricted to the confines of his hunting grounds, and the Neolithic agriculturist to the environs of his village, civilized man of necessity operated far afield. He extended his control upstream to safeguard the water supply for his irrigation system and he sent forth soldiers and traders to obtain by whatever means necessary wood for the builders, the copper and tin for the metallurgists, and gold and silver for the craftsmen. Thus the range of the ancient civilizations was not limited to the immediate locality as had been the case with prehistoric communities. Rather it extended outward until it encompassed entire river valleys and even surrounding regions that yielded necessary raw materials.

*The city came into being for the sake
of life; it is for the sake of good life.*

ARISTOTLE

Chapter

4

*Every city is two cities,
a city of the many poor
and a city of the few rich;
and these two cities are always at war.*

PLATO

Origins of Ancient Civilizations

The first light of civilization dawned on a desert plain scorched by the sun and nourished by two great rivers, the Tigris and the Euphrates. Although at one time it was believed that the Nile valley gave birth to civilization, it is now agreed that the earliest centers were in Sumer, the Old Testament's "land of Shinar." This area comprised the barren, wind-swept plains at the head of the Persian Gulf, in the southern part of what used to be known as Mesopotamia and is now the state of Iraq. It was about 3500 B.C. that certain communities of agriculturists that had developed techniques for cultivating this arid wasteland successfully completed the transition from Neolithic tribalism to civilization.

The date given is an approximation, and is pinpointed merely for the sake of convenience. In fact, no one year, or decade, or even century, can be specified in any meaningful sense. We have seen that the shift to food production did not suddenly occur when someone hit upon the idea of agriculture. Likewise the transition to civilization did not happen at the moment that someone conceived of urban centers and urban civilization. What happened, in short, was not an event but a process. The purpose of this chapter is to examine the nature and origins of this process.

I. NATURE OF CIVILIZATION

Precisely what is meant by the term civilization? Anthropologists point to certain characteristics found in civilizations that distinguish them from the preceding Neolithic cultures. These characteristics include urban centers, institutionalized political authority in the form of the state, tribute or taxation, writing, social stratification into classes or hierarchies, monumental architecture, and specialized arts and sciences. Not all civilizations have possessed all of these characteristics. The Andean civilization, for example, developed without writing, while the Egyptian and Mayan lacked cities as commonly defined. But this cluster of characteristics does serve as a general guide for defining the attributes of the civilizations that emerged at various times in various parts of the world.

The end result was not a uniform type of civilization but rather a striking variety of "styles" of civilization. The earlier Neolithic cultures, as noted in the preceding chapter, represented adaptations to specific environments and hence differed markedly according to the balance between cultivation and stock breeding, and the varieties of plants cultivated and of animals bred. So now the various civilizations differed correspondingly, with the degree of distinctions depending on the degree of isolation in which they developed. Thus the Mayan, Aztec, and Inca civilizations, which emerged independently in the Americas, are clearly distinguishable from those which had taken form earlier in Eurasia. The Eurasian group in turn comprised a diversity of individual civilizations whose distinctiveness depended on their location in relation to the earliest center of civilization in the Middle East. Hence, China, being the most isolated behind desert expanses and mountain barriers, has from earliest times to the present been the most divergent of the Eurasian civilizations.

There remains the question as to why the step to civilization was taken in the first place, particularly in view of the manifold attractions of egalitarian Neolithic society. The answer is suggested by the experience in modern times of the Tanala of Madagascar. Their transition to civilization occurred recently enough to have been recorded by the anthropologist Ralph Linton. Before their shift, the Tanala cultivated dry rice by the slash and burn method. This gave them a good crop the first year, after which the yield progressively declined. Accordingly, the village moved frequently as the fields became exhausted. This mobility precluded individual ownership of land. The village as a whole held general proprietorship, the village elders parcelling out the land as equitably as possible amongst joint families. The several households in each of these joint families worked together, dividing the produce amongst themselves according to need. This was, then, a typical egalitarian tribal society, with no significant economic, political, or social differentiation.

All this changed when some of the families shifted to wet rice cultivation in imitation of neighbors to the east. Since the naturally wet lands were very limited in area, the labor force of an entire joint family was not needed, and the new type of farming therefore was carried on by individual families. These invested so much year-round labor in their rice terraces that they did not return them to the village for reallocation. And since little land was suitable for wet rice cultivation, the formerly classless Tanala society now became divided into a small class of landowners and a large majority who could not hope to own the more productive type of land.

This class division became an actual physical division when the dry-rice farmers were forced to move periodically to fresh lands, while the wet-rice farmers remained on their plots. Warfare also was affected by the new type of economy, as the permanently settled villagers now were willing to spend time and effort to build elaborate fortifications that discouraged the traditional raiding parties. The latter now concentrated on capturing stragglers for slavery, which was assuming new importance. Hitherto slaves had been of little use for slash and burn agriculture, but now they could be used for year-round work on the terraces. Also in place of the previous democracy there developed a society with an absolute king at the head, nobles who held land by royal assignment, commoners who formed the bulk of the population, and slaves who were war captives or their descendants. Finally, a new set of social values evolved, with property becoming the sole means of enhancing the ego. "It was a far cry," concludes the anthropologist Ralph Linton, "from the mobile, self-contained Tanala villages with their classless society and strong joint families to the Tanala Kingdom with its central authority, settled subjects, rudimentary social classes based on economic differences, and lineages of little more than ceremonial importance . . . the transformation can be traced step by step and at every step we find irrigated rice at the bottom of the change." [1]

This transformation of the Tanala is a replica in miniature of the process of change that undermined Neolithic society in the Middle East during the fourth millennium B.C. and culminated finally in the urban revolution and the emergence of civilization.

II. MESOPOTAMIAN ORIGINS

It was in the hills above the Tigris-Euphrates that man had learned to domesticate plants and animals and thereby to achieve the agricultural revolution. It was there also that man now began his next great adventure when he moved down to the river valley and gradually evolved a new and more productive irrigation agriculture and also new social institutions. The interaction of the new technology and institutions set off a chain reaction that culminated eventually in civilization.

The move to the lowlands presented the Neolithic agriculturists with new problems—inadequate rainfall, searing heat, periodic floods, and lack of stone for building. But there were advantages that more than compensated—the date palms that provided plentiful food and abundant, though poor, wood, the reedy marshes with their wild fowl and game, the fish that furnished valuable protein and fat for the diet, and, above all, the fabulously fertile alluvial soil. The potential of this new environment was challenging, and the pioneer agriculturists successfully responded to the challenge by a remarkable feat of adaptation. Thus during the fourth millennium B.C. occurred one of the great technological advances of mankind.

Rainfall was barely sufficient for growing crops in the hilly uplands, but in the valleys below it was quite inadequate. Irrigation was necessary to bring the rich alluvial soils under cultivation, so the pioneer farmers dug short canals leading from the river channels to their fields. The crops were incredibly large compared to those that they had previously wrested from the stony hillsides. Documents dating to 2500 B.C. indicate that the average yield on a field of barley was eighty-six times the sowing! Food was now available as never before—more abundant, more varied, and, thanks to irrigation, more assured. The increased food meant increased population, which in turn made possible more irrigation canals, more new fields, and still more food.

While the technique of irrigation was being worked out, the new craft of metallurgy also was being mastered. This was particularly valuable for the valley settlements where flint was unavailable. At first native metals were treated as unusually tough and malleable stones, and worked cold by hammering and grinding. True metallurgy did not begin until it was learned how to reduce metals from their ores by smelting. Copper seems to have been the first metal so treated, and it was then discovered that upon heating it became liquid and assumed the shape of any container or mold. With cooling it hardened and could be given as good a cutting edge as stone. Furthermore by 3000 B.C. it was widely known in the Middle East and India that a more durable alloy could be produced by adding small quantities of other metals to the copper. Finally they hit on the ideal combination of copper and tin, the resulting bronze being decidedly superior to stone. It was particularly sought after for making weapons, since stone was too brittle to be dependable in battle. On the other hand, bronze was expensive because of the scarcity of both copper and tin, and hence was unavailable for general use, such as toolmaking.

Equally significant at this time was the invention of the plow. In the beginning this consisted simply of a sapling with one lopped and pointed branch left protruding two-thirds of the way down the trunk. A pair of oxen were yoked to the upper end of the trunk while the plowman steered by the lower end as the protruding branch was dragged through the earth. In the light soils of the semiarid Middle East this primitive contrivance was highly functional. By 3000 B.C. it was widely used in Mesopotamia and Egypt and was being introduced in India; by 1400 B.C. it had reached distant China. The significance of the ox drawn plow is that for the first time man was able to use motive power other than that of his own muscles. In this sense the plow was the precursor of the steam engine, the internal combustion engine, the electric generator, and the fission reactor.

By 3000 B.C., wind also was being harnessed to supplement human muscles —in this case to furnish power for water transport. Clumsy square sails appear to have been used first in the Persian Gulf and on the Nile River. They represented the first successful utilization of inorganic force to provide motive power. Crude though the early sail boats were, they offered a far more economic means for heavy transport than pack asses or oxcarts, so that much of the commerce of the ancient civilizations was waterborne.

Another basic invention of this creative millennium was the wheel. In the earliest Mesopotamian models, the wheel and axle were fastened together solidly and the wheels were disks. By 3000 B.C., the axle had been fixed to the cart with the wheel left separate, and shortly thereafter the spoked wheel appeared. Heavy and clumsy though these early carts were, they were much preferable to what had hitherto been available—human shoulders and the

Early agriculture in Egypt, with primitive plow—twelfth century B.C. (Arborio Mella)

pack animal, usually the ass. The wheel also was used early for war chariots, which apparently were driven into the ranks of the enemy until they lost momentum. Then they were used as a fighting platform from which the crew could throw javelins and strike down at the enemy. Another, and more peaceful, use for this invention was the potter's wheel. In its simplest form this was simply a pair of disk-shaped cart wheels with axle attached. The axle was set vertically and the operator spun the lower wheel with his foot while with his hands he spread and shaped the soft clay upon the upper wheel. This mechanism made it possible to mass produce pottery, the first technical product for which this can be said.

These far reaching technological advances went hand in hand with correspondingly far reaching institutional changes. The increase in population enabled some of the villages to grow into towns dominated by a new elite of religious, and later, military and administrative leaders. Their appearance had been made possible by the increased productivity of agriculture, which resulted in food surpluses that could support the growing new class of priests, soldiers, and bureaucrats. This development was not a sudden or a simple one-way process. Much debate has been waged recently on whether the technological change determined the institutional change, or vice versa. This is reminiscent of the debate concerning an earlier stage in man's evolution: whether or not the human brain came first and then created human culture, including speech and toolmaking. It is now agreed that there was interaction back and forth, with speech and toolmaking being both the cause and the effect of brain development. So it appears that technological and social change likewise interacted, eventually precipitating the urban revolution and civilization. The Neolithic cultivators did not at some given time agree—nor were they forced—to provide a surplus for a ruling elite and thus to shift over from the status of tribesmen to that of peasants. Rather it was a gradual process in which *cause* and *effect* were functionally interrelated.

The genesis of the later class differentiation that distinguished civilization may be discerned in the modest village shrines that were centers of socioreligious life but not yet of a full-time priesthood. When the villages grew to towns, the shrines likewise grew to temples with retinues of priests and attendants—the first persons ever to be released from direct subsistence labor. That the priests should have been the pioneer elite group is understandable if they are viewed as the successors of the earlier tribal shamans. The latter had been most influential because of the importance of group agricultural ceremonialism, such as rain making, for Neolithic farmers. Now the new priesthood bore responsibility not only for the traditional supernatural phenomena but also for the growing managerial functions essential for an increasingly complex society.

The accumulative growth of technology and the increasing food surplus had made possible the emergence of the new priestly hierarchies, but the latter in turn contributed to both the technology and the economy. The earliest known examples of writing, which in itself was a priestly invention born of the need for keeping records, attest to the fact that the priesthoods supervised a multitude of economic as well as of religious activities. They kept the records necessary for calculating the time of the annual floods. They assumed the vital managerial functions indispensable for the proper functioning of the growing irrigation facilities, including the rationing of water and the construction and maintenance of dams and canals. They also provided at this time the main stimulus for the crafts, whose output was designed much more for temples than for secular markets.

At this point the growing heterogeneity of society, to which the religious elite had contributed so vitally, began to undermine the position of that elite. The larger and the more complex the towns grew, the more ineffective became purely religious sanctions. At the same time warfare was growing in scale and in frequency. This may have been due to the fact that population growth was outstripping agricultural resources, though the provocative wealth of the temples themselves may paradoxically have contributed to the disorders by inviting raids. The outcome was a shift of power from the priesthood to a new secular elite.

Previously, the occasional threat of outside attack had been met by the assembly of the community's adult males who selected a war leader for the duration. But as the intervals of peace became shorter, the tenure of these war leaders became longer, until they were ensconced as permanent military chiefs, and eventually as kings. Thus the palaces came to rival the temples, until a working partnership was evolved. The priests normally retained their great landholdings and continued their sacred services, while the palace officials constructed walls around their cities and raised large armies, which they employed against neighboring cities and, eventually, for empire building.

One effect of this rise of secular states and empires was a great increase in the output of nonagricultural commodities. The mass production of pottery, the prevalence of articles such as cylinder seals and metal utensils, and the hordes of assorted objects found in some of the more substantial houses, all suggest a new and significant middle class market. Also, a substantial quantity of luxury commodities was absorbed by the burgeoning palace retinues. In addition, the growing militarization required armaments on an unprecedented scale, including not only metal weapons and armor but also more elaborate equipment such as chariots. All this was a far cry from the relatively limited production of earlier times when crafts were geared mainly to meeting temple needs. It should be noted, however, that this change was almost exclusively in volume rather than in technique. What was new was the mass production and not a stylistic or technological innovation.

This mass production had important implications regarding foreign affairs. Most of the crafts were dependent on raw materials brought from the outside, since the lowlands were almost totally devoid of minerals and quality timber. Copper, for example, came from Oman, south of the Persian Gulf, silver and lead from the Taurus Mountains in Asia Minor, and timber from the Zagros Mountains of Iran and from Lebanon on the Mediterranean coast. In order to pay for such imports it was necessary for the various crafts to expand production to provide exports in exchange. The alternative was to conquer the sources of the needed raw materials. That this was not overlooked is evident in the career of Sargon, King of Akkad, in the middle of the third millennium B.C. An epic poem, "The King of Battle," describes how Sargon led his army across unknown mountain passes into the heart of Asia Minor in support of Akkadian merchants who were being maltreated by the local ruler. Eventually Sargon's empire extended "from the Lower to the Upper

Sea"—from the Persian Gulf to the Mediterranean—and he thereby controlled the sources of metals, stone, and timber. Indeed a slightly later source relates that Sargon "did not sleep" in his efforts to promote commerce. "Brisk activity dominates the wharf where the ships are docked; all lands live in peace, their inhabitants prosperous . . . without hindrance ships bring their merchandise to Sumer." [2]

The combined cost of the military and palace establishments bore so heavily on the resources of the early city states that it undermined the position of the traditional assemblies. The latter balked against the onerous levies necessary to meet the rising expenditures, with the result that the assemblies were increasingly bypassed and replaced by permanent, hereditary royal authority.

The centralization of political power was accompanied by growing class differentiation. This is strikingly evident in the corresponding differentiation in grave offerings. During the early period the disparity was minimal, but the more time passed the more pronounced it became. The great majority of the graves had only a few pottery vessels or even nothing at all, reflecting the poverty of the commoners. Those of the well-to-do exhibited "conspicuous consumption" in the form of copper vessels and beads of precious metal. The royal tombs, by contrast, were luxuriously furnished with beautifully wrought weapons and precious ornaments, and included large numbers of palace attendants—men-at-arms, harem ladies, musicians, charioteers, and general servants—who were sacrificed in order to accompany the royal occupant and attest to his power and wealth.

III. DIFFUSION OF CIVILIZATION

Such was the millennia-long evolution from autonomous farm villages to small theocratically-controlled states and eventually to dynastic empires with all of the attributes of civilization as defined above.

Once civilization took root in Mesopotamia and later in the several other regions of Eurasia and the New World, it spread out in all directions. Just as the agricultural revolution had replaced hunting societies with tribal ones, so now the tribal societies in turn were replaced by civilization. By the time tribalism had reached the peripheries of Eurasia, it was being superseded in its core areas. The displacement process continued inexorably as civilization spread out of the original river valleys and spanned adjacent areas of barbarism, until by the time of Christ it extended with virtually no interruption from the English Channel to the China Sea. (See Map VI, "Ancient Civilizations of Eurasia, 3500–1500 B.C.")

If 3500 B.C. is accepted as the approximate date for the emergence of civilization in Mesopotamia, then corresponding approximations may be given for the other centers of civilization: in Egypt, about 3000 B.C.; in the Indus Valley, about 2500 B.C.; in the Yellow River valley of China, about 1500 B.C.; and in Mesoamerica and Peru, about 500 B.C.

The New World civilizations, like New World agriculture, are believed to have developed independently of any Eurasian influences. Whether the beginnings of Chinese civilization were indigenous or stimulated indirectly from the Middle East cannot be answered at present. In the Nile and Indus valleys, civilization got under way as a result of stimulus diffusion from Mesopotamia, meaning that it was not specific techniques and institutions that were adopted, but rather the underlying ideas or principles. The *idea* of writing was taken from Sumer, but distinctive writing systems were evolved in Egypt and India; likewise with state organization, monumental architecture, and so forth.

The net result, then, was the evolution of several civilizations that shared a common general pattern but that nevertheless manifested distinctive characteristics or styles. These styles gradually took form and crystallized during these long millennia of autonomous development, so that to a considerable degree they persist to the present day.

SUGGESTED READING

The pioneer theoretical studies on the advent of civilization are by J. H. Steward, "Cultural Causality and Law: A Trial Formulation of the Development of Early Civilizations," *American Anthropologist,* January-March 1949, and V. Gordon Childe, "Urban Revolution," *Town Planning Review,* XXI (1950), 3–17. Different interpretations are presented in C. H. Kraeling and R. M. Adams, eds., *City Invincible: A Symposium on Urbanization and Cultural Development in the Ancient Near East Held at the Oriental Institute of the University of Chicago, December 4–7, 1958* (Chicago: Univ. of Chicago, 1960); and R. M. Adams, *The Evolution of Urban Society* (Chicago: Aldine, 1966). The relevant volume in the *Foundations of Modern Anthropology Series* (Englewood Cliffs, N.J.: Prentice-Hall) is by L. Krader, *Formation of the State* (1967).

Chapter
5

*There are many sorts of food,
and therefore there are many ways of life,
both of beasts and of men;
they cannot live without food,
and differences in their food have made
differences in their way of life.*

ARISTOTLE

Styles of Ancient

Civilizations

T he development of man's first civilizations several millennia ago can be analyzed in terms of technological innovation, considerations of geography, and economic organization. Though these factors are vital to an understanding of the past, they leave us with little appreciation of the people themselves—how they looked at life, death, and one another. Each of the major ancient civilizations, whether in Mesopotamia, Egypt, Crete, the Indus River valley, or the Yellow River valley, had a distinctive view of life and style of living it. Expressed through art, philosophy, literature, and law, the life styles of the ancients take on substance and color.

Much remains conjecture, for even elementary questions cannot yet be answered. We still do not know, for example, who the Sumerians were, where they came from, and whether they were the first settlers in the Mesopotamian valley or whether they built upon foundations provided by earlier inhabitants. And concerning other ancient peoples, the degree of ignorance is even greater than it is for the Sumerians. Nevertheless certain distinctive life styles are discernible in the various regions, and these are the subject of this chapter.

I. MESOPOTAMIA

Geographic environment affected profoundly the styles of the ancient Eurasian civilizations as it had their preceding Neolithic cultures. In the case of Mesopotamia this is most apparent as regards location, which meant vulnerability to invasions that molded the development of that region from earliest times to the present. Indeed its history comprises in large part a millennia-long struggle between Indo-European invaders from the north and Semitic peoples from the south for control of the fertile river valley.

The first great builders of civilization in Mesopotamia, the Sumerians, appear curiously to have been neither Indo-Europeans nor Semites. Similarities between their language and Chinese suggest some eastern place of origin. In any case it was they who in southern Mesopotamia established the first civilization by successfully harnessing the turbulent waters of the Tigris-Euphrates in an intricate network of irrigation canals. By 3000 B.C., Sumer consisted of twelve separate city states of which Uruk, for example, covered eleven hundred acres and housed perhaps as many as fifty thousand people. The cities fought continually for leadership, and the warfare became steadily more professional and costly. This weakened the Sumerians to the point where they fell subject to the Semites, whose famous leader, Sargon the Great, stands out in history as the first empire builder. Starting from his base at Akkad in the middle of the valley, he first conquered all Sumer and then marched far beyond, eventually winning an empire extending from the Persian Gulf to the Mediterranean.

This was a stupendous realm for the times but it proved short-lived. Sargon's grandson was defeated by new invaders from Iran, and the city state of Akkad was destroyed and disappeared from history. The individual Sumerian cities now reemerged and enjoyed a degree of independence until a strictly Sumerian empire was established by the ancient city of Ur. This lasted for a century from 2113 to 2006 B.C., when a new group of Semitic nomads, the Amorites, invaded the valley and, after protracted fighting, established the Babylonian Empire under their well-known ruler, Hammurabi (ca. 1704–1662 B.C.). As will be noted in the following chapters, this pattern of successive invasions was to persist to modern times, with the Amorites followed by Hittites, Assyrians, Persians, Macedonians, Romans, Arabs, and Turks.

Despite the parade of empires, ancient Mesopotamia was essentially a city civilization and commercial civilization. The cities were the basic units, and each was a sacred entity belonging to its main god. Temples and kings were large-scale capitalists, but much private capital also was invested in land, crafts, trading ventures, and money lending. The majority of citizens earned their livelihood as farmers, craftsmen, merchants, fishermen, and cattle breeders. Each city had a section reserved for the craftsmen—the masons, smiths, carpenters, potters, and jewelers. They sold their handicrafts in a free town market and were paid in kind or in money. The latter consisted of silver ingots or rings which had to be weighed after each transaction.

Outside the city walls were the fields on whose productivity the urban inhabitants ultimately were dependent. Most of the land was held in the form of large estates that belonged to the king or the priests or other wealthy persons.

Diorama showing the city of Ur (Iraq) about 2000 B.C. (Courtesy of the American Museum of Natural History)

Three limestone statues from Khafaje, Sumer, from the early dynastic period, 2700–2500 B.C. (Arborio Mella)

The workers on these estates were allotted individual plots along with seed, implements, and draft animals. In return they provided the labor and, through a variety of arrangements, yielded their surplus produce to the temple or palace or landowner. The basic crops were barley and wheat; the milk animals were goats and cows; sheep supplied the wool that was the chief textile fabric of Mesopotamia. The most common vegetables were beans, peas, garlic, leeks, onions, radishes, lettuce, and cucumbers; the fruits included melons, dates, pomegranates, figs, and apples.

The management of the estates required the keeping of accounts such as the rents received from the tenant farmers, the size of the herds, the amount of fodder needed for the animals and of seed for the next planting, and the intricate details regarding irrigation facilities and schedules. These management and accounting records were inscribed with a reed stylus on clay tablets that were then baked in order to preserve them. This earliest form of writing, known as cuneiform, was obviously not invented for intellectual purposes; rather it was an instrument of administration. As a distinguished scholar has put it, "Writing was not a deliberate invention, but the incidental by-product of a strong sense of private property, always a characteristic of classical Sumerian civilization." [1]

At first the cuneiform consisted of pictographs, so that the scribe drew simplified pictures of oxen, sheep, grain, fish, or whatever was being recorded. Soon the pictographs were conventionalized rather than being left to the artistic fancy of each scribe. This assured uniform writing and reading of records, but a basic problem remained; pictographs could not be used to depict abstract concepts. Sumerian scribes met this difficulty by adding marks to the pictographs to denote new meanings, and, more important, by selecting signs that represented sounds rather than objects or abstractions. This was the essence of the phonetic alphabet that was evolved centuries later, but the Sumerians failed to apply the phonetic principle systematically and comprehensively. They reduced their signs from an original number of about two thousand to some six hundred by 2900 B.C. This was a substantial improvement, but cuneiform remained far more cumbersome than the alphabet developed later by the Phoenicians and the Greeks. Hence there was a need for scribes, who alone had mastered the difficult art of writing and who therefore enjoyed high status and privilege.

Although the origins of writing are to be found in the new circumstances arising from the production of economic surplus, its repercussions were extraordinarily far reaching and fateful. It stimulated intellectual development by making possible the recording and accumulation of factual data, and its transmission to successive generations. Equally significant, it promoted the definition and consolidation of individual cultures by giving permanent written form to religious traditions, which thereby became sacred books, to social customs, which became law codes, and to oral myths and stories, which became classics. Thus writing became the chief means for the cultural integration of the civilizations of mankind.

The Sumerians developed sciences and mathematics, as well as writing, in response to the concrete needs of their increasingly complex society. Their earliest mathematical documents were accounts of flocks, measures of grain, and surveys of fields. Their chief contribution was the development of the first systems for measuring time, distance, area, and quantity. Also, as early as 3000 B.C., they were carefully studying and recording the movements of heavenly bodies, and their motive again was utilitarian. They believed that the will of the gods determined celestial movements, and that knowledge of those movements would enable man to ascertain divine will and act accordingly. Thus Mesopotamian astrologers in the course of many centuries accumulated an enormous amount of data that later was used to develop scientific astronomy.

The religious beliefs of the Sumerians and their successors were profoundly affected by their physical environment, and particularly by the annual flooding of the Tigris-Euphrates. What impressed them was not the periodicity of the inundation but the unpredictability of its timing and volume. The coincidence of heavy rains in the northern areas and deep snow in the Zagros and Taurus mountains frequently produced disastrous floods that devastated farmlands rather than filled irrigation canals. Ninurta, the Sumerian god of the flood, was viewed as a malevolent god rather than a benevolent one. Sumerian literature is filled with lines like these:

> The rampant flood which no man can oppose,
> Which shakes the heavens and causes earth to tremble. . . .
> And drowns the harvest in its time of ripeness.

Fear of the annual floods, together with the ever-present danger of outside invasion, left the Sumerians with a deep feeling of helplessness in a world of uncontrollable forces. "Mere man—his days are numbered," reads a Sumerian poem, "whatever he may do, he is but wind." The Mesopotamian view of life was tinged with an apprehension and pessimism reflecting the insecurity of the physical environment. Man, it was felt, had been made only to serve the gods, whose will and acts were unpredictable. Hence a variety of techniques were employed to fathom the uncertain future. One was the interpretation of diverse omens, and especially dreams. Another was hepatoscopy or divination by inspecting the livers of slaughtered animals. Still another was astrology, which, as already noted, involved the study of the planets for their imagined influence upon, or prognostication of, the destinies of men. Finally, each person had his personal god as a sort of private mentor. Through this personal god, a man could make his wishes and his needs known to the great gods who were much too remote for direct communication.

The Mesopotamians also sought to alleviate the insecurity prevailing between man and man by compiling detailed codes of law. The most outstanding of these was that of Hammurabi, which later served as the basis for the laws of other Semitic peoples, such as the Assyrians, Chaldeans, and Hebrews. The code begins with a prologue by Hammurabi stating that the gods of old had predestined Babylon to be supreme in the world, and predestined him "to cause justice to shine in the land, to destroy the wicked and the evil, that the strong might not oppress the weak." Then followed the laws themselves, some three hundred in all, seeking to regulate all social relationships, clearly and for all time. Thus the code illuminates the society as much as it does the legal system of ancient Babylon. The following are some of its typical features:

1. The application of the *jus talionis,* the principle of *an eye for an eye, a tooth for a tooth:* "If a man has knocked out the eye of a patrician, his eye

shall be knocked out. If he has broken the limb of a patrician, his limb shall be broken." (Laws 196, 197)

2. Class discrimination, so that the lower orders received less compensation: "If a man has smitten the privates of a patrician of his own rank, he shall pay one mina of silver. If the slave of anyone his smitten the privates of a freeborn man, his ear shall be cut off." (Laws 203, 205)

3. The strict requirement of a business society that property be safeguarded: "If a man has stolen goods from a temple, or house, he shall be put to death; and he that has received the stolen property from him shall be put to death." (Law 6)

4. The multitude of "welfare state" provisions, including annual price fixing for basic commodities, limitation of interest rate to twenty per cent, minute regulation of family relationships, assurance of honest weights and measures, and responsibility of the city for indemnifying victims of unsolved robbery or murder. "If the highwayman has not been caught, the man that has been robbed shall state on oath what he has lost and the city or district governor in whose territory or district the robbery took place shall restore to him what he has lost." "If a life [has been lost], the city or district governor shall pay one mina of silver to the deceased relatives." (Laws 23, 24)

5. A static view of the past, present, and future, typical of premodern peoples. Thus the code is presented as part of the divine order for the benefit of mankind under justice, and any later ruler who dares alter the code is colorfully and explicitly cursed: "a reign of sighing, days few in number, years of famine, darkness without light, sudden death, . . . the destruction of his city, the dispersion of his people, the transfer of his kingdom, the extinction of his name and memory from the land . . . his ghost [in the underworld] is to thirst for water." (Laws, Epilogue)

II. EGYPT

The next civilization to emerge—that of Egypt—owed a good deal to the original model that had taken form on the banks of the Tigris-Euphrates. It is believed that one point of contact was the area between the Nile and the Red Sea to which Sumerian traders were attracted by gold deposits. Another area of interaction was in Lebanon, where the Egyptians went to obtain timber. In the course of the trading that ensued, the Egyptians learned about the civilization of Sumer and were sufficiently stimulated so that certain forces already at work in their valley were speeded up, and the advent of civilization correspondingly hastened. But their creation was in no sense a copy of the Sumerian prototype; it was distinctive, reflecting the unique character of the Egyptian people and of their physical environment.

The Nile Valley, in contrast to the Mesopotamian, is exceptionally well protected against outside intervention by the Libyan Desert on the west, the Arabian Desert in the east, the Nubian Desert and precipitous cataracts on the south, and the harborless coast of the Delta on the north. The Egyptian people were left free in their sheltered valley to work out their own destiny. They did not have to cope with periodic inundations of either Semites or Indo-Europeans, and thus were able to preserve their ethnic identity from the time of the pharaohs to the present day. The fellaheen now working on the banks of the Nile resemble closely the figures carved and painted on the ancient temples and pyramids—the same short stature, slim physique, straight black hair, deep-set eyes, and slightly aquiline nose.

Egypt's sheltered existence allowed for political, as well as ethnic, stability. There was no kaleidoscopic succession of empires precipitated by periodic invasions. Instead the Nile River provided a natural cohesion that held the entire valley together as a stable and functioning unit. Its slow but steady current carried northbound traffic effortlessly, while the prevailing north-to-northwest winds made the return trip almost as simple. Thus the Egyptians were provided with a priceless means for reliable communication and transportation that facilitated the unification of the valley about 3100 B.C.

During the preceding centuries, pioneer agriculturists had begun the cultivation of the Nile banks as their counterparts in Mesopotamia had done considerably earlier. The fertile new fields yielded a surplus sufficient to support the diverse specialists that soon congregated in towns. Two separate kingdoms took form—Lower Egypt and Upper Egypt—each comprising about a score of provinces, or *nomes*. About 3100 B.C., King Menes, ruler of Upper Egypt, united the two kingdoms, thereby beginning what is known as the Dynastic Period. Egypt now possessed the basic attributes of civilization, including a system of writing as well as professional administrators, soldiers, religious leaders, and artists.

The outstanding feature of the Dynastic Period was the remarkable political continuity. The so-called Old Kingdom, comprising six dynasties, endured for more than eight centuries from 3100 to 2270 B.C. No comparable period of political stability may be found in the annals of Mesopotamia. Towards the end of the Sixth Dynasty the authority of the kings no longer was absolute, and was increasingly challenged by independent provincial governors. An age of discord followed, known as the First Intermediate Period (2270–2060 B.C.). Upstart kings vied with one another for the support of the nobles, and invaders swept in from Libya and Asia. Finally the Eleventh Dynasty restored order and launched Egypt on the second period of stability, that of the Middle Kingdom (2060–1785 B.C.). The old pattern was repeated, though in obviously telescoped form. In less than three centuries Egypt was experiencing a Second Intermediate Period (1785–1580 B.C.), during which the country was invaded—and for the first time, conquered—by chariot-riding warriors, the Hyksos. As noted in the following chapter, these were but one group in an elemental movement of peoples that overran all centers of civilization in Eurasia in the course of the second millennium B.C.

The civilization of Egypt was generally stable and conservative, but by no means static. During the fifteen centuries between King Menes and the Hyksos, many changes in institutions and practices took place. Yet certain distinctive traits did persist through the centuries. One was the generally confident and optimistic world outlook of the Egyptians in contrast to that of the Sumerians. Just as the unpredictability and ferocity of the annual flooding of the Tigris-Euphrates contributed to the pessimism and insecurity of the Sumerians, so the predictability and gradualness of the Nile floods promoted opposite traits amongst the Egyptians. Whereas the Sumerians regarded their flood god as malevolent, the Egyptians viewed theirs as a deity "whose coming brings joy to every human being." One of the ancient Egyptian poets described the beneficence of the life-giving river as follows:

Is it not surprising . . . to see this great sovereign
Imposing on us . . . neither taxes, nor forced labor?
And who, moreover, faithful to his subjects, is sincere in his promises?
Look how, regularly and progressively,
He keeps his promises and offers gifts to everyone . . .
To Upper Egypt, to Lower Egypt
To the poor and to the rich, to the strong and to the weak,
Without distinction, taking neither side.
These are his gifts, more precious than silver and gold. . . .[2]

Egyptian religious beliefs and practices were extraordinarily complicated. They were made up of many elements—worship of the forces of nature, local sects devoted to the divinities of specific cities and nomes, the evolving beliefs of the priestly hierarchy, and diverse influences from abroad, especially from the East. The names of at least two thousand gods are known to us, yet none of these were regarded by their worshippers with complete submission or awe. The Egyptians believed instead that the deities were to be circumvented or manipulated for their personal or communal benefit. The aid of deities was invoked for unethical as well as ethical purposes, and the elaborate rituals performed in temples were as much incantations as acts of worship. During the later dynasties the idea that eternal afterlife was the reward for those who had been just and good in this life gradually developed. But Egyptian religion, with certain notable exceptions, had little ethical content. Also the mythology and theology lacked coherence, for the Egyptians were generally uninterested in the origins, characteristics, and relationships of their deities.

A predominant feature of Egyptian religious belief concerned death and the physical preparations for the afterlife, especially that of the king. Since his death was not final, his body was embalmed and placed in a gigantic tomb or pyramid, along with food and other necessities. The greatest of these pyramids was that of the Pharaoh Khufu, or Cheops, of the Fourth Dynasty. It covered 13 acres, rose to a height of 481 feet, and contained some 2,300,000 blocks, each weighing an average of 2 1/2 tons. And this was done with the simplest tools—ramps, rollers, and levers; no pulleys and no iron!

It has been said that the Eygptian peasants worked enthusiastically on these pyramids, believing that they were constructing the dwellings of a god on whom their collective well-being would depend. Whatever the justification for this statement—and it may be assumed that, enthusiastic or not, they had little choice in the matter—it does point up the presumed divinity of Egyptian kingship. From beginning to end the pharaoh was a god-king. No distinction was made between the sacred and the secular; indeed the notion was unthinkable. For this reason there was an absence in Egypt of anything corresponding to the Mesopotamian law codes. All law was the expression of the divine authority of the god-king.

This royal authority was enforced by a bureaucracy headed by the vizier— "the steward of the whole land," "the eyes and ears of the king." Other officials included the Royal Sealbearer, who controlled the Nile traffic, the Master of

Largesse, who was responsible for all livestock, and the head of the Exchequer, who maintained branch offices with storehouses throughout the kingdom for the collection of taxes, and, probably, for the distribution of seeds and livestock in bad years. Also there were governors or *nomarchs* to rule each province, or *nome,* and below them came the mayors of the towns and villages. As in other empires, the nomarchs gradually accumulated large estates, became a hereditary official class, enhanced their power and status, and ultimately challenged central authority. This explains in large part the disruption of the Old Kingdom and the ensuing centuries of anarchy. During the Middle Kingdom the pharaohs never regained their original absolute power. Although still popularly invested with divine aura, they found it necessary in practice to share their authority with the priests and the nobles. Hence the Middle Kingdom is sometimes known as the Feudal Age of Egypt, though a strong bureaucracy did keep the nobles in check.

A final distinctive feature of Egyptian civilization was the overwhelming state domination of economic life. Individual property and enterprise were not unknown but neither were they as common as in Mesopotamia. The state not only controlled most production, both agricultural and handicraft, but also directed distribution. Huge government warehouses and granaries were filled with the taxes collected in kind—grains, animals, cloths, and metals. These served to defray state expenses and also provided reserves for years of scarcity. The king, it was said, is "he who presides over the food supplies of all." In addition to the taxes, each community had to provide men for the *corvée,* or forced labor. The pyramids are the best known examples of their work, but these laborers were also used for quarrying and mining and maintaining the irrigation canals.

Egyptian craftsmen were universally recognized for their skills, particularly in luxury products. Their jewelry can scarcely be excelled today; their enamel work and ivory and pearl inlay were superb; they discovered how to make glass in many colors; they were the first to bark-tan leather in the manner still followed in most of the world; and their linen cloth was as fine as has ever been woven. Egyptian technology was perhaps most precocious in devising artificial beauty aids. Medical papyri described procedures for removing wrinkles and darkening gray hair. Among the substances used for cosmetic purposes were kohl for lengthening the eyebrows and lining the outer corners of the eyes, malachite and lead ore for green and gray eye shadow respectively, red ocher for rouge, henna for dyeing the nails, the palms of the hand and the soles of the feet, and human hair for making wigs over which melted beeswax was poured. Ladies who wished to be in the height of fashion gilded their breasts and painted their nipples blue.

III. CRETE

The Minoan civilization of the island of Crete is named after its legendary king, Minos. Until the late nineteenth century the very existence of this civilization was unsuspected. The tales of heroes and gods recounted by Homer in the *Iliad* and *Odyssey* had been dismissed by scholars as folk myths. But they were believed by a German romanticist, Heinrich Schliemann, who vowed he would find and excavate Troy, where Greeks and Trojans had fought over Helen. Schliemann acquired the necessary funds by smuggling tea into Russia and began his search in 1870. He was sensationally successful, unearthing both Troy in Asia Minor and Mycenae in the Peloponnesus, though with disastrous results for archaeology. With more enthusiasm than professional competence, he hopelessly scrambled the remains of a series of superimposed settlements. But the existence of a preclassical civilization in Greece had been proven, and at the end of the century the center of the Minoan civilization was unearthed by the English archaeologist Sir Arthur Evans at Knossos on Crete.

Neolithic communities had been long established on Crete when new settlers with new skills arrived from Asia Minor or Syria early in the third millennium B.C. These found a fertile land, well-known for its fish, its fruit, and especially its olive oil. Also its location in the middle of the eastern Mediterranean was ideal for trading purposes, the waters being safe and the climatic conditions favorable for small vessels propelled by oars or sails. From Crete a mariner could scud along, almost always in sight of land, north to Greece and the Black Sea, east to the Levant coast, south to Egypt, or west to islands and coasts of the central and western Mediterranean. Little wonder that Crete became the entrepôt of the Mediterranean basin. This location, furthermore, was ideal for cultural development as well as commercial. The Cretans were close enough to be stimulated by Mesopotamia and Egypt, yet distant enough to be free to preserve their identity and express their individuality. This they did with such success that their civilization is indubitably the most graceful and zestful of the ancient world.

Minoan artists did not try to impress by mere size, nor did they concern themselves with remote and awful deities or divine kings. Instead they reproduced the life about them on their household utensils, on the walls of their houses, and in their works of art. They found models everywhere; in natural objects such as birds, flowers, sea shells, and marine life of all types; and in scenes from their own everyday life, such as peasants returning from their fields, athletes wrestling with bulls, and women dancing in honor of the Great Goddess. In architecture the Minoans were more interested in personal comfort than outward appearance. The royal palace at Knossos was a sprawling complex that apparently had grown over several centuries. It included not only a throne room, reception chambers, and living quarters, but also storehouses and workshops that occupied most of the complex, as befitted a trading people. Outstanding was an elaborate plumbing and sanitation system that was not surpassed until modern times. The drains were arranged so that the rain water flushed the sewers and kept them clean, and manholes enabled workmen to enter the sewers for repairs.

Women appear to have enjoyed a freedom and social status equal to that of men. Frescoes show them crowding the bleachers at the bull arena and actually participating in the bull wrestling. Some even took part in war, in contrast to the feminine homebodies of Mesopotamia and Egypt, and, for that matter, of classical Greece.

The Minoans do not appear to have constructed great temples or monuments to their gods. Rather they set aside a few square feet in their homes to serve as private sanctuaries. The Knossos complex had a small room which seems to

North entrance to Knossos, site of earliest center of civilization on Crete. (Gabriele Wunderlich)

have been a chapel. The principal centers of worship were nature places—a mountain peak, a forest grove, or a limestone cave. The most important deity was female, the old Earth Mother, who was served by priestesses rather than priests. There are no indications of human or extensive animal sacrifices, the most common offerings being the fruits of the field.

Most Minoans doubtless tilled the soil, but their civilization definitely was amphibious—a thalassocracy, or sea civilization. The forests that covered their mountains provided the timber for constructing vessels in which they sailed from one end of the Mediterranean to the other. With their singlemasted ships they carried back and forth the foodstuffs, ivory, and glass of Egypt, the horses and wood of Syria, the silver, pottery, and marble of the Aegean Isles, the copper of Cyprus, and their own olive oil and pottery. The Minoans doubtless indulged in piracy when the opportunity presented itself. In the *Odyssey,* King Nestor politely asks Odysseus' son, Telemachus, whether he be a trader or a pirate. Both occupations were regarded as perfectly respectable, merely offering the mariner alternate ways of getting what he wanted.

Cretan communities seem to have been socially and economically more egalitarian than their counterparts on the mainland. In place of a few great temples and palaces surrounded by relative slums, the pattern on Crete was the open village, with its outdoor shrine as the center for community life. Families as a rule lived in individual houses built of timber and stucco. Domestic slaves probably were held, though not in large numbers. No buildings that may have been slave quarters have been found, so that the Cretan galleys presumably were rowed by freemen. None of the cities were fortified, indicating that Minoan sea power was deemed sufficient to protect the island. It suggests furthermore that the Cretan communities lived at peace with each other, in contrast to the traditional intercity warfare in Mesopotamia. All in all, it is understandable that ancient writers referred to Crete as "great, fat, and well-fed"—the Isle of the Blessed.

IV. INDUS

About 2500 B.C., or approximately one thousand years after the appearance of man's first civilization at Sumer, another civilization emerged on the banks of the Indus River. It existed in solitary splendor until roughly 1500 B.C., when it petered out for reasons not yet entirely clear. Then it was completely forgotten, so that the Indians assumed their history began with the appearance of the Aryan invaders about 1500 B.C., just as the Greeks of the Classical Age assumed that their history began in, 776 B.C., the year of the first Olympic games. In the 1920's archaeologists were attracted to a desolate spot on the lower Indus River containing several mounds and called by the local people Mohenjo-daro, or Place of the Dead. These mounds already had been raided by the builders of the Lahore-Multan railway in search of bricks for ballast, as well as by local householders who helped themselves to the inexhaustible supplies of bricks as needed. Despite these depredations, excavations revealed that Mohenjo-daro was the site of a succession of flourishing cities, each built upon the ruins of the one before. Further excavations in other parts of the

The city of Mohenjo-daro, showing covered draining running through one of the smaller streets that subdivide the city according to a rigid plan. (Arborio Mella)

Figure of a priest—uncovered at Mohenjo-daro. (Arborio Mella)

Indus Valley and surrounding territories uncovered an ancient civilization several times more widespread than either the Egyptian or Mesopotamian. It encompassed a triangular area roughly one thousand miles on each side, with the base of the triangle along the coast north and south of the mouth of the Indus, and extending northeastward to the foothills of the Himalayas.

Knowledge of this civilization is still at a rudimentary stage, so that further excavations may cause complete revision of current assumptions. The roots of the civilization have been traced back to an amalgam of indigenous Neolithic communities and immigrant farmers from the hills of Baluchistan who moved south into the Indus Valley early in the third millennium B.C. It is believed that the newcomers brought with them some knowledge of the cities and ways of Sumer, which facilitated the emergence of civilization on the Indus as it had earlier on the Nile. Archaeologists have unearthed two large cities and some sixty to seventy towns and villages within the great triangle of civilization, and it may be assumed that more will be found with further excavations.

Like all the other ancient civilizations, that of the Indus was predominantly agricultural. Wheat and barley were the staples, but field peas, melons, sesame, and dates were also grown, as well as cotton, which was first used for cloth making in this valley. Domesticated animals included dogs, cats, humped cattle, buffalo, and possibly pigs, camels, horses, and asses. There was also considerable trade with the outside world, including Mesopotamia, where Indus seals have been found amongst ruins dated at 2300 B.C. Other Indus products discovered on the Persian Gulf island of Bahrain suggest that this was an intermediate point in seaborne trade between Mesopotamia and the Indus.

The Indus cities were unique for their time because they were carefully built according to a central plan rather than haphazardly like rabbit warrens. Each city at its height extended over six to seven square miles. They were laid out on the grid pattern, with wide main streets encompassing large rectangular city blocks some four hundred yards in length and two hundred yards in width, far larger than the average city blocks of today. The buildings were constructed of bricks hardened in kilns, in contrast to the stone used in Egypt and the sun-dried bricks in Mesopotamia. The bricks everywhere were molded in two standard sizes (11 by 5.5 by 2.5 inches, and 9.2 by 4.5 by 2.2 inches), and weights and measures likewise were uniform throughout the Indus lands. Such orderliness and organization seem to have been all pervasive in this civilization. After it reached its maturity about 2500 B.C., it remained virtually static during the following millennium. This was carried even to the point of rebuilding the cities after each destructive flood in such a way that the new city was a duplicate of the old one. Such undeviating continuity of tradition has had no equal, even in Egypt, and has given rise to the theory that the authority regulating this disciplined society may have been spiritual. This hypothesis is supported also by the absence of military equipment and fortifications. But all this is mere speculation, and must remain so until more sites have been excavated and until the Indus script has been deciphered. The script is pictographic and is read from left to right on one line and from right to left on the following line. This is the practice followed in Early Greek and is known as boustrophedon—"as the ox plows."

The causes and circumstances of the decline of the Indus civilization remain obscure. Hitherto it has been widely believed that Aryan invaders were primarily responsible, but it has recently been suggested that the civilization may have been literally drowned in mud. Subterranean volcanic activity, according to this theory, caused a huge upwelling of mud, silt, and sand that dammed the river and formed a huge lake that swamped Mohenjo-daro. After several decades the dam was worn down, the water drained through, and the river resumed its normal course, but in the meantime the city had been ruined. Judging from the multiple layers of silt found in Mohenjo-daro, this disaster occurred at least five times and perhaps more. The net result was irreparable damage to the heart of the Indus civilization, which left the outlying regions in the north too weak to resist the Aryan invaders, and in the south too weak to resist assimilation by native cultures.

63

V. SHANG

Not until about two thousand years after civilization first flowered in Mesopotamia did it appear in the valley of the Yellow River. There it was nourished by the fine compact soil known as loess, which extends from the uplands of North China eastward to the sea. This soil is believed to have been laid by wind action during the Pleistocene period, and in some localities is two hundred to three hundred feet deep. Because of its natural fertility and water-holding quality it is equal to any soil in the world for agricultural purposes. Furthermore the rainfall in North China is scanty, so that, as in Mesopotamia, Egypt, and the Indus Valley, there were no heavy forests to discourage early agriculturists with their primitive stone tools.

Another reason why the Yellow River valley was the center of the first Chinese civilization was that it is the most accessible region from the West. Nomads traversing the Central Eurasian steppes are deflected by mountain ranges towards North China rather than to the south. These nomads, as noted earlier were instruments of cultural cross fertilization as well as of raid and rapine. (See Chapter 1, section III.) This raises the question as to the degree to which the Shang civilization was indigenous or was stimulated by indirect contacts in the Middle East. The generally accepted theory is that the Shang were a relatively small group of Mongoloid invaders from the northwest steppes where they had indirectly acquired from the Middle East a knowledge of bronze and of war chariots. Exploiting the military advantage deriving from the technology, they conquered the Neolithic agricultural communities of North China.

Now a pattern of evolution ensued that was to appear repeatedly in the following millennia after each incursion into the country. The Shang enriched the local culture with the innovations they introduced, but were eventually assimilated, so that the Chinese traditions continued without interruption. The Shang civilization, then, comprised elements that doubtless were ultimately of Middle East derivation if traced back to their early Neolithic origins—elements such as barley, wheat, sheep, cattle, horses, bronze, and the wheel. Yet alongside these were indubitably native East Asian traits that, combined with the foreign adaptations, constituted the great and distinctive Chinese civilization that has persisted with an unequalled record of continuity from the Shang dynasty to modern times.

One of the uniquely Chinese culture traits was the raising of silkworms and the weaving of the fibers into delicate fabrics. Another was the eschewing of animal milk for human consumption, particularly noteworthy in view of the prominence of milk and milk products in the diet of Eurasian nomads. Ancestor worship has also been a prominent feature of Chinese religion from earliest times. Closely related was the importance attached to one's family name, which always preceded the personal name instead of following it as in the West. This reflected the traditional primary role in Chinese society of the family rather than of the individual, the state, or the church. The familiar Chinese style of architecture with the ornate roof supported by rows of wooden pillars also dates back to earliest times.

The Shang technique of bronze casting is particularly noteworthy, having never been surpassed anywhere in the world. The ritual bronze vessels were used in the preparation and offering of sacrificial meats, grain, and wine during the ancestor worship ceremonies. The vessels were of all sizes and shapes, ranging from massive four-legged caldrons and copious jars for storing wine to graceful goblets, exotic sauceboats, animal heads, and memorial masks. The surfaces of these bronzes were richly ornamented with geometric designs and a proliferation of real and imaginary animals. The general design pattern is quite distinct from anything known anywhere to the west, but bears such similarities to patterns in the South Seas and among the Pacific Northwest Indians that a Pacific Basin type of design is recognized.

Most significant for the later history of China and all East Asia was the complex ideographic script found in Shang remains. This is the direct ancestor of modern Chinese writing, thus illustrating again the continuity of Chinese civilization. Whereas the hieroglyphics and cuneiform have for millennia meant nothing to the people of the Middle East, the Shang script is recognizable to modern Chinese. Most of the Shang writing surviving today is found on animal bones and turtle shells that were used for divination purposes, another distinctive Chinese custom. Questions about sickness, dreams, hunting, the weather, or the harvest were inscribed on the bone or shell. Incisions were then made at various points, and red-hot sticks pressed at these points, producing cracks. The shape, arrangement, and direction of these cracks were interpreted for the "Yes" or "No" answer given by the diviner. These shells were carefully buried, so that many have survived and have revealed a good deal about Shang daily life as well as about the Shang script.

Since the Shang dynasty created the first formal political structure in China, it was not able during its existence to establish a bureaucracy comparable to those that had developed through the centuries in Mesopotamia and Egypt. Consequently each district was ruled by its own hereditary noble family, which retained a good deal of autonomy. The authority of the central government under these circumstances depended primarily on the personality of the ruler.

As with the other Eurasian civilizations, the peasants here also were required to yield a portion of their crops to support the nobles, scribes, and officials gathered in the towns. Also they were obliged to serve under their lords in time of war as a light-armed infantry. Only the ruling warrior class could afford the two-horse chariots and the bronze helmets and plate mail that they wore into battle. This monopoly of bronze metallurgy buttressed the sharp class differentiation within Shang society. This was reflected in the contrast between the elaborate palaces and royal tombs on the one hand, and the crude pit dwellings of the common people on the other. It was illustrated also by the costly offerings that were placed in the tombs—bronze ritual vessels, fine silks, jades, marbles, musical instruments, and elaborate weapons. Even more impressive was the mass human slaughter, usually in multiples of ten, that accompanied royal burials. It is unknown whether the hapless victims, presumably slaves or prisoners of war, were sacrificed to propitiate vengeful gods or to become the slaves and concubines of the dead monarch.

SUGGESTED READING

Two lavishly illustrated surveys of the ancient civilizations are *The Epic of Man*, by the Editors of *Life* (New York: Time Incorporated, 1961). and *The Dawn of Civilization* (New York: McGraw-Hill, 1961). Other overall surveys are available in the pertinent chapters of R. Turner, *The Great Cultural Traditions*, Vol. I (New York: McGraw-Hill, 1941); W. H. McNeill, *The Rise of the West* (Chicago: Univ. of Chicago, 1963); and J. Hawkes and L. Wooley, *Prehistory and the Beginnings of Civilization*, UNESCO History of Mankind: Cultural and Scientific Development (New York: Harper & Row, 1963).

Most of the available studies deal with the region best known—the Middle East. These include H. Frankfort, *The Birth of Civilization in the Near East* (Garden City, N.Y.: Doubleday, 1956), Anchor Book; L. Cottrell, *The Anvil of Civilization* (New York: New American Library, 1957), Mentor Book; M. Covensky, *The Ancient Near Eastern Tradition* (New York: Harper & Row, 1966); Jean-Philippe Lévy, *The Economic Life of the Ancient World* (Chicago: Univ. of Chicago, 1964); J. A. Wilson, *The Culture of Ancient Egypt* (Chicago: Univ. of Chicago, 1951), Phoenix Books; L. Cottrell, *The Warrior Pharaohs* (London: Evans, 1969); B. Sewell, *Egypt under the Pharaohs* (London: Evans, 1969); S. N. Kramer, *Sumerian Mythology* (New York: Harper & Row, 1961), Torchbooks; S. N. Kramer, *History Begins at Sumer* (New York: Doubleday, 1959), Anchor Books; R. F. Willetts, *Everyday Life in Ancient Crete* (London: Batsford, 1969); and W. H. McNeill and J. W. Sedlar, eds., *The Origins of Civilization* and *The Ancient Near East* (New York: Oxford Univ., 1968), both of which consist of readings in primary sources. Works dealing with other ancient civilizations are R. Ghirshman, *Iran* (Baltimore: Penguin, 1954), Pelican Book; S. Piggott, *Prehistoric India* (Baltimore: Penguin, 1950), Pelican Book; and W. A. Fairservis, Jr., *The Origins of Oriental Civilization* (New York: New American Library, 1959), Mentor Book.

Chapter
6

*Since conquests are achieved only by
dash and daring, a people accustomed
to the nomadic life and the rough manners
engendered by tne desert can readily
conquer a more civilized people,
even though the latter be more numerous. . . .*

IBN KHALDUN

End of Ancient

Civilizations

In all civilizations there have been poets and thinkers who
have looked to the past with longing. They have regarded prehistoric
man as the "noble savage," untainted by the corrupting influence of
civilization. Long ago, "in the beginning," during that wonderful first
chapter of man's existence, there was paradise on earth. In the Hindu
epics there are passages extolling an idyllic past in which castes were
absent and man could enjoy life in freedom and security. Likewise
Hesiod, an eighth century B.C. Greek poet, described a Golden Age
of long ago, and then traced man's declining fortunes through the Silver and Iron ages to the deplorable present in which the author lived.

This concept of original bliss has some basis in historical fact,
as its universality and persistence suggest. The various civilizations of
the ancient world differed from each other in their respective "styles"—
in their ways of looking at, and going through, life. But all of them
were similar in one basic respect. They all changed man's relations
with his fellow men in the same way. They all substituted a new class
society for the classless society of precivilization times, with profound
repercussions in every aspect of human society, including not only
increased productivity, but also increased social fragility and consequent vulnerability to nomadic invasions. The purpose of this chapter

is to analyze the historical significance of the ancient civilizations and the circumstances of the great invasions of the second millennium B.C. that laid the groundwork for the classical civilizations that followed.

I. HISTORICAL SIGNIFICANCE OF ANCIENT CIVILIZATIONS

So far as economic and social relationships were concerned, the tribesmen before the advent of civilization had enjoyed free and equal access to the natural resources necessary for livelihood. Economic equality and social homogeneity had been the hallmark of their Neolithic villages. But when the tribesmen became peasants they no longer had free access to land and they no longer enjoyed the full product of their labor. Their specific obligations varied from region to region but the net result was everywhere the same. After making the payments required by the state, the priest, the landlord, and the moneylender, they were left almost invariably with only enough for sheer existence. In contrast to the egalitarianism of the Paleolithic hunting bands and the Neolithic villages, the ancient civilizations, as well as those of later periods, inevitably involved stratification into haves and have-nots.

What this meant in human terms was expressed as early as the third millennium B.C. by an Egyptian father taking his son to school and exhorting him to industry by contrasting the wretchedness of both peasants and workers with the blessings of learned scribes and officials.

> Put writing in your heart that you may protect yourself from hard labor of any kind and be a magistrate of high repute. The scribe is released from manual tasks; it is he who commands. . . . Do you not hold the scribe's palette? That is what makes the difference between you and the man who handles an oar.
>
> I have seen the metal-worker at his task at the mouth of his furnace, with fingers like a crocodile's. He stank worse than fish-spawn. . . . The stonemason finds his work in every kind of hard stone. When he has finished his labors his arms are worn out, and he sleeps all doubled up until sunrise. His knees and spine are broken. . . . The barber shaves from morning till night; he never sits down except to meals. He hurries from house to house looking for business. He wears out his arms to fill his stomach, like bees eating their own honey. . . . The farmer wears the same clothes for all times. His voice is as raucous as a crow's. His fingers are always busy, his arms are dried up by the wind. He takes his rest— when he does get any rest—in the mud. If he's in good health he shares good health with the beasts; if he is ill his bed is the bare earth in the middle of his beasts. . . .
>
> Apply your heart to learning. In truth there is nothing that can compare with it. If you have profited by a single day at school it is a gain for eternity.[1]

The coming of civilization involved drastic change in political relationships. The Neolithic villagers had been subject to only rudimentary constraints, whether internal or external. But tribal chiefs and elders now were replaced by king or emperor, and by an omnipresent bureaucracy, including palace functionaries, provincial and district officials, judges, clerks, and accountants. Closely associated with this imperial administration was the ecclesiastical hierarchy that also was an integral feature of civilization. In place of the former shaman who had been a "leisure-time specialist," there now was the priest, a "full-time specialist." [2] This made possible the formulation of an official theology and the organization of a priestly hierarchy. Both the theology and the hierarchy served to buttress the secular order. They invested political institutions and leaders with divine sanction and attributes. The Mesopotamian *ishakku* was the vice-regent of his city's god, while the Egyptian pharaoh was the "living god." This coupling of divine and secular authority provided most powerful support for the *status quo*. It was a rare individual who dared risk swift retribution in this life and everlasting punishment in the hereafter.

As regards culture, the transformation wrought by civilization again was fundamental and enduring. The culture of a Neolithic village had been autonomous and homogeneous. All members had shared common knowledge, customs, and attitudes, and had not depended on outside sources for the maintenance of their way of life. But with civilization, a new and more complex society emerged. In addition to the traditional culture of the village agriculturist, there was now the new culture of the scribes, who knew the mysterious art of writing, of the priests, who knew the secrets of the heavens, of the artists, who knew how to paint and carve, and of the merchants, who exchanged goods with lands beyond deserts and seas. So there was no longer a single culture. Instead there developed what has been called *high culture* and *low culture*. The high culture was to be found in the schools, temples, and palaces of the cities; the low culture was in the villages. The high culture was passed on in writing by philosophers, theologians, and literary men; the low culture was transmitted by word of mouth among illiterate peasants.

The distinction between high and low culture has usually been overlooked because of our dependence upon written sources. Such sources naturally point up the existence of the various high cultures and their individual characteristics rather than the equally significant coexistence of high and low cultures within each civilization. In order to fully comprehend the experiences of mankind since the coming of civilization, it is essential to look within the individual civilizations as well as at them as a group. It is essential, in the words of the anthropologist Robert Redfield, to "slip in by the back entrance, through the villages. . . ." [3] If this is done, one finds everywhere the peasants in place of the Neolithic tribesmen. And all these peasant masses, in all parts of the civilized world, remained in many basic respects the same from the days of Sumer to the present time. Their skin color may have been brown or yellow or white. They may have grown rice or wheat or corn. Yet everywhere, as the historian Oscar Handlin has pointed out, "the peasant masses had maintained an imperturbable sameness." [4]

All the peasantries possessed in common a considerable body of factual information related to agriculture—information regarding the weather, the care of plants and animals, and the processes of combustion and fermentation. All the peasantries also regarded hard labor as a prime virtue and looked down upon townsmen as weaklings who were easily tired. Closely related was a common passion to own a plot of land, a few animals, and the simple tools of field and shop. This meant independence and security, and to attain this all peasantries stubbornly resisted outside intervention, whether by a landlord or by a present-day collective. This peasant "rugged individualism" was balanced, however, by the communal life and relationships of the village. The good neighbor was always ready to offer aid and sympathy when needed, as well as to participate in house raisings, warmings, harvest festivals, and other community affairs.

Relations between the high and low cultures normally were ambivalent and strained. On the one hand the peasants felt superior, regarding country life and agricultural work as morally "good," in contrast to urban life and professions. On the other hand they were economically and politically subject to the city. From there came the landlords, the tax collectors, the prelates, and the soldiers. Their arrogance and arbitrariness made it crystal clear who were the rulers and who the ruled. Whereas the peasants idealized hard work, the elite regarded it as degrading and fit only for the masses who were capable of nothing better. The elite explained their refinements of life, made possible by their exploitation of the peasantry, as the product of their own superior mental and moral qualities. Inevitably the Eurasian peasantries, in the course of millennia, internalized this attitude and became servile and obsequious. And for those who refused to bend the knee, there was always ready at hand the physical violence of the soldier and the psychological violence of the priest. What scars this left on human beings is all too clear in the following report of present-day Indonesian peasants bowing and scraping before Dutch officials while Papuan tribesmen stand erect.

> A Dutch official walked into an office in Hollandia [New Guinea]. Seated at a table were an Indonesian official, still in the Netherland's service, and two Papuan village headmen. The Indonesian jumped to his feet and stood still. The Papuans looked up, smiled and remained seated.
>
> In the bar of a grimy Government hotel, about 9 o'clock one night, a Dutch official asked the Papuan bartender for a beer. The bartender, after five minutes, produced it. He also produced a pointed look at a wristwatch and asked the Dutchman how long he intended to stay.
>
> A Dutch destroyer pulled into a south New Guinea coastal port. Local Dutch officials thought it would be a good idea to show some people from the jungles, still in the head-hunting stage, some real weapons.
>
> Jungle people trekked down, wandered around the ship, and one of them gave the verdict:
>
> "Yes, you have guns. But see these bows and arrows that we have? We think you are not able to use these fine bows and arrows. We can use them. . . ."
>
> Netherlands officials who have seen service in Indonesia, have had to do some considerable adjusting in New Guinea.
>
> In Indonesia they came into a society that had its caste and class distinc-

tions, its own ideas of authority and rights of rulers. They were masters and were treated as masters.

In New Guinea there are no masters and no slaves. Papuan life is a free sort of life. There are no village councils, no great lawgivers or authorities. A man's pretty much his own man, except for the influence on life of demons and spirits.

Between the Dutch and the Papuans there is no bowing and scraping. An Indonesian schoolteacher who tried to convince Papuans that the proper way to show respect was to walk hunched over in front of superiors was told:

"We are men, and men walk straight." [5]

It is evident that the advent of civilization represented a setback for equality between man and man. On the other hand civilization also brought great gains and achievements. Viewed in the light of historical perspective, it constituted a major step forward in the evolution of man. In this respect it resembled the industrial revolution, which initially was responsible for painful social disruption and incalculable human suffering, but which in the long run advanced decisively man's productivity and well-being. So it was with the urban revolution and civilization. The average Neolithic tribesman probably led a more rounded and satisfying life than the average peasant or urban worker. But precisely because tribal culture was comfortable and tension-free, it was also relatively unproductive. (See Chapter 3, section IV.) The exactions of the tax collector, the priest, and the landowner were onerous, but they were also effective in stimulating output. Positive proof of the increased productivity was the enormous population increase in the river valleys. "The vast areas of the new cities as compared with any barbarian [Neolithic] village, the immense cemeteries attached to them, and the stupendous works executed by the citizens, place this conclusion beyond question." [6]

Living standards also rose along with population figures. Certainly the monarchs and the top officials, both secular and ecclesiastical, enjoyed a variety of food and drink, along with an opulence in clothing and accommodations that no tribal chieftain could ever have imagined. The new middle classes—merchants, scribes, lower officials, and clergy—also were able to lead lives that probably were as pleasant and refined as those enjoyed by their counterparts today. Even the masses may in some cases have been better off in the material sense, if not the psycho-social. A British archaeologist has pointed out that, "The sea-fish . . . brought to Lagash from the Persian Gulf and to Mohenjo-daro from the Arabian Sea were probably articles of popular consumption that a Stone Age peasant could never enjoy. The workmen's quarters at Harappa are more commodious than Neolithic huts." [7]

Civilization, with the new art of writing, also made possible the steady accumulation of knowledge and its transmission to successive generations. Innumerable examples of the astonishing technical triumphs of antiquity abound in present-day museums. Various sciences, including mathematics, astronomy, and medicine, also trace their beginnings back to these millennia.

And the very affluence of the urban centers opened new horizons for architects, sculptors, painters, musicians, and poets.

It is true that these precious gains benefitted the few much more than the many who, in the final analysis, bore the costs of the high culture. But the important point so far as the whole history of man is concerned is that the advances *were* made. And it was these advances, accumulating through the millennia, that finally enabled man in modern times to gain such mastery over nature and such productivity through science and technology, that the many are now benefitting along with the few. During the long intervening period the low culture of the villages remained largely unchanged. But the various high cultures underwent continual change—in their religions and philosophies and arts and sciences. These changes will be considered in parts III and IV, after the circumstances of the decline and fall of the ancient civilizations are examined in the following sections.

II. NOMADS ENTER HISTORY

The second millennium B.C. in Eurasia was a period of turbulence—a period of nomadic invasions, of the overthrow of old imperial structures, and of the disruption of old social systems. The ferment was profound and the dislocation was felt from one end of Eurasia to the other. For this reason, the second millennium was an age of transition in the course of which the ancient civilizations disappeared from the historical stage and their place taken by the classical civilizations.

Such wholesale fall and rise of empires, which has occurred more than once in the course of history, raises the question of causation. Was it internal rot or external force that was primarily responsible for political and social demolition throughout Eurasia? It is extremely difficult to answer such a broad question with certainty and precision. The degree to which, in the several regions involved, internal factors were operative as against external cannot be ascertained exactly, though it is safe to assert that both were major factors in determining the course of events.

Beginning with the internal weaknesses, there was first the scarcity and costliness of copper and bronze, which prevented the general use of these metals in making weapons and tools. This gave monarchs and their political and military allies a virtual monopoly of armaments and hence buttressed their privileged position at the top of the social pyramid. It also meant that only a small percentage of the total population was armed, a serious weakness when the old centers of civilization had to face the assault of nomads who were all armed.

The high cost of copper and bronze also deprived the peasantry of metal tools, and perforce they had to rely on stone axes and hoes, and on flint knives and sickles. This lowered productivity considerably, since stone tools were less efficient and durable than metal. Productivity also was curbed by the petering out of technological progress. "The thousand years or so immediately preceding 3000 B.C.," writes the British archaeologist V. Gordon Childe, "were perhaps more fertile in fruitful inventions and discoveries than any period in human history prior to the sixteenth century A.D." [8] This was the millennium, as noted earlier, when man learned to harness the power of wind and of animals, when he discovered the wheel, the art of writing, the technique of irrigation, and the chemical processes involved in metallurgy. (See Chapter 4, section II.) By contrast the third and second millennia B.C. witnessed nothing approaching this great creative outburst; the only comparable inventions during this later period were iron smelting (1400 B.C.) and a truly alphabetic script (1300 B.C.).

One partial explanation for the slowdown in technological growth, according to V. Gordon Childe, was the class differentiation noted in the preceding section. This differentiation undermined incentive for technological innovation. The ruling groups now had an abundant supply of docile labor available in the form of tenants or slaves, but the latter were unlikely to take the initiative in devising or adopting new techniques or devices when any increase in output would benefit others rather than themselves. This brake upon innovation because of social inequity persists to the present day, as indicated by the following comments made recently by a villager in India to an American missionary:

> To a newcomer we may seem suspicious, obstinate, intolerant, backward
> —everything that goes with refusal to change. We did not choose these
> characteristics for ourselves. Experience forced them upon our fathers.
> and the warnings of our father, added to our experiences, have drilled
> them into us. Refusal to change is the armor with which we have learned
> to protect ourselves. If we and our fathers had accepted the new ideas and
> customs commended to us, we might have made greater progress. But
> greater progress would have drawn the eyes of a covetous world toward
> us. And then our lot would have been worse than before. . . . The plow
> that Bala's brother won at your exhibition last spring is better. It is light,
> like our plows, and good for ordinary plowing. But Bala's brother has not
> dared to use it. He is so prosperous that he is afraid of anything that
> makes a show of still greater prosperity. In that he may seem foolish to
> you. But we do not blame him for his caution.[9]

In addition to the weaknesses within, there was the constant threat of three nomadic groups without. In the southern deserts were the Semitic tribesmen, in the Eurasian steppes to the west the Indo-Europeans, and to the east the Mongol-Turkish peoples.

The Indo-Europeans, a cultural rather than a racial group, appear to have originated in the region of the Caspian Sea where they tended their herds of cattle and did a little farming on the side. Being primarily pastoralists, they were ever ready to pack their belongings into their great oxcarts and move on to more promising lands. Entire tribes participated in these migrations— women and children as well as the warriors. Thus they pushed westward to southern Russia and southeastern Europe, so that by 2000 B.C. they ranged in the broad belt from the Danubian Plain to the Oxus and Jaxartes valleys. From this far-flung base they increasingly threatened the centers of civilization that were geographically accessible to them—the Middle East, the Balkan Peninsula, and the Indus Valley.

The original dividing line between the Indo-European peoples in the western part of the steppes and the Mongol-Turkish in the eastern part consisted of the Altai and the Tien Shan Mountains. To the east of this line the steppes are higher and drier, and the climate generally more harsh. The pastures here are not as rich as in the west, and can support sheep, camels, and horses, but not cattle. This geographic imbalance produced a corresponding historic imbalance in the form of a persistent and powerful East-to-West gradient. The peoples of the eastern steppes were attracted to the west, both as refugees and as conquerors. A succession of tribes followed one upon the other—Scythians migrating from the Altai to the Ukraine; Turkish tribes replacing them in Central Asia and later following them westward; and finally the Mongols pushing from the rear until their great eruption in the thirteenth century during which they overran most of Eurasia. These eastern nomads, because of their geographic location, had access not only to Europe, the Middle East, and India, but also to China, where they broke through periodically when the opportunity presented itself.

Because of the East-to-West gradient, the racial composition of the peoples of the western steppes gradually changed from predominantly Caucasoid to predominantly Mongoloid, at least as far west as the Caspian Sea. The shift began late in the first millennium B.C. and continued until the end of the medieval period, when the tide was reversed by the Slavic Russians armed with the weapons of Western technology—muskets and cannon at first, and later machine guns and railroads.

Finally the Semites occupied roughly the area from the Mediterranean to the Tigris and from the Taurus to Aden. Successive waves have appeared through history, emerging apparently from the deserts of Arabia. They used the donkey for transportation until about 1100 B.C., when the domestication of the camel transformed their culture as the domestication of the horse did that of the steppe nomads. With the rise of civilization many Semitic tribes lived on the edges of the cities, developing a symbiotic relationship with the urban dwellers, and always being ready to seize any chance for raid and plunder.

The old centers of civilization on the periphery of Eurasia were irresistible magnets for the surrounding tribesmen. The abundant crops, the barns swollen with grain, and the dazzling luxuries of the cities, all beckoned to the hungry nomads of steppes and deserts. Hence the periodic raids and invasions, particularly of the Mesopotamian cities, which were more vulnerable than those of Crete or the Nile or the Indus. But it was not until the second millennium B.C. that the balance of power throughout Eurasia shifted, and for the first time the nomads threatened the very existence of the great civilizations.

The new military capabilities of the nomads derived from two fateful developments—the domestication of the horse, and, later, the smelting of iron. So far as is known, the earliest domestication of animals took place in the Middle East, where also occurred the earliest riding of animals. Both took place about 5000 B.C., but there was little riding at that early date for the simple reason that the only animals available were the ox, which was too slow, and the onager, or wild ass, which was too small. The practice of animal domestication, however, spread northward to southern Russia where both the onager and the wild horse were to be found. These two animals were domesticated there by 2500 B.C., and soon the horse became favored because it was larger, stronger, and faster. Furthermore the horse gradually increased in size with selective breeding by the southern Russian nomads. A wild horse averages 13 hands (a hand equals 4 inches), whereas a modern domestic horse averages 15–16 hands. When allowed to breed indiscriminately for a few generations, domestic horses soon return to a smaller size, as illustrated by the mustang of the American West.

The first military use that the nomads made of their horse was to harness it to a light-bodied chariot with two spoked wheels, which they developed as an improvement on the clumsy Mesopotamian cart with four solid wheels. The combination of the large horse and easily maneuverable chariot gave the nomads a formidable weapon—the war chariot. The first wave of nomadic invasions in the second millennium B.C. were invasions of charioteers. They rode hard into battle with one warrior in the chariot in charge of the horses and the others shooting arrows from their powerful compound bows. Few infantrymen could stand up for long to the volleys of arrows, let alone to the massed chariot charges that followed.

Towards the end of the second millennium the nomads further increased their military effectiveness by shifting from chariot to cavalry warfare. Their horses were now large and strong enough to bear directly the weight of the rider. Also the nomads developed the bridle and bit for guiding the horse, and the horned saddle and stirrup, which enabled them to ride with both hands free and to launch a shower of arrows at full gallop. This gave the Eurasian nomads unprecedented mobility, so that they were able to outride and outfight the armies defending the urban centers. This was the basis of nomadic military prowess through the Classical and Medieval ages, culminating in the extraordinary conquests of Genghis Khan in the thirteenth century. Not until the superiority of Western firearms was brought to bear were the centers of civilization relieved of the constant threat of nomadic invasion.

The counterpart of the horse for the desert nomad was the camel, of which there were two varieties—the one-humped Arabian, which is adapted to hot desert conditions, and the two-humped Bactrian relative, which is adapted to cold desert conditions. Both can live off land where even the ass would starve, and both can go for weeks on fat stored in their humps and on water stored in their multiple stomachs. Where and when the camel was first tamed is not clear, but by 1000 B.C., transportation and communication across the deserts of Central Asia and the Middle East were dependent on the "ship of the desert."

The discovery of the technique for smelting iron ore also enhanced nomadic military strength. It was not until the middle of the second millennium B.C. that the technique was developed in northeast Asia Minor, and not until the destruction of the Hittite Empire about 1200 B.C. that the local ironsmiths were scattered and their technique became generally known. The reason for this late appearance of iron smelting is the basic difference between the process required for working iron ore and those that had been developed for copper and its alloys.

In smelting copper, the molten metal collects in the bottom of the furnace and the slag floats on top. In iron smelting, at least at the temperature possible with ancient furnaces, the iron is never completely liquefied. It forms instead a gray, spongy mass known technically as the bloom. The discovery that wrought iron could be produced by hammering the red hot bloom was understandably slow in coming. Furthermore the new metal was no improvement over the copper and bronze already available, being less easy to work, requiring more fuel, and losing its cutting edge more easily. Later it was discovered that iron could be hardened by repeated hammering and heating and plunging into cold water (quenching), and bringing the metal into contact with the charcoal fuel, which is an impure carbon. What had to be discovered, then, was not merely a new metal, but a radically new technique of metallurgy, for which the early smiths were unprepared on the basis of their past experience.

Even the improved harder type of iron was always liable to rust, but this was more than compensated for by the fact that iron ore, in contrast to copper and tin, is very widespread and correspondingly cheap. This meant that ordinary peasants now could afford iron tools. Agricultural productivity rose, and the limits of agriculture were extended into heavily wooded areas that hitherto had been impervious to the stone ax. (See Chapter 7, section I.) Equally significant was the effect of the cheap new metal on the Eurasian military balance. Hitherto the poverty-stricken nomads had not been able to afford the expensive bronze weapons in as large quantities as could the rulers of the urban centers. But now iron ore was available in almost every region, and every village smith could forge new weapons that were both superior to, and cheaper than, the old. Thus nomadic warriors now enjoyed not only superior mobility but also iron weapons that were as good and as plentiful as those of the soldiers guarding the civilized areas.

III. NOMADIC INVASIONS IN THE MIDDLE EAST

The combination of the horses and iron weapons precipitated two great waves of nomadic invasion that overwhelmed the centers of civilization. During the first, between roughly 1700 and 1500 B.C., the invaders usually arrived with horse-drawn chariots and bronze weapons; by the second wave between about 1200 and 1100 B.C. they commonly rode on horses and fought with iron weapons. These invasions should not be thought of as vast incursions of hordes that displaced native stock and completely changed ethnic patterns. Rather it was a case of relatively small numbers of invaders who used their superior military technology to establish themselves as warrior elites ruling over subject peoples that far outnumbered them.

The end result was the uprooting of civilization everywhere except in the Middle East. It was not that that region did not suffer invasions; indeed it endured the largest number because of its geographic accessibility. Empires rose and fell in the Middle East in rapid succession, yet civilization itself survived. One reason was that it had been established for a longer period in the Middle East and had sunk deeper roots. Also such large expanses of the Middle East had become civilized by 1700 B.C. that they could not all be overwhelmed and destroyed. Finally, the invaders in the Middle East usually were not raw barbarians fresh from the steppes or desert, but rather semicivilized barbarians who had settled earlier in surrounding lands and who consequently were already partially assimilated by the time of conquest.

About 2000 B.C. the Indo-European Hittites filtered into Asia Minor, probably through the Caucasus. They coalesced with the native peoples and in the course of the following centuries they organized an extensive empire that included much of Syria as well as Asia Minor. They even raided Babylon about 1590 B.C., though they never were able to establish themselves in Mesopotamia. The Kassites were another Indo-European group that came from the Zagros Mountains to the east of Mesopotamia. Taking advantage of the Hittite raid on Babylon they occupied that ancient capital and established a Third Babylonian Dynasty that lasted for several centuries (1600–1100 B.C.). Another invading tribe were the Hurrians, known in the Bible as Horites, who apparently came from the highlands of Armenia. To the north of Babylonia, in the region of Assyria, they created the Mitanni Empire, which reached its height about 1500 B.C. The Hurrians adopted much of Mesopotamian culture and transmitted it to surrounding peoples, including the Hittites in Asia Minor. Even well-protected Egypt did not escape unscathed during the centuries of turmoil. Between 1720 and 1570 B.C. that country was ruled by a very mixed, though predominantly Semitic, group of invaders known as the Hyksos. With their horse-drawn chariots and heavy type of sword and body armor they were able to dominate their country from their base in the delta, though they always remained the hated "Asiatic" foreigners.

By 1500 B.C. this first wave of invasions subsided in the Middle East and a reaction against the intruders set in amongst the indigenous peoples who comprised the vast majority. The Egyptians adopted the military techniques and weapons of the Hyksos to expel them in 1570 B.C. and to establish the Eighteenth Dynasty and the New Kingdom. After this experience with foreign domination the Egyptians sought security in imperial expansion. By the mid-fifteenth century B.C. they controlled Palestine, Syria, Phoenicia, and even reached the Euphrates. Local rulers were allowed to remain on their thrones but power rested with Egyptian garrisons and high commissioners. Likewise in Assyria native leaders successfully overthrew the Mittani Empire and went on to conquer the Kassites. Thus they established the first Assyrian Empire, which dominated the Mesopotamian Valley. These developments left three major powers in the Middle East: the Hittite Empire in the north, the Egyptian in the south, and the Assyrian in the east.

This triangular balance was upset by the second wave of barbarian invasions, which got under way about 1200 B.C. The newcomers were not as devastating as those of the first wave, but they did leave a permanent imprint on the Middle East. They were aided by the fact that the Hittite and Egyptian empires had engaged in a long series of wars that left both exhausted and forced them to evacuate the Syrian-Palestine corridor. Three Semitic peoples moved into the vacuum. The Phoenicians established themselves on the Mediterranean coast where they founded important industrial and trading centers. The Arameans settled in Syria, Palestine, and northern Mesopotamia, and from their base in Damascus they became the masters of the caravan routes, as the Phoenicians were of the sea routes. Finally the Hebrews, who settled in Palestine and Syria, were destined to play a major role in history because of their religion. Meanwhile to the east other invaders such as the Indo-European Medes and the Semitic Chaldeans were infiltrating into Iran and southern Mesopotamia.

About 1100 B.C., a new center of power was taking form, the second

Assyrian Empire. Iron weapons, a disciplined army, an efficient bureaucracy, and iron battering rams mounted on wheels enabled the Assyrians to steadily expand their rule. By the seventh century B.C. their empire, with its capital at Nineveh, included all Mesopotamia, portions of the Iranian plateau, Asia Minor, Syria, Palestine, and Egypt as far south as Thebes. But overextension of the empire and the implacable hostility of the subject peoples ultimately led to disaster. In 612 B.C. a coalition of enemies—Medes and Chaldeans, along with Scythian nomads from the north—destroyed Nineveh and ended forever the role of the Assyrians in history.

The fall of Nineveh was followed by a brief interlude during which the Medes and Chaldeans divided the legacy of the fallen empire. But a new colossus now emerged—the Persian Empire—that was by far the greatest imperial structure to that date. The Persians, related to the Medes and formerly subject to them, first defeated their former overlords. Then under their King Cyrus (550–529 B.C.), and utilizing Assyrian military techniques, they overran in quick succession Asia Minor and the Chaldean Empire in Babylonia. Within a decade after Cyrus' death his successors had conquered both Egypt in the west and the Indian Punjab in the east. Thus the Persian Empire at its height ranged from the Nile River to the Indus and beyond. The entire Middle East now was under one rule and the barbarian tribes were effectively checked.

Despite the turbulence of these long centuries of invasion and the unceasing rise and fall of kingdoms and empires and their rulers, the significant fact is the remarkable degree of cultural continuity. As noted earlier, the demolition of political structures did not mean the extinction of civilization in the Middle East. Rather, the invading barbarians, beguiled by the luxuries of urban life and needing the cooperation of native scribes and bureaucrats and priests, soon adapted to the manners and traditions of their subjects. The Assyrians were typical in this respect, as the following analysis makes clear.

. . . the Assyrians, as well as the Babylonian Chaldeans who succeeded them, self-consciously regarded themselves as the custodians of the archaic culture of the Sumerians and Babylonians. This was the role they cast for themselves and it was a role that they were proud of. Thus the great Assyrian King Ashur-bani-pal gathered together an enormous library, a portion of which was made up of the literary masterpieces of the Mesopotamian past. On thousands of clay tablets, written in cuneiform, a significant legacy of the Mesopotamian past was preserved and venerated. Our knowledge of many of the Mesopotamian myths and ethics comes from such tablet finds. . . . The cultural continuum was likewise exhibited in the pantheons of the gods among the Assyrians and Chaldeans. These gods were really the old Sumerian gods of heaven, air, and earth, and retained the same names. . . . An outstanding achievement of the Assyrians was their art, which in part continued previous Mesopotamian forms and traditions. Although they had plentiful supplies of stone, they followed the earlier Mesopotamian use of brick for most of their buildings, including temples. . . . Assyrian art, for all of its realism, did not free itself of certain archaic Mesopotamian conventions. It lacked, for example, a sense of perspective and always represented figures in profile.[10]

78   *Greece*

In direct contrast to the Middle East, there was little cultural continuum in the peripheral regions of Greece, India and China. Their civilizations lacked the depth in time and space that bolstered those of Mesopotamia and Egypt, and consequently were wiped out in the course of the invasions of the second millennium B.C. The information available on the course of events is much more full and reliable in the case of Greece than the other two regions. One reason is that the Greeks were in relatively close contact with the ancient Middle Eastern civilizations whose written sources have yielded important clues as to what was happening in the Greek world. Furthermore the Greeks themselves were more historically minded than most contemporary peoples, and left correspondingly more revealing records of their doings.

The first Indo-European invaders of Greece were the Achaeans who came sometimes in the twentieth century B.C. They were charioteers with bronze weapons who traditionally have been thought to have infiltrated southward from the Danubian plains, though recent evidence suggests they may have crossed the Aegean from northwestern Asia Minor. Their general level of development was far behind that of the Minoan Cretans, but by 1600 B.C. the newcomers had absorbed much of the Minoan culture that had been transplanted to the mainland, and had established a number of small kingdoms from Thessaly down to the southern tip of the Peloponnesus.

The most advanced settlements were those in the Peloponnesus, being the closest to Crete. Mycenae was the outstanding center in the Peloponnesus, and has given its name to the emerging civilization. All settlements in Mycenaean Greece were strongly fortified, in contrast to the cities of Crete. Massive hilltop citadels were constructed, where the king and his retainers lived. The commoners built their dwellings outside the citadel but in time of danger sought refuge within its walls.

In contrast to the other Indo-European invaders who had established themselves in the Middle East and the Indus Valley, the Mycenaeans took to the sea after the fashion of the Minoans and developed a formidable maritime power. Depending on the opportunities at hand, they raided, they traded, and they founded overseas colonies in Rhodes, Cyprus, and the west coast of Asia Minor. The Mycenaeans exported pottery, olive oil, and hides in return for luxuries such as spices, ivory, and jewelry. In time, their goods were crowding out those of Crete in the markets of South Italy, Syria, and Egypt. Thus the Mycenaeans undermined the former economic hegemony of Crete in the Mediterranean, and by the fifteenth century B.C. they were raiding the great island itself. The unwalled cities, including the capital of Knossos, were taken and destroyed. These disasters, together with a series of devastating earthquakes, led to the virtual extinction of the formerly great Minoan civilization by 1150 B.C.

Meanwhile the Mycenaeans were experiencing a similar fate at the hands of new invaders, the Dorians. Appearing about 1200 B.C. and armed with iron weapons, they captured the Mycenaean citadels and towns one by one. Ad-

The Lion Gate at Mycenae. (Gabriele Wunderlich)

A vase painting showing Mycenaean soldiers. These heavily armed warriors attacked Crete and destroyed the city of Knossos itself, gradually undermining the Minoan civilization. (Marburg-Art Reference Bureau)

ministrative systems disintegrated, rural populations scattered, foreign trade withered, and Greece reverted to an agrarian and pastoral economy. A Dark Age descended and obscured Greece until the rise of the historical city states about 800 B.C.

The main Dorian settlements were in the Peloponnesus, from which the invaders pushed on overseas and founded colonies in Crete, in Rhodes, and on the adjacent coast of Asia Minor. Other Greeks, perhaps Mycenaean refugees, crossed from Athens to the Cyclades Islands and on to the central part of the west coast of Asia Minor. There they established settlements that became known as Ionia, which for a period was the most advanced region of the entire Greek world. Still further north other bands speaking the Aeolic dialect sailed from Thessaly and central Greece to the island of Lesbos and thence to northern Asia Minor. These new Greek colonies in Asia Minor were never able to expand into the interior because of the resistance of a numerous local population. They were confined to the coastal areas, yet they prospered and were destined to play a major role in the general history of the Greek people.

Much more is known of this Dark Age in Greece than of the corresponding post-invasion period in India. This is due in part to the fact that the Greeks had closer contacts with the ancient Middle Eastern civilizations than did the Indians. Traces of these contacts are available in archaeological remains and literary sources and provide clues to early Greek history and culture. More important is the precious heritage of the four great poems left by the Greeks themselves—Homer's *Iliad* and *Odyssey*, and Hesiod's *Works and Days* and *Birth of the Gods*. Homer wrote of war, adventure, and the life of nobles and kings, while Hesiod described the life and lore of the farmer, and the genealogies of the gods. Between them they have left a vivid picture of the primitive agricultural and pastoral society of these centuries. Households were largely self-sufficient, growing their own food and making their cloth with wool from their flocks of sheep. The only full-time traders were foreigners—Phoenicians or Cypriots—who appeared sporadically with trinkets for the commoners and more valuable goods for the nobles. The monotony of the farm work was broken by the occasional visit of a bard who sang of the glories of war and of the exploits of illustrious ancestors.

Each community consisted of the noble families that governed and led in war, and the commoners, including freehold peasants, tenant farmers, and a few craftsmen, hired laborers, and slaves. At the top was the king, whose authority depended on his prowess in war and his leadership qualities in meetings of the council of nobles. Occasionally the king called a meeting of the assembly that included all adult males, but the purpose usually was to mobilize popular support for decisions already reached in conjunction with the nobles. These simple institutions, typical of the Indo-European tribes at this level of development, represented the embryo from which the Greek city state was to develop its organs of government.

India

In India, the Indus Valley civilization experienced the same fate as the Minoan of Crete. About 1500 B.C., it was overrun by tribesmen who had the

military advantage of possessing horses and chariots. The invaders called them‑
selves Aryans, and the land in which they settled Aryavarta, or land of the
Aryans. They were of the Indo-European family of peoples, of which the
western branches had invaded Mesopotamia and Greece, and the eastern, Iran,
where some settled down while others continued eastward to the Indus. It
was not a case of a concerted or planned campaign like those of the Muslims
in later centuries. Rather the Aryans, in small groups, infiltrated a civilization
that obviously had passed its peak and was unable to resist effectively.

As noted earlier, it is not clear whether the Indus civilization collapsed primarily because of the Aryan onslaught or because of seismic cataclysms. (See
Chapter 5, section IV.) Whatever the reason, the fact remains that a primitive
new society emerged in the latter half of the second millennium B.C. Information concerning this society is scanty because the Aryans left no concrete remains, for they used wood or mud for their dwellings and had no large cities.
Thus material available for the reconstruction of Aryan life is the direct
antithesis of that available for the Indus civilization. The latter left a wealth of
material remains and no decipherable written records, whereas the Aryans left
practically no remains and a wealth of literature in the form of Vedas.

The word Veda means knowledge, and for the Hindus the Vedas are a primary source of religious belief as the Bible is for Christians and the Koran
for Muslims. There were originally four Vedas, but the most important is the
Rigveda, which is also the oldest. In the course of time other works were added
to the four Vedas and acquired a similar sacred status. The Rigveda is a
primary source for study of the early Aryans as Homer's epics are for Mycenaean Greece. It is in essence a collection of 1,028 hymns arranged in ten
books, and is as bulky as the *Iliad* and *Odyssey* combined.

The Aryans were tall, with blue eyes and fair skin, and very conscious of
these physical features in contrast to those of the indigenous people whom
they conquered. The latter are referred to in the Vedas as short, black, nose-
less, and as *dasas,* or slaves. The image of the Aryans that emerges from the
Vedic literature is that of a virile people, fond of war, drinking, chariot racing,
and gambling. Their god of war, Indra, was the ideal Aryan warrior: he dashed
into battle joyously, wore golden armor, and was able to consume the flesh of
three hundred buffaloes and drink three lakes of liquor at one time.

When they first arrived in India the Aryans were primarily pastoralists.
Their economic life centered around their cattle, and wealth was judged on
the basis of the size of the herds. As the newcomers settled in the fertile river
valleys, they gradually shifted more to agriculture. They lived in villages consisting of a number of related families. Several villages comprised a clan, and
several clans a tribe, at the head of which was the king. As in Greece, the
king's authority depended on his personal prowess and initiative, and was
limited by the council of nobles, and in some tribes by the freemen.

The outstanding characteristic of this early Aryan society was its basic
difference from the later Hinduism. Cows were not worshipped but eaten.
Intoxicating spirits were not forsaken but joyously consumed. There were
classes but no castes, and the priests were subordinate to the nobles rather
than at the top of the social pyramid. In short, Aryan society resembled much
more the other contemporary Indo-European societies than it did the classical
Hinduism that was to develop in later centuries.

About 1500 B.C. charioteers with bronze weapons also invaded the distant valley of the Yellow River in North China. There they found a flourishing Neolithic culture from which evolved the Shang civilization. The current state of archaeological research does not allow definite conclusions as to the precise relationship between the invasions and the appearance of the civilization. It is generally agreed, however, that it was not a case of wholesale transplantation of foreign elements. Rather the indigenous Neolithic culture provided the solid base, to which the invaders contributed certain innovations and stimuli. Hence the Shang civilization was analyzed in the preceding chapter as one of the ancient civilizations. It follows that the intrusion of charioteers into North China did not produce a sharp cultural break as it did in Greece and India. Rather the distinctively Chinese Neolithic culture continued as a distinctively Chinese civilization, which persisted from the Shang period to the present.

This pattern of continuity is apparent in the transition from the Shang to the Chou dynasty in 1027 B.C. The Chou people had for long lived in the Wei Valley on the fringes of civilization, so that they shared the language and basic culture of the Shang at the same time that they borrowed military techniques from the sheep-herding "barbarians" to the north and west. Consequently when the Chou overran North China there was no interruption in the evolution of Chinese civilization. The writing system continued as before, as did ancestor worship, the methods of divination, and the division of society into aristocratic warriors and peasant masses. Political decentralization also persisted, and indeed became more pronounced under the Chou rulers who assigned the conquered territories to vassal lords. The latter journeyed periodically to the Chou court for elaborate ceremonies of investiture, but gradually this practice lapsed. The lords, ensconced in their walled towns, ruled over the surrounding countryside with little control from the capital.

In 771 B.C. the Chou capital was captured by "barbarians" allied with rebellious lords. The Chou dynasty resumed its rule from a center further to the east that was not so vulnerable to attacks from the borderlands. Thus the dynastic period before 771 B.C. is termed by the Chinese the Western Chou, and the period thereafter the Eastern Chou. During the latter time the Chou kings were rulers in name only. They were accorded certain religious functions and some ceremonial respect, but their domains were smaller than those of their nominal vassals, and their power correspondingly weaker. Indeed they managed to survive until 256 B.C. because they provided spiritual leadership. The dynasty was also a royal priesthood, and as such it was preserved as a symbol of national unity.

Although the Eastern Chou was a period of political instability, it was also a period of cultural flowering. It was a dynamic and creative age when the great works of literature and philosophy and social theory were written. This was the time when the classical Chinese civilization was taking form, corresponding to the classical Greek and Indian civilizations that were evolving at roughly the same time. The origin and nature of these classical civilizations is the subject of Part III.

SUGGESTED READING

A survey of the history of some of the nomadic peoples is given in E. D. Phillips, *The Royal Hordes: Nomad Peoples of the Steppes* (London: Thames & Hudson, 1965). Fuller accounts of various aspects of Central Eurasian history are available in the relevant chapters of E. H. Minns, *Scythians and Greeks* (Cambridge: Cambridge Univ., 1913); M. Rostovtzev, *Iranians and Greeks in South Russia* (Oxford: Clarendon Press, 1922); G. Vernadsky, *Ancient Russia* (New Haven: Yale Univ., 1943); O. Lattimore, *Inner Asian Frontiers of China* (New York: American Geographical Society, 1940); O. Lattimore, *Studies in Frontier History: Collected Papers 1928–1958* (Paris: Mouton, 1962); and W. M. McGovern, *The Early Empires of Central Asia* (Chapel Hill: Univ. of North Carolina, 1939). Interesting analyses of the origins and evolution of horseback riding and of wheeled transport are available in J. F. Downs, "The Origin and Spread of Riding in the Near East and Central Asia," *American Anthropologist*, LXIII (December, 1961), 1193–1203; and S. Piggott, "The Beginnings of Wheeled Transport," *Scientific American*, CCXIX (July, 1968), 82–90.

CLASSICAL CIVILIZATIONS OF EURASIA,

1000 B.C.–A.D. 500

The classical civilizations of Eurasia differed from the preceding ancient civilizations in several basic respects. One was their range, which, with the continuing advance of technology, expanded from river valleys to encompass entire regions such as China, the Indian peninsula, and the Mediterranean basin with its hinterland. No longer was it a case of valley civilizations surrounded by a sea of barbarism. Rather it was now the regional civilizations that expanded steadily outward until they were contiguous to each other, so that civilization stretched in an almost uninterrupted band across the breadth of Eurasia.

The classical civilizations were distinctive in content as well as in range. Like the ancient civilizations, each of these classical civilizations developed its special style. During these centuries, each evolved the social, religious, and philosophical systems that were to persist to modern times. How distinctive the individual styles of the classical civilizations were is apparent in the following paradigm of points of divergence between Chinese and Indian Buddhist civilizations.[1]

[1] A. F. Wright, "Buddhism and Chinese Culture: Phases of Interaction," *Journal of Asian Studies*, XVII (November, 1957), 22.

	CHINESE	INDIAN BUDDHIST
Language	Uninflected, ideographic, and (in its written form) largely monosyllabic; no systematized grammar.	Highly inflected, alphabetic, polysyllabic, with a highly elaborated formal grammar.
Literary modes	Terseness, metaphors from familiar nature, limited imaginative range, concreteness.	Discursiveness, hyperbolic metaphor, unlimited imaginative flights, predilection for the abstract.
Psychology of the individual	No disposition to analyze the personality into its components.	A highly developed science of psychological analysis.
Time and space	Finite, lifetime, milieu, and generation oriented.	Infinite, aeon oriented.
Socio-political values	Familism, supremacy of the secular power, pursuit of the good society.	Individualism (in the Mahayana, universal salvationism), supremacy of spiritual power, pursuit of non-social goods.

Confucianism, Hinduism, Christianity, caste organization, and democratic government all emerged from the remarkable creativity of the Classical Age. This creativity, it should be noted, was not confined to one locality as had been the case at the time of the ancient civilizations. The Middle East then functioned as the center of initiative from which had diffused such fundamental innovations as agriculture, metallurgy, writing, and urban life. But now, during the centuries of the classical period, there existed an equilibrium amongst the Eurasian civilizations, and they interacted as equals. If anything, it was the Middle East that now lagged behind, while what had been the peripheral civilizations of Europe, India, and China now generated most of the innovations that distinguish the Classical Age.

Formerly the things which happened
in the world had no connection
among themselves. Each action interested
only the locality where it happened.
But since then all events
are united in a common bundle.

POLYBIUS

Chapter

7

Incipient Eurasian Ecumene

The most obvious and striking feature of the age of the classical civilization was the existence for the first time of what might be termed an incipient Eurasian ecumene—a Eurasia that was on the way to becoming a functioning unit, an interacting whole. A comparison of the map of Eurasia about 1500 B.C. with that of about A.D. 200 makes clear the substance of this Eurasian ecumene. (See maps VI and X.) The empires of the early period were almost entirely restricted to their respective river valleys, and give the appearance of tiny islands in a vast sea of barbarism. By the first century A.D., however, the Roman, Parthian, Kushan, and Han empires spanned the breadth of Eurasia from the Scottish Highlands to the China Seas. This made possible a modest degree of interaction amongst empires. Of course there had always been certain interregional contacts even at the time of the ancient civilizations, as evidenced by the nomadic invasions in all directions. But now in the Classical Age these interregional contacts were substantially more close, varied, and sustained. And yet, even by the end of the Classical period the Roman and Chinese empires at opposite ends of Eurasia had not been able to establish direct official contact, and possessed no specific or reliable knowledge of each other. Thus Eurasian ecumenism remained at the

87

incipient stage throughout these centuries. The origins, nature, and significance of this incipient ecumenism is the subject of this chapter.

I. Roots of Ecumenism

At the basis of the new Eurasian ecumenism was technological advance. This was to be expected, since from the very beginning of man's history the range of his activities had depended on the level of his technology. When he was at the food gathering stage, the range of the individual band was its hunting ground. As man learned agriculture and metallurgy and shipbuilding, we have seen that his range broadened to encompass, for example, the valley empires of Sargon and of the pharaohs. But now further technological advance made possible a much greater extension of agriculture and civilization, and hence the organization of regional empires that stretched contiguously across the breadth of Eurasia. And this technological advance was basically the discovery and increasingly widespread use of iron.

As noted earlier, iron smelting was developed first in Asia Minor in the middle of the second millennium B.C., and spread from there after the destruction of the Hittite Empire about 1200 B.C. (See Chapter 6, section III.) We have seen that the discovery facilitated the second wave of barbarian invasions at the end of the second millennium B.C., but some centuries elapsed before the new metal was available in sufficient quantities for everyday use. When hoes and axes and plows, as well as weapons, could be made of iron, then the economic, social, and political repercussions were immediate and far reaching.

This stage was reached slowly—about 800 B.C. in India, 750 B.C. in Central Europe, and 600 B.C. in China. In these and other regions the advent of cheap iron led first and foremost to the cutting down of heavy forests hitherto invulnerable to stone-edged axes and wooden plows. But farmers now were able to use their strong and sharp iron axes and their iron-shod plows to extend agriculture from the Middle East eastward across the Iranian plateau and westward across the Mediterranean lands and into Central and Northern Europe. Likewise in India the Aryan newcomers pushed eastward and cut down the forests of the Ganges Valley. At the same time agriculturists in China were extending their operations from the Yellow River Valley southward to the great Yangtze basin.

This expansion of the frontiers of agriculture made possible a corresponding expansion of the ecumene of civilization, which grew more in the half millennium from 1000 to 500 B.C. than in the preceding three millennia from 4000 to 1000 B.C. The basic reason for this was the tremendous increase in productivity that now took place. Not only was agriculture practiced in much larger areas, but the combination of soils and climate in Central Europe and in the monsoon Ganges and Yangtze basins was much more productive than in the comparatively arid Middle East and Indus and Yellow River valleys.

The jump in agricultural productivity meant that a surplus was now available for economic development and for state-building purposes. Trade increased in volume, especially along the rivers that constituted ready-made highways.

Craftsmen appeared in increasing numbers to provide the services needed in the new agricultural communities and the products in demand for the new trade. At first goods and services were exchanged by barter, with obvious inconvenience for both buyer and seller. Then media of exchange were developed, such as measures of grain or, more common, bars of metal. But with every transaction the weight and purity of the metal had to be checked against fraudulent clipping and debasing.

About 700 B.C., the Lydians of western Asia Minor began stamping and guaranteeing pieces of metal as to both quality and weight. Various Greek city states soon improved on this by stamping flat circular coins on both sides. Thus gold and silver coins now facilitated large scale wholesale or interregional trade, and copper coins enabled farmers to sell rather than barter their produce, and artisans to work for wages rather than foodstuffs. The net effect was a great stimulus for all kinds of commerce, a corresponding stimulus for manufacturing and agriculture, and an overall increase in economic specialization with an attendant rise in efficiency and productivity. The manufacturer of cheap goods now had available for the first time a mass market, while the small landholder could turn from subsistence agriculture to specialized farming, whether the mulberry and silkworm in China or olive oil in Greece. The new iron tools also made possible the building of better and larger ships, which, in turn, led to longer voyages and to more trade and colonization. Overseas expansion was impeded at the outset by piracy, which was regarded as normal an activity as brigandage on land. *The Odyssey* describes the half-piratical, half-commercial expeditions of Menelaus and Odysseus in the Aegean Sea, and relates how all participants as a matter of course asked those whom they met whether or not they were pirates. But gradually maritime trade was developed on a regular large-scale basis, with great economic advantage. Transport by sea was many times cheaper than by land, and remained so until the development of an efficient horse harness in the Middle Ages and the building of good roads in the eighteenth century.

By the end of the Classical Age, trade routes circumscribed all of Eurasia in contrast to the local self-sufficiency that prevailed in most regions following the invasions of the second millennium B.C. In addition to the caravan routes across the interior of Eurasia, there were sea routes around the circumference— from the North Sea to the western Mediterranean, from the western Mediterranean to the Levant, from the Red Sea to India, and from India to Southeast Asia and, to a lesser degree, to China. This maritime commerce was accompanied by colonization, especially in the Mediterranean by the Phoenicians and Greeks, and later in Southeast Asia by the Indians.

Side by side with these economic developments were equally significant social and political changes. The military aristocracy that had risen to prominence with the invasions of the second millennium B.C. was being undermined by the new class of merchants, craftsmen, and mariners. The old tribal society was being transformed by monetization; personal services and allegiances were being superseded by the exigencies of the market place.

Equally disruptive was the political consolidation made possible by the economic growth. Tribal chiefs and their advisory councils and assemblies were being replaced by kingdoms and then by empires, whether in Italy or India or China. Nor was it a one way process of economic development stimulating political centralization. A reverse process also operated, for the great new regional empires spanning the Eurasian land mass enforced order and security that promoted long distance trade by land and sea. Regional empires also were able to build and maintain regional road networks that also facilitated commerce.

In the Persian Empire, for example, the so-called Royal Road ran 1,677 miles from Susa, located to the north of the Persian Gulf, westward to the Tigris, and thence across Syria and Asia Minor to Ephesus on the Aegean coast. The route was divided into 111 post-stations, each with relays of fresh horses for the royal couriers. Caravans took ninety days to travel this road from end to end, while the royal couriers traversed it in a week. As the empire was enlarged, branch lines were constructed southwest to Egypt and southeast to the Indus Valley, A few centuries later the Romans constructed their well-known system of roads that were so well engineered that some of them, along with their bridges, are still in use.

At the other end of Eurasia, the Chinese built an elaborate network of both roads and canals. They were able to transport goods from present-day Canton to the Yangtze Valley by an all-water route, thereby promoting their overseas trade. To the northwest they built roads that linked up with the long silk route, which, as will be noted in the following section, traversed the whole of Central Asia to the Middle East. The main highways were lined with trees and provided with stations and guest houses. Road construction and maintenance was the responsibility of central and local officials who were subject to impeachment if they were derelict in their duties. Likewise in India the Royal Highway ran from the Ganges Delta to Taxila in the northwest, near the Khyber Pass, where it connected with the caravan routes west to the Middle East and north to Central Asia.

All these developments involved profound changes in social relationships, in political organizations, in ways of living and earning a livelihood. Such basic and all-inclusive disruption was unsettling and uncomfortable. It led to soul searching—to the posing of new questions and the seeking of new answers. Thinkers were moved to reconsider their respective traditions and to either abandon them or adapt them to the requirements of an age of transition. Speculation concerned such questions as the moral basis of ideal government, the functioning of the social order, and the origin and purpose of the universe and of life.

All over the civilized ecumene, such questions were being posed and discussed about the sixth century B.C. The answers constituted the great philosophical, religious, and social systems of the Classical Age. It was not happenstance, then, that the spokesmen for these systems were all contemporaries— Confucius in China, Buddha in India, Zoroaster in Persia, and the rationalist philosophers in Greece. In all these regions the disruption and the challenge was the same, but the answers varied greatly, and the several Eurasian civilizations set off in decidedly different directions. Indeed it was at this time that these civilizations developed their distinctive philosophical attitudes and social institutions that endured through the centuries and that have characterized them to modern times.

The specific nature of these attitudes and institutions will be analyzed in the following chapters devoted to each of the classical civilizations. The remainder of this chapter will be devoted to an examination of the interrelationships

The Appian Way, "queen of roads," connecting Rome with southern Italy, and still in use today. (Arborio Mella)

Portion of a Greek vase showing Odysseus' encounter with the Sirens, one event of his half-piratical, half-commercial expedition. (Arborio Mella)

amongst these civilizations, or, in other words, the substance of the incipient Eurasian ecumene. Contemporary Eurasians could not have been aware of the parallel developments in their respective civilizations because they had little specific information about each other. But they were definitely aware that the historical stage was expanding—that life was becoming more complex and that a multitude of domestic and external forces impinged on them. Thus the Greek historian Polybius, when starting his history of events from 220 to 145 B.C., observed that, "during this period history becomes, so to speak, an o.ganic whole. What happens in Italy and in Libya is bound up with what happened in Asia and in Greece, all events culminating in a single result."

Two aspects of this new "organic whole" were particularly evident, even to contemporaries. These were interregional commercial bonds and cultural bonds, the subjects of the following two sections.

II. COMMERCIAL BONDS

The principal interregional material bonds were commercial in character, though not exclusively so. This was a time when not only goods moved from one region to another, but people also moved about with their technological skills and their plants. There is a revealing letter, for example, written by the Persian ruler Darius to one of his governors, approving a proposal for transplanting plants and trees from one region to another. "I commend your plan," wrote the King, "for improving my country by the transplantation of fruit trees from the other side of the Euphrates, in the further part of Asia. . . ." [1] How wide-ranging was this interchange is indicated by the fact that cotton, sugar cane, and chickens, all first domesticated in India, spread to both China and western Eurasia during this period. Likewise the Chinese during these centuries obtained for the first time the grape vine, alfalfa, chive, cucumber, fig, sesame, pomegranate, and walnut. In return the Chinese gave to the rest of Eurasia the orange, peach, pear, peony, azalea, camellia, and chrysanthemum. There was a similar interchange of technology, as is evident in the case of that fundamental invention, the waterwheel. The first waterwheel in western Asia was that of Mithridates, king of Pontus, on the south shore of the Black Sea, about 65 B.C. The first waterwheel in China was built soon after, about 30 B.C. The difference between the two dates is much too small for direct diffusion in either direction, and strongly suggests diffusion in both directions from some unknown intermediate source. Such interaction between the various regions of Eurasia was intimately related to trade, and doubtless would have been much less substantial were it not for the efflorescence of local and long-distance trade during the centuries of the Classical Age.

This trade was conducted both by land across Central Eurasia and by sea around the periphery of the land mass. These two general routes were by no means exclusive or independent of each other. A large proportion of the goods were moved along some combination of the two routes, usually by sea between Egypt and India, and by one of several overland routes between India and China. Furthermore, the land and sea routes were competitive, so that excessively high charges or intolerable lack of security in one route normally deflected the trade to the other.

The maritime trade had gotten under way first at the time of the ancient civilizations. Egyptian traders ventured down the Red Sea to East Africa and along the Levant coast to Lebanon. Likewise, Sumerian merchants sailed down the Persian Gulf, along the Arabian peninsula, while their counterparts from the Indus Valley, in ways that remain obscure, appear to have worked their way westward until contact was established, perhaps at the Bahrain Islands in the Persian Gulf. But all of these early seafarers were mere landlubbers compared to the amphibious Minoans of Crete. These argonauts were the great maritime traders of ancient times, plying the Mediterranean from end to end as the unrivalled entrepreneurs of that inland sea.

With the invasions of the Achaeans and Dorians this far-flung commerce dried up and the eastern Mediterranean people sank back to an agrarian and autarchic type of existence. The first to resume the mercantile activities of the Cretans were the Phoenicians. A Semitic-speaking people who had settled along the narrow coastal plains of the eastern Mediterranean, they soon developed a flourishing trade as middlemen. (See Chapter 6, section III.) From the east caravans brought in myrrh, spices, and the products of Mesopotamian craftmanship. From overseas lands came assorted metals, hides, grains, olive oil, and slaves. The Phoenicians themselves manufactured fine furniture, jewelry, metalware, and especially textiles made from the wool of their own sheep and colored by their famous purple dye obtained from shellfish found in large beds along the coast.

In developing this trade the Phoenicians evolved a type of ship rowed by tiers of oarsmen that was fast and seaworthy for the long voyages that were made further and further to the west. In the eleventh century B.C. they began trading with Cyprus where they also founded a colony. Thence they spread out over the Aegean and by the end of the ninth century B.C. they had entered the western Mediterranean and founded trading posts and colonies on the northwest coast of Africa, the south coast of Spain, and on Sicily, Malta, and the Balearic Islands. They even ventured beyond Gibraltar as far afield as Cornwall, England, whence came the eagerly sought after tin. It was at this time that Gades (Cadiz) was founded as a Phoenician trading post on the west coast of the Iberian Peninsula to serve as a way station in the perilous Atlantic trade.

From about 1100 B.C. until the late eighth century B.C. the sailors and merchants of Phoenicia controlled most of the maritime trade of the Mediterranean. Then the Greeks appeared as competitors, spurred on by the same goad of population pressure. First they established trading posts, which later developed into agricultural settlements wherever the land resources made this possible. These settlements were quite independent of the mother city whence they sprang, even though the colonists reproduced the institutions and imitated the religious practices that they had left behind. Thus Greek colonization involved a multiplication of independent city-states rather than an imposition of imperialistic rule.

One principal area of Greek settlement was in Sicily and south Italy, where so many colonies were founded that the region came to be known as Magna Graecia, or Great Greece. On the mainland the Greeks advanced as far north as Naples where they established contact with the Etruscans who were themselves migrants from Asia Minor. These Etruscans, attracted by the local iron resources, had settled there about the ninth century B.C., and then proceeded to develop the earliest urban civilization of Italy. In the western Mediterranean the Greeks were constrained by the Phoenicians who had long preceded them, but they did establish a firm base in northeastern Spain and southern France, where their chief colony was Massilia (Marseilles). Finally the Greeks found a free field in the Black Sea region where they were at first repelled by the cold and foggy climate but where they eventually settled in large numbers because of the economic opportunities. The Black Sea itself provided the annual run of tunny fish, and the native Scythians in present-day southern Russia exchanged their raw materials for Greek-manufactured goods. By the fifth century B.C. the entire Black Sea basin was ringed with flourishing Greek trading posts and settlements.

While the Greeks were prospering on the sea, the Persians were building their empire that eventually extended from the Nile Valley to the Indus. Although a mountain people and ignorant of things maritime, the Persians nevertheless were interested in opening sea routes to facilitate communications between their eastern and western provinces. For this purpose they made use of the experienced Phoenicians and Asia Minor Greeks, both of whom were their subjects. They appointed a Greek mariner, Scylax, to head an expedition that sailed about 510 B.C. from the Indus to Arsinoë at the head of the Red Sea. The Persians also had plans for cutting a canal from the Nile to the Red Sea and appear to have done considerable work toward that goal. Trade flourished under these circumstances, and surpassed anything previously known in volume and in geographic range. Greek, Phoenician, Arab, and Indian mariners plied back and forth between India, the Persian Gulf, Egypt, and the numerous ports of the Mediterranean.

Alexander and his successors continued the work of the Persians by dispatching more expeditions, which enhanced geographic knowledge, and by constructing a series of ports along the Red Sea, through which goods could be transported overland to the Nile and then shipped down the river to Alexandria. The Indian Ocean trade was carried on at this time in two stages. In the first, Indian and Arab traders sailed westward from Indian ports, hugging the coastline until they reached the Arabian peninsula and rounded it to their destination at Aden or Mocha. There they were met by Greco-Egyptian merchants who exchanged their wares for the eastern goods, which they transported via the Red Sea coastal ports to Alexandria.

All this proved to be but the prelude to the great expansion of trade between East and West that blossomed shortly before the Christian era and lasted for about two centuries. One reason for this was China's great westward expansion which opened overland trade routes and facilitated the supply of silk, the most important item in interregional commerce. The precise role of China will be considered shortly in the analysis of overland trade. The other main factor behind the burgeoning trade was the consolidation of the Roman Empire encompassing the entire Mediterranean basin and much of central and northwestern Europe. This establishment of *Pax Romana* eliminated brigandage and piracy, which hitherto had hindered trade, and also removed almost all tolls and exactions. The wealth of the Empire also stimulated trade, particularly because the affluent Roman ruling class had both the taste and the funds for exotic foreign products.

Accordingly the Romans conducted a flourishing trade with all neighboring lands—with Scandinavia to the north, Germany across the Rhine, Dacia across the Danube, and Africa south of the Sahara. The most significant in its general Eurasian repercussions was the commerce with the East. This expanded greatly with the discovery by a Greek mariner sometime in the first century B.C. that the monsoon winds could be used to speed the sailing back and forth across the Indian Ocean. (This was more likely a rediscovery, since Arab sailors appear to have preceded the Greeks—monsoon is derived from the Arab word *mauzim,* or season.) The northeast, or winter, monsoon blows from India towards East Africa from October to April, and the southwest, or summer, monsoon blows in the opposite direction from June to September. No longer was it necessary for the sailors to hug the coasts in a wide, time-consuming arc; now they could scud before the wind directly across the ocean. A merchant could journey from Rome to India in sixteen weeks, including the land stage through Egypt.

"Roman" merchants, mostly Greeks and Syrians, not only undertook such journeys but a few settled permanently in Indian cities, as attested by Indian literary sources. They brought with them glass, copper, tin, linen and wool textiles, and above all, gold coins. In return the Romans wanted pepper and other spices, cotton textiles, precious stones, and, most important, the Chinese silk brought to Indian ports via the overland Silk Road. A few of the more adventurous "Roman" traders, the Marco Polos of their times, made their way further east beyond India. In the second and third centuries A.D. they reached Burma, Malaya, Sumatra, and passed on through the Malacca Strait to Kattigara (Hanoi), from which they at last made direct contact with China. They represented themselves as official Roman envoys in order to further their ends. The Han court doubtless detected the fraud, since the imperial "gifts" were mere products of nearby Southeast Asia that had been bought by the merchants. Nevertheless, the Chinese were flattered by the proffered "tribute" and probably allowed the Westerners to load profitable cargoes of silk.

This direct contact between the Roman and Han empires seemed to promise a new era of economic expansion. It might have been expected that during the third and fourth centuries A.D. maritime trade would have reached unprecedented volume on all the seas surrounding Eurasia. In point of fact the opposite happened because of a combination of internal convulsions and external barbarian attacks on both the Roman and Han empires. But if commerce between Egypt and India declined after the second century, the setback did not extend to the trade between India and Southeast Asia. At the time when Rome and China were left impotent during their time of troubles, India by contrast was reaching her apogee under the Gupta dynasty (A.D. 320–647). Indian civilization, as will be noted in Chapter 9, now came into full flower and exerted great influence on neighboring lands. To the north, across land frontiers, this influence was primarily religious and cultural; to the southeast, across the Bay of Bengal, it was also economic and political. (See the following section.)

Archaeological remains indicate communication between India and Southeast Asia from very ancient times. In the first century A.D. the contacts became more extensive as Indian merchants in growing numbers visited the islands and coastal regions, attracted by the spices and mineral resources. Contemporary Indian literature frequently referred to traders' voyages to Suvarnab-humi—the land of gold. The local peoples were relatively primitive, engaged mostly in rice cultivation, and lacked any elaborate political organization or sophisticated cultural traditions. Consequently, it was relatively easy for Indian merchants and adventurers to marry into leading native families and to propagate their Hindu religion and customs, as well as to impose economic control. The opportunities attracted Brahmans and warriors from the homeland as well as merchants, so that Indian culture was transplanted on a massive scale and a number of Indian kingdoms were established on the islands and mainland.

This Indianization process did not penetrate very deeply at the grass-roots level. As is usual in such cases, it was primarily the leading families that were affected by the newcomers. The average villager carried on much as before, apart from certain tax and labor exactions imposed by the rulers of the new kingdoms. Although the Indian influence was somewhat superficial, it was extraordinarily far flung. Beginning in Malaya and Sumatra, the Indians by the fourth century A.D. were firmly ensconced in distant Borneo and Indochina. At the outset it was the island kingdoms that were most advanced, but toward the end of the third century A.D. they fell behind, perhaps because of the growth of piracy. The center of power shifted to the mainland where Indian immigrants were able to follow land routes across Malaya to Indochina.

Kambuja, in present-day Cambodia, now emerged as a great Hindu kingdom. The Chinese, who called it Fu-nan, have left descriptions of the kingdom that reflect clearly its Hindu character. "There are over a thousand Brahmans from India. The people practice their doctrine and give their daughters to them in marriage so that many Brahmans stay there. They read their sacred book day and night. . . . They make bronze images of their deities. Those with two faces have four arms, those with four faces have eight arms. Each hand holds something." [2]

Such was the nature of the Greater India in Southeast Asia. The parallel with the Greek expansion several centuries earlier in the Mediterranean basin is apparent. In both cases merchants and colonists established footholds in far-flung coastal areas and transplanted their home institutions. The local populations, however, were neither Hellenized nor Hinduized en masse, so that the colonies eventually were assimilated, leaving behind only geographic names and architectural remains as mementoes of past enterprise. For Eurasian history, the significance of both Greater India and Magna Graecia is their contribution in extending the frontiers of civilization—in one case from the south Balkans to the Straits of Gibraltar and to south Russia, and in the other case from south India to Borneo and Indochina.

As far as overland trade was concerned, much depended on the degree to which order and security could be maintained. When large sections of the land routes were under the firm control of some authority, then trade could flourish; when anarchy prevailed, then trade withered. This pattern is clearly apparent in surveying commercial trends through these centuries. A general upward trend is evident in the volume of trade, the result of the technological advances and the expansion of the civilized ecumene. But within this overall trend there were dips and rises related to political conditions. For example, the centuries of the Scythian Empire in western Eurasia, the Chinese empires in eastern Eurasia, and the Mongol Empire embracing most of the continental land mass, were all centuries of secure trade routes and burgeoning commerce.

Very little is known of the earliest overland trade, though fragments have been preserved of the account left by the Greek merchant Aristeas, who lived in the seventh or sixth century B.C. and who claimed to have travelled with Scythian caravans as far east as the T'ien Shan Mountains of Central Asia. In the fifth century B.C. the Greek historian Herodotus wrote an elaborate account of the Scythians, the wagon-dwelling, mare-milking nomads who ruled the steppes between the Don River and the Carpathian Mountains from 700 to 200 B.C. Herodotus' listing of the various Scythian tribes and his description of their customs suggest that detailed information was available to him. This is understandable, for the Scythians lived adjacent to the Greek cities on the north shore of the Black Sea and traded extensively with the colonists. Drawing on the resources of the extensive hinterland they controlled, they exchanged slaves, cattle, hides, furs, fish, timber, wax, and honey, for Greek textiles, wine, olive oil, and sundry luxury items.

In the fourth and third centuries B.C. Scythian power was undermined by new nomadic incursions from the East. During the ensuing confusion long-distance trade evaporated, and over two centuries elapsed before it reappeared. The stimulant this time was provided by the Chinese at the other end of Eurasia who were extending their rule deep into what they called the "Western Region," that is, Central Asia. Their motivation was protection against their dangerous nomadic neighbors, the Hiung-nu, known in European history as the Huns. For many decades the Chinese had bought them off with expensive gifts and cash payments, but now they reversed this appeasement policy and instead sought allies in Central Asia against the Hiung-nu.

In 139 B.C. the great Han Emperor Wu Ti sent an official, Chang Ch'ien, to locate and secure an alliance with the Yue-chi who had been defeated some decades earlier by the Hiung-nu. The Yue-chi, who were the eastern-most of the Indo-European peoples, had fled to the southwest and overrun the Greek kingdom of Bactria (a leftover from Alexander's empire) in present-day Afghanistan. There they settled, and the Chinese envoy found they were too contented and comfortable to resume warfare against the formidable Hiung-nu. So he returned to China, bringing with him a symbol of past Hellenism, the seeds of the vine, as well as a great store of geographical information. The latter was the basis for the ensuing military and diplomatic offensive of China in Central Asia.

Emperor Wu Ti sent a series of great expeditions against the Hiung-nu, eventually forcing the various tribes to submit or to flee into the desert. Indeed it was the Chinese victories that set off a chain reaction of westward migrations that eventually buffetted the Roman Empire and led to the fall of Rome. Having broken the power of the nomads, the Chinese sent a diplomatic mission to the various countries mentioned by Chang Ch'ien in his report. Two former Greek kingdoms, Ferghana and Sogdiana, abused the Chinese missions, presumably feeling safe in their remote location behind the great Pamir Range. But Chinese armies, in a remarkable display of military might, crossed the Pamirs and forced submission to the Han emperor. Thus a great Chinese imperial wedge was driven across Central Asia, eventually establishing contact with the Kushan Empire which was organized in northwest India by the Yue-chi in the first century A.D.

Trade now followed the victorious Chinese banners. Security was assured, and demand had been stimulated by the diplomatic missions, which, in accordance with the custom of the times, bore gifts peculiar to their respective countries. These official exchanges prepared the way for private traders by creating habits and desires. This was particularly true of Chinese silks, which everywhere were in great demand and which comprised at least 90 per cent of China's exports. The remaining 10 per cent included cinnamon, rhubarb, and high grade iron. In return, the Chinese received a wide range of commodities such as furs, woolens, jade, and livestock from Central Asia, amber from the Baltic, and from the Roman provinces, glass, corals, pearls, linen and wool textiles, and, above all, gold.

These goods were transported back and forth by caravans along the famous Silk Road. The main line of this route began in northwest China at Ch'ang-an (Sian), went westward along the Kansu Corridor to the Tarim Basin, which it skirted along both its northern and southern edges, then crossed the Pamirs, continued through Samarkand and Merv in present-day Russian Turkestan, rounded the southern end of the Caspian Sea to Seleucia in modern Iraq, and thence continued to the Roman frontier in the Levant. (See Map X, "Eurasian Ecumene about A.D. 200.")

Despite the existence of this Silk Road, there was no direct commercial intercourse between the Roman Empire and Han China. Roman traders did not go directly overland to China, nor Chinese to Rome. Rather the commerce was conducted by various intermediaries, especially in Parthia or present-day Iran. Both the Chinese and Romans were interested in establishing direct contact but, for obvious reasons, the Parthians were equally interested in preventing it. This is illustrated by the experiences of a Chinese envoy, Kan Ying, who was instructed in A.D. 97 to make his way to Ta Ts'in, the Roman Empire. He reached the Persian Gulf, but there, according to the official Chinese account, he was told by the Parthians:

> "The sea is vast and great; with favorable winds it is possible to cross within three months; but if you meet slow winds, it may also take you two years. It is for this reason that those to go to sea take on board a supply of three years' provisions. There is something in the sea which is apt to make men homesick, and several have thus lost their lives." When Kan Ying heard this, he stopped.[3]

Thus the Parthians misled the envoy not only by exaggerating the dangers of the sea route but also by failing to mention the more direct land route to Syria. The official Chinese account indicated awareness of the situation when it observed that the Romans "always' desired to send embassies to China but the An-hsi [Parthians] wished to carry on trade with them in Chinese silks and it is for this reason they were cut off from communication." [4] The Romans retaliated by encouraging direct sea trade with India, thus eliminating the profiteering middlemen of Parthia. Instead of following the Silk Road westward, the caravans increasingly turned southward through Khotan to ports in northwest India. There the cargoes were picked up by "Roman" merchants, transported briskly across the Indian Ocean with the aid of the monsoons, and unloaded at Red Sea ports.

取蠶

A seventeenth-century Chinese drawing showing the collecting of the cocoons, one of the first steps in the production of silk.

This trade reached such proportions that the Roman historian Ammianus Marcellinus was moved to declare that "the use of silk which was once confined to the nobility has now spread to all classes without distinction, even to the lowest." [5] Doubtless this was an exaggeration, yet the fact remained that many responsible Romans were alarmed by the flow of gold eastward to pay for the popular Chinese silks.

After the second century A.D., this flourishing trade declined gradually with the growing troubles of the Roman and Chinese empires. But it by no means dried up entirely. China continued to produce the silk; the oasis cities through which the Silk Road ran made every effort to maintain the trade on which they had grown rich; and in the West the consumer demand remained unsatiated. Even after Rome fell to the barbarians in the fifth century, Constantinople, or Byzantium, carried on as a great imperial capital with the customary demand for luxury products. On the occasion of the baptism of the infant emperor Theodosius II in 401, we are told that "all the city [Constantinople] was crowned with garlands and decked out in garments made of silk and gold jewels and all kinds of ornaments, so that no one could describe the adornment of the city." [6]

The decline of Roman power, however, accentuated the perennial problem of profiteering middlemen. The Abyssinian kingdom of Axum gained control of the Red Sea in the third century and imposed heavy tolls on the oceanic traffic. Likewise the Persians, ruled by the Sassanids rather than the Parthians after 226 A.D., exploited fully their control of the overland routes. In the fifth century the Byzantine imperial government, partly in order to practice collective bargaining against these middlemen, established a state monopoly in silk importing. Finally in the middle of the sixth century the Byzantines solved the problem by successfully smuggling in from the East some silkworm eggs that were hatched and placed on mulberry leaves. Thus the silk industry got under way in Syria, and then spread to Greece and the western Mediterranean. The West no longer was dependent on Chinese imports, and the Silk Road fell into disuse.

The final blow was the eruption of the Moslem Arabs who conquered the entire Middle East in the seventh century and then expanded into Central Asia where they defeated the Chinese in the battle of Talas in 751. Central Asia now became Moslem and for centuries was a barrier rather than a bridge between China and the West, and also between China and India. Hence the final closing of the overland routes and the shift of trade to the surrounding seas where the Arabs were becoming the leading mariners and merchants. Not until the thirteenth century, when the Mongols conquered all Eurasia from the Pacific Ocean to the Baltic and Black seas, was it possible once more to reopen overland routes and thus clear the way for Marco Polo and his fellow merchants of medieval times.

Despite these various shifts in the direction of trade, one basic fact emerges from this survey. This is the qualitative increase in both the range and volume of commerce that occurred during the Classical Age in contrast to the preceding ancient period. No longer was the scope of commerce confined to individual regions, whether in the Mediterranean Sea or the Arabian Sea or some segment of the Eurasian steppes. Rather trade now became interregional with goods being carried from one end of Eurasia to the other both by sea and by land. This constituted the economic component of the new Eurasian ecumene; the following section will consider the cultural aspect of this ecumene.

III. CULTURAL BONDS

Commercial and cultural bonds were not unconnected or independent of each other. The transplantation of Indian civilization to Southeast Asia was in large part the work of Indian merchants. Likewise, the Greek merchants who followed Alexander's armies spread their Hellenistic culture throughout the Orient. And the course of the diffusion of Buddhism from India to China can be traced along the well-known Silk Road. The most important center of Buddhism in China during the Han period was Lo-yang, a city noted for its colony of "barbarian merchants from the Western Regions." [7]

Cultural movements, however, had their own autonomous dynamism and were by no means entirely dependent upon merchants and trade routes. A fundamental factor affecting cultural developments in the classical world, exclusive of China, was the invention of a simple alphabetic script in the late second millennium B.C. Prior to that time only a handful of professional scribes had been able to read and write the complicated cuneiform script of Mesopotamia and the hieroglyphics of Egypt. The first alphabetic system was devised by Semitic traders in the Sinai Peninsula who adapted the Egyptian signs, with which they had become familiar, to indicate consonantal sounds. But they continued to use many additional symbols for words and syllables, and therefore failed to develop a strictly phonetic alphabet. The Phoenicians completed the transition in the thirteenth century B.C. by developing an alphabet of twenty-two signs denoting simple consonants. The Greeks improved the Phoenician alphabet by using some of its signs to indicate vowels. This Greek alphabet, with some modifications, was spread by the Romans westward and by the Byzantines eastward.

The significance of the alphabet is that it opened the world of intelligent communication to a far wider circle than that of the priests and officials of the old days. The scribes of Egypt and Mesopotamia naturally shunned the new style of writing, and continued to use their traditional scripts almost until the Christian era. China also, in her isolation, continued with her combination phono-pictographic system that has persisted with modifications to the present day. But elsewhere in Eurasia, alphabets were adopted with slight adjustments to fit the different languages. Everywhere the effect was to reduce somewhat, though by no means entirely, or even substantially, the gap between high and low cultures, between urban ruling circles and peasant masses, that had developed with the appearance of civilization. By challenging the monopoly of privileged intellectual cliques that generally supported the *status quo,* the simplified scripts generated a certain ferment in the body politic as well as in traditional piety and learning.

The overall cultural pattern noticeable amongst all Eurasian civilizations during these centuries of the Classical Age was the breakdown of local cultures, which were integrated into the new regional civilizations with their distinctive languages, religions, and social systems. It was much easier for these civilizations to exchange material goods than culture traits. Textiles, spices, and luxury products were universally usable and desirable, whereas ancestor worship, the caste system, and the city-state were irrelevant and unacceptable outside their places of origin. Thus the commercial interregional bonds during this period of incipient ecumenism were generally more extensive and influential than the cultural.

Yet the latter did exist and in some cases were of first-rate historical significance. The first outstanding instance was that of Hellenism which spread from the Greek world eastward to the Orient and westward to Europe. Toward the end of the classical period there were also the great universal religions, especially Christianity and Buddhism, with their claims to the allegiance of all men rather than of any one group.

Considering first Hellenism, derived from the Greek word "Hellas," meaning Greece, its diffusion throughout the Middle East was made possible by Alexander's famous conquest eastward to Central Asia and the Indus Valley. As will be noted in the following chapter, this empire lasted for only a few years during Alexander's lifetime. On his death in 323 B.C. it was divided among his generals, and later partitioned between Rome in the West and the Parthians in the East. It was during these fourth and third centuries B.C. that the military predominance of the Greek soldiers paved the way for the hundreds of thousands of Greek merchants, administrators, and professional men who flocked to the numerous cities built by Alexander and his successors. From the first and most famous Alexandria in Egypt to the farthest Alexandria, Eschata (Kojand) in Afghanistan, these cities served as centers for the diffusion of Greek culture.

Many of the Greek emigrants married local women, Alexander himself setting an example by taking a Persian noblewoman as wife and by arranging the mass marriage of three thousand of his soldiers with Persian women after their return from the Indian campaign. He also enlisted Persian soldiers in his regiments, and adopted the costume of the Persian king and the etiquette of his court. Even though the majority of its inhabitants usually were non-Hellenic, the typical city was basically Greek, with elected magistrates, a council, and an assembly of the citizens. A new form of the Greek language, the *Koine,* or common tongue, became the lingua franca throughout the Middle East. It could be learned relatively easily by those natives who became Hellenized as it was simpler than the Greek of the classical period. The most assimilated of the Middle Eastern peoples were those of Asia Minor who forgot their native languages and spoke the *Koine.* Elsewhere Greek manners, amusements, coinage, and arts were adopted by the upper classes in the cities.

The Greeks responded with a growing cosmopolitanism and respect for foreigners, whom they always had referred to as barbarians. Alexander's father, King Philip, had been urged by the Greek scholar Isocrates to invade Asia in order to deliver its peoples "from barbaric despotism to the tutelage of Hellas." By contrast, another Greek scholar, Eratosthenes, writing several decades after Alexander's death, criticized those who "divided mankind into two classes, Greek and Barbarian. It would be better," he argued, "to distinguish them according to their virtues and their vices, since amongst the Greeks there are many worthless characters, and many highly civilized are to be found amongst the Barbarians; witness the . . . Romans and Carthaginians whose political system is so beautifully perfect." By the first century A.D. the writer Plutarch was claiming that Alexander acted "as one sent by God to be a common ruler and reconciler of all," and that "he bade all men look upon the habitable world as their fatherland. . . ." [8]

The influence of Hellenism extended eastward to northern India and to Bactria and Sogdiana in Afghanistan. These kingdoms flourished for nearly two centuries before falling to the Yue-chi nomads from Mongolia, noted in the preceding section. These Hellenic outposts deep in the heart of Asia exerted a certain recognizable and wide-ranging influence on surrounding peoples. First there were their coins, of brilliant craftsmanship, which constituted, in effect, the beginning of Indian coinage. Then there is the Buddhist text known as the *Questions of Milinda* (that is, Menander, Greek king of Bactria, who conquered part of northwest India) which introduces the Greek dialogue form into Indian literature. In the field of language, a number of Greek words were incorporated into Sanskrit, including those for horse-bit, pen and ink, book, and mine. In science, both Indian astrology and Hindu medicine contain Greek words among their technical terms.

Most significant was the Greek impact on a school of religious art known as Gandharan, after the region of that name in northwest India, which had been under Greek rule. The main products were images of Buddha and relief sculptures representing scenes from Buddhist texts. There is a striking difference between the Buddha images of Gandhara, with their obvious likeness to Apollo, and those from other regions of India. The former were realistic, stressing accuracy of anatomical details such as the delineation of muscles and the addition of mustaches. The latter were idealistic, interested more in projecting a spiritual expression than in presenting an exact likeness. The transmission of Gandharan art style to China has been traced along the Silk Road, trod by Buddhist pilgrims, as well as by merchants. In the process of transplantation, Buddhist sculpture lost much of its naturalness and became austerely abstract. The original Greek realism was confined to such superficial details as the folds of the garments. Thus Greek art style affected all the great civilizations of Asia to an appreciable degree.

Despite this impressive diffusion, Hellenism did not leave a permanent imprint on the Middle East, let alone the remainder of Asia. The basic reason was that its influence had been restricted to the cities where Greek settlers lived and where Greek dynasties had courts. Some of the native peoples were affected but they were almost exclusively of the small upper classes. The great majority in the countryside, and even in many of the cities, continued to speak their own languages and worship their own gods. Thus Hellenism did not sink deep roots and was incapable of surviving through the centuries. When the Islamic conquerors appeared during the Middle Ages they had little difficulty in overwhelming the little islands of Hellenistic culture, so that today, the Greek language and culture survive only in the Greek homeland on the southern tip of the Balkan Peninsula.

Hellenism in the western Mediterranean was slower to take root because the indigenous populations had not yet reached a sufficiently affluent and sophisticated level of civilization. But for that very reason the long-run impact of Hellenism in that region was more durable since there was less competition from the local culture.

As early as the sixth century B.C., the Romans were being influenced by the Greek colonies in southern Italy, but it was not until the third century onward, when the Romans conquered the heartland of Hellenism in the Balkans and the Levant, that they felt the full force of Greek culture. Roman soldiers and officials now came into direct contact with highly educated Greek rulers and administrators, while among the hostages and slaves brought to Rome were many Greeks who served in every capacity—from moral philosopher to contortionist, from laudatory poet to *chef de cuisine*. New intellectual horizons opened for upper-class Romans as they heard the dazzling rhetoric and argumentation of their articulate subjects.

Greeks served as tutors for the leading families, offering instruction in Greek language, rhetoric, philosophy, and literature. By the first century B.C. it was common for young Romans to be sent to Athens or Rhodes for training in the philosophical schools. In the field of literature, the Romans had produced little of significance before the impact of Greek literary works, which consequently proved irresistible. Charmed by the beauties of Greek poetry, drama, and prose, educated Romans were content in the beginning with translations or imitations of the originals. But Roman patrons gradually demanded Roman themes and the expression of Roman values. A national literature came into being which, however, always bore the stamp of its Greek origins, both during the "Golden Age" of Vergil, Horace, and Ovid, and the "Silver Age" of Seneca, Tacitus, and Pliny the Elder and the Younger.

The most obvious manifestation of Greek influence was in the physical appearance of Rome and the other cities of the Empire. All three Greek orders were used—the Doric, Ionic, and Corinthian—though the simplicity of plan and the perfection of proportion and finish that had characterized Greek architecture gave way to baroque richness and to sheer size. The buildings were decorated with sculpture, at first Greek originals imported by wagonloads as booty and later imitated by native artists. Thus towns and cities in Italy, as in the Middle East, began to take on a uniform physical appearance under the influence of Greek art and architecture. Indeed a basic contribution of the Romans to civilization was in appropriating and adapting Greek culture and then spreading it to diverse peoples who had never experienced direct contact with it—Gauls, Germans, Britons, and Iberians. Viewed from this perspective, the "fall" of Rome may be interpreted as the recession of Hellenism before the Germans and Celts, just as it receded in the Middle East before the Moslems.

Much more durable than the impact of Hellenism was that of the two great universal religions, Christianity and Mahayana Buddhism. They began their expansion in the late classical period from their respective places of origin in the Middle East and India, and during the course of the following centuries they won over all Europe in the one case, and most of Asia in the other. The reason for their success is to be found in certain novel characteristics that they shared in common. One was their emphasis on salvation and their promise of an afterlife of eternal bliss. Another was their egalitarianism, so that their brotherhood was open to all who sought admittance—women as well as men, rich and poor alike, slave or free. Finally, both religions stressed a high code of ethics, the observance of which was essential for salvation. This requirement, together with efficient ecclesiastical organization, enabled these two religions to exert effectiv influence on the daily lives of the faithful.

These features were particularly appealing in the later centuries of the Classical Age. These were times of social unrest and moral confusion, especially in the large urban centers. The multitudes in the cities felt uprooted and drifting. For such people, Christianity and Mahayana Buddhism offered solace, security, and guidance. They provided an answer when Pilate, voicing the despairing mood of the times, asked "What is truth?" It was not accidental that the earliest converts to Christianity were the lowly and dispossessed. Likewise, the greatest triumph of Mahayana Buddhism was in China during the time of troubles following the collapse of the Han dynasty, when there seemed to be no solution to man's worldly problems.

Indeed, these satisfying and opportune characteristics of the two religions were evolved precisely in response to the needs of the times. They were not present either in the Judaism from which Christianity had emerged, or in the original Buddhism from which developed the later Mahayana variant.

Judaism was the parochial faith of the Jewish people who about the twelfth century B.C. adopted a national god, Jehovah. "I am Jehovah, thy God. . . , Thou Shalt have no other gods before me." This first of Jehovah's Ten Commandments did not say that Jehovah was the only god in the world. It said, rather, that he was the only god for the children of Israel. Also this Judaistic faith was at this time more social and ethical than mystical and otherworldly. In the words of one of the Jewish prophets, Jehovah cares nothing for ritual and sacrifice; he cares only that men should "seek justice, relieve the oppressed, judge the fatherless, plead for the widow."

But from the sixth century B.C. onward, the Jews changed their religious ideas under the influence of the religions of the Persians and other of their rulers. Also they were affected by the many Jews who lived outside Palestine where, exposed to the tenets of Hellenism, they sought to interpret Judaism in terms of Greek philosophy. Thus the Jews gradually adopted a belief in an afterlife—obedience to God's will would bring eternal happiness in heaven, and disobedience would bring eternal punishment in hell.

Nevertheless, Christianity was a Jewish cult during the lifetime of Jesus and immediately after his crucifixion. But it was universalized by Paul, a Hellenized Jew who lived in the city of Tarsus in Asia Minor. Paul boldly denied that Jesus was sent merely as the redeemer of the Jews. A loving Father had sent His only Son to atone for the sins of all mankind. Therefore Christianity was not a sect of Judaism. It was a new church, a church for Gentiles as well as for Jews. Paul's approach meant that Christianity henceforth could appeal not only to a handful of Jews, but to the millions of Gentiles throughout the Roman Empire.

Hence the steady growth of the new religion despite the official persecution. Finally, in 313 it was tolerated by Emperor Constantine's Edict of Milan, and in 399 it was made the official state religion of the Roman Empire. Then, after the fall of the Empire, Christian missionaries carried the faith to the English and German peoples between 600 and 800, and to the Scandinavian and Slavic peoples between 800 and 1100. With the expansion of Europe, both missionaries and emigrants spread Christianity to all parts of the globe.

The evolution of Buddhism was somewhat similar in that it began, as will be noted in Chapter 9, section II, as a distinct Indian reaction against the injustice of the caste system and the exploitation by the Brahman priestly class.

The founder, Siddhartha (c. 563–483 B.C.), of the Gautama clan, was of noble rank, but he became so distressed by the suffering he saw about him that he gave up his family and material comforts for the life of a wandering ascetic. Finally, in a moment of revelation, he achieved enlightenment and thenceforth was known as Buddha, or the Enlightened One.

The four great truths of Buddhism are: (1) life is sorrow; (2) the cause of sorrow is desire; (3) escape is possible only by stopping desire; and (4) this can only be done by the "eight-fold path" consisting of right belief, right ambition, right speech, right conduct, right living, right effort, right thoughts, right pleasures. The objective of all this effort was Nirvana, literally meaning "emptiness," the "blowing out of the flame."

Buddha had not intended to establish a new religion but after his death his disciples preached his teachings and founded monastic communities that came to dominate the religion. The ideal of these communities was mental and physical discipline culminating in the mystic experience of Nirvana. Satisfying as this was for the monks, it failed to meet the needs of the everyday life of laymen. Hence the evolution of Mahayana, or the Greater Vehicle, as opposed to the Hinayana, or Lesser Vehicle. The Greater Vehicle was "greater" in the sense of its all-inclusiveness. It incorporated more of the concepts of pre-Buddhist Indian thought as well as the religious ideas of the people it converted. In doing so, it turned somewhat from its original contemplative bent and adopted precepts that were easier to comprehend and observe. Salvation now could be attained through faith, even an unthinking act of faith such as the mouthing of the name of Buddha. Also Nirvana changed, at least for the less sophisticated believers, to mean an afterlife in Paradise, and Paradise was more likely of attainment through good works that helped others.

This shift of emphasis from monasticism, asceticism, and contemplation, to charity, faith, and salvation, made Mahayana Buddhism more palatable to non-Indian peoples than the original religion had been, though both forms of the faith won foreign converts. Buddhism spread first to Ceylon and to northwest frontier regions of India in the third century B.C. Then in the first century B.C. it was carried into Central Asia and China, first by traders, then by Indian missionaries, and, most effectively, by Chinese converts who studied in India and then returned to win over their fellow countrymen. So successful were they that by the late fourth century A.D., nine-tenths of the population of northwest China was said to have been converted, and by the sixth century South China had followed suit. From China, Buddhism spread still further: to Korea in the fourth century A.D., to Japan in the sixth century, and later to Tibet and Mongolia. Meanwhile Buddhism in both its Hinayana and Mahayana forms had been penetrating into Southeast Asia. This did not occur at any particular period; rather it represented one aspect of the general Indianization of the region that took place over many centuries.

After these successes Buddhism declined in many countries. In China it reached its peak about 700 but thereafter suffered from internal decay and governmental hostility. Its great land holdings, its vast treasures, and the large numbers of monks and nuns it withdrew from the national economy, all aroused official envy and displeasure and brought on persecution. Between 841 and 855, according to official accounts, 4,600 monasteries and 40,000 shrines were destroyed; 260,000 monks and nuns were defrocked, and, together with their

150,000 slaves, were returned to the tax registers. Buddhism never recovered from this blow, and thereafter it was merely one of "the three religions" (along with Taoism and Confucianism) in which the syncretic Chinese were inter- ested. Likewise, in India, Buddhism eventually gave way to a revival of Hindu- ism, so that virtually no followers are to be found today in its own birthplace. (See Chapter 9, section II.) In Ceylon and in many parts of Southeast Asia, however, Buddhism of the Hinayana variety remains predominant to the present.

Despite this relative decline after its period of greatness, the fact remains that Buddhism in late classical and early medieval times was the predominant religion of Asia. It prevailed in the whole continent except for Siberia and the Middle East, thus giving that vast area a degree of cultural unity unequalled before or after. In doing so, it functioned as a great civilizing force in Asia as Christianity did at the same time in Europe. To many peoples Buddhism brought not only a religion and a set of ethics, but also a system of writing, a type of architecture, and all the other attributes of the great civilizations of India and China that the missionaries spread together with their religion. In the same way, at the other end of Eurasia, Christian missionaries were bringing to the barbaric Germanic and Slavic peoples the civilizations of Rome and of Constantinople, as well as the teachings of Christ. Such was the impact and historical significance of these powerful "cultural bonds" for the new Eurasian ecumene.

During the millennia of the ancient civilizations, the Middle East had been the center of initiative. It was the Middle East that during that period had made the fundamental contributions to mankind—contributions such as agri- culture, metallurgy, urbanism, and imperial organization. But now in classical times this Middle Eastern predominance faded away, except in one area—that of religion. Not only Judaism but also Zoroastrianism have their roots in the Middle East. The latter religion, although observed today by only a handful of Parsis in India, had considerable influence in the Middle East when the Persian Empire was at its height. Furthermore, it stands out in the history of religions as a lofty faith that sought to replace the prevailing gross practices and superstitions of the Persian people with the principles of light, truth, and righteousness.

Yet the fact remains that apart from these religions and other related sects, the Middle East no longer was the vital source of innovation during the Clas- sical Age. After the invasions of the late second millennium B.C., writes one authority, "the creative power of the Ancient Near East appears diminished . . . in the main we observe a codification and consolidation of acquired knowledge." [9] The new ideas and institutions which took shape in classical times, and which have persisted in many cases to the present, were the products of what formerly had been the peripheral regions of Eurasia. Accordingly, the following three chapters are devoted to the civilizations of these regions: the Greco-Roman, the Indian, and the Chinese.

SUGGESTED READING

The various regions of Eurasia are dealt with in the following work, which suffers from the usual defects of multiple authorship; L. Pareti *et al., The Ancient*

World 1200 B.C. to A.D. 500, in *History of Mankind,* Vol. II, International Commission for a History of the Scientific and Cultural Development of Mankind (New York: Harper & Row, 1965). Interregional ties in Eurasia are clearly analyzed in the well written study by G. F. Hudson, *Europe & China: A Survey of their Relations from the Earliest Times to 1800* (London: Edward Arnold, 1931). See also the monumental multivolume study by J. Needham, *Science & Civilisation in China* (London: Cambridge Univ., 1954–), the first volume of which provides an overall survey of China's interaction with the rest of Eurasia, including a theoretical analysis of culture diffusion. Stimulating insights into the Eurasian ecumene from the vantage point of Central Asia are provided by O. Lattimore, *Studies in Frontier History: Collected Papers 1928–1958* (Paris: Mouton, 1962).

Various aspects of the commercial bonds of Eurasia are treated in A. Toussaint, *History of the Indian Ocean* (Chicago: Univ. of Chicago, 1966); D. Harden, *The Phoenicians* (New York: Praeger, 1962); E. H. Warmington, *The Commerce between the Roman Empire and India* (Cambridge: Cambridge Univ., 1928); and Ying-shih Yü, *Trade and Expansion in Han China* (Berkeley: Univ. of California, 1967); J. I. Miller, *The Spice Trade of the Roman Empire, 29 B.C.–A.D. 641* (New York: Oxford Univ., 1969); and above all, C. G. F. Simkin, *The Traditional Trade of Asia* (New York: Oxford Univ., 1969).

For the cultural bonds of Eurasia, see H. G. Rawlinson, *Intercourse between India and the Western World* (Cambridge: Cambridge Univ., 1916); E. Zürcher, *Buddhism: Its Origin and Spread* (New York: St. Martin's, 1962), and also his *Buddhist Conquest of China,* 2 vols. (Leiden: Brill, 1959); R. Grousset, *In the Footsteps of the Buddha* (London: Routledge, 1932); and M. Hallade, *The Gandhara Style and the Evolution of Buddhist Art* (London: Thames and Hudson, 1968).

See the following chapter for bibliographical suggestions concerning Hellenism.

The pupils of Athens have become *Chapter*
teachers of others, and she has made
the term Hellene no longer signify
a race but a mental outlook.

8

ISOCRATES

Greco-Roman Civilization

Of the three chapters dealing with the three classical civilizations, this one on the Greco-Roman civilization is the most lengthy.
One reason is that two distinct though related civilizations are involved,
in contrast to the unitary civilizations of India and China. This bifurcation arises from a basic difference between the historical development at this time of the West on the one hand and of India and China
on the other. In all three instances, civilization spread out from restricted centers of origin to encompass entire surrounding regions—
from the Greek peninsula to the western Mediterranean, from the Indus
River valley to South India, and from the Yellow River valley to South
China. As noted in Chapter 7, section I, iron tools made possible this
expansion by facilitating the extension of agriculture into forested
regions, and of commerce and colonization into new coastal areas.
But at this point the common pattern ends. The newly civilized regions
in India and China remained generally subservient to the original core
areas, whereas in the West, Rome developed a military superiority
that enabled her to conquer not only the Greek homeland in the
Balkans but also the western portions of the ancient Middle East—
Asia Minor, Palestine, Syria, and Egypt. In doing so, Rome began a
new phase of the history of the West, and launched a new, though re-

lated, Western civilization. The history and nature of these two sister civilizations, the Greek and the Roman, is the subject of this chapter.

I. FORMATIVE AGE, 800–500 B.C.

With the Dorian invasions of the twelfth century B.C., Greece lapsed into a "Dark Age." (See Chapter 6, section IV.) The Greece of this period was tribal, aristocratic, agricultural, and confined to the Aegean Basin. By the end of the sixth century B.C. all this had changed. The tribe had given way to the city-state; other social classes had risen to challenge the nobility; industry and commerce had come to play a considerable role; and Greek colonies were to be found scattered on all the Mediterranean shores. These changes constitute the comprehensive transformation of the Greek world that occurred during the formative age and that cleared the way for the subsequent Classical Age. (See Map VII, "Classical Age Empires in the Middle East and Europe.")

A basic factor behind these developments was the geography of the Greek lands. They possessed no rich natural resources—no fertile river valleys or broad plains that, when properly developed and exploited, could support elaborate imperial structures such as those of the Middle East, India, and China. Rather in Greece and on the Asia Minor coast there were successive mountain chains that not only restricted agricultural productivity but also compartmentalized the countryside. Consequently the Greeks had no natural geopolitical center that could have provided a basis for regional integration. Instead, following the invasions, they settled down in isolated villages, usually located near some easily defended high point that provided refuge in time of danger as well as a location for the shrines to the gods. The settlement as a whole was called the *polis,* and the place of refuge the *acropolis,* literally "high town." Where the polis was strategically situated in relation to fertile land or communication routes, it attracted more settlers and became the leading city of the region. In this manner dozens of little city-states emerged, relatively isolated and fiercely independent.

At the outset these city-states depended primarily on subsistence agriculture, herding, and fishing. But by the beginning of the eighth century B.C. this economic self-sufficiency was undermined by population pressure. Land-hungry peasants were forced to take to the sea as pirates or traders or colonists, or, as often happened, some combination of the three. By the fifth century the entire Mediterranean basin, including the Black Sea, was ringed with prosperous Greek colonies that constituted overseas replicas of the mother cities. (See Chapter 7, section II.)

These developments set off a chain reaction that in the end transformed the Greek world. The colonies shipped raw materials and especially grain to overpopulated Greece and in return received wine, olive oil, and manufactured goods, such as cloth and pottery. This trade pattern triggered an economic boom in the homeland. The Greek soil was better suited for olive orchards and vineyards than for wheat fields, and the amount of land under cultivation increased substantially since rocky hillsides could be planted to grape vines and olive trees. Thus the shift to commercial agriculture made it possible to support a population three to four times larger than under the former subsistence agriculture. Likewise the stimulus to manufactures is reflected in the large quantities of Greek pottery unearthed not only all around the Mediterranean but also far into the hinterland—into central Russia, southwest Germany and northeast France. The Greek merchant marine also prospered at the same time in carrying these goods back and forth. Indeed this was the first occasion in history that bulky commodities, as distinct from luxury items, were being traded and transported on such a large scale. Furthermore all this economic activity was efficiently lubricated by the growing use of coin money in which the Greeks pioneered. "Between the sixth and fourth centuries B.C.," concludes an economic historian, "the Greek economy was rocketing. . . . Athenian economics gives one an impression somewhat similar to that of Europe in the nineteenth century, making all necessary allowances for the different eras." [1]

Economic revolution in nineteenth-century Europe stimulated, and in return was stimulated by, social and political revolution. This occurred in Greece also from the eighth century B.C. onward. The commercialization of agriculture meant debts as well as profits, especially for the small landholder. Formerly the nobles had collected rent in the form of a portion of the crop, so that in bad years everyone pulled in the belt for the duration. But now the combination of foreign markets, money economy, and new luxuries left the small farmers vulnerable to mortgages, foreclosures, and even loss of personal freedom. Inevitably this led to bitter class conflict and to popular clamor for debt cancellation and land redistribution. Likewise in the cities new wealthy families emerged that aspired to political recognition commensurate with their economic strength. They could count on the support of the urban poor—artisans, stevedores, and sailors. All these discontented elements, then, struck out against the traditional political system that left power in the hands of the landowning aristocracy.

The movement for change was greatly strengthened in the sixth century when the aristocratic cavalryman was replaced as the decisive figure on the battlefield by the heavily armed and armored infantryman, the hoplite. Massed together in a solid block or phalanx, with a shield on the left hand and a long spear in the right, and trained to maneuver in unison, the hoplites could sweep bristling through the hitherto invincible horsemen. This innovation not only undermined the military basis of aristocratic political authority but also enhanced the status and influence of the independent farmer and artisan who could afford to equip himself for phalanx service.

The combination of economic and military change generated corresponding political change. Having started as monarchies in the Dark Age and having gradually changed to aristocratic oligarchies, the city-states in the seventh century came under the rule of dictators, or tyrants as they were called. These ambitious leaders, usually of noble birth, championed popular demands, won mass support, and seized personal power. The word "tyrant" referred to one who ruled without legal right, and carried with it no sense of moral reproach. Indeed, tyrants commonly favored the interests of the common people against the privileged classes, and often hastened the advent of democracy, though by no means invariably.

Sparta, in the southern Peloponnesus, was the classic example of the opposite trend. About 1000 B.C. the Dorian forefathers of the Spartans had overrun the rich valley of the Eurotas and reduced the native population to the status of *helots,* or serfs. Later in the eighth century the Spartans conquered the rich plains of neighboring Messenia, thereby obviating the need for overseas expansion. But the price paid was heavy and inescapable. Sparta was deprived of the economic and intellectual stimulus of foreign contacts and condemned to a static rural existence. Also the Spartans were forced to organize their state like a military camp in order to keep down the large subject population. Everything was subordinated to military needs. Only healthy infants were allowed to live, the sickly ones being left to die of exposure in the wilderness. From the age of seven, boys lived and trained in the barracks. Until age sixty all men remained under military discipline. Private life was all but abolished and luxury was frowned upon. The morning plunge in the cold waters of the Eurotas, the scanty fare on the mess tables, and the rough timbers of the houses shaped only with the ax were famous throughout Greece. Life consisted almost exclusively of organized amusement, communal meals, public business, and military training and duties. This regimen made the Spartan the best infantryman in all Greece. But it left him no time or inclination for writing plays or carving statues or formulating philosophy.

Meanwhile the Athenians had been developing an altogether different type of society. Far from being a band of invaders camped amidst a hostile population, the Athenians prided themselves on being native inhabitants of Attica. Like the Greeks of other city-states, they began with a monarchy which gave way to an oligarchy of nine *archons* who were the chief executive officers and who were invariably aristocrats. But in contrast to Sparta, the subsequent evolution of Athens was towards democratization. The burgeoning trade created a strong middle class that joined forces with the dispossessed peasantry in demanding political liberalization. In 594 B.C. all parties agreed upon the appointment of Solon as chief magistrate with full powers for reform. His measures for the alleviation of social distress were simple and drastic. He restored to the debtors full title to their land; he freed all citizens who had been enslaved for unpaid debts; and he made such enslavement illegal in the future. In the realm of politics he admitted propertyless citizens for the first time to the Assembly, though this body still possessed little power. Also he made wealthy businessmen eligible to become *archons* and diluted the power of the aristocratic Areopagus, or chief judicial body, by establishing new and more popular courts of justice. In short, Solon's contribution was to create the constitutional base upon which the famed Athenian democracy of later times was to be built.

The three decades following Solon were filled with strife, for many problems remained unsolved. Enslavement was now illegal but the poor still found it difficult to earn a living, and likewise the aristocrats, though somewhat curbed, could still block popular legislation. Under these circumstances Pisistratus established himself as the first tyrant of Athens about 560 B.C. During his thirty-year rule he divided the estates of the aristocrats and distributed them amongst landless peasants and helped the urban poor with large-scale public works that beautified the city. Pisistratus was succeeded by his sons who proved incapable, so that more strife ensued until the advent of Cleisthenes, who gained control about 506 B.C. He abolished the old tribes, setting up ten new ones that in reality were based on territorial divisions rather than kinship. This innovation contributed much to undermining the political power of the aristocrats. Also he established a new Council of 500 for which all male citizens over thirty years of age were eligible, and which had authority to prepare measures for submission to the Assembly, as well as supreme executive and administrative power. With these reforms of Cleisthenes, Athens by 500 B.C. had emerged as a democracy while Sparta remained a militarized and regimented society.

II. CLASSICAL AGE, 500–336 B.C.

In his famous funeral speech commemorating the Athenian soldiers who had fallen in battle against the Spartans in 431, Pericles declared, "Our city is open to the world. . . . Athens is the school of Greece." This boast was fully justified. During the fifth century B.C. Athens overshadowed Sparta and all other Greek cities. This was the golden age of Periclean Athens which is synonymous with the golden age of Classical Greece.

One reason for the dazzling preeminence of Athens was the leading role of the city in the fateful defeat inflicted upon the great Persian Empire. This was due partly to the good fortune of the Athenians in discovering the Larium silver lodes shortly before the Persian Wars. Their decision to use the treasure for naval construction provided them with two hundred triremes of latest design, a fleet that proved decisive in the ensuing struggle.

The root of the war was the Persian conquest of the Greek city-states in Asia Minor during the mid-sixth century B.C. Heavy-handed Persian interference in their domestic affairs led the cities to revolt in 499. They appealed to the homeland cities for aid and received a positive response, partly because the Persian Empire at this time was expanding across southern Russia and menacing the Balkans from the north. Despite the naval assistance from across the Aegean, the Asia Minor cities were overwhelmed by 494. The Persian Emperor Darius now resolved to chastise the obstreperous Greeks and sent out an expedition that landed at Marathon, to the northwest of Athens, in 490. Although the Athenians fought almost alone, thanks to inter-city rivalries, their phalanxes inflicted a stunning defeat on the invaders. The effect on Greek morale was enormous. "These were the first Greeks," wrote the historian Herodotus, "who had the courage to face up to Persian dress and the men who wore it, whereas up to that time the very name of the Persians brought terror to a Greek."

Ten years later the Persians came again with much larger forces, and this time by land through Thrace and Thessaly. A mixed force under Spartan command fought gallantly to the last man at the pass of Thermopylae. The Persians pressed on to Athens, which they sacked, but the Athenian fleet destroyed the Persians in nearby Salamis. An allied Greek fleet followed the retreating Persians across the Aegean and won another naval victory. Soon the Asia Minor cities were freed from Persian rule, and the Greeks emerged as the victors over the greatest empire in the world.

The repercussions of the Greek triumph were momentous. First and foremost, it saved the Greeks from being engulfed in an oriental despotism, thereby allowing them to preserve their identity and to make their unique contribution to human civilization. Plato recognized this when he wrote: "If the common

The pass at Thermopylae. In ancient times this pass was narrower than it is now and was the only passageway into Greece from the north. It is historically famous as the site where Leonidas and his Spartans in 480 B.C. fought to the last man against the Persians. (Arborio Mella)

resolution of Athenians and Spartans had not warded off the impending enslavement, already we might almost say that the Greek communities would be jumbled together and Greeks confounded with Barbarians, as those under Persian tyranny now live broken up and tacked together in miserable confusion." [2]

The success of the Greeks, and especially of the Athenian fleet, also furthered the cause of democracy, for the rowers who drove the ships into battle were citizens who could not afford to equip themselves as hoplites. Thus the urban poor now assumed a military role even more important than that of the propertied hoplites. This naturally strengthened the movement for more democracy, which reached its apogee during the Age of Pericles (461–429 B.C.).

Although an aristocrat by birth, Pericles was an earnest democrat who completed the transference of power to the Assembly, of which all adult male citizens were members. This body was the sovereign power in the affairs of Athens. Holding forty regular meetings a year and extraordinary sessions as required, it not only settled general questions of policy but made detailed decisions in every sphere of government—foreign affairs, military operations, finance. Pericles also introduced pay for service in most public offices so that the poor could afford to assume such offices. In addition he established an array of popular courts in which final decisions were rendered by juries on which all citizens could serve if chosen by lot. Pericles was quite justified, then, in proudly stating in his funeral oration in honor of the Athenian heroes who fell in battle with the Spartans in 431:

> Our form of government does not enter into rivalry with the institutions of others. We do not copy our neighbor, but are an example to them. It is true that we are called a democracy, for the administration is in the hands of the many and not of the few. But while the law secures equal justice to all alike in their private disputes, the claim of excellence is also recognized; and when a citizen is in any way distinguished, he is preferred to the public service, not as a matter of privilege but as the reward of merit. Neither is poverty a bar, but a man may benefit his country whatever be the obscurity of his condition. [3]

Finally the prominent role of Athens in the Persian Wars led the city to a course that eventually culminated in imperialism. Whereas Sparta was immobilized by her static economy and the constant threat of a helot revolt, Athens took the lead in organizing a confederacy of Asiatic Greeks and islanders. Known as the Delian Confederation because its headquarters were originally on the small island of Delos, its purpose was collective security against possible further Persian attacks. It was theoretically an alliance of equals, the constitution providing each member with only one vote in the periodic meetings. But from the start Athens provided the executive leadership and the generals and also collected tribute from cities unable or unwilling to furnish ships. Step by step Athens tightened her hold: the treasury of the Confederation was moved from Delos to Athens; Athenian coinage became the common medium of exchange; and members were denied the right of secession. Thus by 450 B.C. the Confederation had become an empire, and the power of Athens extended, in the words of Euripides, from Ionia "to the outward Ocean of the West."

Athenian imperialism was relatively enlightened and beneficient, as indicated by the fact that most of Athens' allies remained loyal until the very end of the ensuing Peloponnesian War. And when they did revolt, the instigators were dissident oligarchs, for the people usually viewed the Athenian assembly not as an oppressor but as a defender against their own oppressive compatriots. Nevertheless the outbreak of the Peloponnesian War in 431 B.C. was probably inevitable, given the expansionist dynamism of Athens and the resulting apprehension of Sparta.

Since one was a maritime power and the other a land power, the fighting dragged on indecisively for ten years. The Spartan armies raided Attica each year but could not penetrate the long walls that joined Athens to the sea and protected her supplies. The Athenians for their part, badly hurt by the great plague of 429 B.C. which carried off almost half the population, including Pericles, could only make random raids on the coast of the Peloponnesus. Then in 415 the fatal decision was made to send the fleet to capture Sicily and cut off Sparta's grain supply. "Fleet and army," wrote Thucydides, "perished from the face of the earth, nothing was saved." Athens' allies now revolted; the Spartans finally destroyed the long wall; and Athens was starved into capitulation in 404 B.C. Athens was left shorn of its fleets, its empire, and even its vaunted democracy, for the Spartan victors imposed a short-lived oligarchic regime.

This ruinous war left the Greek world exhausted and solved none of its problems. Spartan high-handedness caused Thebes and Athens to unite together in a new league for mutual protection. In 371 the Thebans inflicted on the Spartans their first major military defeat in two hundred years. For the next decade Thebes was supreme on the Greek mainland, but then internecine rivalries prevailed again and the city-states once more were engulfed in a confused anarchy of shifting alliances and petty wars. The stage was set for the subjugation and forcible unification of Greece by foreign power. In 338 B.C. Philip of Macedon smashed the combined armies of Thebes and Athens at Chaeronea. He deprived the Greek cities of most of their autonomy, but before he could proceed further he was assassinated in 336 B.C. His successor was his world famous son, Alexander the Great.

The Classical Age was over; the Hellenistic Age was beginning .Before turning to the latter we shall pause to consider the civilization of the Classical Age, generally accepted as one of the great triumphs of the human mind and spirit.

III. Civilization of the Classical Age

The "Golden Age of Pericles," "the Greek Miracle," "the Glory That Was Greece"—these are some of the hyperboles commonly used in referring to the civilization of fifth-century Greece.

We shall see that this civilization had its shortcomings, yet this extravagant praise is understandable and largely deserved. Why is this so? What was the basis of the Greek "genius"? It may be safely assumed that it was not literally a matter of genius—that the Indo-Europeans who migrated to the south Balkans did not happen to be genetically superior to those who migrated to the Middle East or India or Western Europe. Rather the answer must be sought by comparing the historical development of the Greeks with that of the other Indo-Europeans who settled in other regions of Eurasia.

Such comparison suggests two explanations for the extraordinary achievements of the Greeks. In the first place they were located close enough to the earliest centers of civilization in Egypt and Mesopotamia to profit from their pioneering accomplishments, and yet not so close that they could not retain their individuality. Indeed, the main significance of the outcome of the Persian Wars was precisely that it insured the Greeks that they would be able, so to speak, to have their cake and eat it too.

The second factor behind the Greek achievement was the emergence and persistence of the polis which provided the essential institutional framework for the cultural blossoming. The polis, it should be noted, was not a uniquely Greek institution. In India, for example, the Aryan immigrants in the earlier stage of their development also had what amounted to city-states in certain regions. Megasthenes, the Greek Seleucid ambassador to Pataliputra about 302 B.C., recognized "free cities" in the Maurya Empire to which he was accredited. But these were eventually absorbed by the territorial monarchies that came to dominate the Indian peninsula. The Greeks alone were able to preserve their city-states for several centuries.

One reason was the mountainous terrain, which did not afford a geopolitical base for an enveloping regional empire. (See section I of this chapter.) Another was the direct access to the sea enjoyed by most of the Greek city-states, which gave them economic sustenance and strength as well as intellectual stimulation. It is true that the Greeks paid a heavy price for their polis fragmentation in the form of continual wars that eventually led to unification imposed from the outside by Macedon and then by Rome. But in return they enjoyed their centuries of freedom within their respective states, and this appears to have been at least a prerequisite for the great creative outburst of the fifth century.

The classical Greek civilization was not pristinely original. Like all civilizations, it borrowed heavily from what had gone before, in this case the Middle Eastern civilizations. But what the Greeks borrowed, whether art forms from Egypt or mathematics and astronomy from Mesopotamia, they stamped with the distinctive quality of their minds. And this was, in the final analysis, an openmindedness, an intellectual curiosity, an eagerness to learn, a commonsense approach. When the Greeks traveled abroad, which they did more than others as traders, soldiers, colonists, and tourists, they did so with a critical eye and skeptical mind. They questioned everything and tested all issues at the bar of reason. In Plato's *Apology*, Socrates maintains that the individual must refuse, at all costs, to be coerced by human authority or any tribunal, to do anything, or think anything, which his own mind condemns as wrong—". . . the life which is unexamined is not worth living. . . ." Socrates also pointed out the public value of free discussion, upon which he based his defence in the trial for his life.

And now, Athenians, I am not going to argue for my own sake, as you may think, but for yours. . . . For if you kill me you will not easily find another like me, who, if I may use such a ludicrous figure of speech, am a

sort of gadfly . . . . and all day long and in all places am always fasten-
ing upon you, arousing and persuading and reproaching you. . . . I
would have you know that, if you kill such a one as I am, you will injure
yourselves more than you will injure me.[4]

This free thought was uniquely Greek, at least in such pervasiveness and
intensity. Unique also was the secular view of life, the conviction that the chief
business of existence was the complete expression of human personality here
and now. This combination of rationalism and secularism enabled the Greeks
to think freely and creatively about human problems and social issues and to
express their thoughts and emotions in their great literary, philosophical, and
artistic creations, which are relevant and compelling to the present day.

These unique qualities of the Greeks are reflected clearly in their religious
thought and practices. They viewed their gods as being similar in nature to
themselves, differing only in superior power, longevity, and beauty. By believing in such divinities the Greeks felt securely at home in a world governed
by familiar and comprehensible powers. The relationship was essentially one
of give and take; in return for prayers and sacrifices the gods were expected to
demonstrate their good will. The religious tie consisted of "common shrines and
sacrifices" as Herodotus stated, rather than of an organized church or a common faith. The Greek religion never formulated a common body of doctrines or
a sacred book, though Homer's *Iliad* and Hesiod's *Theogony* summed up prevailing religious concepts. The quality of this religion becomes evident when
contrasted with that of the Mesopotamians. According to Mesopotamian explanations of the origins of things, the human race had been specifically created
to build temples for the gods and to feed them with offerings. Such duties, in
fact, constituted the *raison d être* of mankind. How different was the conception of the sixth-century Greek philosopher Xenophanes:

> Mortals think that the gods are begotten, and wear clothes like their
> own, and have a voice and a form. If oxen or horses or lions had hands
> and could draw with them and make works of art as men do, horses would
> draw the shapes of gods like horses, oxen like oxen; each kind would rep-
> resent their bodies just like their own forms. The Ethiopians say their gods
> are black and flat-nosed; the Thracians, that theirs are blue-eyed and red-
> haired.[5]

Religion in Classical Greece was an integral element in polis life and accordingly penetrated every aspect of that life. It offered an interpretation of
the natural world, a consecration of daily work and of social institutions, and
also was one of the chief sources of inspiration for poets and artists. Every
Greek temple was a focus of local and national culture. Many specialized, more
or less accidentally, in the development of particular arts. Round the worship
of the legendary Aesculapius on the island of Cos grew up a brotherhood of
miracle-workers who became the first scientific physicians. Outstanding was the
renowned Hippocrates, whose medical treatises were resolutely clinical in tone.
He diagnosed each case on the basis of objective observation, eschewing magical
causes or cures for disease. Regarding the "sacred" disease, epilepsy, he wrote,

"It seems to me that the disease called sacred is no more divine than any other. It has a natural cause, just as other diseases have. Men think it divine because they do not understand it. . . . In Nature all things are alike in this, that they can all be traced to preceding causes." [6]

Likewise round the worship of Dionysus, the wine god, grew up a company of actors who passed from dramatizing the ritual cult of the god to creating profound tragedy and uproarious comedy. This literature is inconceivable apart from its setting in fifth-century Athens. The plays were produced before the assembled citizens at regularly held religious festivals organized and financed by the state. This close relation between the author and his audience was responsible for the balance and normality of Athenian drama. Aeschylus, in his *Persians,* presented a dramatized version of the victory at Salamis before the very citizens who had won that victory. Sophocles in his tragedies referred frequently to the gods, yet he was not interested primarily in religious problems. Rather he was chiefly concerned with human beings, noble and admirable, confronted with forces beyond their control, committing awful deeds, and suffering terrible retribution. The heroism and suffering of Oedipus in the face of overwhelming adversity are the essence of tragedy and express something of the meaning of human life and of the problems common to all men.

If Sophocles was not deeply interested in conventional religion, Euripides was positively skeptical. He wrote unsparingly of the weakness of the gods and satirized those who deemed them superior to men. Euripides was generally critical and a dedicated fighter for unpopular causes. He championed the rights of the slave and the foreigner, urged the emancipation of women, and attacked the glorification of war. The same is even more true of Aristophanes, whose comedies were filled with social satire. Himself a conservative who yearned for the good old days, he ridiculed democratic leaders and policies. In the *Lysistrata* he presented a group of women who, appalled by the endless bloodshed, refused to sleep with their husbands until they forsook war. In the *Knights,* Aristophanes mocks democratic institutions through a general who is trying to persuade a sausage-seller to unseat Cleon, the democratic leader.[7]

SAUSAGE-SELLER. Tell me this, how can I, a sausage-seller, be a big man like that?

GENERAL. The easiest thing in the world. You've got all the qualifications: low birth, marketplace training, insolence.

SAUSAGE-SELLER. I don't think I deserve it.

GENERAL. Not deserve it? It looks to me as if you've got too good a conscience. Was your father a gentleman?

SAUSAGE-SELLER. By the gods, no! My folks were scoundrels.

GENERAL. Lucky man! What a good start you've got for public life!

SAUSAGE-SELLER. But I can hardly read.

GENERAL. The only trouble is that you know anything. To be a leader of the people isn't for learned men, or honest men, but for the ignorant and vile. Don't miss this golden opportunity.

Greek art also was the distinctive product of a polis civilization. Art and architecture found their highest expression in the temples, the civic and religious core of polis culture. These temples were the revered dwelling places of the protecting gods and goddesses, such as Athena for whom the Parthenon was built as a shrine in Athens. Sculpture, the handmaiden of architecture, served to decorate the houses of the gods. Master sculptors, such as Phidias and Praxiteles, worked on temple walls and pediments and also carved statues for the interiors. In contrast to the realism of later Roman sculpture, their works represented a synthesis or generalized representation rather than a copy of individual models. Nor should Greek coins be overlooked in this connection, for they afford some of the finest examples of the sculpture of the times. In conclusion, all of Greek art embodied the basic Greek ideals of balance, harmony, and moderation. This is evident in a comparison of the Parthenon with an Egyptian pyramid or a Mesopotamian ziggurat, or of a Greek statue with the relatively crude and stilted sculptures of all Middle Eastern peoples to that time.

The same contrast is manifest in philosophical speculation. The sixth-century rationalist philosophers of Ionia on the Asia Minor coast were the first to challenge the traditional supernatural explanations of the nature of the world. They posed the basic question "What is the stuff of which the world is made?" Thales speculated that everything originally was water, because this substance is found in liquid, solid, and vapor form. Heraclitus thought fire was the prime element because it was so active and could transform everything. Anaximenes believed it was air, arguing that it became fire when rarefied, and wind, cloud, water, earth, and stone when condensed. In the light of modern science these efforts may appear naive, but what is important is that the question was asked and the answer was sought by the free use of reason and without recourse to divine intervention. In the same manner, the Greeks at this time took the astronomical observations of the Egyptians and Mesopotamians and purged them of their astrological associations, and they also took their mathematical lore, which had remained at the empirical stage, and developed it into a coherent logical structure.

In response to the growing complexity of Greek society, philosophers about the mid-fifth century B.C. turned their attention from the physical universe to human beings and their problems. This was particularly true of the Sophists, of whom Protagoras was the outstanding spokesman. "Man is the measure of all things," he maintained, by which he meant that there are no absolute truths since everything is relative to the needs of man himself. This emphasis on man led the Sophists to condemn slavery and war, and to espouse most popular causes. On the other hand many Greeks, especially those of conservative persuasion, feared that the relativism of the Sophists endangered social order and morality. Typical was Socrates, who was profoundly disturbed by the political corruption of his day and by the absence of any certain guide to correct living. Out of his never ending conversations with his friends evolved the science of dialectics, which tests provisional definitions through questions and answers until universally recognized truths are reached. In this way, Socrates maintained, concepts of absolute truth or absolute good or absolute beauty could be discovered. And these would provide enduring guides for personal conduct, in contrast to sophist relativism, which had been used to rationalize private license and public corruption.

Socrates' disciple Plato (427–374 B.C.) was an aristocrat who shared with his friends their pride in Athens and their distrust of the Athenian people. Distrust deepened into hatred when Athenian democracy condemned Socrates to death. Plato's goal, therefore, was a society that preserved aristocratic privileges and yet was acceptable to the poorer classes. Accordingly he divided the citizens of his ideal Republic into four grades: guardians, philosophers, soldiers, and the masses that did the work. This class differentiation was to be permanent, and was to be justified by a myth or "noble lie" about God creating men of four kinds: gold, silver, brass, and iron. Plato hoped at one point that the ruler of Syracuse would accept and apply his teachings, but when this did not materialize he returned to Athens and for the next forty years instructed small groups of disciples. Everything that exists on earth, he taught, is an inferior copy of a corresponding spiritual idea, so that the entire physical world is an imperfect copy of a perfect idea. Virtue, according to Plato, is knowledge, not of the unsteady material world but of the real world of ideas.

The other great thinker of this period was Aristotle (384–322 B.C.), who began as Plato's disciple but who, following his master's death, founded the Lyceum. Aristotle was a collector and rationalizer rather than a mystic, a logician and scientist rather than a philosopher. He took all knowledge for his province, so that he ranged more widely than anyone before or since. His outstanding contributions were in logic, physics, biology and the humanities; indeed he established these subjects as formal disciplines. As a great encyclopedist, he sought orderliness in every aspect of nature and of human life. Thus he balanced the classes of the social world with corresponding orders in the natural world, beginning with minerals at the bottom, then vegetables, animals, and finally man at the top. This gradation justified the division of human beings into born masters and born slaves:

> . . . from the hour of their birth some are marked out for subjection, others for rule; . . . the art of war is a natural art of acquisition, for it includes hunting, an art which we ought to practice against wild beasts and against men who, though intended by nature to be governed, will not submit; for war of such a kind is naturally just.[8]

No account of Classical Greece would be complete without reference to Herodotus and Thucydides who related the stirring events of their times and in so doing created a new literary genre—history. Herodotus had lived first among the Asia Minor Greeks who had fallen under Persian rule. He then lived in Athens where the Persians had suffered their epochal defeat. Herodotus ascribed this fateful outcome to the democratic constitution of the Athenians, so that his *History* is the first great tribute to democracy. The moral of his tale may be illustrated by the words he attributes to a Greek who speaks of his countrymen to the Persian king: "For though they be free men, they are not in all respects free; Law is the master whom they own, and this master they fear more than your subjects fear you. Whatever it commands they do; and its commandment is always the same; it forbids them to flee in battle, whatever the number of their foes, and requires them to stand firm, and either to conquer or die." [9]

Thucydides' history was very different, being of the Peloponnesian War in which Athens, after twenty-seven years of bitter struggle, was finally beaten to her knees. Whereas Herodotus eulogized victory and glory, Thucydides analyzed defeat and suffering. His sympathies were unquestionably with Athens, whose armies he had led as a general. But he sternly suppressed his emotions and set for himself the task of ascertaining objectively the causes of the disaster. Although he did not use the phrase, he nevertheless said in effect that he was seeking to create a science of society.

> Of the events of the war I have not ventured to speak from any chance information, nor according to any notion of my own; I have described nothing but what I either saw myself or learned from others of whom I made the most careful and particular enquiry. The task was a laborious one, because eye-witnesses of the same occurrences gave different accounts of them, as they remembered or were interested in the actions of one side or the other. And very likely the strictly historical character of my narrative may be disappointing to the ear. But if he who desires to have before his eyes a true picture of the events which have happened, and of the like events which may be expected to happen hereafter in the order of human things, shall pronounce what I have written to be useful, then I shall be satisfied. My history is an everlasting possession, not a prize composition which is heard and forgotten.[10]

Having presented the remarkable achievements of the Greeks in so many fields, it is customary to point out certain failings. Women were accorded inferior status; slaves were exploited; and these slaves, together with the *metics*, or resident aliens, though comprising a majority of the population, were denied Athenian citizenship. All this is true but largely irrelevant. Classical Greece should be judged by contemporary standards rather than by present-day practices, or even worse, by utopias.

As regards citizenship, the Athenians, like all other Greeks, regarded themselves as a kinship group, so that one became citizen only by descent and not by residence, however long. It is also noteworthy that the metics, as voluntary immigrants, were free to leave whenever they wished. Yet many lived permanently in Athens, and made generous gifts to their adoptive city, suggesting a certain degree of contentment and loyalty. Likewise, slavery, despite its many deleterious effects, which will be analyzed in the last section of this chapter, was not as widespread as commonly assumed. The great majority of citizens—two thirds to three quarters—had no slaves and worked for their living as farmers, artisans, shopkeepers, and seamen. It is not true, as often stated, that the average Athenian was able to spend his days watching plays, serving on public bodies, and discussing philosophy and politics, because he had slaves to support him.

Classical Greece, then, should be judged not by what it failed to do but by what it did. If this be the criterion, then the contributions and their historical significance stand out clearly and overwhelmingly. The spirit of free inquiry, the theory and practice of democracy, the major forms of art and literature and philosophical thought, and the emphasis on individual freedom and individual responsibility—all these comprise the splendid legacy of Greece to mankind.

IV. HELLENISTIC AGE, 336–31 B.C.

The Hellenistic Age derives its name from the new civilization that emerged with the diffusion of Classical Greek culture throughout the Middle East following Alexander's conquests. (See Chapter 7, section III.) On succeeding his father, Philip, in 336 B.C., Alexander first crushed a revolt in Thebes with a severity that persuaded the other Greek cities to acquiesce in his rule. Then in 334 B.C., he led his Macedonian soldiers eastward against the Persians. Crossing the Hellespont, he overran first Asia Minor, then Syria, Egypt, Mesopotamia, and Persia itself, capturing Darius' capital, Persepolis, in 330 B.C. Next year the conqueror pushed on to the Hindu Kush and Bactria, and from there marched on into India, penetrating as far as the Punjab. Only the refusal of his men to advance any further persuaded Alexander to return to Babylon where he died of malarial fever in 323 at the age of thirty-three.

Rival generals now fought for control of the great empire until by the beginning of the third century three succession states emerged. One of these was Macedon, which now reverted to being a modest, Hellenized, national kingdom that dominated, though did not directly rule, the Greek city-states to the south. Egypt, ruled by the Ptolemies, was the most viable of the succession states because of its natural riches and strong sea and desert defences. The largest state, comprising the Asian provinces of the empire, fell to the Seleucids. Precisely because of the extent of their holdings they fought a continual and losing battle against a host of surrounding enemies. They ceded first the Indus provinces to the Indian king Chandragupta (see Chapter 9, section III), then Asia Minor to Celtic invaders, and Persia and Mesopotamia to the Parthians. Finally in the first century B.C., Rome conquered the remaining provinces along the Mediterranean coast, along with Macedon and Egypt, thereby ending the Hellenistic Age and beginning the Roman.

Although Alexander's empire proved ephemeral, the succession states did survive more or less intact for three centuries, during which time the Middle East became Hellenized. Thousands of Greek merchants, administrators, teachers, professional men, and mercenary soldiers emigrated from their city-states to Egypt and the Asian provinces, attracted by the unprecedented opportunities afforded by those rich lands. Thus were laid the foundations for the new Hellenistic civilization, a hybrid creation that differed from the classical parent stock in virtually every respect.

The political framework was altered basically because the polis was undermined and rendered sterile. The Greek city-states, trying to survive, experimented with federal union. The Achaean League included the states of the Peloponnesus excepting Sparta, and the Aetolian Federation included nearly all of central Greece excepting Athens. Although often described as federal organizations, these leagues actually were confederacies that delegated little power to central authority. They proved too weak and too late, so that the city-states functioned within the orbit of one or another of the neighboring empires until the coming of the Roman legions.

As for the cities in the succession states, they never resembled the classical polis. They were rent internally by the distinctions between the Greek immigrants and the native people. Furthermore they were always completely subordinate to one or another imperial structure. If the citizens suffered from tyrannical, or, even worse, from weak kings, they could do very little about it. The real decisions were made in the courts or on battlefields rather than in meetings of popular assemblies. Thus the citizens understandably concentrated on accumulating wealth and enjoying life, leaving the poor and the slaves to shift for themselves as they could. The civic spirit and social cohesion of the old polis gave way to self-centeredness and class strife.

Economic conditions and institutions also changed fundamentally. The Greek homeland suffered economic eclipse as well as political. It had depended on the export of wine, oil, and manufactured goods in return for foodstuffs and raw materials from the overseas colonies. But by the fourth century these colonies had taken root and developed their own industries and vineyards and olive orchards. The home cities, as noted above, had experienced earlier a boom similar to that of Europe in the nineteenth century. So now they were dwarfed by their former colonies just as Europe after the nineteenth century was dwarfed by the United States and the Soviet Union, and essentially for the same reason.

Although the Greek lands suffered economic decay, many Greeks waxed rich by emigrating to the Middle East, which was now open to them. They had much to contribute with their enterprising spirit and their advanced commercial and banking methods. They discovered and circulated the huge gold and silver hoard of the Persian dynasty. Also they introduced, or put to wider use, technological inventions such as the suction and piston pumps, the water mill, the worm screw, and a hydraulic machine. The Greeks also directed large-scale public works and state enterprises, including irrigation systems, mines, quarries, salt pans, "royal lands," and workshops for luxury fabrics and ceramics. The net result was an increase in regional economic integration with a corresponding increase in regional commerce and productivity. The proceeds, however, were grossly maldistributed. Speculators took advantage of rising profits to reap great fortunes, while slaves increased in number and free workmen declined in status. It was a period, in short, of greater productivity but also greater economic inequality and social strife. "Those in possession," wrote Isocrates, "would sooner have flung their property into the sea than have assisted the poor, and the poorest derived less satisfaction from seizing the wealth of the rich than from the act of depriving them of it." [11]

The average person during this Hellenistic Age was buffeted not only economically but also psychologically. He felt lost in the large new cities with their teeming multitudes uprooted from their traditional milieu. In the old polis, life had been relatively simple. Law, morality, religion, and duties were all clearly defined and generally accepted. Now all this was gone and the citizen found himself in a formless world, particularly since the Hellenistic cities frequently were torn by racial and cultural as well as class divisions. The rulers tried to cultivate a mystique of personal loyalty, adopting titles such as Savior and Benefactor. But such expedients offered no lasting solution. Each person remained confronted with the question of how to conduct himself in face of the impersonal and overwhelming forces of his time.

The response of intellectuals tended to be withdrawal from worldly affairs and turning from reason to mysticism. This was reflected in the vogue for

Spear bearers displayed on a wall in Darius' capital, Persepolis. (Arborio Mella)

The ruins of Persepolis. (Arborio Mella)

romantic adventure and utopian literature. When depicting an ideal society, authors described not a city-state on the rocky soil of Hellas but a rainbow-tinted fairyland at the world's end. Especially popular in contemporary fiction were utopian island communities located in the Indian Ocean, blessed with natural riches that satisfied all material needs, and inhabited by people who lived "simply and temperately . . . without jealousy and strife." This escapist tendency was reflected also in the philosophies of the day, such as Cynicism, Skepticism, Epicureanism, and Stoicism. Though very different in many respects, they were generally concerned with the pursuit of personal happiness rather than of social welfare. Their underlying motive was to reconcile politically impotent man to the uncertainties of life in an economically insecure and war-ridden world.

If philosophy was the religion of the cultivated upper classes, very different was the religion of the lower classes. They turned to cults of oriental origin—Mithraism, Gnosticism, the Egyptian mother-goddess Isis, and the astral religion of the Chaldeans. All these had in common the promise of salvation in after-life. All satisfied the emotional needs of the harried masses with comforting assurances of a paradise to come. Thus the secularism and rationalism of Classical Greece now gave way to mysticism and otherworldliness.

In view of these trends in philosophy and religion, it is surprising to note that more progress was achieved in science in the Hellenistic Age than in any other period prior to the seventeenth century. This was due in part to the economic opportunities afforded by Alexander's conquests. The greatly expanded markets provided incentive to improve technology in order to increase output. Also the continual wars amongst the succession states, and between them and outside powers, created a demand for more complex war engines. Equally stimulating was the direct contact between Greek science and that of the Middle East—not only of Mesopotamia and Egypt, but also, to a certain extent, of India. Finally, the Macedonian rulers of the Hellenistic states, brought up in the aura of the prestige of Greek learning, generously supported scientific research. This was particularly true in Egypt, where the Alexandria Museum and Library constituted in effect the first state-supported research institute in history. It included astronomical observatories, laboratories and dissecting rooms, botanical and zoological gardens, and a library of from 500,000 to 700,000 volumes. From all over the Mediterranean world, in an early version of the "brain drain," came philosophers, mathematicians, physicians, botanists, zoologists, astronomers, philologists, geographers, artists, and poets—all attracted by the congenial and stimulating atmosphere, by the superb facilities, and by the free meals and lodgings and enviable salaries.

In mathematics the outstanding name was Euclid, whose *Elements of Geometry* systematized a large part of mathematical knowledge into one single edifice of deductions from axioms. In astronomy, Hipparchus invented most of the instruments used until modern times and compiled the first star catalogue. Ptolemy's compilation of Hellenistic astronomical knowledge is the best known work and remained the standard text until the Renaissance. Most original was Aristarchus, who was the first to grasp the enormous size of the universe and to place the sun rather than the earth in the center. His views received little support, being considered impious as well as contrary to everyday experience.

Thus Ptolemy's geocentric system remained generally accepted throughout medieval times. The progress in astronomy facilitated advances in scientific geography. Eratosthenes, the director of the Alexandria Museum, calculated the earth's circumference at 24,700 miles. This was only 250 miles off, and was not improved until the eighteenth century. He also drew a map of the inhabited world with a grid of latitudes, and concluded from the ebb and flow of tides in the Atlantic and Indian Oceans that the seas were one and that Europe, Asia, and Africa constituted a huge island.

Perhaps the outstanding contributions of Hellenistic science were in medicine and mechanics. The Museum encouraged anatomical research, so that physicians now comprehended for the first time the role of the heart in blood circulation, the significance of the pulse, the functions of sensory and motor nerves, and the convolutions of the brain. Much of this knowledge was passed on by the great encyclopedist of medicine, Galen, whose writings were so impressive that doctors dared not question him and strike out in new directions until modern times. In mechanics the outstanding figure was Archimedes, the founder of hydrostatics, the laws of floating bodies, which were used thereafter for testing the purity of metals. He also devised ingenious war machines and formulated the principles of the screw, the pulley, and the lever. It was in connection with the latter that he is quoted as having said: "Give me place to stand, and I will move the world."

In conclusion, the historical significance of the Hellenistic Age is that it brought the East and West together, breaking the separate molds that had formed through history. Men now for the first time thought of the entire civilized world as a unit—an ecumene. At first the Greeks and Macedonians went to the East as conquerors and rulers, and imposed a pattern of Hellenization. But in the process they themselves were changed, so that the resulting Hellenistic civilization was an amalgam rather than a transplantation. And in the long run the religions of the East made their way West and contributed substantially to the transformation of the Roman Empire and medieval Europe.

V. EARLY REPUBLIC, TO 264 B.C.

In 217 B.C. a peace conference was held in Greece to try to end the incessant wars amongst the city-states. A delegate of the Aetolian League, pointing to the titanic struggle between Rome and Carthage in the western Mediterranean, warned that whoever won would be a menace to Greece. "For it is evident even to those of us who give but scanty attention to affairs of state, that whether the Carthaginians beat the Romans or the Romans the Carthaginians in this war, it is not in the least likely that the victors will be content with the sovereignty of Italy and Sicily, but they are sure to come here." [12] The warning proved prophetic. Peace was patched up, but within five years there was war again. During the following century, Rome, having destroyed Carthage, turned eastward and imposed her rule upon both Macedon and the Greek cities, and ultimately upon the entire Hellenistic East.

What were the origins of this Italian city that was to affect so profoundly the course of world history? Actually many similarities are noticeable between the early histories of the Greeks and the Romans. Both were of the same ethnic stock, for just as the Indo-European Achaeans and Dorians filtered down the Balkan peninsula to Greece, so the Indo-European Latins filtered down the Italian peninsula to the south bank of the Tiber River. Among the Latin communities formed at the time was Rome, located at the lowest point at which the Tiber could be conveniently bridged and the highest to which small ships could ascend. This strategic position, similar to that of London on the Thames, made Rome from the outset more mercantile and more open to foreign influences than other Latin settlements.

The chief foreign influences came from two civilized peoples who had come from overseas to settle in Italy—the Etruscans and the Greeks. (See Chapter 7, section II.) The Etruscans, who arrived about 800 B.C., probably from Asia Minor, settled to the north of the Tiber and then conquered the Latins to the south. Before their rule was overthrown they bequeathed to the Romans some of their gods and goddesses, a knowledge of the arch and the vault, and the typically eastern practice of divination by examining animal entrails. The Greeks, who appeared shortly after the Etruscans, established colonies in southern Italy and Sicily, including Tarentum, Syracuse, and Naples. Among their contributions to the Latins were the alphabet, some art and mythology, and certain religious concepts and practices, including the identification of Roman gods with Greek counterparts—Zeus, Hermes, and Artemis became Jupiter, Mercury, and Diana.

About 500 B.C. Rome expelled its last Etruscan king and began its career as an independent city-state. Within a few years it had conquered the surrounding peoples and controlled the entire Latin plain from the Apennine Mountains to the sea coast. Roman institutions during this formative period were similar to those of the early Greek cities. The king originally held the *imperium,* or sovereign power, restrained only by an advisory council of aristocrats and a popular assembly that could only approve or disapprove legislation. Then, as in Greece, the monarchy was abolished and the patricians became the dominant element in society. The *imperium* formerly held by the king was now delegated to two consuls who were elected for one year periods and who were always patricians. The Senate, which was the principal legislative body, also was an aristocratic body and remained so even after some commoners, or plebeians, were admitted.

The divergence between the development of Rome and of the Greek city-states occurred when Rome accomplished what had proven beyond the capacity of the Greek cities—the conquest and unification of the entire peninsula. Why was it that Rome could master the Italian peninsula whereas no Greek city was able to unify the Greek lands, let alone the whole of the Balkan peninsula? One reason was the marked difference in terrain. The Balkans are a jumble of mountains; indeed the name "Balkan" is derived from the Turkish word for mountain. The crisscrossing of ranges is very prevalent in Greece, whereas in Italy by contrast there are only the Apennines which are not as difficult to cross and which run only north and south without transverse ranges. Consequently the Italian peninsula is not so compartmentalized, and is correspondingly easier to unite and keep united. There was no Balkan counterpart, for example, to the system of Roman roads that knitted Italy into one unit, especially the Appian Way from Rome to Brindisium on the heel of the Italian boot.

Detail of an Etruscan relief dating from the sixth century B.C. *This wood relief, sheathed in bronze, shows two warriors in combat. (The Metropolitan Museum of Art, Rogers Fund, 1903)*

In fact this road is still extant and was used by the British and American troops that landed in southern Italy in 1943.

Another reason for the success of the Romans was their enlightened treatment of the other Italian peoples. Athens had levied tribute and never extended its citizenship. Rome granted full citizenship to about a fourth of the population of the peninsula, and Latin citizenship to the remainder, which carried substantial but not complete privileges. Autonomy was enjoyed by all, the only restraint being loss of control over foreign relations and compulsory manpower levy for military service. This policy saved Rome, for her Italian allies remained loyal during the critical years when Hannibal was rampaging irresistibly up and down the length of the peninsula.

Finally, the Romans prevailed because of the superior military force and strategy that they developed. In fighting their neighbors they learned that the traditional phalanx of 8000 men was too large and unwieldy, especially in mountainous terrain. So they organized their soldiers into "maniples," or "handfuls," of 120 soldiers. Thirty of these, or 3600 men, constituted a legion, which also had cavalry to protect its flanks. In addition to the traditional helmet, shield, lance, and sword, the Romans equipped the legion with an effective assault weapon—the iron-tipped javelin. This was flung at the enemy from a distance, after which the legionnaires attacked on the run, maneuvering skillfully to exploit any break in the opposing ranks.

By 295 B.C. the Romans had won central Italy and pushed south against Tarentum, the prosperous Greek city in the "instep" of the peninsula. The Tarentines called in the help of the Greek king Pyrrhus of Epirus, ranked by Hannibal as second only to Alexander in generalship. Pyrrhus won two "Pyrrhic victories," but he could not afford his heavy losses, whereas the Romans, though losing even more, could draw from a pool of 750,000 Italian fighting men. So Pyrrhus withdrew in 272 B.C. with the insightful observation "What a battleground I am leaving for Rome and Carthage!" Only eight years later, in 264 B.C., Rome and Carthage were at war in Sicily.

Before considering the Punic Wars—so named after the Latin word *punicus* for Phoenician—it is necessary to note a certain democratization of Roman institutions. Since the plebeians had provided the manpower for the victorious legions, they were in a position to demand political concessions. When their demands were denied, they resorted to the novel but effective device of a walkout (*secessio*) and literally withdrew en masse from the city until their demands were met. One of the first gains won in this fashion by the plebeians was the right to choose officials known as Tribunes to defend their interests. The Tribunes were elected by the new Plebeian Assembly, which also cared for other matters of concern to the masses. Other concessions included the writing down of the laws so that they would be known to all and limitation of the amount of land that could be owned by any one individual.

Thus by 265 B.C. Rome, the mistress of Italy, was undergoing a process of democratization. Conceivably this could have culminated in the first democratic national state in the history of the world. But if this were in fact a possibility, it was effectively eliminated by the series of overseas wars in which Rome was now involved. The wars transformed Rome into a great empire, but they also transformed as profoundly her domestic institutions, and one of the many casualties was the trend towards democratization.

VI. LATE REPUBLIC, 265-27 B.C.

The transformation of Rome from an Italian republic to a great empire was sudden and spectacular and was reminiscent of the conquests of Alexander. Indeed there were certain common basic factors that help to explain the explosive expansion of both Macedon and Rome. Each had evolved superior military instruments and techniques, and each enjoyed the vital advantage of social vigor and cohesion in contrast to the social decrepitude and fragmentation of the Persian Empire and the Hellenistic succession states.

Rome's great rival, Carthage, had started as a Phoenician colony but had become fully independent when Alexander destroyed Tyre in 332 B.C. Thanks to her near monopoly of the transit trade in the western Mediterranean, Carthage had waxed rich and powerful. With her wide-ranging fleets and mercenary troops she dominated northwest Africa, southern Spain, Sardinia, Corsica, and western Sicily. At first there was no direct conflict between Rome and Carthage for the simple reason that the one was a land power and the other a sea power. But they did clash when the Romans conquered southern Italy, for they feared Carthage's growing influence on the island that was so close to their newly-won possessions.

The First Punic War (264-241 B.C.) forced the Romans for the first time to turn to the sea. They built a fleet and by turning naval battles into boarding operations they doggedly wore down the Carthaginians and conquered Sicily. The struggle to the death between the two great powers was now inevitable. Rome spent the next twenty years subduing the Celtic tribes in the Po Valley, thereby increasing her reserve of peasant soldiers. Carthage, to compensate for the loss of Sicily, consolidated her hold on Spain. It was from this base that the great Carthaginian strategist, Hannibal, carried out his daring invasion of Italy in 218 across the Alps, thus beginning the Second Punic War (218-201). He defeated the Romans in battle after battle, particularly in his great masterpiece of Cannae (216). But the loyalty of Rome's allies robbed him of victory. When a Roman army landed near Carthage, Hannibal was recalled, undefeated, from Italy, to be defeated on his home ground. Once again Rome had exhausted her opponent, and in 201 Carthage was forced to accept a peace leaving her only her small home territory, her walls, and ten ships—enough to chase off the pirates. Despite this catastrophic defeat, the Carthaginians made a remarkable economic recovery. But this served only to alarm Rome to the point of ruthlessly provoking the Third Punic War (149-146). Carthage itself was captured, the city completely destroyed, and the populace enslaved.

With these Punic Wars, Rome was caught in a chain reaction of conquest leading to further conquest. One reason was her overwhelming strength; with Carthage out of the way she was now the number one power in the Mediterranean. Also conquest was manifestly profitable, as booty, slaves, and tribute poured in from each new province. Finally, there were the inevitable commitments and challenges associated with far-flung imperial frontiers. For example, Philip V of Macedon had aided Hannibal during the Second Punic War, so Rome, after having disposed of Carthage, turned on Macedon. The ensuing war proved to be the first of a series in which the Romans skillfully played off against each other the several Middle Eastern powers—Macedon, Seleucid Syria, Ptolemaic Egypt, and the rival Aetolian and Achaean leagues of Greek city-states.

Thus the Romans overran and annexed in quick succession Macedon, Greece, the Asia Minor states of Pergamum, Bithynia and Cilicia, then Seleucid Syria, and finally Egypt in 31 B.C. In this manner the Romans took over the Hellenistic succession states of the East, though in Asia they acquired only the provinces along the Mediterranean coast. All the interior had fallen to Parthia, which henceforth was to be Rome's chief rival in the East. Meanwhile Julius Caesar had gained fame by conquering (58–49 B.C.) all of Gaul between the English Channel and the Mediterranean. Finally the permanent occupation of Britain was begun in the first century of our era and was consolidated with the construction of a line of fortifications between the firths of Clyde and Forth. This marked the limits of Roman rule in northern Europe.

Rome did not treat her newly acquired provinces as generously as she had her earlier Italian allies. The Senate appointed governors who were given a free hand so long as they sent back home an adequate flow of tribute, taxes, grain, and slaves. The result was unconscionable exploitation and extortion. The maladministration of Governor Gaius Verres in Sicily (73–71 B.C.), described in the following indictment by Cicero, was neither exceptional nor atypical:

> Countless sums of money, under a new and unprincipled regulation were wrung from the purses of the farmers; our most loyal allies were treated as if they were national enemies; Roman citizens were tortured and executed like slaves; the guiltiest criminals bought their legal acquittal, while the most honourable and honest men would be . . . condemned and banished unheard; strongly fortified harbours, mighty and well defended cities were left open to the assaults of pirates and buccaneers. Sicilian soldiers and sailors, our allies and our friends, were starved to death; fine fleets, splendidly equipped, were to the great disgrace of our nation destroyed and lost to us. Famous and ancient works of art, some of them the gifts of wealthy kings . . . —this same governor stripped and despoiled every one of them. Nor was it only the civic statues and works of art he treated thus; he also pillaged the holiest and most venerated sanctuaries; in fact, he has not left the people of Sicily a single god whose workmanship he thought at all above the average of antiquity or artistic merit.[13]

The Roman homeland was affected almost as adversely by these policies as the subject territories. Many of the small farmers in Italy had been ruined by the ravages of Hannibal's campaigns and by the long years of overseas service during the following wars. Then came the influx of cheap grain and of droves of slaves from the conquered provinces. The peasants were forced to sell out to the new class of ultrarich who were eager to accumulate large estates because agriculture still was considered the only respectable calling for gentlemen. Thus the second century B.C. saw the growth in Italy of large plantations (*latifundia*) worked by slaves and owned by absentee landlords. The dispossessed peasantry drifted to the towns where they lived in squalid tenements and competed once again with slaves for such work as was available. The authorities took care to provide them with "bread and circuses" (*panis et circenses*) in order to keep them quiet. Despite the insecurity and rootlessness, city life at least was exciting and alluring. Poets were loud in their praise of rustic virtues, but the peasants themselves thought otherwise and continued to flock to Rome—the "common cesspool" as it was termed by the contemporary historian Sallust.

The political fruits of empire were as bitter as the economic. The earlier trend towards democratization was reversed because the Senate had directed the victorious overseas campaigns and gained greatly in prestige and power. Also the new urban mobs offered no basis for popular government since they were always ready to sell their votes or to support any demagogue who promised relief from their troubles. Equally disruptive was the changing character of the armed forces. Imperial obligations required a large standing army, so that it no longer sufficed to call up property owners for short-term militia service. Rather the ranks were opened to volunteers, and so dispossessed peasants enlisted for long periods. Rome's legions accordingly changed from a citizen army to a professional one. The soldiers' first loyalty now was not to the state but to their commanders to whom they looked for a share of the booty and of any land that might be available for distribution. The generals increasingly came to regard the legions entrusted to them as their client armies and used them to advance their personal fortunes.

The cultural repercussions of imperial expansion also were disruptive. The traditional Roman virtues had been those of poor, hard-working peasants. But when wealth began to pour into the capital, the ancient homilies concerning thrift, abstinence, and industry were soon forgotten. The last days of the Republic were marked by a wild scramble for money, the sort of ostentatious waste to be expected from *parvenues,* and a callous indifference to all human values. "Rome," grumbled a contemporary, "has become a city where paramours fetch a better price than plowlands, and pots of pickled fish than plowmen."

In light of the above, it is understandable that the period from the end of the Punic Wars in 146 B.C. to the end of the Republic in 27 B.C. was one of crisis—of class war, slave revolts, and increasing military intervention in politics. A gallant reform effort was made at the outset by Tiberius Gracchus and his brother Gaius. They sought to use their elective positions as Tribunes to push through a moderate program of land distribution. But the oligarchs would have none of it and resorted to violence to gain their ends. Tiberius was murdered in 133 B.C. along with three hundred of his followers. Twelve years later Gaius was driven to suicide, and the senatorial class resumed its sway.

The fate of the Gracchi brothers made it clear that no leader could prevail without superior forces at his disposal. So it was the generals who now took the stage, spurred on by popular acclaim won by their roles in the perennial frontier wars. One of these generals was Marius, victor over the Numidian tribes of North Africa, who pitted himself against Sulla, hero of the campaign against King Mithridates in Asia Minor. For several years there was virtual civil war between their two factions until Sulla made himself the sole master of Rome. He strove, until his retirement in 80 B.C., to restore the Senate to its ancient role as arbiter of Roman politics. In fact the Senate did grow so strong and dictatorial that Rome was a republic only in name. Yet the primacy of the Senate did not restore stability. In fact, the great Spartacus slave revolt broke out in 73 B.C. and for a while threatened the very existence of the state. In the end the resources of empire prevailed, and Spartacus fell fighting, and the roads to Rome were lined with his crucified followers.

The survival of Rome and her empire depended on the establishment of the rule of one man who could draw on the strengths of all elements of society. This is apparent in retrospect, but the great contribution of Julius Caesar was that he perceived it clearly at the time and acted accordingly. As conqueror of Gaul he had gained fame and also built up a powerful and devoted army. In 49 B.C. he crossed the river Rubicon, which separated his province from Italy, and in a series of brilliant campaigns defeated the forces of the Senate under his rival Pompey. Caesar was now the undisputed master of the empire. Precisely what he would have done with his mastery cannot be known, for he was murdered by representatives of the old oligarchy in 44 B.C.

His death was followed by another thirteen years of political jockeying and armed strife between his adopted son and heir Octavian and the political adventurer Mark Antony. With his naval victory over Antony and Cleopatra at Actium (31 B.C.), Octavian was supreme. He was only thirty-three years old at the time, the age at which the great Alexander had died. But Octavian had forty-four years of life ahead of him, during which he laid the foundations for two golden centuries of imperial peace and stability.

VII. EARLY EMPIRE, 27 B.C.–A.D. 284

In 27 B.C. the Senate conferred upon Octavian the titles of Augustus and Imperator, symbolizing the transformation of Rome from republic to empire. Octavian professed to prefer the republican title of "First Citizen" (*Princeps*), but in practice he grasped full powers, in emperor-like fashion, at the expense of both the Senate and the Plebeians. He created a centralized system of courts under his own supervision and assumed direct control over provincial governors, punishing them severely for graft and extortion. He standardized taxes and made their collection a state function rather than a private business operated by rapacious tax farmers. He kept close check on the army, seeing to it that the soldiers were well provided for and that they swore allegiance directly to him. He also created a permanent navy that suppressed piracy and safeguarded the transportation of both commodities and troops to all parts of the empire.

By these measures Augustus, as he came to be known, created an efficient administrative system that ensured the *Pax Romana* that was to prevail for two centuries. It is true that the four emperors following Augustus—Tiberius (14–37), Caligula (37–41), Claudius (41–54), and Nero (54–68)—were unworthy of their high office. But the empire weathered their misrule and then blossomed under a succession of "five good Emperors"—Nerva (96–98), Trajan (98–117), Hadrian (117–138), Antoninus Pius (138–161), and Marcus Aurelius (161–180). It was during these reigns that the Roman Empire reached its apogee, both in geographic extent and in the quality of its civilization.

In the extreme north, the imperial frontier was defined by the fortifications built from the Forth to the Clyde. In the northeast, the Rhine and the Danube provided a natural frontier, which further east curved north of the Danube to encompass Dacia (modern Rumania). Both Asia Minor and Egypt were Roman possessions, but between the two the frontier ran close to the Mediterranean coast, leaving the interior to the Parthians and, after A.D. 224, to the Sassanians. Likewise in North Africa the Romans controlled the coastal territories between Egypt and the Atlantic, with the Sahara as their southern limit.

This huge area, with its strong natural frontiers, constituted a prosperous and virtually self-sufficient economic unit. Various factors contributed to the flourishing nature of the imperial economy during these centuries, including the honest and efficient administration, the monetary stability, the large-scale public works, and the extensive trade, both within and without the empire. The internal free trade ensured unhindered distribution of wheat, papyrus, and glassware from Egypt; linens, woolens, and fruits from Syria; wool, timber, and rugs from Asia Minor; wine, oil, and manufactured goods from Italy; grains, meats, and wool from Gaul; and a variety of minerals from Spain and Britain. The Romans also imported certain goods from the outside: amber, furs, and slaves from the Baltic Sea area; ivory, gold, and slaves from sub-Saharan Africa; and, most important, various luxury items from Asia, including perfumes, precious stones, spices, and, above all, silk. (See Chapter 7, section II.) Thanks to this thriving domestic and foreign trade, staples and luxuries poured into the capital from as near as Gaul and as far as China—enough staples to feed and clothe over a million people, and enough luxuries to satisfy the extravagances of the rulers of the Western world.

In the cultural field, a basic achievement of the Romans was the extension into Central and Northern Europe of urban civilization with all that that entailed. In this respect their role in the West was similar to that of the Greeks in the Middle East. In the third century B.C., after Alexander, the Greeks founded dozens of cities from which Hellenistic culture spread as far as the Indus and the Jaxartes. So now the Romans founded cities such as London and Colchester in Britain, Autun and Vaison in Gaul, and Trier and Cologne in Germany. These cities, varying from 20 to 500 acres in size, were a distinct improvement on the relatively squalid hill-top forts and villages of the Celts and Germans. Even the slaves' quarters in these cities were more hygienic than the hovels of the contemporary native villagers. Furthermore the cities possessed public bathhouses for the comfort of the body and public theaters for the pleasures of the mind, as well as residential blocks and public markets and shops. It was these cities that comprised the basic cells of the imperial culture as well as of the imperial body politic.

The great city of the empire, of course, was Rome. It sprawled over five thousand acres and its population during the second century A.D. is estimated at a little over one million. This was gigantic for a period when there was little of the technology that makes modern cities viable. It would be this lack that doubtless would have most impressed a modern visitor to ancient Rome.

Such a visitor would have noted the complete absence of sanitation facilities in the crowded tenements of the poor, their place being taken by elaborate public latrines with seats of marble and decorated with statues of gods or heroes. An inevitable by-product of this arrangement was the emptying of chamber pots into the streets. That this was not a rare occurrence is indicated by the many references to this practice in Roman law. Noteworthy also was the total lack of street lighting, so that on moonless nights the capital was plunged in impenetrable darkness. Everyone locked himself in his home; no one dared venture out except for the wealthy with their escort of slaves who carried torches and protected them against robbers. The poet Juvenal observed bitingly at the time that to go out for an evening dinner without having made your will was to expose yourself to the reproach of carelessness.

Certain other features of Rome, however, would have been found all too familiar by our mythical visitor; in particular, there was the gulf between the few rich and the many poor. Cicero, for example, was by no means one of the wealthiest senators, yet he had a half dozen country-houses, each with a complete staff of domestics and gardeners. When a visitor commented to the military hero Lucullus that one of his country villas was well designed for summer use but uninhabitable in winter, he replied laughingly, "Do you think that I have so much less sense than cranes and storks that I do not change my residence with the seasons?" On the other hand, the common assumption that the wealthy of Rome were gluttonous and depraved is quite unjustified. There was a traditional upper-class decorum and etiquette that condemned those who made public displays of their vices and excesses. Indeed the most common creed in society circles at this time was Stoicism, which stressed devotion to duty and the brotherhood of man. The average member of Rome's upper class, then, did not drag himself from orgy to orgy, but rather pursued a relatively quiet life of luxurious and sensible pleasure.

Yet, whatever their restraint or excesses, the wealthy lived very differently from the poor. For the latter, housing was scarce, rents were high, and wages low. The crowded tenements in which they lived were rickety firetraps, especially in the less expensive upper floors where no water was available. Eleven aqueducts supplied Rome with abundant water, but it was piped mostly to the homes of the rich and to public baths and fountains. The streets below the tenements teemed with life and reverberated with noise. Hawkers bawled their wares, money changers rang their coins, tinkers pounded their hammers, snake charmers played their flutes, and beggars rehearsed their misfortunes to passersby. Night provided no relief. Transport carts were banned from the streets in daytime, so immediately after sunset appeared a great procession of carts, beasts of burden, and their drivers. According to Juvenal, this night traffic condemned Romans to perpetual insomnia unless they lived in isolated villas. "What sleep is possible in a lodging?" he asked. "The crossing of wagons in the narrow, winding streets, the swearing of drovers brought to a standstill would snatch sleep from a sea-calf or the emperor Claudius himself." [14]

Life under such conditions was made tolerable by the mass entertainment provided by the state. Most popular were the chariot races and gladiatorial contests. The largest of the six race courses in Rome was the Circus Maximus with 140,000 seats. Although the charioteers were of lowly origins, usually slaves, they gained great fame and fortune if they were steady winners. Innumerable copies of their portraits were posted in the streets and on tenement walls. The gladiatorial fights, staged in the Colosseum with 50,000 seats, were cruel spectacles that assumed various forms. Some pitted ferocious animals—bears, elephants, rhinoceroses, lions—against each other or against armed men. Others set gladiators, usually equipped with different types of weapons, to fight one

A relief from the column of Antonius Pius showing Roman foot soldiers surrounded by cavalry. (Alinari-Art Reference Bureau)

A detail from a relief showing the decapitation of German nobles by Roman soldiers. (Anderson-Art Reference Bureau)

another to death. Particularly revolting was the scale of these blood baths. Five thousand beasts were killed on the day Titus inaugurated the Colosseum, and Trajan once had ten thousand Dacian prisoners fight each other to the finish.

A better use of leisure was provided by the sumptuous public baths of Rome. These were so elaborate that those of Diocletian covered 32 acres; Caracalla's spread over 27 acres. Such establishments were, of course, much more than simple bathing pools. In addition to hot, tepid, and cold baths, they provided exercise facilities, lounging halls, gardens, and libraries. They were, in short, "athletic clubs" on a grand scale, and they admirably promoted the ideal of "a healthy mind in a healthy body."

Finally the Rome of these centuries was also the center of imperial culture. This culture, as noted earlier, was essentially Greek-derived, particularly in such fields as literature, art, and philosophy. (See Chapter 7, section III.) But in engineering and law, the Romans, with their bent for practicality, had important contributions of their own to make. Typically, the Romans achieved little in abstract science but excelled in the construction of aqueducts, sewer systems, bridges, and roads. The roads were superbly built, with a bottom layer of large stones set in firm soil, a middle layer of gravel, and a top layer of large slabs of stone. They were carefully cambered so that the surface water drained off into the ditches on each side. These famous roads, together with their bridges, were so well engineered that they continued to be used through the Middle Ages, and in some cases even to the present day. Likewise, Roman architecture, in contrast to the Greek, was concerned primarily with secular structures such as baths, amphitheaters, stadia, and triumphal arches.

Perhaps the most important single intellectual contribution of the Romans was their body of law based on reason rather than custom. Their original laws, as set down in the Twelve Tablets about 450 B.C., were simple and conservative, typical of a peasant people. With the growth of commerce and of empire, life became more complicated and these laws no longer sufficed. Typical was the problem of an alien in Rome who might be arrested and his property seized. What law would be applicable in such a case, particularly in view of the contemporary concept that a people carried their law with them wherever they went. The Romans established a special court to try such cases, and as a result of its operations they realized that among foreign peoples there were many legal systems but only a few almost universal legal principles. Hence the formulation of a new body of law—the *jus gentium,* or law of the peoples—which they accepted as applicable to themselves as well as to others.

The final legal concept evolved by the Romans was that of *jus naturale,* or natural law. This stemmed not from judicial practice but from the Stoic idea of a rational god ruling the universe. Or, in Cicero's words, it was law above mere custom or opinion, "implanted by Nature, discoverable by right reason, valid for all nations and all times." While jurists did not regard this as an automatic limitation upon Roman civil law, they did view it as an ideal to which human legislation should conform. This basic principle represents one of Rome's great contributions and remains operative to the present day. In fact, Roman law, as systematized later in Justinian's Code in the mid-sixth century, constitutes the basis for the present legal systems of the Latin countries of Europe, of the Latin American states, of the Province of Quebec, and of the state of Louisiana.

VIII. Late Empire, a.d. 284–467

The great days of Rome came to an end with the death of Marcus Aurelius in 180. For some time his predecessors had passed on the succession to adopted sons of proven talent, a system that had made possible a string of unusually capable rulers. But Marcus Aurelius allowed his true son, Commodus, to succeed him. The results were disastrous. Commodus avoided his duties as head of the empire and spent most of his time at chariot races and gladiatorial contests. After his assassination in 193 he was followed by rulers who were for the most part equally incompetent. The Praetorian Guard, a highly trained and well-paid body created by Augustus to protect the security of the capital, now got out of control, and an emperor remained in power only while he had the support of this body. During the period from 235 to 284 there were almost two dozen emperors, and only one of them died a natural death. This disintegration in the center inevitably weakened the frontier defenses. Outlying provinces were overrun by the German tribes in the West and by the revived Persian Empire of the Sassanians in the East.

This imperial decay of the third century was checked with the advent of the strong and capable emperors Diocletian (284–305) and Constantine (312–317). Among the policies they adopted to hold the empire together was a rigid regimentation imposed step by step in response to specific urgent needs. Because agricultural lands were being left untilled, villages were required to pay a collective tax on abandoned lands. Because inflation was mounting, the famous Edict of Prices (301) set maximum prices for thousands of commodities and services, with specified variations according to quality. Interest rates were soaring, so they were limited to between 6 and 12 per cent, depending upon the degree of risk. Shortages of certain products brought on export prohibitions, as in the case of foodstuffs and "strategic products" such as iron, bronze, weapons, army equipment, and horses. These controls were extended to the point of a virtual caste system. Constantine required every soldier's son to be a soldier unless unfit for service. Similarly agricultural laborers were tied to the land on a permanent and hereditary basis. The tendency was to extend this to all crafts and professions that were deemed indispensable or that had recruitment difficulties.

Another policy during this time of troubles was decentralization, which proved necessary with the deterioration of the imperial economy. Diocletian divided his realm in two, keeping the eastern half for his own administration and appointing a co-emperor for the western. This division was hardened when Constantine built a new capital on the site of the old Greek colony of Byzantium on the Bosphorus. The choice was inspired, for Constantinople, as the new city soon came to be called, was easily defended thanks to the narrows at each end of the straits, and also provided ready access to both the vital Danube and Euphrates frontiers. Thus Constantinople became one of the great cities of the world, and served as the proud capital of the East Roman, or Byzantine, Empire for centuries after Rome and the Western empire had passed away.

Another policy of these later centuries that was to affect the future profoundly had to do with relations btween Christianity and the imperial government. It was Constantine who made the fateful decision to seek stability and cohesion through cooperation with Christianity rather than its suppression. This represented the culmination of a centuries old trend in religious attitudes and practices. The vicissitudes of daily life during this later imperial phase were leading increasing numbers to turn for solace to salvation religions, as had happened earlier in the Hellenistic East. (See section IV of this chapter.) Spiritual needs no longer wére satisfied by the cult of emperor and the official polytheism. Brotherhoods that celebrated the mysteries of Oriental gods now provided satisfying explanations of the world, rules of conduct, and release from evil and from death.

The most successful of the new religions was Christianity. It offered the doctrine of One God, the Father Omnipotent, in place of the polytheism of the Greco-Roman gods and the diffuse monotheism of the oriental cults. It brought the solace of a Redeemer, Jesus, who was not an ambiguous figure in a mythological labyrinth, but who miraculously lived an earthly life, even though he was the Son of God. "I bring you tidings of great joy which shall be to all people." Christianity also guaranteed salvation to the believer, but instead of a starry eternity, it restored him to life through a personal resurrection foreshadowed by the Resurrection of Christ himself. Perhaps most important of all, Christianity provided fellowship when times were disjointed and common people felt uprooted and forsaken. All Christians were brothers, and their meetings were often called *agape*, meaning "love" in Greek. They assisted one another, and by their devotion and self-denial they set an inspiring and contagious example. Thus at a time when the laws and philosophy of the old order were becoming irrelevant and unviable, Christianity offered relevance and hope for the meek and the humble.

By the time of the great fire of 64 the Christians had become so numerous that Nero deemed it politic to blame them for the disaster and to begin the first of numerous persecutions. But this merely hallowed the memory of the martyrs and spurred the proselytizing efforts. After a final major persecution early in the fourth century, Emperor Constantine issued the Edict of Milan (313) excusing Christians from pagan rituals and granting their religion the same toleration accorded to all others. Finally Emperor Theodosius (379–395) made Christianity in effect the state church. The old Roman aristocracy and the apostate Emperor Julian (361–363) fought a stubborn rearguard action to preserve pagan practices, but by the end of the fourth century Christianity reigned supreme.

Just as the emperors adopted Christianity with the aim of furthering social cohesion, so for the same reason they adopted the pomp and circumstance of oriental court etiquette. In contrast to Augustus who had dubbed himself "First Citizen," Diocletian took the name of Jovian, the earthly representative of Jupiter, while Constantine, after his conversion to Christianity, assumed sacred status. The power of the emperor henceforth was considered to be derived from the gods rather than delegated by citizens. Accordingly, court ritual now made the emperor remote and unapproachable, bedecked in a jeweled diadem and a robe of purple silk interwoven with gold. All subjects were required to prostrate themselves, while a privileged few were allowed to kiss the border of the emperor's robe. High imperial officials were correspondingly beatified— the treasurer became "count of the sacred largesses," and the imperial council was known as the "sacred consistory."

With these measures the emperors of the third and fourth centuries strove valiantly to halt the imperial decline. If resolve and effort alone were needed, they would have been spectacularly successful. In fact they did stabilize the situation somewhat, but only temporarily. The net effect of their herculean endeavors was to postpone rather than to avert the end. Beginning in 406 the West Roman emperors were powerless to prevent permanent large-scale incursions of Franks, Burgundians, Visigoths, and Vandals in Gaul, Spain, and Africa. Nor could they prevent the ultimate indignity of the sack of Rome by barbarians in 410 and again in 455. Finally in 476 Romulus Augustulus, the last of the West Roman emperors, was forced to abdicate by Odoacer, the German, or Hunnic, leader of a band of mercenary soldiers.

Though generally taken to mark the end of the West Roman Empire, this incident, which attracted little attention at the time, was merely the culmination of a process of disintegration that had extended over two centuries. To understand the reason for this "fall of Rome," if the traditional cataclysmic phrase may be used, it is necessary to determine the dynamics of this prolonged but inexorable descent to oblivion.

The instrument responsible for the "fall" was, of course, the German barbarians. Thus a French historian has concluded, "Roman civilization did not die a natural death. It was murdered." [15] There is some justification for this verdict, particularly if it is kept in mind that the innumerable small tribes known to the Romans in the earlier centuries amalgamated later to form the larger political units of the Franks, the Alamanni, and the Goths. Yet even then it was not a case of irresistible hordes sweeping everything aside by sheer weight of numbers. Historians estimate that only about 100,000 Ostrogoths invaded Italy, and an equal number of Visigoths subjugated Spain and southern France. The Vandal force that crossed the Straits of Gibraltar to North Africa totalled about 80,000 men, or 1 per cent of the native population of that province.

So the question still remains—why the "fall"? An American historian has recently stated that "though war was the apparent cause of death . . . the organic disease of the Empire was economic." [16] In fact, this "organic disease" is discernible not only in the Roman Empire but in the Hellenistic states, in Classical Greece, and even in the earlier ancient civilizations. All were afflicted by the same basic problem of low productivity. This stemmed from the failure to advance technology significantly after the Neolithic age, which had produced such core inventions as metallurgy, the plow, the wheel, the sail, and the solar calendar.

The underlying cause for this technological retardation appears to have been the institution of slavery, which was an integral and universally accepted part of all these civilizations. Even in Classical Greece, where slavery never was as rampant as in Rome, Aristotle, as noted above, asserted that some men were born to rule and some to be ruled, and if the latter refused to accept their preordained fate, then it was "naturally just" that they should be hunted down as though they were "wild beasts."

The repercussions of this slavery institution were manifold and pernicious. It deprived the slave of any incentive to improve on the traditional operations of his craft. It also deprived the master of any incentive to technological innovation so long as plenty of slave labor was available. Thus when an obelisk was to be erected during the reign of Vespasian in the present-day Piazza San Pietro in Rome, an inventor of the time suggested an engineering technique that would have greatly facilitated the operation. But the emperor preferred manual slave labor so as not to leave the slaves unemployed. Likewise the water-mill, though known in the eastern provinces of the empire as early as the first century B.C., was not adopted in Rome until the fourth century when the supply of slaves had shrunk.

Equally harmful was the natural tendency of a slave-owning society to associate manual labor with slaves and hence to regard such labor as beneath the dignity of freemen. Thus the Greek essayist Plutarch stated that the great Archimedes

> . . . did not think the inventing of military engines an object worthy of his serious studies, but only reckoned them among the amusements of geometry. Nor had he gone so far, but at the pressing instances of Hiero of Syracuse, who entreated him to turn his art from abstracted motions to matters of sense, and to make his reasonings more intelligible to the generality of mankind, applying them to the uses of common life.
>
> The first to turn their thoughts to mechanics, a branch of knowledge which came afterwards to be so much admired, were Eudoxus and Archytas, who confirmed certain problems, not then soluble on theoretical grounds, by sensible experiments and the use of instruments. But Plato inveighed against them, with great indignation, as corrupting and debasing the excellence of geometry, by making her descend from incorporeal and intellectual, to corporeal and sensible things, and obliging her to make use of matter, which requires much manual labor, and is the object of servile trades. Mechanics were in consequence separated from geometry, and were for a long time despised by philosophers.[17]

In these various ways, then, the institution of slavery tended to inhibit technological innovation during the millennia following the egalitarian Neolithic age. Slavery also had the economic effect of depressing the internal market by restricting domestic purchasing power, since slaves obviously were not able to purchase the fruits of their labor.

For some time these basic structural weaknesses were masked by imperial expansion, with the resulting flood of booty, tribute, foodstuffs, and slaves. But there were limits to the expansion of empires at that level of technological development—limits set by logistical and communications requirements. Thus Rome, like China, was able to advance just so far and no further. When that point was reached, and the imperial frontiers became fixed, or even began shrinking, then the hitherto hidden structural defects became visible.

A page from the Ashburnham Pentateuch, written in the Latin language, believed to be the only Visigothic illuminated manuscript, gives some indication of the enduring effect that Rome had on the barbarian tribes that had contributed to her fall. (Bibliothèque Nationale, Paris)

The army, which hitherto had been a profitable source of slaves and material wealth, now became a heavy but inescapable burden. Likewise the bureaucracy, having become swollen during the period of expansion, now proved insupportable in a period of contraction. The excessive expenditures led to inflation that eventually reached runaway proportions. In Egypt, for example, a measure of wheat that cost 6 drachmai in the first century A.D. rose to 200 in 276, 9,000 in 314, 78,000 in 334, and to more than 2 million soon after 334. With such inflation, coinage became worthless and there was some reversion to barter. This trend was hastened by the growing diffusion of industry to the countryside and to the provinces. The diffusion occurred for a variety of reasons, including the deterioration of imperial communication facilities and the drop in the supply of slaves which necessitated tapping new labor pools. The shift of industry from the cities to villages and large country estates meant the agrarianization of the empire. The large estates became increasingly self-sufficient, boasting craftsmen of every kind as well as agricultural laborers. And the more self-sufficient they became, the more the imperial economy disintegrated into autarchic units.

This economic decentralization inevitably was accompanied by political decentralization. With the decline of trade and the shrinkage of state revenues, the imperial edifice no longer could be supported and slowly it began to crumble. This was a factor behind the desperate efforts of Diocletian and Constantine to buttress the structure by imperial fiat. But the disease was "organic" rather than superficial, so all the regimentation, with its propping and bracing, was of no avail in the long run. Regimentation, however, was not the cause of imperial decay, but an ineffective remedy that was tried to halt the decay. "Crisis preceded regimentation," as an economic historian has pointed out.[18]

It follows that a major reason why the West Roman Empire "fell" and the East did not, was precisely that the economy of the West was less advanced and less strong. Italian agriculture was never as productive as that in the alluvial valleys of the Middle East. The grain harvest in Italy "was on an average no more than four times the sowing." [19] The rich soils of Central and Northern Europe had to await medieval technological advances for effective exploitation. Likewise industry in the West was of relatively recent origin and generally lagged behind that in the East. This was true of Italy, and much more so of Gaul, the only other western province where industry had taken root. Thus although the whole Roman Empire was wracked by "organic disease," the western part, being the least robust, was the first to succumb, while the eastern survived to live for another millennium.

Despite its demise, the West Roman Empire did leave a rich legacy. Most apparent are the material remains—the amphitheaters, arenas, temples, aqueducts, roads, and bridges. Equally obvious is the linguistic bequest in the form of the Romance (or Romanized) languages of Europe. Roman law, as noted above, is very much alive in the legal systems of numerous countries in Europe and the Americas. The organization and ritual of the Catholic church owe much to Roman imperial structure and religious traditions. Finally the *Pax Romana,* which had brought two centuries of relative peace and prosperity, left a tradition of imperial unity in place of the city-state particularism of the Greeks. It was this tradition during the following centuries that fired the imagination and ambition of barbarian princes throughout Europe to become *imperator* or *basileus* or tsar.

SUGGESTED READING

A full annotated bibliographical survey is provided by M. Chambers, *Greek and Roman History* (2nd ed.), American Historical Association, Service Center for Teachers of History, Publication No. 11 (Washington, 1965).

Recent surveys of both Greece and Rome are available in C. Roebuck, *The World of Ancient Times* (New York: Scribners, 1966); C. G. Starr, *History of the Ancient World* (New York: Oxford Univ., 1965); T. W. Africa, *The Ancient World* (Boston: Houghton Mifflin, 1969); and T. B. Jones, *From the Tigris to the Tiber: An Introduction to Ancient History* (Homewood, Ill.: Dorsey, 1969). For Greece alone, see the standard text by J. B. Bury, *A History of Greece to the Death of Alexander the Great*, 3rd ed. (London: Macmillan, 1951); and the readable analyses by W. Durant, *Life of Greece* (New York: Simon & Schuster, 1939) and R. W. Livingstone, ed., *The Legacy of Greece* (Oxford: Clarendon, 1921). On specific aspects of Greek history and civilization there are A. R. Burn, *Persia and the Greeks: The Defence of the West* (London: Edward Arnold, 1963); W. S. Ferguson, *Greek Imperialism* (Boston: Houghton Mifflin, 1913); J. M. Cook, *The Greeks in Ionia and the East* (New York: Praeger, 1962); T. J. Dunbabin, *The Western Greeks* (Oxford: Clarendon, 1948); A. Andrewes, *The Greek Tyrants* (London: Hutchinson, 1956); A. H. M. Jones, *Athenian Democracy* (Oxford: Blackwell, 1957); M. P. Nillson, *History of Greek Religion* (Oxford: Oxford Univ., 1949); B. Farrington, *Greek Science*, 2 vols. (Baltimore: Penguin, 1949); M. Hadas, *History of Greek Literature* (New York: Columbia Univ., 1950); and R. Flacelière, *Daily Life in Greece at the Time of Pericles* (New York: Macmillan, 1965).

For the Hellenistic world, see the standard survey by W. W. Tarn and G. T. Griffith, *Hellenistic Civilization* (London: Edward Arnold, 1952); the definitive biography by W. W. Tarn, *Alexander the Great*, 2 vols. (Cambridge: University Press, 1948); the detailed analysis by M. Rostovtzeff, *Social and Economic History of the Hellenistic World*, 3 vols. (Oxford: Clarendon, 1941); and the readable M. Hadas, *Hellenistic Culture: Fusion and Diffusion* (New York: Columbia Univ., 1959).

There are several good one-volume studies of Rome, including A. E. R. Boak and R Hudson, *A History of Rome to 565 A.D.*, 3rd ed. (New York: Macmillan, 1945); R. H. Barrow, *The Romans* (Baltimore: Penguin, 1951). See M. P. Charlesworth, *The Roman Empire* (New York: Oxford Univ., 1951) for the first three centuries; for the later period, see A. H. M. Jones, *The Decline of the Ancient World* (London: Longmans, 1966). Special topics are treated in J. Carcopino, *Daily Life in Ancient Rome* (New Haven: Yale Univ., 1940); L. Homo, *Roman Political Institutions* (New York: Knopf, 1930); S. Dill, *Roman Society from Nero to Marcus Aurelius* (London: Macmillan, 1904); M. I. Finley, ed., *Slavery in Classical Antiquity: Views and Controversies* (Cambridge: W. Heffer, 1960); and C. Bailey, ed., *The Legacy of Rome* (New York: Oxford Univ., 1923). Finally the problem of why Rome "fell" is analyzed in the following two convenient collections of readings, which also provide excellent bibliographies on the subject: S. N.

146 Eisenstadt, ed., *The Decline of Empires* (Englewood Cliffs, N.J.: Prentice-Hall, 1967); and D. Kagan, ed., *Decline and Fall of the Roman Empire* (Boston: D. C. Heath, 1962).

*I consider that my duty
is the good of the whole world.*

ASHOKA

Indian Civilization

Turning from Greece and Rome to India, we enter an altogether different world. The differences are not simply those that might naturally emerge from contrasting physical environments—differences in occupations, diet, habitation, dress, and the like. The differences were much more far reaching and fundamental. There was nothing in the West remotely resembling basic Indian concepts and institutions such as caste, *ahimsa,* or nonviolence, reincarnation, and *karma,* or the law of moral consequences. These were not merely esoteric abstractions of Indian thought. Rather they constituted the bedrock of Indian civilization, molding the thought and daily lives of all Indians. And the pattern that resulted was so distinctive and so enduring that Indian civilization to the present day has distinguishing characteristics that mark it off from all other Eurasian civilizations.

Such distinctiveness also characterizes the civilization of China, as will be noted in the following chapter, but this is to be expected, given the unparalleled geographic and historical isolation of that country. In India, by contrast, the beginnings appeared to be basically similar to those of the other regions to the west where Aryan invaders had settled—the Iranian plateau and the Balkan and Italian peninsulas. As noted earlier (Chapter 6, section IV), the Aryan tribes that descended upon India about 1500 B.C. possessed the same physical features, the same pastoral economy, the same social institutions, the same gods, and the same epics as did, for example, the Achaeans and the Dorians. Furthermore the Indo-Aryans were not isolated in their subcontinent to anywhere near the degree that the Chinese were on the eastern extremity of Eurasia. The mountain ranges of northwest India are not impassable, so that armies and merchants and pilgrims crossed back and forth through the centuries. In fact, during much of the time there was more interaction between northern India and the Middle East and Central Asia, than between northern India and the southern part of the peninsula.

The question naturally arises, then, why the Indo-Aryans should have developed a civilization so basically different from those of their kinsmen to the west. The scanty evidence available does not allow for a specific or definitive answer, but the most simple and plausible explanation is that the Indo-Aryans were Indianized. In contrast to the Achaeans or Dorians or Latins, who settled in relatively uncivilized areas, the Indo-Aryans encountered in the Indus Valley a highly developed civilization with large urban centers and a dense population. (See Map VIII, "Classical Age Empires in India.") This native population, although subjugated and despised, was too numerous and too advanced to be exterminated or pushed aside or assimilated, leaving few traces of the original culture. Instead, as the Aryan pastoralists settled down and took up agriculture, they perforce lived in close proximity with the prior inhabitants of their new land. After some centuries of such coexistence and intermarriage, the inevitable result was a cultural synthesis. The circumstances and nature and consequences of this synthesis are the subject of this chapter.

I. Aryan Impact

Following their penetration into the Indus Valley, the Aryans concentrated in the more rainy parts of the Punjab where the pasture was adequate for their herds. It is noteworthy that in an early epic, the Rigveda, the rivers of the Punjab are spoken of quite often, while the Ganges is mentioned only once. Gradually, however, the Aryans began to spread into the heavily forested basin of the Ganges. Their expansion was slow at first, with only stone, bronze, and copper axes being available. But iron was introduced about 800 B.C. and their pace gained speed. The main occupation now shifted from pastoralism to agriculture. Furthermore, the monsoon climate of the Ganges Valley made possible rice cultivation, which was much more productive than the wheat and barley grown in the Punjab. Thus the center of population density shifted from the northwest to the east, which consequently became the seat of the first powerful kingdoms.

The shift to agriculture stimulated various crafts necessary for the new villages, including carpentry, metallurgy, weaving, and tanning. Agriculture also promoted trade, with the river serving as the natural highway for transporting surplus foodstuffs. Barter was the common practice at first, with the cow as the unit of value in large-scale transactions. When coins appeared, the earliest weight standards, significantly enough, were exactly those of the pre-

Aryan Indus civilization. Towns grew out of villages that were strategically located for trade or that had specialized in particular crafts.

This economic growth in turn facilitated political consolidation. Originally the Indo-Aryans, like their relatives in the West, were organized under tribal chiefs assisted by councils of elders and general assemblies. With economic development the tribes gave way to kingdoms in the Ganges plain and to republics in the Punjab and in the foothills of the Himalayas. Of these early states the kingdom of Magadha in the lower Ganges soon rose to preeminence because of its location on two main trade routes and its control over rich iron ore deposits. With these advantages Magadha was to serve as the base for the formation of both the Maurya and Gupta empires. Noteworthy in this regard is the dictum of Kautilya, the chief minister of the first two Mauryan emperors: "The treasury is based upon mining, the army upon the treasury; he who has the army and treasury may conquer the whole wide earth." [1]

The Nanda dynasty in the fourth century B.C. was the first to exploit systematically the resources of Magadha for state building purposes. They built canals, organized irrigation projects, and established an efficient administrative system for the collection of taxes. The Nandas have been described as the earliest empire builders of India. In fact, they laid the foundations of empire but were not destined to actually fashion the first imperial structure. This was to be the historic role of Chandragupta Maurya, the young adventurer who usurped the Nanda throne in 321 B.C. and went on to build the famous empire named after him.

These economic and political developments were paralleled by fateful changes in social structure. Originally the Indo-Aryans, like other Aryans, were divided into three classes, the warrior nobles, the priests, and the common people. They had none of the restrictions associated with caste, such as hereditary professions, rules limiting marriages to within castes, and taboos as to dining companions. But by 500 B.C. the caste system was functioning with all its essential features. Although many theories have been advanced as to its origins, it is generally agreed that color was a basic factor. Indeed the Sanskrit word for caste, *varna,* means color.

Being so conscious of the difference in complexion between themselves and the dark natives, the Aryan newcomers dubbed them *Dasas,* or slaves. With their strong sense of racial superiority, the Aryans strove to prevent admixture with their despised subjects. Accordingly they evolved a system of four hereditary castes. The first three comprised their own occupational classes, the priests (*Brahmans*), the warrior nobles (*Kshatriyas*), and the farmers (*Vaishyas*). The fourth caste (*Shudras*) was reserved for the Dasas, who were excluded from the religious ceremonies and social rights enjoyed by their conquerors.

This arrangement ceased to correspond to racial reality with the passage of time. Aryan tribes frequently made alliances with Dasa tribes to wage war against other Aryan tribes. Also Aryan settlers mingled with the natives who then adopted Aryan speech and customs. In such cases the Dasas' priests became Brahmans, and their chiefs, Kshatriyas. Thus today the black south Indian Brahman is no less aristocratic for that reason, nor is the light-skinned, grey-eyed untouchable of some northern Indian regions any more elevated because of his pale complexion. In response to these realities, traders and some landowners were classified as Vaishyas, while cultivators and general laborers became Shudras.

Within these four broad divisions have grown up a bewildering variety of castes which have four basic features in common. One is characteristic employment, so that bankers and merchants often belong to the Vaishya caste. Another feature of caste is the hereditary principle, expressed in complex marriage regulations and restrictions. Caste also involves further restrictions as to food, water, touch, and ceremonial purity. Finally each caste has its *dharma,* or moral code, which stipulates such duties as maintenance of the family unit and performance of prescribed ceremonies at marriage,. birth, and death.

Outside this system are the pariahs, or untouchables, comprising today about a seventh of the Indian population. They are condemned to trades or crafts regarded as unclean because their function involves some ritual defilement or the taking of human or animal life. These occupations include hunters, fishermen, butchers, executioners, gravediggers, undertakers, tanners, leather workers, and scavengers. Involvement in these occupations has led in turn to social segregation. Untouchables live in isolated villages or in quarters outside town limits, and are required to use their own temples and wells. They have to be most careful to avoid polluting members of the castes by any kind of physical contact or, in extreme cases, by even coming within their sight. For this reason, until recent decades they never moved outside their quarters or villages without striking a pair of clappers together to warn others of their approach.

The untouchables are further subjected to psychological disabilities as crippling and degrading as the physical. The doctrine of karma holds that one's status in present life has been determined by the deeds of previous lives. The untouchables therefore are held responsible for their present plight because of past sins, and their only hope for improved status in future lives is dutiful performance of present duties.

It is this combination of social and religious sanctions that has enabled caste to function to the present day. It should be added that with its manifold provisions for mutual aid, caste does provide security so long as one abides by its injunctions. Thus it continues to serve as the steel framework of Hindu society. And although it has been attacked by reformers and undermined by the exigencies of modern industrial society, caste nevertheless remains essentially in operation in rural India where three-fourths of the total population continues to live.

II. REFORMATION AND COUNTER-REFORMATION

Caste, with its basic tenets of dharma, karma, and reincarnation, is part and parcel of the Hindu religious system. Originally the Aryans had typical tribal gods personifying natural forces, such as Indra, god of thunder and war, Agni, god of fire, and Soma, god of their sacred intoxicant of the same name. Gods of this nature were appropriate for pastoralists, but as the Aryans settled down to agriculture they perforce turned to new deities. Hence the advent of the "great gods" of Hinduism—Brahma, the Creator, Vishnu, the gracious Preserver, and Shiva, the Mighty and the Destroyer. It is not accidental that

Shiva Nataraja—Shiva as Lord of the Dance. Bronze sculpture dating from about A.D. 1000. (The Metropolitan Museum of Art, Purchase 1964. Harris Brisbane Dick Fund)

Brahma. Relief dating from about A.D. 600–700. (Arborio Mella)

these new gods, particularly Shiva, bear striking resemblances to finds in the Indus Valley sites. At this time, the Aryans naturally appropriated native religious ideas and practices that had evolved through the millennia in the ancient agriculture-based civilization.

With the new gods came also a growing concentration of power in the hands of the priestly class, or Brahmans. This innovation also was derived probably from pre-Aryan religious tradition. The Brahmans, who in some regions were in contact with native religious leaders, presumably learned of the magical claims and practices of their counterparts in the Indus civilization, the remains of which impart so strong an aura of theocratic regimentation. Whatever the historic prototypes in the distant past, the Brahmans effectively exploited their mastery of the Vedas, or hymns, that were recited aloud during rituals and sacrifices. These were transmitted orally through the generations, and were considered so sacred that they were memorized word for word, sound for sound. As the custodians and transmitters of this precious heritage, the Brahmans were able to assert and enforce their claims as the leaders of Hindu society, superior to the Kshatriya, or secular heads.

With time the Brahmans challenged even the status of the deities by emphasizing the significance of the rituals over which they presided. They set forth these claims in the Brahmanas, or prose manuals designed to interpret the Vedas and guide the ritual. These often consisted of a combination of puerile speculation and shrewd formulas that buttressed priestly pretensions. At a more mundane level the Brahmans enjoyed numerous prerogatives and exemptions because of the sacred nature of their functions. Donors of gifts were assured definite reward in this, as well as in subsequent, lives. "Gift of land" was rated most highly for it "liberated from all sin." Thus the Brahmans acquired vast estates, including entire villages. Also they were exempt from all taxes since they were deemed to have discharged such debts through "acts of piety." And being sacrosanct, the Brahmans could not be sentenced to death or to any type of corporal punishment. Finally the doctrines of karma, reincarnation, and dharma provided virtually irresistible means for Brahman control of the mind. There was little chance for individual assertiveness when one's station in life was the inescapable result of one's own past actions, and when hope in future life rested exclusively on faithful observance of stipulated caste duties, regardless of how onerous or degrading they might be.

The Brahman pretensions and exactions were one factor in the religious reformation in India in the sixth and fifth centuries B.C. Another was the economic growth noted above, which created a wealthy merchant, or Vaishya, caste that resented the special privileges enjoyed by the two upper castes. Finally there was the tension between the Brahmans and the non-Aryans who had been admitted to the Hindu fold but who resented the priestly domination. Thus the Shakya tribes in the Nepal hills from which the Buddha came are thought to have been of Mongolian stock. This combination of factors lay behind the ferment in Indian religious and intellectual circles during these centuries. The demand arose for moshka, or freedom—for something more meaningful and satisfying than prescribed rituals and rigid doctrines.

One manifestation of the unrest was a trend towards asceticism. Some of the most active minds, alienated by the society about them, concentrated on pure introspection. They developed techniques for disciplining or "yoking" (yoga) the senses to an inward focus, culminating in that state of trance or ecstasy which mystics describe as "enlightenment" and sceptics call "self-hypnotism." Out of this inward searching and speculating developed many reform movements, of which only two have survived to the present—Jainism and Buddhism. The founders of both, it might be noted, began as ascetics and then challenged in more practical and systematic fashion the Brahman establishment.

Jaina ideas were in circulation as early as the seventh century B.C., but it was the teacher Mahavira (ca. 540–467 B.C.) who gave them shape and institutional organization. Born into a non-Aryan noble family, he renounced the material world at age thirty and roamed as a naked ascetic for twelve years before attaining enlightenment. The sect he founded came to be known as Jainas, or followers of the Jina (conqueror) as he was called. A basic tenet of his teaching was that not only animals and insects, but "stocks and stones and trees" had each a separate soul. Accordingly he stressed the importance of respecting life in any form. The Jaina priest going about his duties will sweep the path before him to avoid stepping on any insects, and the pious Jaina wears a cloth over his nose to prevent insects being drawn up his nostrils. About a million Jainas live today in West India (Gujarat), but their influence on Hindu society has been far greater than this number suggests. They, together with the Buddhists, were responsible for the central doctrine of ahimsa, or nonviolence, which eventually was accepted within the general body of Hinduism. Mahatma Gandhi, although not a member of this sect, was strongly influenced by its teachings.

Jainism never spread outside India, but Buddhism became a powerful force in Central Eurasia and in East and Southeast Asia. In doing so it played a major role in the creation of a Eurasian ecumene during the Classical Age. (See Chapter 7, section III.) So far as India was concerned, the significance of Buddha's teachings is that they posed a more fundamental challenge to Hinduism than did Jainism. He had no place for caste or for Brahmans, and, like the later Protestants, he held that the scriptures should be understood by the laity. Accordingly he taught in the vernacular of the Gangetic plain and eschewed magic, sacrifices, and obscure writings.

Apart from its spectacular successes in the outside world, Buddhism within India was a serious rival to Hinduism for several centuries. But it never became the dominant faith, and after A.D. 600 it went into decline. By the end of the twelfth century, when the Moslem Turks arrived, it survived only in a few localities and in a debased form. One reason for this paradoxical disappearance of a great religious movement from the land of its birth was that it failed to provide for the usual crises of life. It offered no ceremonies for birth, marriage, death, and other critical turns in the lives of the laity. By contrast the Brahmans were ready with their rites, which fact assured their survival despite the attacks of the reformers. More important, the Brahmans themselves embraced reform. In their philosophical texts, the Upanishads, they set forth their own paths to moshka—to freedom and release.

The supreme spirit permeating the universe, they taught, was Brahman, a being capable of all knowledge and feeling. He was the universal soul and the all-pervading breath; all else was illusion. The individual soul—Atman—was a spark of the supreme being. By transmigration it passed from state to

Fifteenth-century representation of the infant Mahavira with his mother. It was Mahavira (about 540–467 B.C.) who consolidated Jaina ideas and gave them institutional organization. (Arborio Mella)

state until it attained release by reabsorption into Brahman. This identification of the individual soul and the Soul of the universe was the ultimate goal that holy men sought to reach by discipline, meditation, and withdrawal from the world of the senses. Thus seekers after truth now could abandon the world within the fold of Hinduism.

155

Although Buddhism as a practicing faith disappeared in India, it has survived to the present by virtue of its basic tenets being incorporated in Hinduism. The Hindu counter-reformation triumphed precisely because it accepted Buddhist ideas in partnership. The original Hinduism with its nature worship and sacrifice and power propitiation was transformed by the philosophy of the Upanishads, by the compassion of ahimsa, and by the spiritual and moral discipline of dharma.

III. Maurya Empire

Turning from religious movements to political developments, the outstanding event was the emergence of India's first imperial structure, the Maurya Empire. As noted earlier in this chapter, the migration of the Aryans to the Ganges Valley had shifted the center of gravity to that region, and particularly to the kingdom of Magadha. Meanwhile the northwest provinces had been going their own way, dissociated from the rest of India by virtue of their close ties with Persian civilization. In fact, Emperor Darius crossed the Hindu Kush mountains about 518 B.C. and made the western Punjab the twentieth satrapy of his empire.

According to Herodotus, this proved to be a lucrative accession. "The Indians, who are more numerous than any other nation with which we are acquainted, paid a tribute exceeding that of every other people." [2] Herodotus also tells us that when Xerxes invaded Greece in 480 B.C., his army included Indians who "wore cotton dresses, and carried bows of cane, and arrows also of cane, with iron at the point." [3] This testimony from Herodotus is significant in illustrating the fact that only with foreign invasions and foreign historical accounts do we have specific factual data on India's early history. A civilization that regarded the material world as an illusion was understandably unconcerred as to exact details of time and place. History was of interest only for the light it could throw on the perennial truths of Hindu philosophy. Consequently history, myth, and imagination are inextricably combined in the few Indian sources available. Hence the importance of the accounts left by the more materialistic and historically minded foreign visitors.

After the Persian invasion the mists fall again until the appearance of Alexander two centuries later in 327 B.C. His intrusion was more a raid than a full-fledged invasion. He stayed only two years, and less than a decade after his departure Greek authority in the Punjab had completely disappeared. Not a mention of Alexander is to be found in contemporary Indian sources. And yet his campaign did have significant influence on the future development of India.

Least important are the accounts left by Alexander's companions of their impressions of India. Unfortunately none of these has survived, though information taken from them has been passed down as fragments in the writings of later historians and geographers. These describe harbors, articles of trade, appearance of cities, native dress, and strange customs such as polygamy, caste regulations, and burning of the dead. But this matter-of-fact reporting was spiced with the fantastic by tales of people 10 feet high and 6 feet wide, of mouthless people who sustain themselves by vapors, of rain falling in the form of brass pellets, and of eels in the Ganges 300 feet long.

More practical was the contribution of Alexander's army and fleet in opening or reinforcing land and sea trade routes. This swelled the east-west trade from northwest India through Afghanistan and Iran to Asia Minor and Levant ports. The Greek colonies planted throughout the Middle East by Alexander doubtless contributed much to this trade, and the Hellenistic states that followed Alexander promoted it for two centuries.

Most important for Indian history was Alexander's role in creating a political vacuum in northwest India by overthrowing several local kingdoms and republics. Chandragupta Maurya promptly filled the void and founded the empire named after him. In 322 B.C., three years after Alexander's departure, Chandragupta, then an ambitious young general, unseated the Nanda dynasty of Magadha and founded his own. In the following years he extended his rule steadily northwestward until his empire extended from the Ganges to the Indus, including the deltas of both rivers. At the same time he organized a powerful army and an efficient administration to sustain his realm. Thus when Seleucus became king of the Middle East as one of the successors to Alexander and attempted to recover Alexander's Indian provinces, Chandragupta easily repelled the Greek forces.

A year later, in 304, Seleucus was forced to accept a peace by which he abandoned the Indian provinces to the Maurya emperor and bestowed upon him the hand of a Greek princess in marriage. In return he obtained 500 elephants, which he used to good effect against his rivals in the Hellenistic world. This settlement marked the advent of the Maurya Empire as one of the great powers of the age. In the capital of Pataliputra, in Magadha, resided for several years the Greek ambassador, Megasthenes, whose observations are a valuable source, even though available now in only secondary form. Chandragupta's son, Bindusara (ca. 298–273 B.C.), appears to have conquered the Deccan, while his grandson, the famous Ashoka (273–232 B.C.), subjugated Kalinga, or eastern India. Thus the Maurya Empire under the latter ruler encompassed the entire Indian peninsula except for the southern tip.

The structure and functioning of this empire is indicated in the book *Arthashastra* [The theory of political economy], by Chandragupta's mentor, Kautilya. A thoroughgoing realist, Kautilya was devoted to "the goddess of wealth, whom thousands of kings have rejected." His goal was to transform waste land, "as unproductive as a barren cow," into a "good country," which he defined as follows:

> Possessed of capital cities both in the centre and at the extremities of the kingdom . . . powerful enough to put down neighboring kings; free from miry, rocky, uneven and desert tracts, as well as from conspirators, tigers, wild beasts and large tracts of wilderness . . . containing fertile lands, mines, timber forests and elephant forests and pasture grounds . . . not depending upon rain for water . . . rich in various kind of

commercial articles; capable of bearing the burden of a vast army and
heavy taxation; inhabited by agriculturists of good and active character
. . . —these are the qualities of a good country.[4]

At least some of these qualities were to be found in the Maurya Empire.
Well kept highways thronged with merchants and soldiers, royal couriers and
mendicant fakirs, and enough vehicles to necessitate a regular highway code.
The conquest of Kalinga on the east coast stimulated trade, and an Admiralty
department maintained waterways and harbors. Numerous temple inscriptions
attest to the wealth and generosity of trade and craft guilds that provided endowments. The capital, Pataliputra, known as the "city of flowers," was famous
for its parks, its public buildings, its river frontage of over nine miles, and its
educational institutions to which students flocked from all parts of the empire
and from abroad.

All this was supported by "the king's sixth" of the harvest, which in practice
was more commonly raised to a fourth, leaving the peasants with barely enough
for existence. Law was severe and order ruthlessly maintained. The army
reputedly numbered 700,000 men, with 9,000 elephants and 10,000 chariots.
Spies were efficient and ubiquitous, sending in a stream of reports to the capital
by messenger and carrier pigeon. Torture, of which eighteen varieties are recited in the *Arthashastra*, was frequently used as a means of punishment and to
extort confessions. All in all, it was an efficient, harsh, bureaucratic society,
embodying Kautilya's dictum that "Government is the science of punishment."

Ashoka's reign represented a basic and unique departure from this traditional
type of imperial rule. Having conquered the kingdom of Kalinga in a particularly bloody campaign, Ashoka underwent a spiritual experience that he described as follows in his thirteenth rock edict:

> One hundred and fifty thousand persons were carried away captive, one
> hundred thousand were slain, and many times that number died. . . .
> The Beloved of the Gods, conqueror of the Kalingas, is moved to remorse
> now. For he has felt profound sorrow and regret because the conquest of
> a people previously unconquered involves slaughter, death, and deporta-
> tion. . . . Even those who escaped calamity themselves are deeply af-
> flicted by the misfortunes suffered by those friends, acquaintances, com-
> panions and relatives for whom they feel an undiminished affection. Thus
> all men share in the misfortune, and this weighs on the King's mind.[5]

From this moment Ashoka devoted himself to promoting and materializing
the teachings of the Buddha. He aspired to a future with "security, mastery
of the senses, equanimity and gentleness in the hearts of all beings." After the
fashion of the Persian rulers, he inscribed his edicts on rocks, in caves, and
on specially built pillars. These edicts were more in the nature of state sermons
than formal laws. They enjoined typically Buddhist virtues—simplicity, compassion, mutual tolerance, and respect for all forms of life. In contrast to
Kautilya, who thought primarily of the state, Ashoka was interested more in
people. Hence his numerous public works that brought no direct profit to the
state—hospitals and medical care at state expense, orchards and resting places

on highways, distribution of alms to all sects, and Buddhist missions to several foreign countries.

Ashoka was not an Indian Constantine as is sometimes asserted. He did not make Buddhism the state faith, nor did he persecute the other sects. To the contrary, he made generous contributions to Brahmans and Jainas and helped the worthy of whatever denomination. It was not a change of religion, then, but of general attitude. He laid most stress on toleration and nonviolence, not only because they were morally desirable but also because they would promote harmony in his huge and diverse empire. This proved successful during his reign, for Ashoka ruled with popular acclaim for forty-one years. But within half a century after his death his dynasty was overthrown and his empire destroyed.

This has been the pattern of Indian history to modern times. In contrast to China, where imperial unity was interspersed with short intervals of fragmentation, in India it was precisely the opposite—brief unity and prolonged fragmentation. This is not to say that India did not possess unity. She did, but it was cultural rather than political. And this culture emphasized loyalty to the social order rather than to the state, as evidenced in the higher status accorded to caste than to any political institution. Thus the culture that enhanced unity in one sphere undermined it in another.

IV. INVADERS, TRADERS, AND MISSIONARIES

With the end of the Maurya Empire early in the second century B.C. there followed five hundred years of confusion and obscurity. But one constant factor is discernible throughout this period. This is the increasing interaction between India and the outside world, with manifold repercussions in all areas—political, economic, and cultural.

First there was the impact of the Greeks, known in India as the Yavanas, who remained a force in the northwest for two centuries after Alexander. As noted in Chapter 7, section III, they stimulated Gandharan art, set a model for Indian coinage, and, above all, promoted trade between India and the Middle East. Next came a series of invaders who displaced the Greeks and in some cases pushed further to the south. The Parthians, called Pahlavas by the Indians, originated in the Caspian Sea area, and first wrested control of Iran and Mesopotamia from the Seleucids. Then, from about 140 B.C., bands of these people infiltrated into northwest India, forcing the Greeks northward and finally occupying the lower Indus Valley.

After the Parthians came the Scythians, or Shakas as they were known in India. Forced out of Central Asia by the Yue-chi, they overwhelmed the Greeks in Bactria about 130 B.C., crossed the Hindu Kush Mountains, spread into the Punjab, and finally settled in Gujarat. There they mixed with the native population to form the Maratha people who were to figure prominently in later Indian history.

Finally came the Kushans, who succeeded in uniting the Yue-chi horde of which they were a part and then crossed the Hindu Kush Mountains into the Punjab in the first century B.C. In the next century they extended their rule

Lion capital from Ashoka column in Sarnath. This work, on display in the New Delhi Museum, dates from the reign of Ashoka (273–232 B.C.) and is one of the many monuments that this ruler of the Maurya Empire ordered erected in honor of the memory of the Buddha. (Arborio Mella)

southward, probably as far as the Narbada River between Hindustan and the Deccan. Under their best known ruler, Kanishka, who ruled from about A.D. 130 to 160, their empire included the Punjab, Kashmir, the Indus and Upper Ganges valleys, Afghanistan, and parts of present-day Chinese Turkestan. It was an empire that straddled the busiest commercial routes of the time and encompassed regions permeated by Indian, Hellenistic, Persian, and, to a lesser degree, Chinese influences. Kushan coins have been found in Scandinavia, Ethiopia, and various Roman provinces, as well as in Asian Lands. These coins bear the names and effigies of gods from the Hellenic, Persian, and Indian pantheons. Kanishka depicted both the Buddha and Persian divinities on his coins and protected Jainism and Brahmanism impartially. Likewise he adopted at one and the same time the Indian imperial title *maharaja* ("great king"), the Parthian title, which in Sanskrit was *rajatiraja* ("king of kings"), and the Chinese title, which in Sanskrit was *devaputra* ("son of Heaven").

During the third century the Kushan Empire declined and faded out. The immediate reason appears to have been the advent of the vigorous Sassanian dynasty in Persia (A.D. 226), which expanded eastward into Afghanistan. This disrupted the ties between the original Central Asian base of the Kushans and their provinces in India. By the end of the third century the Kushan Empire had disintegrated, leaving a power vacuum between the Ganges basin and the borders of Persia. This cleared the way for the next great Indian empire, the Gupta, just as a similar vacuum earlier had preceded the empire of the Mauryas.

In retrospect, the unprecedented interaction between India and the outside world during this half millennium between 200 B.C. and A.D. 300 stands out clearly. The empires of the Greeks, the Pahlavas, the Sakas, and the Kushans all were based at least as much in Central Asia or the Middle East as in India. All fostered the profitable trade along the routes running from northern India westward to the Middle East and northward to Central Asia and China. This was also the period of flourishing overseas commerce that brought Roman traders to southern and western India, and Indian traders to Southeast Asia. (See Chapter 7, section II.)

In the realm of culture, Indian Buddhist missionaries during these centuries were carrying their message to all the surrounding countries. The begging priest could move among hostile or disordered peoples with impunity since he was too poor to be worth robbing and also was surrounded with the aura of supernatural dedication. There was little incentive for robbing or injuring such a man, since the only return was the possibility of retribution from above. Hence the diffusion of Buddhism and Brahmanism from India to the surrounding countries, with all the cultural accretions involved in such transfer of religions. (See Chapter 7, section III.) Nor was the culture flow exclusively one-sided. The succession of invaders from the north brought with them a variety of Greek, Persian, and Central Asian influences. And by sea there came to India in the first century A.D. a new religion—Christianity. According to legend, St. Thomas arrived about A.D. 52 on the Malabar coast of southwest India where he established a number of churches. Thence he travelled overland to the east coast where his preaching, however, was strongly opposed, and where he was killed in A.D. 68 near Madras. His work in the Malabar region, however, bore fruit, for considerable Christian communities exist there to the present day.

V. GUPTA CLASSICAL AGE

In the fourth century A.D. the great Gupta Age began—a time when the invaders of the preceding centuries were assimilated and when various cultural trends reached fruition. This was the classical period of Indian civilization, comparable to the Early Empire or Augustan Age in the West. The Gupta Empire, like the Maurya, had as its base the Magadha state in the Ganges Valley. This state had managed to preserve its independence following the Maurya collapse, and then, with the end of the Kushans, it began to expand once more into the resulting vacuum.

The Gupta era began with the accession of Chandragupta I about 320, and reached its height under his grandson, Chandragupta II, who reigned from 375 to 415. He expanded his empire until it stretched from the Indus to the Bay of Bengal, and from the northern mountains to the Narbada River. These frontiers constitute the traditional limits of Hindustan, a point deserving emphasis. Politically, the Gupta Empire was a north Indian empire and did not encompass the entire peninsula. Indeed south India at this time was in many ways a world apart, with the Vindhya range still an effective barrier dividing the peninsula in two. The peoples of the south spoke Dravidian languages— Tamil, Telugu, and Kanarese—in contrast to the Indo-Aryan speech of the north. On the other hand, the south had accepted the Hindu and Buddhist religions and social customs and used Sanskrit as its language of scripture and learning. Thus a single civilization bound together the diverse peoples despite their disparate ethnic and linquistic backgrounds and the existence in the south of several independent kingdoms.

The Gupta Empire appears to have enjoyed marked prosperity. This was enhanced by the currency reform of Chandragupta II who introduced standard gold and silver coins. The volume of trade reached new heights, both within the peninsula and with outside countries. The degree of security under Gupta rule is reflected in the drop of interest rates on loans for overseas trade from 240 per cent during the Maurya period to 20 per cent at this time. One of the chief industries was textiles—silk, muslin, calico, linen, wool, and cotton— which were produced in large quantities for both domestic and foreign markets. Other important crafts included metallurgy, pottery, carving, and the cutting and polishing of precious stones.

Judging from the reports of Chinese Buddhist pilgrims, Gupta rule was milder than that of the Maurya. Fa-hien, who spent the years 401 to 410 in India, travelling from monastery to monastery, was impressed by the state services and by the general prosperity. Although the dynasty was Hindu, he observed no discrimination against Buddhists. The countryside was peaceful and prosperous, and not overrun by police and spies as under the Maurya. Fa-hien also noted that:

> The people are numerous and happy; they have not to register their households, or attend to any magistrates and their rules; only those who cultivate the royal land have to pay (a portion of) the gain from it. If they want to go, they go; if they want to stay on, they stay. The king

governs without decapitation or (other) corporal punishments. Criminals are simply fined, lightly or heavily, according to the circumstances. Even in cases of repeated attempts at wicked rebellion, they only have their right hand cut·off. The king's body-guards and attendants all have salaries . . . . in the markets there are no butchers' shops and no dealers in intoxicating drink.[6]

In linguistics and literature, this was the period of the triumph of Sanskrit. Hitherto the learned and rather archaic language of the Brahmans, Sanskrit now staged a comeback, spreading to administration and secular literature. Poetry and prose flourished with the stimulus of lavish royal patronage. Outstanding were the works of Kalidasa, "the Indian Shakespeare," who rendered ancient legends and popular tales into both dramas and lyrics. His *Sakuntala* was translated into English in the late eighteenth century, and has since been widely acclaimed and presented on foreign stages. Perhaps the greatest cultural achievement of the Gupta era was the redaction into final form of the two great national epics, the Mahabharata and the Ramayana. Dating back to many centuries before Christ, the early versions of these works have been entirely lost. Today they are known only in the form in which they were left by Gupta writers. In this form they have remained the classics of Hindu literature and the repositories of Hindu tradition. Their heroes and heroines are a part of the life of the people; their mine of stories has been used by generations of writers and their philosophical poem, the *Bhagavad Gita,* is the supreme scripture of the Hindus.

In the field of science the Gupta period was outstanding. Contact with Greeks resulted in mutually beneficial exchange of ideas. Aryabhata, born in A.D. 476 at Pataliputra, is one of the greatest figures in the history of astronomy. He taught that the earth is a sphere, that it rotates on its own axis, that lunar eclipses are caused by the shadow of the earth falling on the moon, and that the length of the solar year is 365.3586805 days—a calculation with a remarkably slight margin of error. Another great scientist, Varamihira, was learned in Greek sciences and was so gifted that he made significant contributions to virtually all natural sciences.

The greatest achievement doubtless was the formulation of the theory of zero and the consequent evolution of the decimal system. The base could have been· any number; the Hindus probably chose ten because they counted on their fingers. With this system, individual numbers were needed only for 0, 1, 2, . . . 9. By contrast, for the ancient Greeks each 8 in 888 was different. And for the Romans, 888 was DCCCLXXXVIII. The difficulty of division and multiplication with these systems is apparent. The simple Hindu numerals were carried westward by Arab merchants and scholars, and so became known as "Arabic numerals." Despite their obvious advantage they were long scorned as pagan and as too vulnerable to forgery; one stroke could turn 0 into 6 or 9. It was not until the late fifteenth century that Hindu-Arabic numerals prevailed in the West and the door was opened to modern mathematics and science. In retrospect, this Indian contribution stands out as comparable to the invention of the wheel, the lever, or the alphabet.

SUGGESTED READING

Excellent and convenient bibliographical guides are provided by the publications of the American Historical Association's Service Center for Teachers of History: R. I. Crane, *The History of India* (Washington, 1958); and K. W. Morgan, *Asian Religions: An Introduction to the Study of Hinduism, Buddhism, Islam, Confucianism, and Taoism* (Washington, 1964).

The most useful collection of source materials is available in W. T. de Bary *et al., Sources of Indian Tradition* (New York: Columbia Univ., 1958), which includes sections on Brahmanism by R. N. Dandekar, on Jainism and Buddhism by A. L. Basham, and on Hinduism by V. Raghavan and R. N. Dandekar.

The best general histories are by P. Spear, *India: A Modern History* (Ann Arbor: Univ. of Michigan, 1961); R. Thapar, *A History of India*, Vol. I (Baltimore: Penguin, 1966); K. M. Panikkar, *A Survey of Indian History*, 3rd ed. (Bombay: Asia Publishing House, 1956); D. D. Kosambi, *Ancient India: A History of its Culture and Civilization* (New York: Pantheon, 1965); and A. L. Basham, *The Wonder that was India* (London: Sedgwick and Jackson, 1956).

Important works on individual subjects are by K. M. Sen, *Hinduism* (Baltimore: Penguin, 1961); E. J. Thomas, *The Life of Buddha as Legend and History* (New York: Barnes and Noble, 1956); N. Macnicol, ed., *Hindu Scriptures* (New York: Dutton, 1938); Swami Prabhavananda and F. Manchester, *The Upanisads; Breath of the Eternal* (New York: Mentor, 1957); J. H. Hutton, *Caste in India* (London: Oxford Univ., 1946); V. A. Smith, *Asoka* (Oxford: Clarendon, 1920); and the collection of secondary readings by O. L. Chavarria-Aguilar, ed., *Traditional India* (Englewood Cliffs, N. J.: Prentice-Hall, 1964). Finally, much interesting material is to be found in J. Auboyer, *Daily Life in Ancient India from Approximately 200 B.C. to A.D. 700* (London: Weidenfeld and Nicolson, 1961), and M. Edwardes, *Everyday Life in Early India* (London: Batsford, 1969), a beautifully illustrated analysis of life in India between 300 B.C. and A.D. 700.

Chapter When the right men are available,
government flourishes.
10 When the right men are not available,
government declines.

<small>CONFUCIUS</small>

Chinese Civilization

C hinese civilization is characterized by cohesion and continuity as compared with the disparateness and discontinuity of Indian
civilization. There has been no sharp break in China's evolution comparable to that occasioned in India by the appearance of the Aryans
or the Moslems or the British. There were, of course, numerous
nomadic incursions into China, and even a few dynastic take-overs.
But it was not the Chinese who were forced to adopt the language or
the customs or the pastoralism of the invader. Rather it was the invader
himself who invariably was quickly and completely Sinicized.

One reason for this was the greater isolation of China, so that
she was invaded only by the nomads of the northwest. She did not
have to cope with the succession of peoples with relatively sophisticated cultures who invaded India and who consequently were able
to retain in varying degrees their ethnic and cultural identity. The
Chinese were all Mongoloids to begin with, as were their nomadic
invaders and the relatively primitive tribes that they assimilated in
the course of their expansion eastward to the Pacific and southward to
Vietnam. Thus the Chinese enjoyed racial and cultural homogeneity
throughout their history. During the Classical period this homogeneity
was further cemented, as we shall see, by the standardization of the

writing system, which enabled speakers of widely differing dialects to communicate with each other. In India, by contrast, there are today fourteen "national languages," one of which is English, which serves, in Nehru's words, as "the link" amongst the other thirteen.

As important as cultural homogeneity in China has been the remarkable political unity that has persisted through the ages. This can be explained to a considerable degree by the unique secularism of Chinese civilization—the only great civilization that has at no time produced a priestly class. To be sure, the emperor was also a priest who made the sacrifices to heaven in behalf of all his subjects, but this religious function was always secondary to the business of governing. Consequently, the great division between religious and laity, between Church and State, which existed in the other Eurasian civilizations, had no place in China. Nor was there any counterpart to India's epics, steeped in metaphysics and concerned with personal salvation. Rather the Chinese had their classics which emphasized the life of man in society, and particularly the relations between the members of a family and between a king and his subjects. This strong secular bent provided a firm underlying foundation for political organization and stability. This was further cemented during these centuries by a unique Chinese institution—a civil service recruited on the basis of public competitive examinations. It was two thousand years before anything comparable appeared in the West, or anywhere else for that matter.

These, then, are some of the background factors that help explain the Chinese civilization and history that will be analyzed in this chapter.

I. AGE OF TRANSITION

The period of the Eastern Chou (771–256 B.C.) was on the surface inauspicious, with its powerless dynasty and its feudal lords constantly at war with one other. (See Chapter 6, section IV.) Yet this was also a period of basic socio-economic change that determined the course of China's evolution decisively and permanently. The root cause for this change here, as in India, was the introduction of iron. It came late in China, not appearing significantly until about 600 B.C. But by the fifth and fourth centuries B.C. it was leaving its mark on Chinese society and government.

The pattern of its impact was familiar. New and more efficient iron tools made possible the extension of agriculture from the original Yellow River place of origin southward towards the heavily-wooded Yangtze basin (corresponding to the diffusion in India from the Indus to the Ganges). Iron tools also facilitated extensive drainage projects in the valleys, canal building for long-distance hauling of bulky commodities, and well digging for irrigation purposes in the dry northwest lands.

All this meant a very substantial increase in productivity, which in turn stimulated trade and industry and culminated in the monetization of much of the economy. Money had been used earlier, usually in the form of cowrie shells. Now copper coins appeared and were increasingly used in all branches of the economy. Most involved in this monetization was a new class of free and wealthy merchants and craftsmen. They were no longer dependent on feudal lords as they had been in the past. Rather they now constituted a new monetary aristocracy that soon challenged the primacy of the feudal lords.

With this monetization, land now became a form of property that was bought and sold. Wealthy merchants acquired large holdings, and nobles sought to increase their revenues by appointing agents to collect more rent directly from the peasants instead of the customary amount traditionally obtained from the village headman.

This economic change was accompanied by political change—by a fundamental shift from feudal decentralization to state centralization. The economic growth and monetization provided the rulers of the various feudal states with the financial resources needed for centralization. This was particularly so because the newly reclaimed lands could be administered outside feudal relationships and hence rents were contributed directly to the princes' exchequers. Also the princes increasingly established profitable monopolies in the production and distribution of iron and salt. The result was that the princes were able to transform fiefs they had formerly parcelled out to nobles into administrative units staffed by officials of their own central government. This was a gradual development, but where it did occur, it greatly increased the resources and power of the ruler, and correspondingly enfeebled the Chou dynasty in the capital. Indeed a basic reason for the success of the rulers of Ch'in in conquering all China was precisely that they pioneered in these measures and profited accordingly. We will discuss this in section III of this chapter.

II. PHILOSOPHERS AND CLASSICS

The disruption and reorganization that we have described profoundly affected Chinese thinkers. It forced them to reassess their traditions and to either abandon them or adapt them to the requirements of a period of transition. Thus the Eastern Chou period was a time of great intellectual ferment and creativity, reminiscent of the achievements under comparable circumstances of the rationalist philosophers in Greece and of the Buddha and other religious reformers in India.

Because of the secular, this-worldly nature of Chinese civilization, its outstanding thinkers tended to be primarily practical politicians interested in winning over to their views the rulers of the various states. In the course of their travels and disputations, they attracted disciples and gradually formed various schools of philosophy. So intense was this intellectual activity that the Chinese refer to this as the period of the "Hundred Schools." Here we shall consider a few of these schools that persisted through the centuries and influenced significantly the evolution of Chinese civilization.

Although the founders of these various schools often were bold innovators, almost all of them looked for inspiration in a supposedly golden age in the distant past. This tendency is to be found in most civilizations; golden ages are depicted in the *Iliad,* the *Aeneid,* and the Vedas, as well as in Chinese writings. But consciousness and veneration of the past was exceptionally strong amongst the Chinese. Hence they carefully preserved and studied the writings of earlier ages, which they considered indispensable for the conduct of both private and public affairs.

The most important of these ancient works were the *Five Classics* associated with Confucianism. According to the order in which they are usually discussed, the first of these is the *Classic of Changes,* or *Book of Divination.* This was replete with popular omen lore and auguries, such as:

> If a ram butts a hedge
> and cannot go back or in,
> your undertaking will completely fail.[1]

The second work is the *Classic of Documents,* or *Book of History.* This consists of historical documents and speeches from the early Chou centuries, though some of the materials are now known to be later forgeries. The third is the *Classic of Songs,* or *Book of Poetry,* an anthology of some three hundred poems dating mostly from the early Chou period. The fourth work is the *Record of Rituals,* or *Book of Rites,* a collection of materials ranging from the broadest philosophical pronouncements to the most detailed rules for the conduct of everyday life. The final work is the *Spring and Autumn Annals,* a brief chronicle of events between 722 and 481 B.C. that affected the state of Lu or occurred in that state. This was Confucius' native state, and according to tradition he compiled the *Annals* from earlier local records.

Turning from these Classics to the philosopher-teachers that studied and made use of them, the most outstanding by all odds is Confucius. His influence has been so overwhelming and enduring that the Chinese way of life during the past two thousand years can be fairly characterized with the one word—Confucianism. Born in 551 B.C. to an impoverished family of the lower aristocracy, Confucius (the Latinized form of K'ung-fu-tzu, or Master Kung) had to make his own way in the world. And the world he faced was unpromising, with feudal anarchy rampant, and no higher power, spiritual or temporal, to attract national loyalty. Confucius was moved by this to wander from court to court seeking a ruler who would adopt his ideas for successful government. He did hold a few minor posts, but his influence in the world of practical politics was negligible. So he turned to the teaching of young men who, he hoped, might be more effective in implementing his precepts.

Confucius at last had found himself. He proved to be a teacher of rare enthusiasm and skill. What he taught, and the nature of his personality, are set forth in the *Collected Sayings,* or *Analects,* the oldest parts which appear to have been put into writing a century or so after his death. This is not an epic of self-sacrifice crowned by martyrdom, but the record of an engaging personality—sensible, kindhearted, distressed by the folly of his age, convinced that he could restore tranquility, and withal, possessing a saving sense of humor.

Confucius' teachings were fundamentally conservative. He had no notion of tampering with the existing social order and relationships. "Let the ruler be a ruler and the subject a subject; let the father be a father and the son a son." But while insisting on the right of the rulers to rule, he was equally insistent that they should do so on the basis of sound ethical principles. Like Plato, he wanted the kings to be sages, and this they could be if they possessed the five virtues of a gentleman—integrity, righteousness, loyalty, altruism, and love, or human-heartedness.

Confucius also was a rationalist in an age of gross superstition and fear of the supernatural. Men firmly believed in the prophetic significance of dreams, in the arts of divination, and in the dread power of the spirits of the dead. But Confucius, while recognizing spirits and Heaven, largely ignored them in his teachings. "Recognize," he said, "that you know what you know, and that you are ignorant of what you do not know." And again, "If you do not know about the living, how can you know about the dead?"

Confucius' teachings were far from being generally accepted, let alone implemented, during his lifetime. Yet in the end they prevailed and became the official creed of the nation. One reason was his basic conservatism, his acceptance of the *status quo,* which naturally appealed to those at the top. Another was his emphasis on ethical principles, which he insisted were the prerequisites for the proper exercise of authority. Finally Confucius provided a philosophy for officialdom, for the bureaucrats who became indispensable with the establishment of imperial government two and a half centuries after his death. As a famous Confucianist reminded the founder of the Han dynasty: "You have won the empire on horseback but you cannot rule it from horseback."

In the second century B.C. Confucianism was declared the official dogma of the empire, and the Classics became the principal study of scholars and statesmen. Until the fall of the Manchu dynasty more than two thousand years later, in 1911, the teachings of Confucius reigned supreme in the land. Indeed they persisted even later, for Generalissimo Chiang Kai-shek urged dedication to the principles of Confucianism as the solution for the problems of the Republic. To the present day the Nationalist regime on Taiwan observes Confucius' birthday as Teachers' Day, a national holiday.

After Confucianism, the most influential Chinese philosophy was Taoism. This is understandable, for the two doctrines supplement each other neatly, satisfying between them both the intellectual and emotional needs of the Chinese people. While Confucianism emphasized decorum, conformity, and social responsibility, Taoism stressed individual whim and fancy, and conformity to the great pattern of nature. This pattern was defined as Tao, or the Road or Way, so that the disciples are known as Taoists. The key to conforming with Tao was abandonment of ambition, eschewing of honors and responsibilities, and a meditative return to nature. The ideal subject had big bones, strong muscles, and an empty head, while the ideal ruler "keeps the people without knowledge and without desire . . . and fills their stomachs. . . . By non-action nothing is ungoverned."

Altogether different from both Confucianism and Taoism were the doctrines of the Legalists. They were practicing statesmen rather than philosophers and were interested in reorganizing society in order to strengthen the princes they served and to enable them to wage war and unite the country by force. They viewed the nobility as an anachronism to be replaced by state military forces, whereas the mass of the people were to be coerced into productive work. They regarded merchants and scholars as nonessential and diversionary, and therefore not to be tolerated. All aspects of life were to be regulated in detail by laws designed to promote the economic and military power of the state. Rulers were to be guided not by the traditional virtues of humanity and righteousness extolled by the Confucianists, but by the exigencies of *Realpolitik,* whatever they might be.

Figure of an archer, possibly Yen-mo, the god of Death. This glazed earthenware statue was found in a Tang dynasty tomb and is presently in the Victoria and Albert Museum, London. (Arborio Mella)

The efficacy of these doctrines was demonstrated when they were adopted by the Ch'in rulers, who proceeded to subjugate the other princes and to

establish the first empire. They then extended their regimentation with customary ruthlessness to the entire country, but the result, as we shall see, was a reaction that led to the overthrow of the empire a few years after the death of its founder. Legalism was discredited and Confucianism, as noted, was enthroned permanently as the official creed. Yet this, in a sense, represented a victory for the Legalists, for it was their tenet that there should be a single official doctrine buttressed by government patronage and support. It is true that the triumphant Confucianists never developed the persecuting fervor characteristic of guardians of official orthodoxies. Rather they contented themselves with a monopoly of social respectability and of governmental posts. And so the memory of other schools faded away, while Taoism, absorbing all sorts of popular superstitions and demon lore, became the religion of the uneducated masses and was tolerantly despised by the Confucian literati.

III. CH'IN EMPIRE

China's millennia-long history has been marked by three great revolutions that basically changed her political and social structure. The first in 221 B.C. ended the feudal system and created a centralized empire; the second in 1911 ended the empire and established a republic; while the third in 1949 put in power the current Communist regime.

The first of these revolutions was engineered by the leaders of the northwest state of Ch'in in the Wei Valley. This location in itself contributed to the victory, for the valley is largely inaccessible and easy to defend. The Ch'in rulers were able to attack the other states to the east without fear of any enemy action in their rear. The frontier location also served to keep the Ch'in military forces in fighting trim because of the constant wars against the barbarian nomads. In fact the Ch'in were amongst the first Chinese to use steel in place of bronze weapons, and cavalrymen in place of charioteers. Important also in the Ch'in triumph was the conquest in 318 B.C. of the great food-producing plain of Szechwan. This added greatly to the area and strength of Ch'in, placing it in somewhat the same relationship to the other Chinese states as Macedonia had been to the Greek cities. Finally the Ch'in rulers were able and ambitious realists who pioneered in applying Legalist doctrines and concentrating all power in their hands. (See Map IX, "Classical Age Empires in China.")

With these advantages, the Ch'in leaders extended their possessions steadily, overcoming the surrounding states one by one. Contemporaries referred fearfully to the "wild beast of Ch'in," and likened its relentless expansion to that of a "silkworm devouring a mulberry leaf." By 221 B.C. the Ch'in ruler was master of all China, and he adopted the title of *Shih Huang-ti*, or "First Emperor." His successor would be "Second Emperor," and so on down the generations for "ten thousand years," meaning forever.

The new emperor proceeded to apply to all China the Legalist doctrines that had succeeded so brilliantly in his home state. He abolished all feudal states and kingdoms, reorganizing his vast realm into administrative areas, or commanderies, each with a set of officials appointed by, and responsible to, the central government. Also he disarmed all soldiers except his own, required the old aristocratic families to reside in his capital where they could be kept under surveillance, and planted Ch'in garrisons throughout the country. The new emperor also imposed economic centralization by standardizing weights, measures, and coinage.

In the light of future history, one of the most important innovations was the scrapping of the numerous ways of writing the characters of the language that had been developed in the kingdoms. In their place was substituted a standardized script that was intelligible from one end of China to the other. This proved to be a most effective and enduring bond of unity because of the nature of Chinese script. This is based not on a limited number of signs expressing the phonetic elements of a word; it consists rather of a large number of symbols or characters, each one of which denotes an object or an abstract concept. The system is precisely that used in the West for figures. All Westerners know what the symbol "5" means, even though they call it five, fünf, cinque, or cinq. So it is with Chinese characters, or ideographs, which have meaning but no sound. They are ideas, like numerals, which every reader can sound according to his own dialect. Thus the new Ch'in standardized script, which has continued with modifications to the present, could be read and understood by all educated Chinese, even though they spoke dialects that often were mutually unintelligible. And for the same reason, the script was equally comprehensible to foreign peoples, so that educated Japanese, Koreans, or Vietnamese can read Chinese without being able to speak a word of it. The significance of this for future Chinese national unity and for Chinese cultural influence throughout East Asia can well be surmised.

Whatever their justification in the light of later history, these innovations at the time impinged on many vested interests and aroused passionate opposition. This was especially true of the scholars, for whom Legalist doctrines and policies were anathema. The First Emperor accordingly decided to deprive them of their intellectual props by ordering the "Burning of the Books." All the Classics were consigned to the flames, except those dealing with subjects of utilitarian value, such as medicine, agriculture, and divination. The plan really failed, for scholars hid their books at great risk or else memorized entire texts before surrendering them. Later, after the fall of the dynasty, the greater part of the traditional literature was recovered from the hidden books and from the memories of old men. The persecution, however, effectively dampened the intellectual ferment that had characterized the Chou period; the Golden Age of Chinese thought was over.

This intellectual loss should be balanced against the indubitable economic gain through more efficient utilization of human and natural resources. The standardization of weights, measures, and coinage facilitated economic growth. Also a network of trunk roads was built, radiating from the capital to the most distant frontiers. To maximize the value of these roads, the emperor standardized the length of the axles of the two-wheeled Chinese carts—an essential measure because the wheels cut deep ruts in the friable sandy soil, so that every cart had to follow the existing ruts or be fitted with new axles. The emperor also utilized the new national unity and strength to extend the frontiers southward to present-day Vietnam. To the northwest the nomads were beaten back, and to keep them back the famous Great Wall was built, running 1400 miles from Inner Mongolia to the ocean. So great was the loss of life on this stupendous project that even today, more than two thousand years later, people still speak of the fact that a million men perished at this task, and that every stone cost a human life. Just as the scholars cursed the emperor for the "Burning of the Books," so the common people cursed him for the building of the Great Wall.

It was this general detestation, together with the lack of a competent successor, that explains the popular revolt and the end of the dynasty in 207 B.C., only four years after the death of the First Emperor. But although Ch'in rule was so short-lived, it left a deep and permanent imprint on China. The country had been transformed from a congeries of feudal states into a centralized empire, which it remained until the twentieth century. It is only appropriate that the occidental name for China is derived from the Ch'in.

IV. HAN EMPIRE

The First Emperor had abolished feudalism in one stroke, but the succeeding Han emperor, more pragmatic and cautious, first restored feudalism a bit and then whittled it away to insignificance. At the outset, he granted fiefs to his sons and close relatives, but these holdings were all smaller than the former feudal states of the Chou period. Furthermore they were interspersed among commanderies under the direct rule of state officials. Then in 127 B.C. a decree was issued limiting the inheritance of the oldest son to one half the fief, the remainder to be distributed among the other sons. Thus the fiefs shrank steadily in size and importance, becoming merely large estates. The imperial structure erected by the First Emperor was gradually restored, though without the original terror and oppression. Thus the Han Empire flourished for four centuries, about the same length of time as the Roman Empire.

The Han Empire also resembled the Roman Empire in its vast territorial expanse. During the first sixty years the Han rulers concentrated on national recuperation and dynastic consolidation. But under the "Martial Emperor," Wu Ti (141–87 B.C.), the imperial frontiers were greatly extended in all directions. Tribal territories in the south were incorporated, though several centuries of Chinese immigration and assimilation of the local peoples were necessary before this part of the empire became predominantly Chinese-speaking. The greatest expansion occurred to the west, where Chinese expeditions drove across Central Asia, establishing contact with the Kushan Empire in northwest India and vastly increasing the volume of trade along the Silk Road. (See Chapter 7, section II.)

The nomadic Hsiung-nu had the advantage of superior cavalry forces, supported by a limitless supply of horses. In fact, the Chinese had to trade with the nomads for the horses needed by their own cavalry units. But the Chinese had a new weapon that proved decisive. This was the crossbow which they invented sometime late in the feudal wars. Fitted with a string drawn by a winding mechanism and released by a cocking piece, the crossbow had greater range and penetrating power than the ordinary bow. Because of this weapon

The legendary Emperor Shun and his court. Among the ministers is Yü the Great (d. 2197 B.C.), who founded the Hsia dynasty, the first historical dynasty. Late Ch'ing drawing. (Courtesy of the New York Public Library)

and the marshalled resources of a great empire, China's frontiers during the Han period began to take on roughly modern lines.

The Han Empire was comparable to the Roman Empire in population as well as territorial extent. A census taken in the year A.D. 1, and believed to be reasonably accurate, showed the empire to have 12.2 million households with a total of 59.6 million people. By contrast the population of the Roman Empire at the time of Augustus (27 B.C.–A.D. 14) is estimated at 30 to 50 million people in Europe, somewhat fewer in Asia, and not quite 20 million in Africa.

At the head of the Han realm stood the emperor, entrusted with full temporal authority but also responsible for the physical well-being and prosperity of his subjects. The sanctity of the emperor's person was emphasized in his daily activities—in the long ceremonies of court or shrine over which he presided; in the prescribed robes for each occasion; in the army of officials, courtiers, eunuchs, and women that waited on him; in the elegant carriages in which he travelled; and finally in the majestic mausoleum prepared for the time when his mortal remains would be laid to rest with appropriate solemnity.

Below the emperor were two senior officials corresponding to a modern prime minister and a head of civil service. These men were in constant touch with the emperor and were responsible for the actual operation of government. Beneath them were nine ministries entrusted with the following functions: religious ceremonials, security of the palace, care of the imperial stables, punishment of criminals, receipt of homage and tribute from foreign leaders, maintenance of records of the imperial family, collection of state revenues, and management of the imperial exchequer.

In addition to the central government there was a provincial bureaucracy that administered, in descending order, commanderies, prefectures, districts, and wards. Officials at the grass roots level were assigned such basic tasks as collection of tax in grain, textiles, or cash; arresting of criminals; maintenance of roads, canals, and granaries; and upkeep of the imperial post, with its horses and chain of stations.

In the first century B.C. this bureaucracy is said to have comprised some 130,000 officials, or only one for every 400 or 500 inhabitants. This small number in relation to the total population was typical throughout Chinese history, and is to be explained by the restricted role of the imperial government. "Governing a country," according to a Chinese proverb, "is like cooking a small fish: neither should be overdone." Consequently Chinese governments did not assume responsibility for the social services taken for granted in the modern world, as is evident from the ministerial duties listed above. Rather the main role of government was collection of revenue and defense of the country against external attack, and of the dynasty against internal subversion.

The bureaucracy was a privileged, but not hereditary, elite. During the Han period, a unique system was originated for the selection of civil service personnel by means of competitive public examinations. In 124 B.C. a sort of imperial university was established for students destined for government service. This was steadily expanded, so that the student body totalled three thousand by the second half of the first century B.C., and thirty thousand before the end of the Han era. In their later, fully developed form, the examinations were on three levels, and each led to the award of one of three degrees that roughly corresponded to those of bachelor, master, and doctor in Western universities. In principle the examinations were open to all, but candidature involved such a prolonged study that only the sons of the well-to-do could qualify. On the other hand, poor boys not infrequently were given the opportunity to study by village, clan, or guild endowments.

Since the examinations were based on the Confucian Classics, the empire in effect was run by Confucianists and according to Confucian principles. Each official was assigned to a post outside his home province to ensure that he would not use his position to build up local family power. The result was an administrative system that was far more efficient and responsive than any other prior to modern times. Indeed this civil service based on merit was a major factor in the continuity of the Chinese imperial system from the time of the First Emperor to the twentieth century. There was another side, however, to this examination system. Being based on total acceptance of a single body of doctrine, it engendered a rigid orthodoxy and an intellectual arrogance that was to prove China's undoing centuries later with the intrusion of the West.

Although China was to suffer grievously in modern times because she lagged in science and industry, during the Han period it was a very different story. China then drew technologically abreast of the rest of Eurasia, and in many fields took a lead that she was to maintain until recent centuries. Some of the more important Chinese inventions of these centuries were the water-powered mill, the shoulder collar for horses, which greatly increased their efficiency, and the techniques for iron casting, paper making, and pottery glazing. Rag paper, dating from about A.D. 100, soon replaced cumbersome wooden and bamboo slips for writing. But paper is not as durable as wood, and since it was developed by the Chinese long before printing, it can be held responsible, paradoxically, for the loss of certain books. Although a great invention of incalculable importance in later times, paper making may have been premature from the standpoint of the preservation of Chinese literature. Pottery glazes, however, which were eventually developed into porcelain or china, were an undiluted blessing. They not only reached the level of artistic creation, but they also represented a major advance in hygiene, since smooth porcelain was more sanitary than the rough pottery or wooden utensils hitherto available.

The outstanding Han contribution in literature was in the field of historical writing. This was to be expected from a people who looked to the past for guidance in dealing with the present. Their Five Classics contained a good deal of assorted historical materials. But now in the first century B.C. appeared a history much more comprehensive and sophisticated than any to that date.

This was the *Shih chi,* or *Historical Records,* written by a father-son team, though authorship is commonly attributed to the son, Ssu-ma Ch'ien, who wrote the major part. As court astrologer, he had access to the imperial library and archives. Also he had the advantage of extensive travelling throughout the empire, during which he made use of the resources of local libraries. The history he wrote was not so much an original work as a compilation of all available historical materials. It was only when dealing with contemporary matters and personalities that he himself expressed personal judgments and wrote original history. As he explained modestly, "My narrative consists of no more than a systematization of the material that has been handed down to us. There is therefore no creation; only faithful representation."

This method had obvious disadvantages, especially the lack of dramatic quality and stylistic unity found in early historians such as Herodotus. On the other hand it did assemble and preserve for posterity a tremendous quantity of historical materials from contemporary books and archives. The *Historical Records* was in effect a universal history, equivalent to a work of approximately 1,500,000 words. Its 130 chapters included chronological records and tables of the various dynasties, biographies of Han notables, and essays on varied topics such as rituals, music, astrology, astronomy, economic matters, and foreign peoples and lands. Future Chinese historians paid Ssu-ma Ch'ien the tribute of copying his method, so that Chinese historiography has transmitted through the millennia a mass of data unequalled by that of any other country over so long a period.

All Chinese historians also shared a belief in the "Mandate of Heaven" concept. They held that a king ruled as the deputy of Heaven only so long as he possessed the virtues of justice, benevolence, and sincerity. When he no longer demonstrated these virtues and misruled his kingdom, he was automatically deprived of the Mandate of Heaven, and rebellion against him was then not a crime but a just punishment from Heaven through the medium of the rebels. Thus Chinese historians, although often aware of the social and economic factors behind dynastic decline, subordinated them to what they considered to be a more basic underlying consideration—the moral qualifications of the ruler. Chinese historiography, then, tended to be more a compilation of sources than the personal analyses of individual historians, and the organizational framework was based on the rise and fall of dynasties interpreted in accordance with the workings of the Mandate of Heaven.

V. IMPERIAL DECLINE

The traditional interpretation of Chinese history as a succession of repetitive dynastic cycles obscured fundamental changes that occurred in certain periods behind the cyclical facade. It is true, of course, that dynasties did rise and fall. The founder of a line naturally was a man of ability, drive, and action. But his descendants, after a few generations of upbringing in a court atmosphere, were likely to be effete and debauched. Sometimes a strong ruler or a capable and devoted minister managed to halt the deterioration. But the overall trend was downhill, until successful revolt removed the dynasty and restarted the familiar cycle.

More fundamental than this dynastic cycle, however, was what might be termed the economic-administrative cycle. This began with the security and prosperity common at the outset of every major dynasty. The restoration of peace led to population increase, greater production, correspondingly greater revenues, and full government coffers. But a combination of personal ambitions, family influences, and institutional pressures inevitably led the emperors sooner or later to overextend themselves. They squandered their human and financial resources on roads, canals, fortifications, palaces, court extravagances, and frontier wars. Thus each dynasty began to experience financial difficulties about a century after its founding.

To meet the deficits the government raised taxes, which bore most heavily on the small peasant proprietors that were the backbone of Chinese society. At the beginning of each dynasty they constituted the majority of the peasantry. But as taxes increased, more and more of them lost their plots to the large landowners and became tenants. The landowners, having political influence commensurate with their wealth, paid negligible taxes, so that the more their holdings increased, the more the government revenues declined, and the more the taxes rose on the diminishing number of small peasants. Thus a vicious circle was set in motion—rising taxes, falling revenues, neglected roads and dikes, declining productivity, and, eventually, famines, banditry, and full scale peasant uprisings. Meanwhile frontier defences were likely to have been neglected, inviting raids across the frontiers by the nomads. Often it was the combination of internal revolt and external invasion that brought down the tottering dynasty and cleared the way for a new beginning.

This was essentially the pattern of the Earlier Han dynasty. The "Martial Emperor," Wu Ti (141–87 B.C.), had won great victories and extended China's frontiers deep into Central Asia. But in doing so he overstrained the imperial resources. He resorted to a variety of measures to cope with the crisis, including currency debasement, sale of ranks, and reinstitution of government monopolies on salt, iron, and liquor. Although he managed to remain solvent for the duration of his reign, his successors sank deeper into trouble as the number of tax-paying small peasants declined. Large-scale revolts broke out, and even at the court various omens were interpreted as portents from Heaven that the end of the dynasty was drawing near.

In fact the dynasty was briefly ousted (A.D. 9–25) by Wang Mang, a powerful minister who had already dominated the court for some three decades. He boldly tackled the basic economic problem by decreeing nationalization of the great private estates and their distribution amongst the tax-paying peasants. This and other reforms alienated the wealthy families, who opposed the usurper bitterly. At the same time a disastrous change in the lower course of the Yellow River made millions homeless and drove the uprooted peasants into banditry and rebellion. The nomads took advantage of the disorders to invade the country and sack the capital, where Wang Mang died at their hands in A.D. 23. He was succeeded on the throne by a distant cousin of the former Han emperor.

The history of the Later Han (A.D. 25–222) was basically the same as that of its predecessor. During the lengthy wars of the interregnum many of the old aristocrats and landowners had been wiped out. Tax returns, therefore, were adequate at the beginning of the revived dynasty. But again the tax-paying peasantry began to be squeezed out, and the downward spiral once more was under way. Great rebellions which broke out in 184 in East China and in Szechwan were not crushed until 215. The dynasty never recovered from this ordeal.

The situation resembled that of the last days of Rome. The decimation of the small peasants had decimated also the original peasant draft army. This was replaced by professional troops, whose first loyalty was to their generals, who thus were able to ignore the central government. Great landowners also defied the government by evading taxes and enlarging their holdings by various legal and extra-legal means. Helpless peasants, fleeing the barbarian invaders or government tax collectors, became the virtual serfs of these landowners in return for economic and physical security. The great families converted their manors into fortresses, virtually taking over the functions of government in their respective localities. Their estates were largely self-sufficient, so that trade declined and cities shrank correspondingly. Thus the Han dynasty passed from the historical stage in A.D. 222 in a swirl of peasant revolts, warlord coups, and nomadic raids. China entered a prolonged period of disunity and disorder similar to that in the West following the collapse of the Roman Empire.

SUGGESTED READING

Excellent and convenient bibliographical guides are provided by the following publications of the American Historical Association's Service Center for Teachers of History: C. O. Hucker, *Chinese History* (Washington, 1958); and K. W. Morgan, *Asian Religions: An Introduction to the Study of Buddhism, Islam, Confucianism, and Taoism* (Washington, 1964). The standard full-scale, meticulously annotated bibliography is by C. O. Hucker, *China: A Critical Bibliography* (Tucson: Univ. of Arizona, 1962). The standard work on China's geography is G. B. Cressey, *Land of the 500 Million: A Geography of China* (New York: McGraw Hill, 1955). The best general history is E. O. Reischauer and J. K. Fairbank, *East Asia: The Great Tradition* (Boston: Houghton Mifflin, 1958). Noteworthy cooperative works are: R. Dawson, *The Legacy of China* (Oxford: Clarendon, 1964), and the forthcoming *Cambridge History of China*.

Pearl Buck's famous novel *The Good Earth* (New York: John Day, 1931) provides a classic picture of peasant life and attitudes, while Lin Yutang, *My Country and my People* (New York: Reynal and Hitchcock, 1935) is a readable though somewhat idealized presentation of traditional upper-class intellectual and aesthetic values. A convenient and reliable collection of primary materials regarding Chinese intellectual and religious development is W. T. de Bary *et al.*, *Sources of Chinese Tradition* (New York: Columbia Univ., 1960). Concerning the greatest figure in Chinese culture there is H. G. Creel, *Confucius, the Man and the Myth* (New York: John Day, 1949); and A. Waley, *The Analects of Confucius* (London: Allen and Unwin, 1938).

Noteworthy studies of specific subjects are a collection of readings: *The Chinese Civil Service,* ed. J. M. Menzel (Boston: D. C. Heath, 1963); L. Cottrell, *The Tiger of Ch'in: The Dramatic Emergence of China as a Nation* (New York: Holt, 1962); H. G. Creel, *Chinese Writing* (Washington: American Council on Education, 1943); and the multivolume study *Science and Civilisation in China* by J. Needham, *et al.* (London: Cambridge Univ., 1954–). Finally, an evocative portrait of everyday existence at various social levels during the Han period is provided by M. Loewe, *Everyday Life in Early Imperial China* (New York: Putnam, 1968).

MAPS

The range of human activity throughout history has been determined by the level of technological development. The more primitive the technology, the more constricted the range; and, conversely, the more advanced the technology, the more extensive the range. Thus in Map I, Tentative Global Distribution of Hominids and Homo Sapiens, the Australopithecines with their primitive pebble tools and lack of clothing are restricted to the warm African savannas; Homo erectus with his superior tools and clothing and control of fire has expanded into the temperate zones of Eurasia; while Homo sapiens with his still more complex technology has pushed further into northern Eurasia, the Americas, and Australia.

Technological advance has involved not only range extension but also population growth. The more advanced the technology, the more efficient the exploitation of the physical environment and hence the larger the population that can subsist in a given region. Map II, World Population Growth, depicts the population "explosions" resulting from each technological revolution from Paleolithic times to the present.

The population explosions were naturally limited to those races that participated in the technological revolutions. Consequently, as shown in Map III, Global Race Distribution, certain races have increased to their present dominant status, while others have dwindled to insignificance.

179

With the agricultural revolution, the disparity in population growth not only resulted in the rise of certain races and the fall of others, but also caused an increase of agriculturists and a decrease of hunters. The agriculturists, possessing the more advanced technology, far outstripped the hunters, as depicted in Map IV, Recession of Hunters, and in Map V, Expansion of Agriculturists.

The agricultural revolution made possible the rise of civilizations, which were at first limited to the fertile river valleys where agriculture was most productive. Thus the early civilizations, as shown in Map VI, Ancient Civilizations of Eurasia, 3500–1500 B.C., were small islands in the surrounding seas of barbarism. These ancient civilizations were overwhelmed during the second millennium B.C. by Indo-European and Semitic nomadic invasions, which thereby cleared the ground for the succeeding classical civilizations.

The classical civilizations and empires encompassed entire regions rather than isolated river valleys. The development of these regional empires in Europe, India, and China is presented in Maps VII, VIII, and IX. These regional empires together comprised a Eurasian ecumene—a continuous belt of civilizations and imperial structures across the breadth of Eurasia. The political, religious, and economic components of this new entity are depicted in Map X, Incipient Eurasian Ecumene About A.D. 200.

The classical civilizations, like the ancient ones, were in many cases overthrown by a new wave of Eurasia-wide invasions, as pictured in Map XI, Barbarian Invasions in Eurasia, 4th–5th Centuries A.D. In most of Eurasia, imperial structures eventually were reconstituted and stabilized, but in the West the short-lived Carolingian Empire was overthrown by a new wave of invasions by Moslems, Magyars, and Vikings (Map XII, Continued Barbarian Invasions in the West, 9th–10th Centuries). Two other great waves of invasions profoundly affected medieval Eurasia—that of Islam beginning in the 7th century, and that of the Mongols in the 13th century (Map XIII, Expansion of Islam to 1500, and Map XIV, Mongol Empire at the Death of Kublai Khan, 1294).

Destructive though these invasions were initially, they did forge bonds and create a Eurasian ecumene more closely knit than that of the classical period (Map X). This new medieval ecumene, with its network of trade routes and wide-ranging travellers, is depicted in Map XV, Eurasian Ecumene about 1300.

In the late Middle Ages, Western Europe passed from an attitude of self-defense, as depicted in Map XII, and took the offensive. This expansionism was the product of a combination of factors, including technological advances, economic growth, population upsurge, and religious militancy. The result was a series of crusades, motivated at least as much by secular considerations as by religious ones, and launched in all directions, as depicted in Map XVI, Expansionism of the Medieval West.

Because of Western Europe's lead in global exploration, it is often overlooked that in the early 15th century the Chinese undertook a series of expeditions that were far more ambitious and wide ranging than anything in the West at that time, as illustrated in Map XVII, Early 15th-Century Chinese and Portuguese Voyages.

As striking as the difference between the Chinese and Portuguese voyages was the contrasting fate in Eastern Europe of the Byzantines and the Russians. The Byzantine Empire, which had encompassed the Mediterranean basin under Justinian I, shrank during the following centuries, albeit with periodic comebacks, until by the fifteenth century it comprised only two minuscule footholds, one in the Peloponnesus and the other around the city of Constantinople. This contraction is depicted in Map XVIII, Decline of the Byzantine Empire. To the north, by contrast, the gathering of the Russian lands was being achieved under the leadership of Muscovy. Map XIX, The Growth of Muscovy, depicts this unifying process to the end of Ivan III's reign in 1505.

Meanwhile developments comparable to those in Eurasia had been unfolding in the non-Eurasian world, though at a slower pace. The advent of agriculture and iron metallurgy in sub-Saharan Africa stimulated economic growth, commerce, and empire building (Map XX, African Empires and Trade Routes). In the Americas, agriculture was developed independently and most successfully, as reflected in the large number of plants that were domesticated. But the Americas suffered from isolation, so that iron metallurgy never reached the New World as it did sub-Saharan Africa from Eurasia. Nevertheless, the flourishing agriculture did provide a base for state structures comparable to those of sub-Saharan Africa, as shown in Map XXI, Amerindian Empires.

As a result of the historical evolution depicted in the above maps, the various regions of the world had reached varied levels of development by 1500, when the Europeans began their overseas expansion which for the first time brought all the regions into direct contact with each other. This disparity in development, as shown in Map XXII, Culture Areas of the World about 1500, is of basic historical significance, for it determined the course and speed of European expansion during the following centuries. The more retarded the overseas territories, the more swift and overwhelming the European intrusion, and, conversely, the more advanced the overseas territories, the more effective and prolonged their resistance to the Europeans.

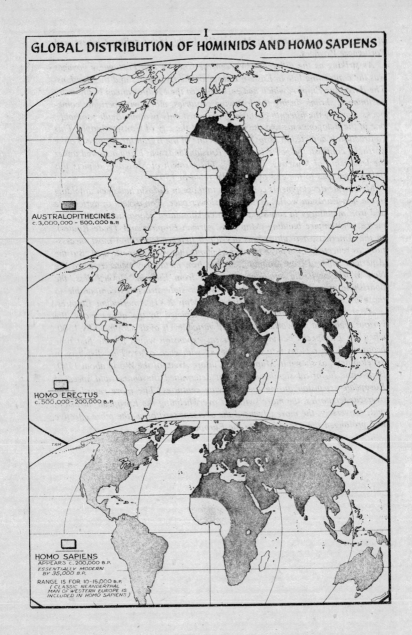

AUSTRALOPITHECINES
c. 3,000,000 – 500,000 B.P.

HOMO ERECTUS
c. 500,000 – 200,000 B.P.

TRM

HOMO SAPIENS
APPEARS c. 200,000 B.P.
ESSENTIALLY MODERN
BY 35,000 B.P.

RANGE IS FOR 10-15,000 B.P.
(CLASSIC NEANDERTHAL
MAN OF WESTERN EUROPE IS
INCLUDED IN HOMO SAPIENS)

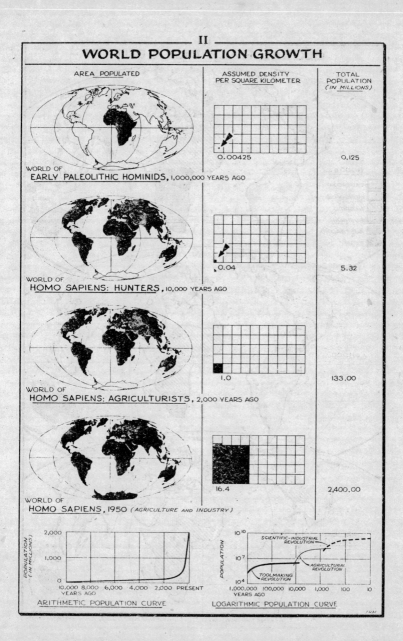

II
WORLD POPULATION GROWTH

AREA POPULATED	ASSUMED DENSITY PER SQUARE KILOMETER	TOTAL POPULATION (IN MILLIONS)
WORLD OF **EARLY PALEOLITHIC HOMINIDS**, 1,000,000 YEARS AGO	0.00425	0.125
WORLD OF **HOMO SAPIENS: HUNTERS**, 10,000 YEARS AGO	0.04	5.32
WORLD OF **HOMO SAPIENS: AGRICULTURISTS**, 2,000 YEARS AGO	1.0	133.00
WORLD OF **HOMO SAPIENS**, 1950 (AGRICULTURE AND INDUSTRY)	16.4	2,400.00

ARITHMETIC POPULATION CURVE

POPULATION (IN MILLIONS)
2,000
1,000
0
10,000 8,000 6,000 4,000 2,000 PRESENT
YEARS AGO

LOGARITHMIC POPULATION CURVE

POPULATION
10^10
10^7
10^4
1,000,000 100,000 10,000 1,000 100 10
YEARS AGO

SCIENTIFIC-INDUSTRIAL REVOLUTION
AGRICULTURAL REVOLUTION
TOOLMAKING REVOLUTION

183

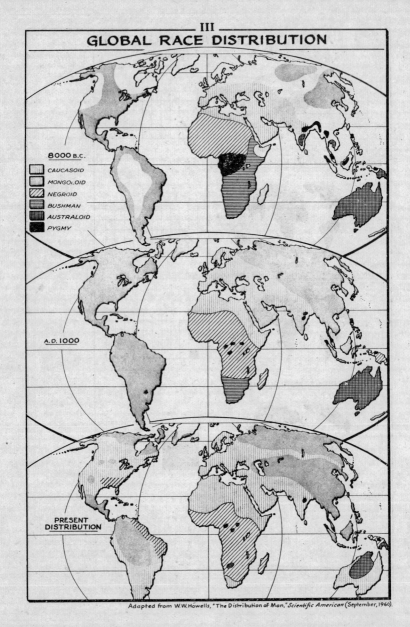

III
GLOBAL RACE DISTRIBUTION

8000 B.C.

☐ CAUCASOID
☐ MONGOLOID
☐ NEGROID
☐ BUSHMAN
☐ AUSTRALOID
■ PYGMY

A.D. 1000

PRESENT
DISTRIBUTION

Adapted from W.W.Howells, "The Distribution of Man," *Scientific American* (September, 1960).

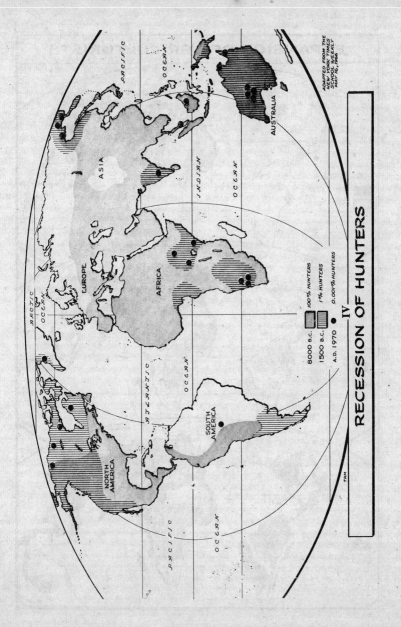

RECESSION OF HUNTERS

IV

8000 B.C. 100% HUNTERS
1500 B.C. 1% HUNTERS
A.D. 1970 0.001% HUNTERS

ADAPTED FROM THE
NEW YORK TIMES
SCHOOL WEEKLY
MAY 16, 1966

EXPANSION OF AGRICULTURISTS

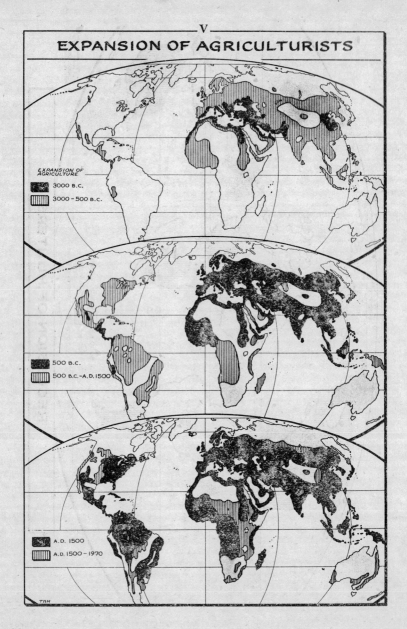

EXPANSION OF
AGRICULTURE

3000 B.C.

3000 - 500 B.C.

500 B.C.

500 B.C.-A.D. 1500

A.D. 1500

A.D. 1500 - 1970

TRH

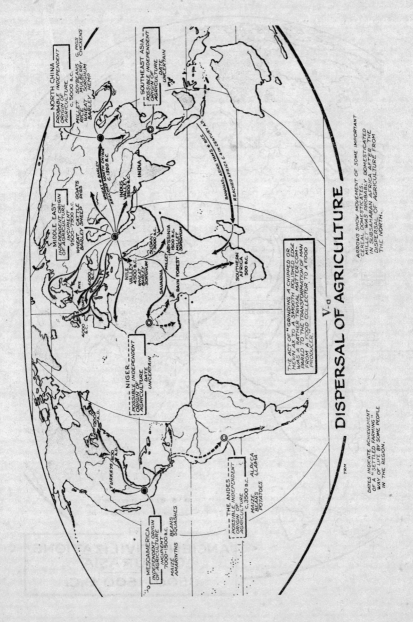

DISPERSAL OF AGRICULTURE

V-a

NORTH CHINA
PROBABLE INDEPENDENT
ORIGIN OF AGRICULTURE.
C. 5000 B.C.
MILLET
RICE
WHEAT
BARLEY
SOYBEANS
MULBERRY
HEMP
PIGS
CHICKENS

SOUTHEAST ASIA
POSSIBLE INDEPENDENT
ORIGIN OF
AGRICULTURE.
DATE
UNCERTAIN

MIDDLE EAST
INDEPENDENT ORIGIN
OF AGRICULTURE.
INCIPIENT
9500–7500 B.C.
WHEAT CATTLE GOATS
BARLEY SHEEP PIGS

INDIA

NIGER
POSSIBLE INDEPENDENT
ORIGIN OF
AGRICULTURE
DATE
UNCERTAIN

WHEAT NORTH CHINA
BARLEY C. 1300 B.C.

INDUS
VALLEY
3500 B.C.

NILE
VALLEY
4000
B.C.

WHEAT
BARLEY
SORGHUM

SUDAN

ABYSSINIA
3500 B.C.
MILLET
SORGHUM

SAVANNA

RAIN FOREST

SOUTHERN
AFRICA
500 B.C.

BANANAS, ASIAN YAMS & RICE A.D.
REACHED AFRICA C. 4TH CENTURY

**THE ACT OF "GRINDING A CHIPPED OR
HEWN AX TO A SMOOTH POLISHED EDGE
WAS A RATHER TRIVIAL MATTER COM-
PARED TO THE TRANSFORMATION OF MAN
FROM A FOOD COLLECTOR TO A FOOD
PRODUCER."**

MESOAMERICA
INDEPENDENT ORIGIN
OF AGRICULTURE
7000–1500 B.C.
MAIZE AMARANTHS
BEANS
SQUASHES

THE ANDES
POSSIBLE INDEPENDENT
ORIGIN OF
AGRICULTURE
3300 B.C.
MAIZE ALPACA
BEANS LLAMA
POTATOES

TURKEYS 1500 A.D.

1500 B.C.

DATES INDICATE ACHIEVEMENT
OF A SETTLED FARMING
WAY OF LIFE BY SOME PEOPLE
IN THE REGION.

ARROWS SHOW MOVEMENT OF SOME IMPORTANT
CEREAL DOMESTICATES.
MILLET WAS PROBABLY DOMESTICATED
IN SUB-SAHARAN AFRICA AFTER THE
DISPERSAL OF AGRICULTURE FROM
THE NORTH.

TRM

187

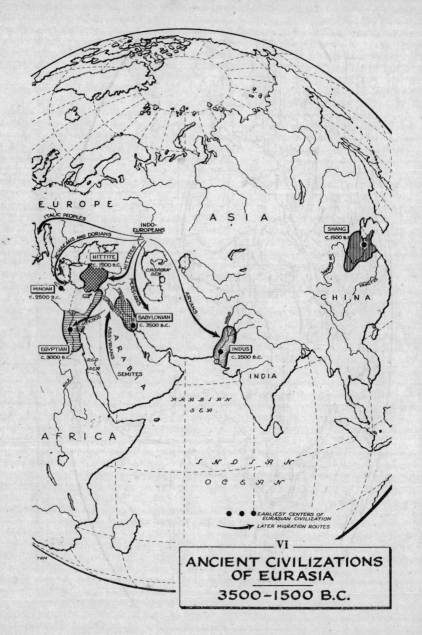

EUROPE

ASIA

ITALIC PEOPLES

ACHAEANS AND DORIANS

INDO-EUROPEANS

SHANG
c. 1500 B.C.

HITTITE
c. 1500 B.C.

HITTITES

CASPIAN SEA

MINOAN
c. 2500 B.C.

PERSIANS

ARYANS

CHINA

BABYLONIAN
c. 3500 B.C.

HYKSOS

ASSYRIANS

INDUS
c. 2500 B.C.

INDUS

EGYPTIAN
c. 3000 B.C.

RED SEA

ARABIA

NILE

SEMITES

INDIA

ARABIAN SEA

AFRICA

INDIAN OCEAN

● ● ● EARLIEST CENTERS OF
       EURASIAN CIVILIZATION
⟶   LATER MIGRATION ROUTES

VI
ANCIENT CIVILIZATIONS
OF EURASIA
3500–1500 B.C.

TRM

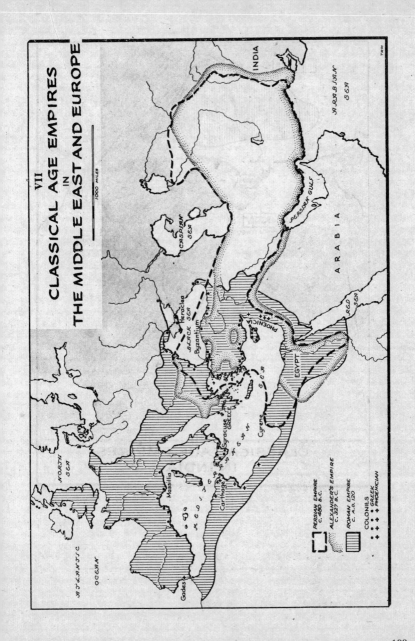

CLASSICAL AGE EMPIRES
IN
THE MIDDLE EAST AND EUROPE

VII

1000 MILES

PERSIAN EMPIRE
c. 400 B.C.

ALEXANDER'S EMPIRE
c. 327 B.C.

ROMAN EMPIRE
c. A.D. 120

COLONIES
• • • GREEK
+ + + PHOENICIAN

ATLANTIC OCEAN

NORTH SEA

Gades

Massilia

Carthage

Syracuse

GREECE

Byzantium

Heraclea

BLACK SEA

CASPIAN SEA

INDIA

ARABIA

PERSIAN GULF

RED SEA

EGYPT

PHOENICIA

Cyrene

MEDIT. SEA

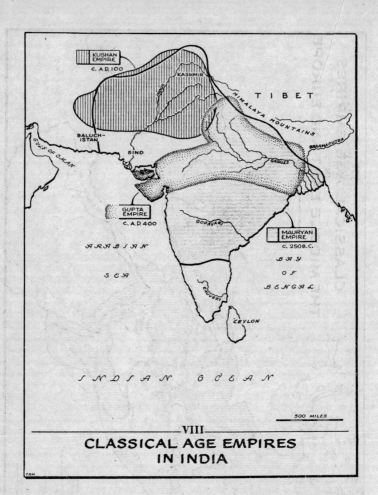

KUSHAN
EMPIRE
C. A.D. 100

KASHMIR

TIBET

HIMALAYA MOUNTAINS

BALUCH-
ISTAN

SIND

BRAHMAPUTRA

GANGES

GUPTA
EMPIRE
C. A.D. 400

GODAVARI

MAURYAN
EMPIRE.
C. 250 B.C.

ARABIAN

SEA

BAY

OF

BENGAL

CAUVERY

CEYLON

INDIAN OCEAN

500 MILES

VIII
CLASSICAL AGE EMPIRES
IN INDIA

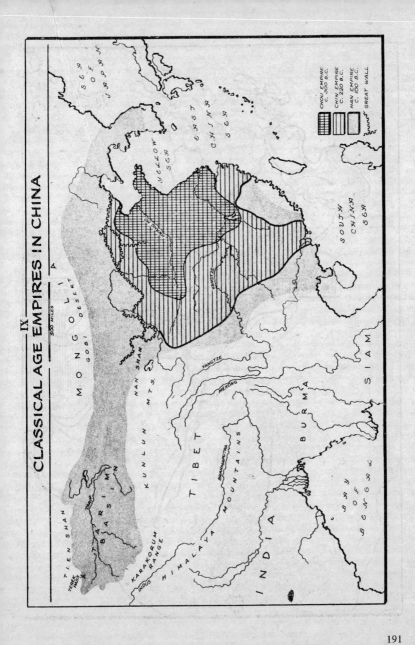

CLASSICAL AGE EMPIRES IN CHINA

IX

300 MILES

CHOU EMPIRE
C. 300 B.C.

CHIN EMPIRE
C. 220 B.C.

HAN EMPIRE
C. 100 B.C.

GREAT WALL

SEA OF JAPAN

EAST CHINA SEA

YELLOW SEA

SOUTH CHINA SEA

HWANG HO

YANGTZE

MONGOLIA

GOBI DESERT

TIEN SHAN

TARIM BASIN

TARIM

NAN SHAN

KUNLUN MTS.

KARAKORUM RANGE

INDUS

HIMALAYA MOUNTAINS

TIBET

BRAHMAPUTRA

YANGTZE

MEKONG

BURMA

SIAM

INDIA

BAY OF BENGAL

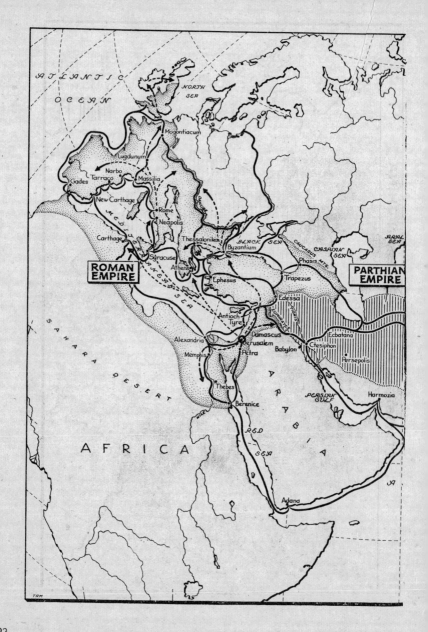

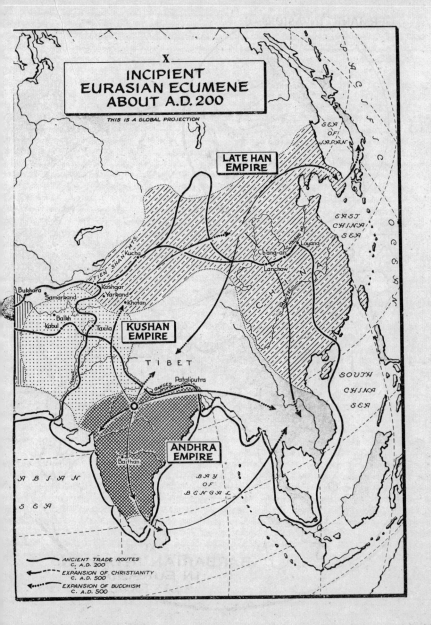

X

INCIPIENT
EURASIAN ECUMENE
ABOUT A.D. 200

THIS IS A GLOBAL PROJECTION

LATE HAN
EMPIRE

SEA
OF
JAPAN

PACIFIC

EAST
CHINA
SEA

TIEN SHAN MTS.

Kucha

C'hang-an

Loyang

Kashgar

C H I N A

Bukhara

Samarkand

Yarkand

Khotan

Lanchow

Huang Ho

Balkh

Kabul

Taxila

KUSHAN
EMPIRE

T I B E T

GANGES

Pataliputra

SOUTH
CHINA
SEA

Yangtze

ANDHRA
EMPIRE

Baithan

ARABIAN

SEA

BAY
OF
BENGAL

OCEAN

ANCIENT TRADE ROUTES
C. A.D. 200
EXPANSION OF CHRISTIANITY
C. A.D. 500
EXPANSION OF BUDDHISM
C. A.D. 500

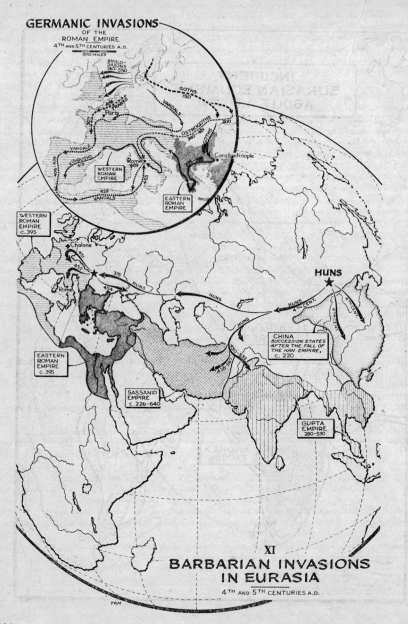

GERMANIC INVASIONS
OF THE
ROMAN EMPIRE
4TH AND 5TH CENTURIES A.D.
500 MILES

ANGLO-
SAXONS
367-550

GOTHS
150

VANDALS

Paris

OSTROGOTHS
340-485

GOTHS
200

VANDALS

VISIGOTHS

Rome
489

Constantinople

WESTERN
ROMAN
EMPIRE

429

VANDALS

EASTERN
ROMAN
EMPIRE

WESTERN
ROMAN
EMPIRE
c. 395

Chalons
451

452

Rome

454

HUNS

378

HUNS

HUNS

HUNS

HUNS

HUNS

4TH CENT.

4TH CENT.

HUNS

EASTERN
ROMAN
EMPIRE
c. 395

CHINA
SUCCESSION STATES
AFTER THE FALL OF
THE HAN EMPIRE,
c. 220

SASSANID
EMPIRE
c. 226-640

428-561

532

GUPTA
EMPIRE
280-530

XI
BARBARIAN INVASIONS
IN EURASIA
4TH AND 5TH CENTURIES A.D.

TRM

CONTINUED BARBARIAN INVASIONS IN THE WEST

9TH AND 10TH CENTURIES

500 MILES

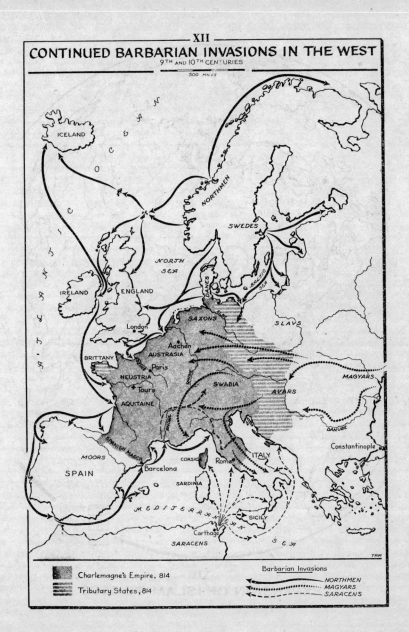

ICELAND

NORTHMEN

SWEDES

NORTH SEA

BALTIC SEA

IRELAND

ENGLAND

London

DANES

SAXONS

SLAVS

BRITTANY

Aachen

AUSTRASIA

NEUSTRIA

Paris

Tours

SWABIA

AVARS

MAGYARS

AQUITAINE

DANUBE

SPANISH MARCH

ITALY

Constantinople

MOORS

Barcelona

CORSICA

Rome

SPAIN

SARDINIA

MEDITERRANEAN

SICILY

Carthage

SARACENS

SEA

Charlemagne's Empire, 814

Tributary States, 814

Barbarian Invasions

NORTHMEN

MAGYARS

SARACENS

TRM

XIII
EXPANSION OF ISLAM TO 1500

EUROPE

HUNGARY

RUSSIAN
STATES

Kiev

Vladimir

*KHANATE OF
KIPCHAK*
GOLDEN HORDE

Sarai

Constantinople

GREAT SIBERIAN

Karakorum

Shangtu

Khanbaligh

*KHANATE OF
THE GREAT KHAN*

*KHANATE OF
CHAGHADAI*

Samarkand

Kashgar

CHINA

Foochow

Baghdad

*KHANATE OF
PERSIA*
ILKHAN

Balkh

TIBET

ARABIA

Mecca

RED SEA

INDIA

AFRICA

ARABIAN
SEA

INDIAN
OCEAN

TRM

XIV
MONGOL EMPIRE
AT THE DEATH OF KUBLAI KHAN
1294

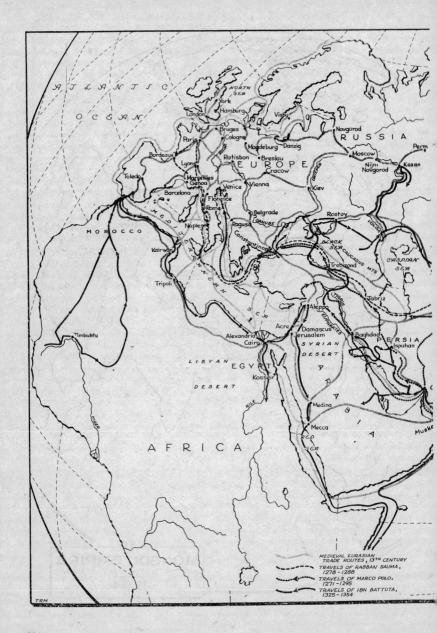

MEDIEVAL EURASIAN
TRADE ROUTES, 13TH CENTURY

TRAVELS OF RABBAN SAUMA,
1278 – 1288

TRAVELS OF MARCO POLO,
1271 – 1295

TRAVELS OF IBN BATTUTA,
1325 – 1354

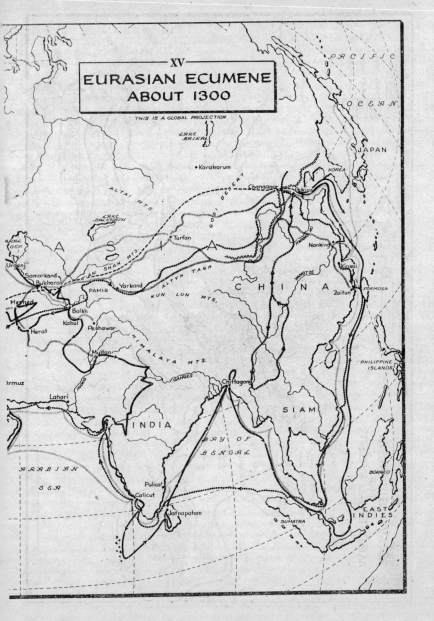

XV

EURASIAN ECUMENE
ABOUT 1300

THIS IS A GLOBAL PROJECTION

PACIFIC

OCEAN

JAPAN

LAKE BAIKAL

• Karakorum

KOREA

ALTAI MTS.

GOBI DESERT

Changanor

Peking

LAKE BALKHASH

A   S   I   A

Turfan

TIAN SHAN MTS.

Nanking

YANGTZE

ARAL SEA

Urgenj

Samarkand
Bukhara

Yarkand

ALTYN TAGH

KUN LUN MTS.

CHINA

FORMOSA

Kinsai

Zaitun

PAMIR

Meshed

Balkh

Kabul

Peshawar

Herat

HIMALAYA MTS.

PHILIPPINE
ISLANDS

Multan

Ormuz

Lahari

INDUS

GANGES

Chittagong

SIAM

INDIA

BAY OF BENGAL

ARABIAN

SEA

Pulicat

Calicut

BORNEO

Jafnapatam

EAST
INDIES

SUMATRA

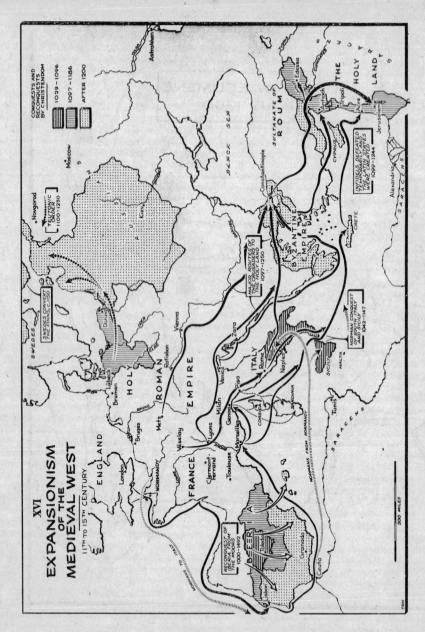

XVI

EXPANSIONISM
OF THE
MEDIEVAL WEST

11TH TO 15TH CENTURY

CONQUESTS AND
RECONQUESTS
BY CHRISTENDOM

1029 - 1096
1097 - 1186
AFTER 1200

TEUTONIC
ORDER
1100-1250

SWEDES CONQUER
THE FINNS, c.1150

INFIDELS DEFEATED
TEMPORARILY AND
LATIN KINGDOMS
WERE CREATED
1099-1244

MAJOR ROUTES OF
THE CRUSADERS TO
1097-1250

NORMAN CONQUEST
OF SOUTH ITALY
AND SICILY
1042-1147

RECONQUEST OF
IBERIA FROM
THE MOORS
1000-1492

500 MILES

ENGLAND

HOLY ROMAN EMPIRE

FRANCE

ITALY

IBERIA

THE HOLY LAND

BYZANTINE EMPIRE

SULTANATE OF ROUM

SARACENS

London · Bruges · Metz · Ratisbon · Vienna · Bremen · Lubeck · Danzig · Novgorod · Moscow · Astrakhan · Kiev

Rhine · Elbe · Oder · Volga · Dnieper · Danube

Lyons · Vézelay · Clermont-Ferrand · Toulouse · Marseilles · Genoa · Milan · Venice · Pisa · Zara · Rome · Naples · Sardinia · Corsica · Malta · Sicily · Crete · Cyprus

Constantinople · Black Sea · Euphrates · Tigris · Edessa · Antioch · Tripoli · Acre · Jerusalem · Alexandria

Granada · Toledo · Ceuta · Tunis

NORMANS FROM NORMANDY · NORMANS TO ITALY

TRH

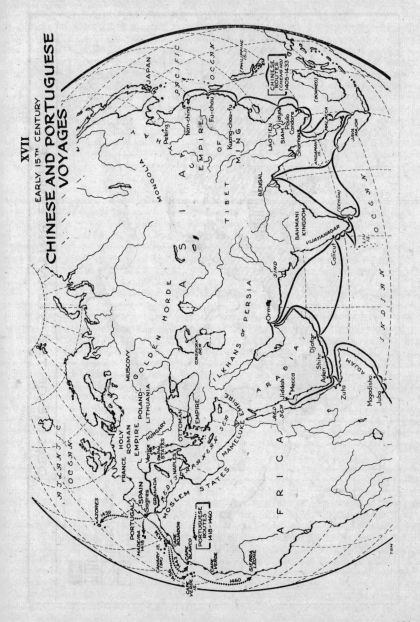

XVII

EARLY 15TH CENTURY

CHINESE AND PORTUGUESE VOYAGES

CHINESE ROUTES (CHENG HO) 1405–1433

PORTUGUESE ROUTES 1418–1460

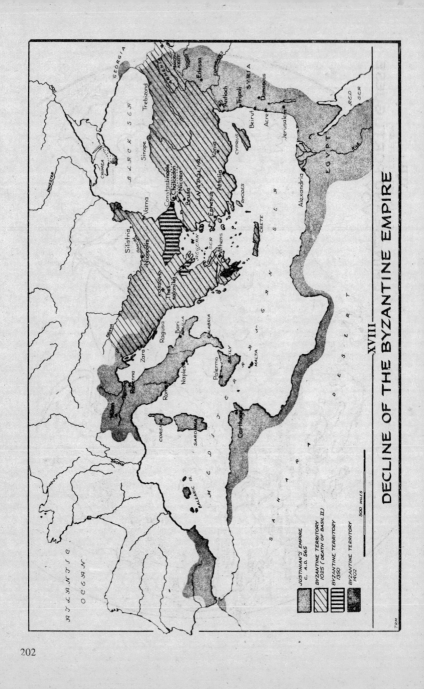

DECLINE OF THE BYZANTINE EMPIRE

XVIII

JUSTINIAN'S EMPIRE
c. A.D. 565

BYZANTINE TERRITORY
1025 (DEATH OF BASIL II)

BYZANTINE TERRITORY
1360

BYZANTINE TERRITORY
1402

500 MILES

XIX
THE GROWTH OF MUSCOVY

ARCTIC OCEAN

WHITE SEA

Archangel

GULF OF BOTHNIA

LAKE LADOGA

GULF OF FINLAND

Kargopol

Ustyug

Perm

Novgorod

Vologda

Nijnii Novgorod

BALTIC SEA

Riga

Tver

Moscow

Smolensk

Kaluga

Samara

Minsk

Pensa

Warsaw

NIEMEN

Lemberg

Kiev

Kursk

Voronezh

DNIEPER

CARPATHIAN MTS.

DNIESTER

Sarai

URAL

DON

VOLGA

DANUBE

BLACK SEA

CAUCASUS MTS.

CASPIAN SEA

Constantinople

URAL MOUNTAINS

PECHORA

OB

DVINA

VOLGA

OKA

500 MILES

MUSCOVY IN 1300

MUSCOVY, EXPANSION, 1300-1462

MUSCOVY, EXPANSION, 1462-1505

TRM

203

AFRICAN EMPIRES AND TRADE ROUTES

TRADE
ROUTES

DONKEY
CARAVANS

CAMEL
CARAVANS

HEAD
PORTERAGE

LESSER
HEAD PORTERAGE

PORTUGUESE
CARAVELS

ARABIAN
DHOWS

GHANA EMPIRE
EARLY
11TH CENT.

MALI EMPIRE
14TH CENT.

SONGHAI EMPIRE
EARLY
16TH CENT.

TO INDIA & CHINA

TO INDIA & CHINA

1000 MILES

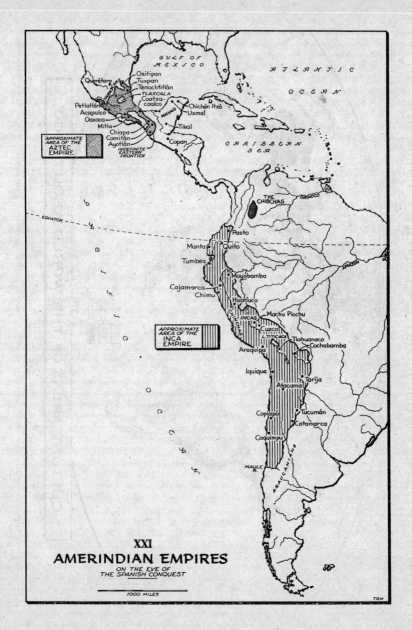

GULF OF MEXICO

ATLANTIC OCEAN

Querétaro
Oxitipan
Tuxpan
Tenochtitlán
TLAXCALA
Coatza-coalco
Chichén Itzá
Petlatlán
Acapulco
Uxmal
Oaxaca
MAYAS
Mitla
Tikal
Chiapa
Comitán
Ayotlán
Copan
INDEFINITE EASTERN FRONTIER

APPROXIMATE AREA OF THE AZTEC EMPIRE

CARIBBEAN SEA

THE CHIBCHAS
ORINOCO

EQUATOR

Pasto
Manta
Quito
Tumbez
Moyobamba
Cajamarca
Chimu
Huanuco
Machu Picchu
INCAS
Cuzco
L. TITICACA
Tiahuanaco
Cochabamba
Arequipa
Iquique
Atacama
Tarija
Copiapó
Tucumán
Catamarca
Coquimpu

APPROXIMATE AREA OF THE INCA EMPIRE

MAULE R.

ARAUCANIANS

XXI
AMERINDIAN EMPIRES
ON THE EVE OF THE SPANISH CONQUEST

1000 MILES

TRM

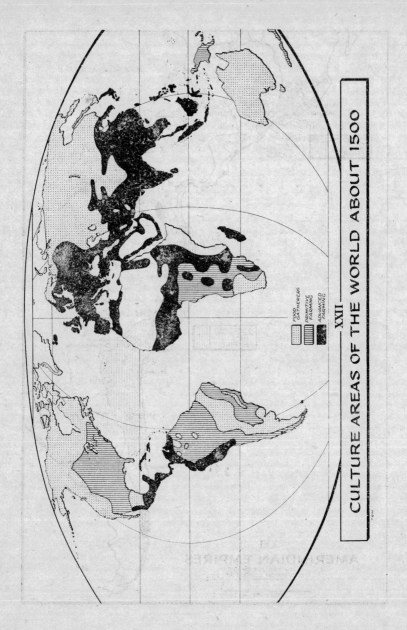

FOOD
GATHERERS

PRIMITIVE
FARMING

ADVANCED
FARMING

XXII

CULTURE AREAS OF THE WORLD ABOUT 1500

All in all, the invasions gave the coup de grace to a culture which had come to a standstill after reaching its apogee and seemed doomed to wither away. We are reminded of the cruel bombings in our own day which destroyed ramshackle old buildings and so made possible the reconstruction of towns on more modern lines.

ROBERT LOPEZ

Chapter

11

End of Classical

Civilizations

The great civilizations of Greece, Rome, India, and China dominated the Eurasian ecumene in classical times. Yet in the end, the nomads and pastoralists of the frontier regions overran these civilizations and fundamentally altered the course of global history. Beneath the seeming invulnerability of the empires lay roots of decline that invariably brought on decay and eventual disintegration. Technological stagnation and arrested productivity combined to expose the classical civilizations to the onslaught of the barbarians from the third to the sixth centuries.

The effect of the nomadic invasions varied from region to region. Northern China and northern India were overrun but retained their distinctive civilizations. Southern China and southern India escaped invasion because of their remoteness. Byzantium and Persia proved powerful enough to repel the invaders. The West, however, suffered repeated and protracted incursions by Germans, Huns, Moslems, Magyars, and Vikings, so that the old order was uprooted to a degree unequalled anywhere else in Eurasia. Ironically, however, this destruction was a primary reason for the primacy of the West in modern times, for a new civilization was able to emerge out of the ashes of the old, a civilization better adapted to the demands of a changing world. The purpose of this chapter is to describe the significance and decline of the classical civilizations and to determine how and why the West started on the road to global dominance.

I. HISTORICAL SIGNIFICANCE OF CLASSICAL CIVILIZATIONS

The classical civilizations, like the preceding ancient civilizations, were by definition founded on class differentiation. They rested in the final analysis on the labor of peasant masses that furnished the surplus that supported the ruling elites.

Despite differences in detail, the overall social structure of the various Eurasian civilizations was similar. At the head of each was the ruling king or emperor. Next came the nobility and top officials—Roman senators, Iranian warrior-nobles, Indian princes, and Chinese marquises and Grand Administrators. Another privileged group in all civilizations was the priestly hierarchy —Indian Brahmans, Iranian magi, Christian priests, and the secularist Confucian literati. Traders and merchant enterprisers were also present everywhere, carrying on manufacturing, mining, wholesale and retail trade, organized transportation, and moneylending. Finally at the bottom of the pyramid, and comprising the great majority of the total population, were the workers in agriculture and the crafts. Some were free; others were serfs or slaves, with the proportion varying according to region and period.

Greece at first was an exception to this general pattern, consisting of small city-states with elected magistrates, and governments based on citizen assemblies and councils. Herodotus made clear the contrast between these republican city-states and the contemporary Persian Empire with its autocratic monarch and its satraps appointed from the center as governors of provinces. But this Greek exception proved short-lived. It is true that Xerxes failed to conquer Greece, and that Alexander instead conquered Persia, but this did not represent a victory for the Greek city-states. Alexander and his successors adopted the manners, methods, and institutions of the Persian autocracy. Likewise in Rome the republic gave way to autocratic emperors who created a vast imperial bureaucracy on models derived from Egypt and Persia via the Hellenistic kingdom. By the time of Constantine, the Roman Empire bore a far greater resemblance to the Persian Empire than it did to Periclean Athens or Cicero's Rome.

Inextricably bound up with this social stratification was economic stratification. Everywhere there was gross inequity in the distribution of wealth. Everywhere the privileged lived in provocative luxury as contrasted with the poverty and misery of the rural and urban workers. The following passage from an essay written in Han China in the first century A.D. is typical of abundant contemporary testimony regarding the plight of the peasantry in the classical civilizations:

> The gambler came upon a farmer clearing away weeds. He had a straw hat on his head and a hoe in his hand. His face was black, his hands and feet were covered with callouses, his skin was as rough as mulberry bark and his feet resembled bear's paws. He crouched in the fields, his sweat mixing with the mud. The gambler said to him, 'You cultivate the fields

in oppressive summer heat. Your back is encrusted with salt, your legs look like burnt stumps, your skin is like leather, that cannot be pierced by an awl. You hobble along on misshapen feet and painful legs. Shall I call you a plant or a tree? Yet you can move your body and limbs. Shall I call you a bird or a beast? Yet you possess a human face. What a fate to be born with such base qualities.' [1]

This grinding poverty of the great majority may be compared with the affluence of the well-to-do, as depicted in the following account adapted from a contemporary source of the Han period:

Opulent families lived in multi-storeyed houses, built with intersecting cross-beams and rafters that were richly carved and decorated on all visible surfaces. . . . In the inner rooms of the house the beds were carefully furnished with wooden fittings cut from the choicest timber; fine embroideries were hung up as drapes, and screens were set to overlap each other and ensure privacy. There was a shocking profusion of fine silk among the rich . . . . the wealthier classes wore choice furs of squirrel or fox, and wild duck plumes . . . . it was quite a common thing at a banquet to be regaled with one dish after another, with roasts and minced fish; kid, quails and oranges; pickles and other relishes. . . .

Naturally the rich families needed adequate means of transport up and down Ch'ang-an's streets [capital of Han Empire], and you could see their carriages drawn up in rows, gleaming in silver or gold and fitted with every sort of gadget. The horses themselves were neatly decked and shod, and caparisoned with breastplates and pendant jewelry. They were kept in check by means of gilt or painted bits, with golden or inlaid bridles. . . . With these extravagances there should be borne in mind the comparative cost of keeping the horses alive, as a single animal consumed as much grain as an ordinary family of six members.

There was no shortage of entertainment for the rich, who would amuse themselves looking at performing animals, tiger-fights and foreign girls. Musical performances were no longer restricted to special occasions such as folk festivals, and the tunes and dances were far more sophisticated than they had been in the past. Rich families now kept their own five-piece orchestras with bells and drums, and their house choirs. . . . [2]

Two very different standards of living inevitably meant two very different cultures within each civilization. Neolithic cultural homogeneity had given way with the advent of the ancient civilizations to the low culture of the villages and the high culture of the schools, temples, and palaces of the cities. (See Chapter 6, section I.) This bifurcation continued in the classical civilizations, with the core of all the Eurasian high cultures now being the "sacred books"— the Iranian Zend-Avesta, the Indian Vedas, the Buddhist Canon, the Chinese Classics, and the Christian Old and New Testaments. Since these texts were the basis of knowledge, they dominated education. This was often carried to the point of wholesale memorization and arid scholasticism. The Chinese examination, the Indian debate, and the Hebrew and Christian colloquies between masters and pupils, all tested students' mastery of an approved body of learning.

The sacred books also were used to inculcate loyalty and obedience. Repudiation of official teachings or challenge to the social order were branded as crimes punishable in this world and in the next. The "hells" which were so prominent in all high cultures were eternal concentration camps for those who dared resist their secular or religious leaders. Normally this threat of punishment in the afterlife effectively buttressed the *status quo*, though peasant wit everywhere suggests that not all were unquestioning believers. "There are three blood suckers in this world," runs a north Indian proverb, "the flea, the bug, and the Brahman."

Low culture in the classical civilizations remained essentially the same as in the ancient civilizations. There was the same body of lore related to the everyday occupations in the fields, workshops, and homes. And to appease or control the feared supernatural forces, there were everywhere similar rites, rituals, and superstitions that had little relationship to the official religions professed by the high cultures. In India, for example, the peasantry was unaware of the lofty philosophical formulations of the Upanishads. But it was all too aware of cruel goblins, of vampires that ate raw flesh, and of spirits stalking the earth at night, vomiting fire, and devouring the putrefied flesh of corpses. Likewise a student of Chinese religions has observed that,

. . . . instead of dividing the religious life of the Chinese people into three compartments called Confucianism, Buddhism, and Taoism, it is far more accurate to divide it into two levels, the level of the masses and the level of the enlightened.

The masses worship thousands of idols and natural objects of ancient, Buddhist, Taoist, and other origins. . . . The enlightened, on the other hand, honor only Heaven, ancestors, and sometimes also Confucius, Buddha, Lao Tzu, and a few great historical beings, but not other spirits. . . . The masses believe in astrology, almanacs, dream interpretation, geomancy, witchcraft, phrenology, palmistry, the recalling of the soul, fortune-telling in all forms, charms, magic, and all varieties of superstitions. The enlightened are seldom contaminated by these diseases. The masses visit temples and shrines of all descriptions. The enlightened avoid these places, except the Temple of Heaven, ancestral halls, the Confucian temple and occasionally the temples of great historical personages. The ignorant regard religious ceremonies as magic; the enlightened regard them merely as pure form. The ignorant are fatalistic, believing that spirits have direct control over their fortunes and misfortunes; the enlightened are not believers in fate in this sense. . . . The ignorant people go to deities primarily to seek blessings, particularly those of children, wealth, and long life. The enlightened people worship not to seek favors, but to pay respect.[3]

In addition to this common class basis, the classical civilizations also shared a common durability and permanence. Despite the interaction amongst these civilizations, reflecting the new Eurasian ecumenism, the fact remains that they

A page from an early manuscript of a codification of Roman law made by the Visigothic king Alaric II. This page shows a barbarian king, a bishop, a count, and a duke. Codifications such as this one contributed to the preservation of the principles of Roman law. (Bibliothèque Nationale, Paris)

all retained their individuality during these centuries. There was no case of one dominating or imposing a permanent imprint on the other. The impact of Hellenism on the Middle East proved ephemeral, while Buddhism failed to displace Confucianism in China, and was Sinicized in the process.

The reason for this regional independence is that the agrarian-based civilizations of pre-modern times lacked the technical and economic resources for extending their control beyond their respective regions. Interregional hegemony was not feasible until the scientific and industrial revolutions of modern times, which were to provide the West with the power and the dynamism to overwhelm not only Eurasia but the entire globe. Since all the Eurasian civilizations had the same agricultural base, none of them had power and organization sufficiently superior to overcome the regional pride and self-consciousness that had developed everywhere. How strong this was can be seen in this case of a Chinese Buddhist monk, Hsüan-tsang, who spent the years from 629 to 645 visiting monasteries in India, and then decided to return to his country.

> The monks of Nalanda [monastery], when they heard of it, begged him to remain, saying: 'India is the land of Buddha's birth, and though he has left the world, there are still many traces of him. What greater happiness could there be than to visit them in turn, to adore him and chant his praises? Why then do you wish to leave, having come so far? Moreover China is a country of . . . unimportant barbarians, who despise the religious and the [Buddhist] Faith. That is why Buddha was not born there. The mind of the people is narrow, and their coarseness profound, hence neither sages nor saints go there. The climate is cold and the country rugged—you must think again.'

> The Master of the Law (the Chinese Buddhist) replied, 'Buddha established his doctrine so that it might be diffused to all lands. Who would wish to enjoy it alone, and to forget those who are not enlightened? Besides, in my country the magistrates are clothed with dignity, and the laws are everywhere respected. The emperor is virtuous and the subjects loyal, parents are loving and sons obedient, humanity and justice are highly esteemed, and old men and sages are held in honour. Moreover, how deep and mysterious is their knowledge; their wisdom equals that of spirits. They have taken the Heavens as their model, and they know how to calculate the movements of the Seven Luminaries; they have invented all kinds of instruments, fixed the seasons of the year. . . . How then can you say that Buddha did not go to my country because of its insignificance?' [4]

This incident makes clear why the individual classical civilizations have persisted to modern times. Only with the disruptive expansionism of the West did the philosophies and religions and social institutions of the Classical Age begin to give way in the various regions of Eurasia. And even so, they are still very much alive today, as demonstrated by the continued vitality of Roman law and of the Roman Catholic church in the West, and of Hinduism and of caste in India.

II. Roots of Decline

The classical civilizations were all able to preserve their identity because they all remained agricultural civilizations. Or, in other words, they all remained technologically stagnant through the millennia. John Maynard Keynes perceived and emphasized this immobility.

> The absence of important technological inventions between the prehistoric age and comparatively modern times is truly remarkable. Almost everything which really matters and which the world possessed at the commencement of the modern age was already known to man at the dawn of history. . . . At some epoch before the dawn of history . . . there must have been an era of progress and invention comparable to that in which we live today. But through the greater part of recorded history there was nothing of the kind.[5]

Keynes's observation is fully justified. The Neolithic age preceding civilization had been, in fact, remarkably precocious in its technology. It was then that man invented the wheeled cart, the sailboat, and the plow, discovered the chemical processes involved in metallurgy, worked out an accurate solar calendar, and learned how to harness the power of animals and of the wind. After the urban revolution, this headlong advance was arrested. During the following millennia only three discoveries were made that compared in significance with those of the earlier period. These were iron, the alphabet, and coinage. All three, significantly enough, were discovered not in the old centers of civilization along the Nile and the Tigris-Euphrates, but rather in peripheral and less constraining environs—the Caucasus frontier region and the Aegean commercial cities.

Apart from these three great inventions, the advances made at this time were based on the earlier discoveries, merely refining the skill with which they were used or increasing enormously the scale on which they were applied. In many cases even such modest gains remained unrealized, even though they would have yielded rich returns. For example, the ancient harness developed for use with oxen was applied to the horse in such a way that the animal could not pull without choking. The result was that at least two-thirds of the power of the horse was wasted. A sensible functional harness had to wait for the Middle Ages. Until then horse traction was suitable only for lighter loads; heavy loads were pulled by human beings. Witness the carvings showing the thousands of men engaged in pulling and hauling during the construction of the pyramids and the ziggurats. Another example was the water mill which made its appearance in Asia Minor and in China in the first century B.C. This invention was potentially a great labor saver in view of the many hours of tedious work by women and slaves in grinding corn. Yet water mills were not built in Rome until the fourth century, and even then they were comparatively rare.

Significantly enough, only war provided a motivating force sufficient to balance slightly the prevailing technological lethargy. The Greeks invented ingenious ratchet-equipped catapults and wheeled assault towers pulled by block and tackle, as well as the so-called "Greek fire," (8th century A.D.) a petroleum-based incendiary that proved efficient for setting fire to enemy ships and siege machinery. But these were obviously not wealth-producing and could not solve the basic economic problem of the old civilizations.

Since labor productivity was not raised by new inventions, wealth could be increased only by bringing new areas under cultivation, or by conquest and exploitation. But virgin lands were not limitless; indeed extensive fertile regions throughout the Mediterranean basin now were being eliminated as sources of food because of large-scale erosion that was becoming a serious problem. Likewise empires could not expand indefinitely, for there were strict limits beyond which they could not extend because of the level of their military technology. Thus a point of diminishing returns was inescapable when the pressure of burgeoning military and bureaucratic establishments became too much for the productive capacities. A vicious circle then set in, as noted above, particularly in the case of the fall of the Han and Roman empires concerning which more information is available. Rising taxes and increasing impoverishment fomented uprisings in the cities and countryside, which invited nomadic incursions and ultimately led to successful internal revolt or external invasion, or a combination of the two. Hence the cyclical nature of imperial history in pre-modern times. A historian, analyzing the decline of the Roman Empire, emphasized, in conclusion, technological backwardness:

> The Roman Empire, we must not forget, was technically more backward than the Middle Ages. In agriculture a two-field system of alternate crops and fallow was usually followed, and the potentially richest soils were little exploited. The horse collar had not been invented, so that oxen had to be employed for plowing and for carting. Water mills existed, but seem to have been relatively rare, and corn was generally ground by animals or by human labor in hand querns. Yet with this primitive technique, agriculture had to carry an ambitious superstructure far heavier than that of any medieval state. No medieval kingdom attempted, as did the Roman Empire, to support, as well as a landed aristocracy and the church, a professional standing army, and a salaried bureaucracy.[6]

In retrospect it is clear that the cycle could have been broken only by technological advances that would have provided the economic underpinnings necessary for the imperial edifices. But technology was moribund, and the basic reason was that the ruling establishments everywhere knew how to expropriate existing wealth but did not know how to create new capacity for producing more wealth. They were capable of siphoning off astonishingly large surpluses from their peasant subjects, as evident in the stupendous amounts of capital and labor invested in pyramids, ziggurats, cathedrals, and palaces. But technological innovation required something more than efficient organization and coercion, and all the agricultural civilizations failed to achieve this *something more*—which was why they remained agricultural.

The widespread presence of slavery was one reason for the technological standstill. It was usually simpler and cheaper to put slaves to work than to design and construct new machines. Thus the inventors of the time usually produced gadgets intended not to save labor but to amuse or to facilitate religious ritual. Hero of Alexandria in the first century A.D. used his knowledge of steam power to construct a device that opened temple doors. Likewise, in the same century, Emperor Vespasian in Rome forbade the use of a machine that would erect columns inexpensively, commenting, "Let me provide food for the common folk." Laudable though this sentiment might be, the fact remains that it made the cities of the classical empires parasites of the country rather than centers of productive industry.

Slavery also inhibited technology by fostering a negative attitude toward work. Since labor was the lot of the slaves, it came to be regarded as demeaning for any free citizen. Even in civilizations where slavery was not so prevalent, this attitude toward labor existed; witness the cult of the long fingernail in China. Sharp social stratification naturally promoted an upper-class contempt for work and workers, and slavery merely served to accentuate this attitude. As Aristotle wrote in his *Politics,* "in the best governed polis . . . the citizens may not lead either the life of craftsmen or of traders, for such a life is devoid of nobility and hostile to perfection of character." Likewise the Roman philosopher Seneca, in a letter to Lucilius in A.D. 65, expressed the same scorn for manual labor, which, he said, should be proffered with "bowed body and lowered eyes":

> Some things we know to have appeared only within our own memory; the use, for example, of glass windows which let in the full brilliance of day through a transparent pane, or the substructures of our baths and the pipes let into their walls to distribute heat and preserve an equal warmth above and below. . . . Or the shorthand which catches even the quickest speech, the hand keeping pace with the tongue. All these are the inventions of the meanest slaves. Philosophy sits more loftily enthroned: she doesn't train the hand, but is instructress of the spirit. . . . No, she's not, I say, an artisan producing tools for the mere everyday necessities.[7]

Precisely this isolation of the philosopher from the artisan arrested the technological growth of the Eurasian civilizations. It was the interaction between the two—the ordered speculation of the philosopher and the practical experience and traditional lore of the artisan—that enabled the West to achieve its great scientific and industrial revolutions in modern times, and thereby make its unique contribution to man's development. But such interaction proved impossible in the classical civilizations because of the sharp social cleavages and the resulting social attitudes. The lofty intellectual lacked interest and the depressed artisan lacked incentive.

This technological stagnation explains the cyclical nature of Eurasian imperial history during the pre-modern millennia. Empires rose and fell in a basically similar pattern. None was able to break through to a new level of development. Hence the repetitive cycles in contrast to the dynamism of modern industrialized societies. W. W. Rostow has described as follows this common feature of the agricultural civilizations prior to Britain's epochal and pioneering 'take-off" with her industrial revolution.

> . . . limitations of technology decreed a ceiling beyond which they could not penetrate. They did not lack inventiveness and innovations, some of

high productivity. But they did lack a systematic understanding of their physical environment capable of making invention a more or less regular current flow, rather than a stock of *ad hoc* achievements inherited from the past. . . .

It followed from this productivity ceiling that food production absorbed 75 per cent or more of the working force and that a high proportion of income above minimum consumption levels was spent in non-productive or low-productive outlays: religious and other monuments, wars, high living for those who controlled land rents; and for poorer folk there was beggar-thy-neighbor struggle for land or the dissipation of the occasional surplus in an expensive wedding or funeral. Social values were geared to the limited horizons which men could perceive to be open to them; and social structures tended to hierarchy. . . .[8]

III. Barbarian Invasions

The period from the third to the sixth centuries was one of Eurasia-wide invasions comparable to the bronze and iron invasions of the second millennium B.C. And just as the earlier invasions effectuated the transition from the ancient to the classical civilizations, so these later invasions ended the classical civilizations and heralded the medieval. (See Map XI, "Barbarian Invasions in Eurasia, 4th–5th Centuries A.D.")

The general direction of nomadic movement was from east to west because of the geographic steppe gradient—the lure that the better watered and more fertile lands of the western steppes held for the nomads of the east. (See Chapter 6, section II.) The main invasion routes followed the corridor of grassland that stretched across Central Eurasia, beginning in the environs of Peking and ending in the Hungarian plains of Central Europe. This is why so many of these nomadic peoples ended their wanderings in present-day Hungary, which they made their base for raids into the surrounding European countries.

A basic factor behind the invasions was the constantly increasing interaction between the nomads and the surrounding centers of civilization. In many of these centers, nomads were used as slave or mercenary soldiers, a practice that frequently proved the entering wedge for either a military coup in the imperial capital or for an invasion by the fellow-tribesmen of the barbarian mercenaries. Another factor was the gradual settling down of nomadic peoples, often in regions adjacent to imperial frontiers. This shift from nomadism to agriculture normally led to population growth and greater economic and military strength, which invariably was used if imperial weakness held out the promise of success. Invasions also were often the end result of a lengthy shock transmission process. A defeat before the Great Wall of China or the formation of an aggressive tribal confederacy in Mongolia frequently deflected the train of nomadic buffer shocks westward, culminating eventually in nomadic incursions across the Oxus or Danube or Rhine rivers.

Because of the Eurasia-wide scope of the invasions, a great variety of peoples were involved. Han China, Gupta India, and Sassanian Iran usually were assaulted by Turco-Mongols, often referred to as Huns. But the Roman Em-

Terracotta mounted figure from Central Asia dating from the Hunnic period. This statue, from a private collection in Paris, possibly represents the Hunnic leader Attila himself. (Arborio Mella)

The Oseberg longship, excavated in 1904, is the best preserved Viking ship in the world and is on display in the Viking Ship Museum in Oslo, Norway. (Norwegian National Travel Office)

pire, being at the western terminal of the invasion route, was the object of attack, at one time or another, of all the peoples along that route, as well as of surrounding barbarians. The procession included assorted Germanic tribes, Iranians, Balto-Slavs, and Vikings, as well as the Turco-Mongols.

The outcome of the invasions varied as much as their personnel. In China, the Han Empire finally succumbed to Turco-Mongol invaders in A.D. 222. Three separate kingdoms emerged, Wei, north of the Yangtze, Wu, in the south, and Shu, in the west. After decades of warfare, Wei defeated its rivals and established in 265 a new dynasty, the Chin. This dynasty ruled all China until 316, when a new wave of invaders overran the entire northern half of the country. The Chin court fled south to Nanking, whence it ruled the Yangtze Valley and those regions of the south settled by the Chinese. China remained divided in two in this manner until finally reunited by the Sui dynasty in 589.

These centuries are called by Chinese historians the "Age of Confusion." The southern half of the country was ruled by a succession of Chinese kings, while the northern part was governed by assorted Turco-Mongol conquerors. The Chinese considered the southern kings to be the legitimate heirs to the Han dynasty and denied the title Emperor to the northern rulers. In reality both halves of the country during these centuries were usually fragmented. But it was northern China that suffered the most disruption, being exposed to the long succession of barbarian invasions. "Under their impact," observes one authority, "a pastoral economy might conceivably have replaced the agricultural economy of North China, and Altaic language might have taken the place of the Chinese." [9]

The West Roman Empire under similar circumstances did undergo, as we shall see, such a basic transformation. But North China was saved, primarily because the native Chinese population so greatly outnumbered the nomadic invaders. The north at that time was still by far the most populous part of the country, and therefore was able to absorb the nomadic influx without undergoing radical change. In fact large numbers of Chinese migrated from north to south during these troubled centuries to escape the barbarian ravages, so that not only did the north remain Chinese, but the south was substantially Sinicized. Thus with reunification of the entire country by the Sui dynasty in 589, China resumed her normal course, as distinctively Chinese as during the Han period.

Turning to India, the invasions there occurred much later, for the Gupta Empire was at its height when China already was beset with her "Age of Confusion." During the fifth century, however, the eastern branch of the Huns, or the "White Huns" as they are called, crossed the Oxus River and drove south to India, while the western branch advanced over the Russian steppes to Europe. Under the impact of the Hun onslaught the Gupta Empire disintegrated during the first half of the sixth century. Very little is known of events during the remainder of the century, so that it may be presumed that there was much strife and probably further invasions.

The veil of obscurity lifted briefly during the first half of the seventh century when a feudatory ruler, Harsha, succeeded by a combination of diplomacy and force of arms in uniting most of northern India. His empire was loosely organized, however, consisting of powerful independent monarchs who recognized his suzerainty more as a personal homage than as subordination to imperial authority. Thus with Harsha's death in 647, after a brilliant reign of forty-one years, his ramshackle structure fell to pieces. Once more the veil of obscurity descended upon India, and remained down until the thirteenth century when the Moslem Turks appeared and gradually imposed their rule over most of the country.

The intervening several centuries were marked by recurring invasions and disunity. No empires emerged with bureaucratic organization like that of the Maurya or Gupta. Instead there were transitory clan supremacies or kingdoms based upon individual personalities. Also there were migrations into India on a large enough scale to form new cultural and social groups. An outstanding example is that of the Rajputs, a sturdy and brave people who gave their name to the area known as Rajputana in northwest India. They were a military aristocracy who were soon absorbed into the Hindu caste of Kshatriyas, or warriors. They became intensely proud of their Hinduism and for some time dominated north and central India. In fact they remained prominent to the nineteenth century, and to a degree even to the present.

Their experience is significant because it helps explain why India, despite the long centuries of turmoil and invasions, was not fundamentally changed. The newcomers were assimilated into the prevailing caste system, so that it was much more a case of their adapting to India's civilization than the other way around. Thus India, like China, emerged from her time of troubles with the civilization that she had evolved during classical times modified but not transformed.

IV. Germans and Huns in the West

In Europe, however, the pattern of events was precisely the opposite; there it was transformation rather than modification. The most numerous invaders in that region of Eurasia were the Germans who occupied the Central and East European lands from the Baltic to the Danube, and from the Rhine to the Russian plains. They were organized in tribes, amongst the more important being the Franks, Vandals, Lombards, and the Ostrogoths and Visigoths. All shared the same general religious beliefs and institutions, and all spoke closely related dialects, so that they could understand each other. Fortunately for the Romans, however, they had little consciousness of unity. They were as ready to fight against each other as against the Romans, thus enabling the Roman Empire to survive as long as it did.

The institutions and customs of these Germanic peoples require attention, for they were destined to comprise a basic element in the new civilization that was to emerge in the West after the fall of Rome. The contemporary Roman historian, Tacitus, described the Germans as a cattle people who rated their wealth by the number of their animals. Cattle rustling, in fact, was a major cause for strife amongst them. The Franks who had settled along the Rhine, had made the greatest advance from the pastoralist stage to the agricultural. Consequently they had increased most rapidly in numbers and general strength, in contrast, for example, to the Visigoths along the lower Danube who remained more dependent on their herds. This, however, gave them greater mobility, which compensated, at least initially, for their smaller numbers.

The social organization of these tribes consisted of three main elements.

At the top were the nobles who were usually hereditary and who were the large landholders. Most Germans were freemen who customarily owned their own plots of land. Those who did not were obliged to work for the nobles as sharecroppers. At the bottom was a class of men neither free nor slaves. They were bound to the land but could not be sold apart from it. This form of bondage, similar to that of the Roman *colonus,* was the source of the institution of serfdom that prevailed in Western Europe in medieval times.

The main source of authority in these tribes was the assembly of freemen. It selected the king, if there was one, and also the military leader for each campaign. Tacitus noted that the Germans usually chose their kings on the basis of inheritance, but their war chiefs by their valor and ability on the battlefield. The chief weapon was a long, straight, double-edged sword with a broad point, and was used for slashing rather than thrusting. Young men were given the right to carry a sword after solemn rites that were the origin of the later medieval ceremony by which a squire was raised to knighthood. Each outstanding warrior leader had a retinue of young followers, or *comitatus,* who fought beside him in battle and owed him loyalty and obedience. In return the chief provided arms and subsistence as well as a share of the war booty. This institution contributed to the later system of feudalism, which was based on the loyalty of knights to their feudal lords.

Tacitus described the Germans as great eaters, heavy drinkers, and confirmed gamblers. On the other hand he praised their high moral standards, which he held up as a model for his fellow Romans. He also stressed their hospitality as universal and unstinted. During the winter season groups would go from house to house, staying at each until the owner's supplies were exhausted. This is reminiscent of the later medieval arrangement by which a king or noble was entitled, as a part of his feudal dues, to so many days of entertainment for himself and his entourage. The general cultural level of these Germans is suggested by the fact that they knew how to weave and to make metal implements and wheeled vehicles, but did not know how to write.

Such were the people who began to press upon the imperial frontiers as early as the first century B.C. At that time the Roman legions were strong enough to hold the line with little difficulty. But with the decline of the empire the army also weakened and the Romans were hard pressed to maintain control. They resorted to diplomacy to play off one tribe against another, and they also accepted, since they had no choice, the settlement of whole bands of German warriors on the Roman side of the border in return for their aid against the tribes on the other side. This policy worked so long as the Romans were able to keep their allies in check. But by the fourth century they could no longer do so and the floodgates burst.

The onslaught was triggered by dread new invaders that the Europeans had never seen before—the Huns. Their appearance and their deliberate policy of frightfulness terrorized both the Romans and the Germans. The contemporary Roman historian, Ammianus Marcellinus, described them as "almost glued to their horses," and "so monstrously ugly and misshapen that you might suppose they were two-legged animals. . . ."

When provoked they fight, entering battle in wedges and uttering various savage yells. As they are agile and quick they purposely scatter in an irregular line and deal terrible slaughter as they dart about. . . . None has a fixed dwelling: without home or law or stable livelihood, they roam about like refugees with the wagons in which they live. . . . None of them can tell you his origin, for he was conceived in one place, born far from there, and brought up still farther away.[10]

Apparently displaced from their original pasture lands in Central Asia by a newly-formed confederacy, the Huns headed westward and crossed the Volga in 372. There on the Russian steppes they quickly defeated the easternmost German tribe, the Ostrogoths, and then terrorized the neighboring Visigoths into seeking refuge across the Danube River on Roman territory. Two years later, in 378, the Visigoths, exasperated by what they considered to be harsh treatment by Roman officials, defeated and killed the East Roman Emperor in the Battle of Adrianople. This destroyed the legend of Roman invincibility, so that during the following decades Italy and Gaul as well as the Balkan Peninsula felt the scourge of German and Hunnic invasions.

The Visigoths under Alaric marched to Italy, sacked Rome in 410 (an event that shocked the imperial world at the time but that soon was to be repeated), and eventually settled in southern Gaul and northern Spain where they founded the first German kingdom on Roman territory. Behind the Visigoths came the Huns who established their base on the Hungarian plains whence they raided both the eastern and western provinces of the empire. Under their feared leader, Attila, they appeared in 452 before the undefended gates of Rome, where, according to an implausible tradition, Pope Leo I persuaded the Hun chieftain to spare the capital. In any case Attila turned northward without sacking the capital, and a year later was found dead one morning with a burst artery beside a German princess that he had married the day before. His empire collapsed with his death and the Huns disappeared from European history.

The Hunnic devastations, however, had shattered Roman control over the western provinces and German tribes now migrated across the frontiers virtually at will. The Vandals crossed the Rhine, pushed their way through Gaul and Spain, and crossed the Straits of Gibraltar to North Africa where they established a kingdom. From their new base they turned to sea raiding, and in 455 one of their expeditions sacked Rome. Meanwhile the Burgundians were occupying the Rhone Valley, the Franks were spreading out and sinking deep roots in northern Gaul, while the Angles, Saxons, and Jutes promptly invaded England when the last Roman soldiers departed in 407. The local Celtic population fled to the mountains of Scotland and Wales, so that Anglo-Saxon stock now became the dominant ethnic strain in England. Thus it was that the West Roman Empire passed under the control of new German succession kingdoms, a passing symbolized by the deposition of the last emperor, Romulus Augustulus, by the German Odoacer, in 476. (See Chapter 8, section VIII.)

To this point the course of events in Europe was familiar. The West Roman Empire had succumbed to the barbarians as had the Han and Gupta empires. Furthermore it appeared in the sixth century that the aftermath of imperial disintegration in the West would be the same as that in China. Just as the Sui dynasty had finally united China in 589, so Europe at about the same time seemed to be on the road to reunification by the Frankish kings and the East Roman emperors.

Fifteenth-century French illuminated manuscript depicting the sack of Rome by Alaric and the Goths in A.D. 410. In the upper left corner of the painting, St. Augustine is shown offering his book The City of God *to the pope. It was the sack of Rome by the Goths that prompted Augustine to write this famous work. (Bibliothèque Nationale, Paris)*

The Franks had originated in the lower Rhine Valley whence they had emigrated in the fifth century to northern Gaul. There they played a modest role in the turbulent history of the times until, under the leadership of the Merovingian kings, they became the most powerful people in the West. The most outstanding of the Merovingians was Clovis (481–511), who united the Frankish tribes, defeated the Romans, Byzantines, and Visigoths, and welded together a kingdom stretching from the Pyrenees across Gaul and well into Germany. A principal reason for his success was his conversion to Catholicism, which won him the support not only of the Pope but also of the indigenous Gallo-Roman population. It appeared that the Merovingians might be able to recreate the West Roman Empire, enlarged by the addition of the Frankish lands on the eastern bank of the Rhine.

This imperial ambition was shared by the rulers at Constantinople. While the West Roman Empire had been falling apart, the East Roman Empire remained intact, thanks to its naval power, its superior financial resources, and the natural strength of its capital located on the straits between Europe and Asia. Thus Constantinople survived the barbarian invasions which overwhelmed Rome, and, in fact, endured another half millennium before falling to the Turks in 1453. During those centuries the empire developed a distinctive civilization, a mixture of Greek, Roman, Christian, and Eastern elements. To emphasize this distinctiveness, the empire is commonly referred to as the Byzantine Empire, so named after the original Greek colony on the site of Constantinople.

After the western provinces had become German kingdoms, the suzerainty of the Byzantine emperors perforce was restricted to the eastern half of the original empire—that is, to the Balkan Peninsula, Asia Minor, Syria, and Egypt. This contraction was unacceptable to Justinian the Great (527–565) who was an Illyrian by birth and a westerner at heart. He spoke and thought in Latin, and was determined to recover the western lands and to restore the original Roman Empire. One of his generals, Belisarius, with a small number of heavily armed troops, conquered the Vandal kingdoms in North Africa in one year. Southeast Spain also was recovered from the Visigoths, but eighteen years of bitter fighting was needed to subdue the Ostrogoths in Italy. Thus within two decades almost all the Mediterranean had become once more a Roman lake, and Justinian expressed the hope "that God will grant us the remainder of the empire that the Romans lost through indolence."

V. CONTINUED INVASIONS IN THE WEST

But this was not to be. The West did not follow the path of China. Instead a new wave of invasions smashed the fragile new imperial structures of the Franks and the Byzantines, and left the West once more in turmoil and disunity. Again it was a confederacy in Mongolia that pushed hordes of refugees westward along the invasion route to Europe. Like their Hunnic predecessors, these Avars, as they came to be known in the West, used the Hungarian plains as a base from which they launched raids in all directions.

These raids set off migrations that had far reaching repercussions. They forced the Germanic Lombards into Italy (568) where they drove out the Byzantines from most of the peninsula, thus blasting Justinian's hopes for an imperial restoration. The Avars also pushed Slavic tribes southward into the Balkan Peninsula where they dispersed the Latinized Illyrians and Dacians into isolated mountain areas. The Slavic newcomers sank roots in the northern Balkans as agriculturists, while the dispossessed Illyrians and Dacians remained in obscurity until modern times when they reappeared as the Albanians in the western Balkans and as the Rumanians north of the Danube. Thus during the seventh century the Balkan Peninsula attained its modern ethnic pattern, with Greeks in the south, the Albanians in the west, the Rumanians in the northeast, and the Slavs occupying a broad band from the Adriatic to the Black Sea.

In the eighth century hopes were aroused again for western imperial unity by the spectacular successes of the Carolingian dynasty, which had replaced the Merovingians. The successors of Clovis had proven a sorry lot—the *Rois fainéants,* or "do-nothing kings." The kingdom was held together, however, by strong willed ministers who held the office of "mayor of the palace." The most outstanding of these was Charles Martel, the Hammer, who was the power behind the throne from 714 to 741. His greatest achievement was the defeat at the Battle of Tours (732) of the Moslems who had overrun North Africa and Spain, and had advanced into southern France. (See Chapter 13, section III.)

Martel's son, Pepin the Short, was not content to remain the minister of "do-nothing" kings and in 751 deposed the last Merovingian and established what came to be known as the Carolingian dynasty. The name is derived from Charlemagne, the son of Pepin, and the most famous of the line. During his long reign from 768 to 814 Charlemagne campaigned ceaselessly to extend his frontiers. He conquered the Saxons in northwest Germany, dispersed the Avars in Hungary, annexed the Lombard kingdom in Italy, and forced the Moslems back over the Pyrenees. By the end of the eighth century he was the undisputed master of the West, his empire extending from the North Sea to the Pyrenees and from the Atlantic Ocean to the Slavic lands in Eastern Europe. In recognition of his supremacy, Pope Leo III crowned him as emperor on Christmas Day in the year 800. And the assembled multitude, relates Charlemagne's secretary and biographer, shouted, "To Charles Augustus, crowned of God the great and pacific Emperor of the Romans, life and victory!"

The scene reflects the tenacity of the dream of imperial unity. But it was destined to remain a dream, for soon after Charlemagne's death Europe was inundated by new waves of attacks from the south, the east, and the north. In the south, Moslem pirates and adventurers conquered the islands of Crete and Sicily, and also raided all the Mediterranean coasts with devastating effect on maritime trade. In the east, still another nomadic host from Central Asia, the Magyars, reached the Hungarian plains in 895 and followed the example of the preceding Huns and Avars in raiding the surrounding lands.

Most wide ranging were the incursions of the Norsemen, or Vikings. They were the equivalent on sea of the nomads on land. In place of horses they built fast ships with shallow draught that gave them unrivalled speed and mobility. The Vikings from Norway sailed westward to Iceland, Greenland, and North America. With their comrades from Denmark they raided the British Isles and the west coast of Europe, and even forced their way through the Straits of Gibraltar and ravaged both shores of the Mediterranean. Since Sweden faces

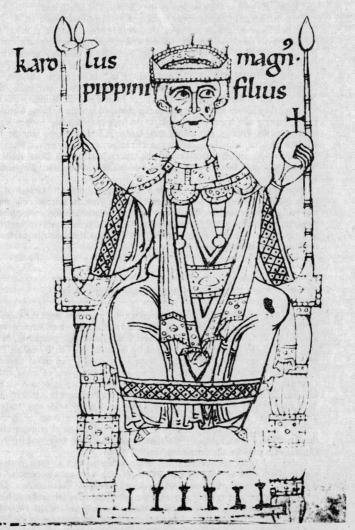

karolus magn̄
pippini filius

*Charlemagne—ninth-century drawing in the collection of the
Courtauld Institute, London. (Arborio Mella)*

eastward, the Vikings from that country crossed the Baltic to the Russian rivers and followed them to their outlets in the Caspian and Black seas.

Thus the whole of Europe was enveloped by these daring raiders. At first, in the late eighth and ninth centuries, they were interested only in plunder, and they destroyed countless monasteries and towns. Few regions were safe, for the Norsemen with their shallow draught ships were able to penetrate up the rivers far into the interior. In the churches of the time was heard the prayer, "From the wrath of the Northmen, O Lord, deliver us." In the tenth and eleventh centuries the Vikings began to settle down in the overseas territories, thus occupying and ruling large parts of northern France and the British Isles. But wherever they settled they were eventually absorbed into the existing Christian state. The king of France, for example, in the hope of forestalling further depredations by the Vikings, recognized their leader in 911 and gave him the title of duke of what came to be known as Normandy, a name derived from the Norsemen who settled there. One of the descendants of this Duke Rollo of Normandy was William the Conqueror who successfully invaded England in 1066.

Meanwhile the Carolingian Empire had crumpled under the impact of the triple assault of Moslems, Magyars, and Vikings. Western Europe once more was reduced to a shambles. The lowest point was reached in the tenth century. At no time since the end of the Roman Empire did the present seem so wretched and the future so bleak. (See Map XII, "Continued Barbarian Invasions in the West, 9th–10th Centuries.")

VI. HISTORIC UNIQUENESS OF THE WEST

From this survey of the invasions marking the transition from the classical to the medieval eras, it is apparent that the various regions of Eurasia were affected quite differently. South China and South India were unscathed, being geographically too remote to be reached by the invaders. The Byzantine Empire, with its resourceful diplomacy, financial resources, and naval strength, successfully repelled through the centuries a long succession of assailants—Germans, Huns, Avars, Slavs, Persians, and Arabs. Persia was equally sucessful under its Sassanian dynasty, which replaced the Parthians in A.D. 226. The Sassanians united the country by appealing to Persian pride, by reviving Zoroastrianism as a state religion, and by organizing a force of heavily armored cavalrymen. Thus Persia was able to repel waves of nomads along the Oxus River while fighting Byzantium to an exhausting draw that left both empires easy prey for the oncoming Moslem Arabs.

China and India, as noted earlier, did not fare so well in their northern regions. Both were overrun by barbarians yet both were able to preserve the distinctive civilizations that they had developed during the Classical Age. Thus a Chinese of the first century B.C. Han period would have felt quite at home had he been resurrected, for example, in the early eighth century A.D. He would have found the contemporary T'ang dynasty essentially the same as the Han, and he would have noted the same people, the same language, the same Confucianism and ancestor worship and imperial administration and so forth.

This points up the uniqueness of the historical experience of the West. If a Roman of the first century B.C. had been resurrected in the Europe of 1000 or 1500 or 1800, he would have been astonished by the German peoples in many parts of the old empire and by the strange new ways of life. He would have found the Latin language replaced by several new Germanic and Romance languages; the Roman togas replaced by blouses and trousers; the ancient Roman gods cast aside for the new Christianity; the Roman imperial structure superseded by a conglomeration of new nation states; and the old ways of earning a living rivalled by new agricultural techniques, by commerce with hitherto unknown parts of the globe, and by new crafts with strange machines that saved labor and that ran without the traditional human or animal power.

The explanation, of course, is that only in the West was a classical civilization permanently submerged and superseded by something fundamentally new. Everywhere else in Eurasia the various regional civilizations either escaped the invaders (South China and South India), or repelled them (Byzantium and Persia), or endured and survived them (North China and North India). Only in the West was the classical civilization shattered beyond recall despite repeated attempts at restoration over several centuries.

Since it was precisely this uniqueness that made possible the global primacy of the West in modern times, its origins require attention. As noted in section II of this chapter, technological stagnation was a basic structural weakness of the classical civilizations. But since this was true of all of them, why did only the West European civilization founder?

A comparison of West European institutions and experiences with those of the rest of Eurasia points to certain conclusions. In the first place Western Europe was not as productive in classical times as, for example, China. The monsoon winds provide most of East Asia with ample rainfall during the summer growing months, in contrast to Europe where most of the rain comes in the sterile winter months. This, together with the greater solar heat in the lower latitudes, allows more intensive and prolonged cultivation in East Asia, including two crops per year in many localities. Furthermore, rice, the principal crop of East Asia, produces a much larger yield per acre than wheat, rye, and the other cereals grown in the West. According to one estimate, rice on a given plot of land yields caloric value that is five times as great as that of wheat on the same land.[11] The net result was a far greater productivity in China than in the West, which led to the correspondingly denser population found in China from the advent of agriculture to the present day. This superiority in productivity and in population in turn made China more capable of supporting the empire's bureaucratic and military establishments, and of resisting, or, if necessary, absorbing, barbarian invaders.

Another was the absence in the West of anything comparable to the Chinese writing system, which provided lasting cultural homogeneity, and to the Chinese examination system, which provided administrative efficiency and stability. Finally, the Roman Empire had to cope with more formidable enemies on its frontiers. Being located on the western receiving end of the steppe invasion route, Europe bore the brunt of attacks by virtually all the nomadic peoples. Furthermore, the Roman Empire's Germanic neighbors were more numerous than the nomads on China's northwestern frontier, while the neighboring

Persians and Arabs were more advanced and posed a more serious and lasting military threat than did China's nomadic neighbors. Hence the prolongation of the invasions in the West far beyond their duration in the rest of Eurasia.

It will be recalled that at one point North China faced the prospect of pastoralism replacing agriculture and of Altaic languages replacing Chinese. The restoration of unity and order by the Sui dynasty eliminated this prospect, but in the West the invasions continued in prolonged succession. The Avars undid the work of Justinian and Clovis, and the Moslems, Magyars, and Vikings demolished the empire of Charlemagne. Hence the unique denouement in the West—the irrevocable dissolution of the imperial structure and of its classical civilization.

This outcome is of such significance that it can fairly be described as a major turning point in world history. It was such a fateful turning point because the wholesale demolition cleared the ground for long overdue innovation. A historian recently presented the following conclusion concerning the demise of the Roman Empire: "All in all, the invasions gave the *coup de grace* to a culture which had come to a standstill after reaching its apogee and seemed doomed to wither away. We are reminded of the cruel bombings in our own day which destroyed ramshackle old buildings and so made possible the reconstruction of towns on more modern lines." [12] But this "culture" was no different from all the others of Eurasia, which also were at a "standstill." These others, however, managed to survive the invasions and to gain a new lease on life. But it was the old life that was prolonged, while the West, with the death of the Roman Empire, was able to start a new life—to make a new beginning.

The import of this new beginning becomes evident if it is recalled that during the ancient period the Middle East had been the center of initiative from which had diffused the fundamental innovations of those millennia. But during the classical period it was Europe, India, and China that generated most of the innovations, while the Middle East lagged behind. And the reason was precisely that the ancient civilization of the Middle East had survived the invasions of the second millennium B.C., while the ancient civilizations of the peripheral regions had gone under, leaving the way clear for a fresh start—for the emergence of the new classical civilizations.

So it was during the transition from the classical to the medieval civilizations. But this time the existing classical civilizations survived everywhere except in the West. For this reason the West alone was free to strike out in new directions and to evolve during the medieval age a new technology, new institutions, and new ideas—in short, a new civilization. And in modern times this new civilization proved its superiority over the "standstill" civilizations of the rest of Eurasia—indeed of the entire world—as inevitably and irresistibly as at an earlier time the agricultural civilizations had triumphed over tribal cultures.

SUGGESTED READING

The problem of the rise and fall of empires is considered in the following collection of readings: S. W. Eisenstadt, ed., *The Decline of Empires* (Englewood

Cliffs, N.J.: Prentice-Hall, 1967). Various viewpoints regarding the decline of Rome are presented by D. Kagan, *Decline and Fall of the Roman Empire* (Boston: D. C. Heath, 1962); and in S. Mazzarino, *The End of the Ancient World* (London: Faber and Faber, 1966). For a discussion of the invaders of the Roman Empire, see one of the many editions of Tacitus, *Germania,* and also E. A. Thompson, *A History of Attila and the Huns* (Oxford: Clarendon, 1948); E. A. Thompson, *The Goths in Spain* (London: Oxford Univ., 1969); and G. Jones, *A History of the Vikings* (New York: Oxford Univ., 1968). The developments following the invasions are analyzed in the standard account by F. Lot, *The End of the Ancient World and the Beginning of the Middle Ages* (New York: Knopf, 1931); in the following study which stresses the role of Byzantium and Islam, J. L. LaMonte, *The World of the Middle Ages: A Reorientation of Medieval History* (New York: Appleton-Century-Crofts, 1949); in A. Dopsch, *The Economic and Social Foundations of European Civilization* (New York: Harcourt, 1937), which revises earlier theories concerning the economic breakdown after the decline of Rome; in W. C. Bark, *Origins of the Medieval World* (Stanford: Stanford Univ., 1958), which stresses the creativity of the early Middle Ages in the West; and in R. S. Hoyt, ed., *Life and Thought in the Early Middle Ages* (Minneapolis: Univ. of Minnesota, 1967), which also interprets this period as one of transition and transformation. Finally there is this biography of a central figure of the times: R. Winston, *Charlemagne: From the Hammer to the Cross* (Indianapolis: Bobbs-Merrill, 1954).

MEDIEVAL CIVILIZATIONS OF EURASIA, 500–1500

Like the Classical Age, the Medieval Age was heralded by invasions—by the Dorians, Aryans, and Chou in the first instance, and by the Germans, Huns, and Turks in the second. There the parallel ends, however, for the medieval centuries, unlike the classical, were punctuated by continued invasions that affected virtually all regions of Eurasia. Beginning in the seventh century, there were the invasions of the warriors of Islam who overran not only the entire Middle East where they originated, but eventually North Africa, Spain, the Balkans, India, Southeast Asia, and much of Central Asia. Even more extensive were the conquests of the Turks and the Mongols during the half millennium between 1000 and 1500, encompassing as they did the great bulk of the Eurasian land mass from the Baltic Sea to the Pacific Ocean.

These great conquests, despite their fury and range, nevertheless did not uproot civilization in most of Eurasia as the earlier incursions of the Dorians, Aryans, and Chou had done. By medieval times most civilizations had sunk roots too deep to be extirpated so easily. Thus the traditional civilizations everywhere survived. In China, for example, the native Ming dynasty supplanted the Mongol Yuan, and the country reverted with a vengeance to age-old ways. In the sprawling Moslem world the indigenous Greco-Roman, Iranian, Semitic, and Egyptian traditions were not obliterated but rather fused into the syncretic civilization of Islam. Likewise the East Roman Empire continued .

without interruption for a full millennium as the Byzantine Empire, so that its inhabitants referred to themselves in modern times as "Romaioi," or Romans.

The one exception to this general pattern, as noted in the preceding chapter, was in the West. There, and there alone, the prevailing classical civilization was torn up root and branch. Only in the West, therefore, was the ground sufficiently cleared for the emergence of a new civilization that was free to develop along fresh lines in contrast to the traditional civilizations of the rest of Eurasia.

It was this unique feature of the West that enabled it to develop the economic vigor, the technological proficiency, and the social dynamism to expand overseas and to gain control of the sea routes of the world. With this fateful development the Medieval Age came to an end. But it ended, it should be noted, not with land invasions by Eurasian nomads, as did the ancient and classical periods, but rather with the maritime enterprise of the West. The overseas activities of Western explorers, merchants, missionaries, and settlers marked the transition from medieval to modern times, and from the Eurasian to the global phase of world history.

What has emerged is a sense of the Chapter
remarkable complexity of the interplay
between the Occident and East Asia
from Roman and Han times onward.
This involved a two-way traffic, in many
items, along many routes, and of varying
density in different periods . . . . despite
difficult communication, mankind in the
Old World at least has long lived
in a more unified realm of discourse
than we have been prepared to admit.

LYNN WHITE, JR.

Eurasian Ecumene

J ust as an incipient Eurasian ecumene differentiated the Classical Age from the Ancient Age, so now a full-fledged Eurasian
ecumene differentiated the Medieval Age from the Classical Age. The
incipient stage had been attained as a result of improved technology,
particularly the large-scale production of iron, with its manifold repercussions in all aspects of life. (See Chapter 7.) Likewise the full
ecumene was now facilitated by further technological advance, especially in shipbuilding and navigation. But more significant during these
centuries was a political consideration—the existence for the first
time of tremendous empires that encompassed not merely river valleys
as in the Ancient Age, or entire regions as in the Classical Age, but
that reached across several regions to embrace a large proportion of
the entire Eurasian land mass.

It has been seen that the great Alexander knew nothing of the
Ganges Valley or of China, and that virtually no direct relations existed
between the Roman and the Han empires at the opposite ends of
Eurasia. The reason is that Alexander's empire was pretty much confined to the Middle East, with only a precarious foothold in India,
while the Roman and Han empires were for all practical purposes
restricted to the western and eastern tips of Eurasia. In striking con-

trast, the medieval period witnessed first the Islamic Empire, which by the mid-eighth century stretched from the Pyrenees to the Indian Ocean, and from Morocco to the borders of China. In later centuries Islam expanded much further into Central Asia, Southeast Asia, and Africa's interior. Even more impressive was the thirteenth century Mongol Empire that included Korea, China, all of Central Asia, Russia, and most of the Middle East—the greatest Eurasian empire to that time and ever since. (See Map XIV, "Mongol Empire at the Death of Kublai Khan, 1294.")

Empires of such unprecedented dimensions eliminated the age-old regional isolation by making possible direct contact and interaction amongst the various parts of the land mass. This chapter will consider the nature of the resulting new bonds—commercial, technological, religious, and intellectual.

I. Eurasian Sea Trade

In classical times, the existence of the large Roman and Han empires at the opposite ends of the Eurasian trade routes stimulated commerce all along the line, and conversely, the disintegration of these empires undermined and reduced this commerce. It revived, however, and reached new heights during medieval times with the appearance of the Islamic, and later the Mongol, Empire.

The Moslem conquests unified the entire Middle East, through which ran all the trans-Eurasian trade routes—both the land routes that terminated at various Black Sea and Syrian ports, and the sea routes that ran through the Red Sea and the Persian Gulf. Particularly flourishing was the trade across the Arabian Sea with the Malabar coast of southwest India. Sizeable settlements of Moslem merchants, mostly Arabs and Persians, grew up in the ports of India and Ceylon. From west to east were shipped horses, silver, wrought iron objects, and linen, cotton, and woolen fabrics, which were exchanged for silks, precious stones, teak, and assorted spices.

Moslem merchants went on from India and Ceylon to Kalah Bar (Kedah) on the Malay coast, whence some sailed on to Sumatra and Java, while others went through the Malacca Straits and then north to Kanfu (Canton) in South China. The customary schedule was to leave the Persian Gulf in September or October, sail with the northeast monsoon to India and Malaya, and arrive in the China Sea in time for the southern monsoon to Canton. There the Moslem merchants spent the summer, and then returned with the northeast moonsoon to the Malacca Straits and across the Bay of Bengal, arriving back in the Persian Gulf in the early summer—making a round trip of a year and a half.

After the first Moslem reached Canton in 671, considerable numbers settled there as they had in the various Indian Ocean ports. They were granted autonomy by the local authorities, so that they selected their own headman who was responsible for maintaining order in their section of the city. The descendants of some of these Moslem families later entered the Chinese civil service as Marco Polo was to do later. By 758 the Moslems were numerous enough to attack Canton, and as a result the Chinese closed the port to foreign trade. Reopened in 792, Canton continued to be a center for Moslem traders until 878 when they were massacred by rebellious Chinese bands. Thereafter

Moslem and Chinese merchants met at Kalah Bar in Malaya to exchange their commodities.

With the advent of the Sung dynasty (960–1127), the Chinese ports again were reopened to foreigners. During the Sung period the Chinese made considerable progress in shipbuilding and navigation, so that by the end of the twelfth century they were replacing the Moslems in the waters of East and Southeast Asia. By the time the Mongols conquered China and founded the Yuan dynasty (1279–1368), Chinese ships were the largest and best equipped, while Chinese merchants were settling in various ports in Southeast Asia and India. Marco Polo, who in 1291 accompanied a Mongol princess around southeast Asia to Iran, witnessed and described the vigor of Chinese maritime enterprise, as did also the Arab traveller Ibn Battuta, who fifty years later chose to make his way from India to China on a Chinese junk. Noteworthy also is the nature of China's imports and exports, which reflected her leading position in the world's economy during this period. Apart from fine cotton textiles, the imports were raw materials such as hides and horses from Central Asia, and fine woods, gems, spices and ivory from South Asia. Conversely, Chinese exports, apart from some minerals, were manufactured goods such as books, paintings, and especially porcelains and silks.

During the Ming dynasty (1368–1644), Chinese maritime activity reached its height, culminating in a remarkable but short-lived naval domination of the Pacific and Indian Oceans in the early fifteenth century. This was manifested by the series of seven expeditions sent out between 1405 and 1433 under the superintendency of the chief court eunuch, a certain Cheng Ho. These expeditions were unprecedented in their magnitude and in their achievements. The first comprised 62 ships and 28,000 men, and sailed as far as Java, Ceylon, and Calicut. On the return a flotilla of Sumatran pirates tried to block the way but they were completely annihilated. The later expeditions pressed on further, reaching as far as the east coast of Africa and the entrances to the Persian Gulf and the Red Sea. More than thirty ports in the Indian Ocean were visited by the Chinese, and everywhere they persuaded or compelled the local rulers to recognize the suzerainty of the Ming emperor. And all this at a time when the Portuguese were just beginning to feel their way down the coast of Africa, not reaching Cape Verde until 1445! (See Map XVII, "Early 15th-Century Chinese and Portuguese Voyages.")

These extraordinary Chinese expeditions were suddenly halted by imperial fiat in 1433. The reasons for their beginning as well as for their ending remain a mystery. It is surmised that the expeditions may have been launched to compensate for the loss of foreign trade over the land routes with the disintegation of the Mongol Empire, or to enhance the prestige of the imperial court, or to find the emperor's predecessor who had disappeared underground as a Buddhist monk. Likewise it is speculated that the expeditions may have been halted because of their excessive cost or because of the traditional rivalry between court eunuchs and Confucian bureaucrats. In any case the withdrawal of the Chinese left a power vacuum in the waters of East and South Asia. Japanese pirates harried the coasts of China, while in the Indian Ocean the Moslem Arabs regained their former primacy. But adept though they were as merchants, the Arabs lacked the unity and the resources to develop the formidable naval power that the Chinese had briefly marshalled. Thus when the Portuguese sailed around Africa into the Indian Ocean in 1498, they encountered no effective resistance, and proceeded to establish their hegemony of the West.

II. EURASIAN LAND TRADE

Meanwhile a great revolution in land trade had occurred with the rise of the Mongol Empire. For the first and only time in history one political authority extended across the breadth of Eurasia—from the Baltic Sea to the Pacific, and from Siberia to the Persian Gulf. A mid-fourteenth century Italian handbook summarized the commercial significance of this *Pax Mongolica* in describing a trade route running across Central Asia from its beginning point at Tana at the mouth of the Don River.

> The road you travel from Tana to Cathay is perfectly safe, whether by day or by night, according to what the merchants say who have used it. . . . You may reckon that from Tana to Sarai [on the Volga] the road is less safe than on any other part of the journey; and yet even when this part of the road is at its worst, if you are some sixty men in the company you will go as safely as if you were in your own house.[1]

When Kublai Khan in 1264 moved his capital from Karakorum in Mongolia to Peking, this automatically opened China to the European merchants trading along the trans-Eurasian routes. The first Europeans to arrive at Kublai's new court were not diplomatic emissaries but two Venetian merchants, Nicolo and Maffeo Polo. Of greater economic importance than this access to China was the access for the first time to the source of spices in India and the East Indies. Hitherto spices had reached Europe via two routes: through the Red Sea and Egypt, or to the Persian Gulf and then by caravan routes to ports on the Black Sea or the eastern Mediterranean. The first route was controlled by the Arabs who shipped the spices to Egypt, and by the Venetians who loaded cargoes at Alexandria for distribution in Europe. The second route was dominated by the Mongol ruler (Ilkhanate) of Persia and Mesopotamia, and by the Genoese who awaited the spices at the port terminals.

The Genoese, however, were not content only to sail the Black Sea. They ascended the Don River from the Azov Sea in small, light vessels, which they transported, probably on ox-wagons, across the narrow neck of land to the Volga and thence to the Caspian Sea and to Persia. Thus the Genoese were able to reach the Persian Gulf and to go directly to India and the East Indies where they discovered how cheap the spices were in their places of origin and what fabulous profits had been made during the past centuries by the succession of middlemen between the producers in Southeast Asia and the consumers in Europe.

This revival of overland trade during the *Pax Mongolica* proved short-lived. One reason was the expulsion of the Mongols from China in 1368 and the general disintegration of the Mongol Empire. This led to a recrudescence of fragmentation in Central Asia and hence to the disruption of trans-Eurasian trade. More important was the conversion of Ilkhan Ghazan (1295–1304) to Islam, which automatically barred to European merchants the transit route to the spice islands. Almost all spices henceforth were shipped along the Red Sea-Nile route, with golden profits for the Arab and Venetian middlemen. But other Europeans were unwilling to continue paying exorbitant prices, particularly since they now knew from where the spices came and at what cost. Hence the search for a new route around the Moslem barrier—a search that was to culminate in da Gama's epochal voyage around Africa.

III. TECHNOLOGICAL DIFFUSION

The great Moslem and Mongol empires affected not only the flow of trade within Eurasia but also the diffusion of technology. An outstanding example is the lateen sail, a tall, triangular, fore-and-aft sail that has always been used on Arab craft. In the Mediterranean, by contrast, the Egyptians, Phoenicians, Greeks, and Romans had used a square sail which is easier to handle in bad weather. But the Arab sail is much more maneuverable, being able to keep closer to the wind and to tack on rivers and narrow waters. For this reason it soon superseded the square sail in the Levant, and by the eleventh century it had become the normal rig throughout the Mediterranean. Today this triangular sail is known as the "Latin," or "lateen," sail, though it was the Arabs who, with the Moslem invasions, introduced it into the Mediterranean. And from there it spread to the Atlantic where, during the fifteenth century, Portuguese and Spanish ship designers combined the square sail on the foremast with the lateen on the main and mizzen. The resulting hybrid three-masters were capable of sailing in all reasonable weathers, and thus made possible the long ocean voyages of Columbus and da Gama.

The Moslem Empire, straddling North Africa, the Middle East, and South Asia, had contact with all regions of Eurasia and thus served as a conduit or intermediary in the interchange of knowledge and techniques as well as of articles of trade. An example of this interchange may be seen in the following account left by an Arab physician and scientist who lived in Baghdad between 850 and 925. This shows how the Chinese learned from the Moslems about Galen, a Greek physician of A.D. 130 to 200, whose numerous writings had been translated into Arabic.

> A Chinese scholar came to my house and remained in the town about a year. In five months he learnt to speak and write Arabic, attaining indeed eloquence in speech and calligraphy in writing. When he decided to return to his country, he said to me a month or so beforehand, 'I am about to leave. I would be very glad if someone would dictate to me the sixteen books of Galen before I go.' I told him that he had not sufficient time to copy more than a small part of it, but he said, 'I beg you to give me all your time until I go, and to dictate to me as rapidly as possible. You will see that I shall write faster than you can dictate.' So together with one of my students we read Galen to him as fast as we could, but he wrote still faster. We did not believe that he was getting it correctly until we made a collation and found it exact throughout. I asked him how this

could be, and he said, 'We have in our country a way of writing which we call shorthand, and this is what you see. When we wish to write very fast we use this style, and then afterwards transcribe it into the ordinary characters at will.' But he added that an intelligent man who learns quickly cannot master this script in under twenty years.[2]

This revealing account is unusual because during the medieval period the Chinese usually were the donors rather than the recipients in the Eurasian interchange. In earlier times, it is true, it had been the other way around. During the ancient and classical periods such basic inventions as the wheel, windlass, and pulley diffused in all directions from Mesopotamia, the swape and crank from Egypt, the windmill from Persia, and iron smelting from Asia Minor. But during the first fourteen centuries of the Christian era, China was the great center of technological innovation, and transmitted to the rest of Eurasia a multitude of inventions. (See Table 1.)

The English philosopher Francis Bacon wrote in 1620,

> It is well to observe the force and virtue and consequences of discoveries. These are to be seen nowhere more conspicuously than in those three which were unknown to the ancients, and of which the origin, though recent, is obscure and inglorious; namely, printing, gunpowder, and the magnet. For these three have changed the whole face and state of things throughout the world, the first in literature, the second in warfare, the third in navigation; whence have followed innumerable changes; insomuch that no empire, no sect, no star, seems to have exerted greater power and influence in human affairs than these mechanical discoveries.[3]

All three of these inventions, whose historical significance Bacon correctly appraised, were of Chinese origin. The oldest existing example of block printing—printing in which a single block of wood is engraved for each page printed —is a Chinese Buddhist sacred text from the year 868. The first invention of separate movable type also is Chinese, the work of a simple artisan who between 1041 and 1049 made movable type of baked clay. In later centuries the Chinese substituted wood and various metals for the clay. The diffusion of these inventions has been traced from China to the Middle East and thence to Europe, where the first example of block printing dates back to 1423, followed in 1456 by the first book printed with movable type—Gutenberg's *Bible*.

Gunpowder was used in China for fireworks as early as the T'ang dynasty (618–906). By 1120 the Chinese had evolved a weapon known as the "fire-lance" comprising a stout bamboo tube filled with gunpowder. This was almost certainly the precursor of the metal-barrel gun, which appeared about 1280, though it is not known whether it was first contrived by Chinese or Arabs or Europeans.

The earliest definite reference to magnetism is found in a Chinese book of about 240 B.C., but for centuries thereafter the compass was used only by geomancers for magical purposes. By 1125, however, it was applied for navigation purposes, and apparently the Arab merchants who came to China learned of this instrument and introduced it into Europe.

TABLE 1. Transmission of Techniques and Inventions *

Technique or Invention	Approx. lag in centuries
From China to the West	
Square-pallet chain-pump	15
Edge-runner mill	13
Edge-runner mill with application of water-power	9
Metallurgical blowing-engines, water-power	11
Rotary fan and rotary winnowing machine	14
Piston-bellows	14
Draw-loom	4
Silk-handling machinery (a form of flyer for laying thread evenly on reels appears in the +11th century, and water-power is applied to spinning mills in the +14th)	3–13
Wheelbarrow	9–10
Sailing-carriage	11
Wagon-mill	12
Efficient harness for draught-animals: Breast-strap (postilion)	8
Collar	6
Cross-bow (as an individual arm)	13
Kite	12
Helicopter top (spun by cord)	14
Zoetrope (moved by ascending hot-air current)	10
Deep drilling	11
Cast iron	10–12
'Cardan' suspension	8–9
Segmental arch bridge	7
Iron-chain suspension-bridge	10–13
Canal lock-gates	7–17
Nautical construction principles	10
Stern-post rudder	4
Gunpowder	5–6
Gunpowder used as a war technique	4
Magnetic compass (lodestone spoon)	11
Magnetic compass with needle	4
Magnetic compass used for navigation	2
Paper	10
Printing (block)	6
Printing (movable type)	4
Printing (metal movable type)	1
Porcelain	11–13
From the West to China	
Screw	14
Force-pump for liquids	18
Crankshaft	3
Clockwork	3

* Adapted from J. Needham, *Science and Civilisation in China* (London: Cambridge Univ. Press, 1954), 242–43.

In addition to these three basic inventions, the Chinese gave much more to their Eurasian neighbors. In A.D. 105 they invented paper, the prerequisite for printing. Chinese prisoners of war who were taken to Samarkand in 751 introduced the paper-making process to the Arabs, who in turn spread it to Syria, Egypt, Morocco, and in 1150, to Spain. From there it passed on to France and the rest of Europe, displacing parchment as it went. Its value is evident in the fact that to produce one copy of the Bible on parchment, the skins of no less than three hundred sheep would be required.

Other Chinese inventions that spread throughout Eurasia with profound repercussions were the stern-post rudder which appeared in Europe about 1180 at the same time as the compass, the foot-stirrup which made possible the heavily-armored feudal knights of medieval Europe, and the breast-strap harness which rests on the horse's shoulders and allows it to pull with full force without choking as had been the case with the old throat harness. Finally the Chinese domesticated numerous fruits and plants which were spread throughout Eurasia, usually by the Arabs. These include the chrysanthemum, the camellia, the azalea, the tea rose, the Chinese aster, the lemon, and the orange, the latter still being called the "Chinese apple" in Holland and Germany.

In conclusion it should be noted that the transmission of these and other inventions occurred in clusters that obviously relate to facilitating political events. Thus the Crusades may be considered responsible for the twelfth-century cluster of the compass, stern-post rudder, paper-making, and the idea of the windmill, while the *Pax Mongolica* likewise stimulated the fourteenth-century cluster of gunpowder, silk machinery, printing, and the blast furnace for cast iron.

IV. EURASIAN RELIGIONS

The medieval period was characterized not only by an unprecedented trans-Eurasian exchange of goods and technologies, but also by an unprecedented diffusion of religious creeds. In the case of Christianity and Buddhism, this began towards the end of the classical period and continued during the medieval. (See Chapter 7, section III.) But by all odds the outstanding religious innovation during the medieval centuries was the appearance of Islam. Apart from its teachings, which will be noted in the following chapter, the new religion profoundly affected extensive regions of Eurasia and Africa as a result of its spectacular eruption from the Arabian Peninsula following the death of Mohammed in A.D. 632.

The expansion of Islam, the details of which will be noted later, occurred in two stages. During the first, from 632 to 750, it spread over the Middle East and then west to the Pyrenees and east to Central Asia. The net effect was the virtual transformation of the Mediterranean into a Moslem lake. But the second stage of expansion between 1000 and 1500 made the Indian Ocean also a Moslem preserve, for during these centuries Islam expanded much further—into India, Southeast Asia and Africa.

The vast extension of the domains of Islam naturally alarmed the beleaguered rulers of Christendom who were now effectively isolated on the western tip of Eurasia. This explains their ambivalent reaction to the appearance of the

النَّخْلُ نَحَا لَهَهَا صَنْعَةُ العَسَلِ ❀ وَزَعَمُوا أَنْ فِيهِ خَلْقَ اللهُ الْجَنَّةَ وَلَمْ يَذْكُرُهُ فِي قَوْلِهِمْ مَا فِيهِ وَيُبَيِّنُهُ
حَتَّى الحَقِّ وَاليَقِينُ التَّشْبِيهِ الْقَطِيعِ مِنْ قَوْلِهِمْ أَنْ فِيهِ غَيْرَ مِنْ شَجَرٍ طُوبَى يَدَ وَلَمْ بَاقِ قَلَى إِذَ ذَلِكَ
بَلِ اعْتَقَدُوا جَمْلَاكَا هُوَ ❀ وَيَلِي الْيَوْمُ الثَّانِي مِنْ هَذَا الشَّهْرِ صَوْمُ تَطَوُّعِ سُنَّةَ أَيَّامٍ مَتَى البِيِّضُ فِي
الرَّابِعِ مُبَاهَلَةٌ البَّيْتَ عَلَيْهِ السَّلَامُ مَعَ نَصَارَى نَجْرَانَ وَلَخْرَاجِهِ لِلْحَسَنِ وَلْحُسَيْنِ مَقَامَ ابْنَائِهِ
وَفَاطِمَةَ مَقَامَ نِسَائِهِ وَعَلَى بِنَا بِأَبِي طَالِبٍ تَرَهُ لِلَى نَفْسِهِ بِمَا بَدَأَ اللهُ تَعَالَى بِهِ فِي آيَةِ الْبَاهِلَةِ ❀

Fifteenth-century Arab manuscript from the collection of the National Library, Paris, showing Mohammed and his daughter Fatima. (Arborio Mella)

Mongols in the thirteenth century. They were appalled and terrified by the devastation and slaughter that marked the seemingly irresistible advance of the Mongol horsemen. In 1260 Pope Alexander IV in his bull *Clamat in auribus* addressed to all the princes of Christendom an appeal for unity in face of the common danger: ". . . take provident action against a peril impending and palpably approaching . . . the scourge of Heaven's wrath in the hands of the inhuman Tartars, erupting as it were from the secret confines of Hell. . . ."

Yet, as seen through Western eyes, the picture was not all black. The Mongols had subjugated the Christian Russians, who were adherents of the schismatic Greek church. Furthermore the most crushing blows had been dealt by the Mongols against Islamic Persia and Mesopotamia. When the Moslems in desperation appealed to the Christian rulers for aid, the normal reaction was that expressed by the Bishop of Winchester: "Let us leave these dogs to devour one another." Some Westerners went further in regarding the Mongol invaders as a divine intervention in behalf of the Christian cause and as potential allies against the hereditary foe Islam. They even cherished the hope that the new barbarians might be converted to the true faith as the Magyars and Vikings had been before them. Being ignorant of civilization and with no sophisticated religious beliefs or organized priesthood to sustain them, the Mongols seemed ripe for conversion and for assimilation.

The Western Christians, however, were not alone in their designs on the Mongols. Representatives of three other religions were then competing for the soul of Asia. Most aggressive was Islam, which then was spreading from Persia across the Oxus River into Central Asia, where it won over some Turkish tribes. Buddhism also had become familiar to the Mongols in the course of its diffusion from its Indian home to China along the Silk Road of Turkestan. Finally there were the Nestorian Christians, whose origins go back to the Council of Ephesus (431) when they were condemned as heretics. They then withdrew from the Roman Empire into Persia, and later, under pressure from advancing Islam, moved along the overland routes through Central Asia to China. Thus they were able to convert various Turkish tribes, and then as the Mongol Empire expanded, these Christianized Turks entered its service as administrators, translators, interpreters, and envoys.

While these Nestorian Christians naturally entertained high hopes of converting the Mongols, the Western Christians dispatched two missions to the court of the Grand Khan in Karakorum in northern Mongolia. The first (1245–47) was led by the Italian Franciscan John de Piano Carpini, and the second (1253–55) by the Flemish Franciscan William de Rubruquis. Both envoys reached the Mongol court and found the Khans interested in all foreign religions. Friar William was asked to intone a psalm in the Western mode and to explain illustrations in the Bible. But a few days later he found the Khan intently studying burnt shoulder blades of sheep. If they were completely intact, he believed he could begin a projected campaign with assurance of victory, but if he saw the slightest crack he would make no move. The traditional magicians, or shamans, were very influential at the court, and the friars were unable to win over any members of the royal family. "We believe that there is only one God," declared Mangu Khan to Friar William. "But as God gives us the different fingers of the hand, so he gives to men divers ways. God gives you the Scriptures, and you Christians keep them not. . . . He gave us diviners, we do what they tell us, and we live in peace." [4] Likewise an alliance against Islam proved impossible, for the Mongols demanded submission rather than partnership—"all of you, without exception," declared Mangu Khan, "must come to tender us service and pay us homage . . . the Commandments of the Eternal are what we impart to you." [5] The missions were successful, however, in providing the West with the first reliable information concerning the appearance, customs, and military tactics of the new barbarians.

Immediately following Friar William's return, there arose the hope once more of a victorious Christian-Mongol alliance that would end once and for all the menace of Islam. This hope was nurtured by the great victories won by Genghis Khan's grandson, Hulagu, who was a Buddhist, and whose wife was a Christian. With the aid of Christian soldiers from the kingdoms of Armenia and Georgia, Hulagu had between 1258 and 1260 captured and sacked the Caliphate capital, Baghdad, and had then overrun all of Syria to the Mediterranean coast. It was confidently expected that he would as easily overwhelm Egypt and North Africa, and would then join Western Christendom in conquering Spain, thus completing the final extirpation of hated Islam from the face of the earth.

But contrary to these expectations the Mongols were repulsed in 1260 by the Mamelukes of Egypt in the decisive battle of Ain Jalut (Goliath's Spring) in Palestine. The Mongols reeled back and Egypt and the Islamic world were saved. Indeed this defeat apparently impressed on the minds of the superstitious Mongols a conviction of the superior power of the Moslem God and thus hastened their conversion to Islam. The result, therefore, was not the elimination of Islam but the eventual conversion to Islam of the Mongols in the Middle East and Central Asia, while the easternmost Mongols turned to Buddhism. (For details of these campaigns, see Chapter 14, section IV.)

In the West, hope still was held for the great but mysterious realm of Cathay, which was known to be free of Islam. Neither Carpini nor Rubruquis had reached China, but they were told that it was only twenty days' journey from Karakorum and that it was a country of unparalleled wealth. When Kublai Khan in 1264 moved his capital to Cambaluc (from Khan Baliq or the Khan's headquarters—the modern Peking) China for the first time became accessible to Europeans. The first to arrive were two Venetian merchants, Nicolo and Maffeo Polo. Kublai welcomed them warmly, questioned them about Europe, and gave them letters to deliver to the Pope. In these letters he asked for a hundred missionary-scholars to come to his court to instruct his people and to dispute with representatives of other religions.

In making this request it is doubtful that Kublai was motivated by zeal for Christianity. More likely he wanted trained men for his bureaucracy, since he had only recently conquered China and did not wish to risk too high a proportion of Chinese in the higher offices. In fact he did employ large numbers of foreigners in his service, and he was careful to maintain a balance amongst the various elements in order to safeguard his authority. Whatever the Khan's motives in requesting missionaries, the Papacy dispatched only two Dominicans who got as far as Asia Minor before turning back because of unsettled conditions on the road.

In 1289 Pope Nicholas IV sent John of Montecorvino, a veteran of fourteen years' missionary work amongst the Moslems in the Levant to the Mongol court. Friar John took the sea route from the Persian Gulf to India, the Malacca

Straits, and Kanfu (Canton), whence he went overland to Cambaluc (Peking). He was allowed to remain in the capital and to preach, so that within six years after his arrival in 1292 he had built a church with a campanile and with a choir of 150 boys whose Gregorian chants pleased the imperial ear. When the Papacy learned of this success it sent reinforcements, enabling Friar John to start another mission in Kanfu. By the time of the friar's death in 1328 several thousand converts had been won over in China.

This progress had been made possible by the positive attitude of the Mongol rulers who deliberately encouraged all alien religions, whether Moslem, Buddhist, or Christian, as counterweights to the dominant Confucian establishment in China. Accordingly the Christian missionaries received liberal allowances from the imperial treasury that enabled them to build a friary with "apartments fit for any prelate." This unexpected affluence proved short-lived, however, for it depended entirely on the support of the Khan. But as Marco Polo reported, "All the Cathaians detested the Great Khan's rule because . . . he put all authority into the hands of Tartars, Saracens, or Christians, who were attached to his household and devoted to his service, and were foreigners in Cathay." Thus when the Mongols were expelled from China in 1368, the various foreign elements they had patronized were expelled along with them, including the Catholic missions. Western Christianity was not to gain a foothold in China again until da Gama's voyage established a direct sea route between the two extremities of Eurasia and paved the way for the arrival of the Jesuits in the sixteenth century.

V. EXPANDING HORIZONS

Although the Europeans failed to win over the Mongols as allies or as co-religionists, they did, thanks to the *Pax Mongolica,* broaden immeasurably their horizons and gain a new Eurasian perspective. This was very different from the early medieval period when the collapse of the Han and Roman empires severed the trans-Eurasian ties of classical times. Parochialism set in, and in the West this was accentuated by the tenets of triumphant Christianity. The Bible became the main source of geographical knowledge, so that Jerusalem was regarded as the center of the earth, while the Nile, Euphrates, and Ganges were believed to have a common source in the Garden of Eden.

The expansion of Islam in the seventh and eighth centuries further narrowed European horizons by erecting a constricting barrier across North Africa and the Middle East. It was not until the twelfth century when the Crusaders began to return from the Levant with their tales that first-hand information of the outside world again became available. Yet even then the Mediterranean remained the axis of the world, and knowledge of the lands to the east and south was meager in the extreme.

The great breakthrough came with the *Pax Mongolica,* which made possible the transition from a Mediterranean to a Eurasian perspective, just as Columbus and da Gama later were to effect a corresponding transition from a Eurasian to a global perspective. The travels of merchants, missionaries, and prisoners of war revealed the existence of a great empire in the Far East that not only equalled but surpassed Europe in population, wealth, and level of civilization.

Nor was this a one-way process, for the East now became aware of the West as well as vice versa. Marco Polo, who opened the eyes of the West to Cathay, had his counterparts in China and the Middle East.

We know of Chinese trading colonies in Moscow, Tabriz, and Novgorod during this period, while Chinese engineers were employed on irrigation projects in Mesopotamia. Also there are records of Chinese bureaucrats who accompanied Genghis Khan on his campaigns and inspection tours from one end of Eurasia to the other. In addition there was the Nestorian monk Rabban Bar Sauma, who was born in Peking and who travelled in 1278 to the Ilkhan's court in Baghdad. From there he was sent by the Mongols to Europe to seek Christian help against Islam. Starting out in 1287, he travelled to Constantinople, Naples, Rome, Paris, and London, meeting en route both Philip IV of France and Edward I of England. The most wide-ranging of these medieval travellers was the Moslem Ibn Battuta (1304–1378). Starting from his native Morocco, he made the pilgrimage to Mecca and journeyed on through Samarkand to India where he served as judge and also as ambassador to China. Returning later to Morocco, he resumed his travels, crossing north to Spain and then south to the interior of Africa, where he reached Timbuktu. When he finally returned to Morocco and settled down, he had travelled no less than 75,000 miles.

By all odds the most important traveller for the Western world was the famous Marco Polo. Accompanying his father and his uncle on their second journey to China, he arrived at Kublai Khan's court in 1275. He favorably impressed the Khan and served him for seventeen years in various capacities that required him to travel throughout the country. As an official he carefully observed the inhabitants and resources of the lands through which he journeyed, noting such things as "a kind of black stone, which is dug out of the mountains like any other kind of stone and burns like wood." In 1292 he escorted a Mongol princess on a voyage around southeast Asia and across the Indian Ocean to Persia where she was to be the bride of the Ilkhan. Marco Polo then continued westward to his native Venice, arriving there in 1295 after an absence of twenty-five years. Shortly afterward he was captured in a battle with the Genoese, and while in prison he dictated his account of his travels.

The book opens with this passage, which gives some idea of what a thrilling eye-opener it was for the people of the time.

> Emperors and Kings, dukes and marquesses, counts, knights and burgesses, and all ye, whoever ye be, who wish to know of the various races of men, and of the diversities of the different regions of the world, take this book and have it read to you. You shall find in it all the mighty wonders, all the great singularities of the vast regions of the East—of the Greater Armenia, of Persia, of Tartary, and of India, and of many a country besides—set down by us clearly and in due order, as they were recounted by Messer Marco Polo, called Millione, a wise and noble citizen of Venice, who saw them with his own eyes. . . . And all who read this book or hear it read, must believe it, as all the things contained in it are true. For I tell you that ever since the Lord our God did with his own hands mould our first father Adam, there never was up to the present day any man, Christian or Pagan, Tartar or Indian or of any other race what-

soever, who knew and explored so great a part of the various regions of the world and of its great marvels, as this Messer Marco knew and explored. . . .[6]

Marco's stories were as exciting as this introduction promised. He told of the Grand Khan's palace with its gardens and artificial lakes, its elephants with harnesses of silver and precious stones. He told also of roads that were paved and raised above the surrounding ground so that they might drain easily, of the Grand Canal through which merchant vessels passed each year, of ports with ships larger than any known in Europe, and of lands which produced spices, silk, ginger, sugar, camphor, cotton, salt, saffron, sandalwood, and porcelain. Marco described also all the fabulous countries he visited and heard about while escorting the Chinese princess to Persia—Singapore, Java, Sumatra, Ceylon, India, Socotra, Madagascar, Arabia, Zanzibar, and Abyssinia.

It all seemed so fantastic and exaggerated that he was dubbed Il millione, "the man who talks in millions." Actually he had provided Europeans with the most comprehensive and authoritative account of China available to the mid-sixteenth century. The title of his book is significant—*The Description of the World*. In fact this work had suddenly doubled the size of the known world for westerners. Marco Polo opened up new vistas for his contemporaries fully as much as Columbus was to do two centuries later. Indeed it was his tantalizing picture of Cathay and the Spice Islands that beckoned the great explorers onward as they sought a direct sea passage after the Moslems had blocked the overland routes.

SUGGESTED READING

The most important single work dealing with all types of interaction within Eurasia is the first volume of J. Needham, *Science and Civilisation in China* (London: Cambridge Univ., 1954). The maritime trade is described by G. F. Hourani, *Arab Seafaring in the Indian Ocean in Ancient and Early Medieval Times* (Princeton: Princeton Univ., 1951); and by A. Toussaint, *History of the Indian Ocean* (Chicago: Univ. of Chicago, 1966). The overland trade is admirably analyzed by G. F. Hudson, *Europe and China: A Survey of their Relations from the Earliest Times to 1800* (Boston: Beacon, 1961). An analysis of Eurasian trade in general is given in C. G. F. Simkin, *The Traditional Trade of Asia* (London: Oxford Univ., 1969).

For technological exchange, the basic work is the multivolume study by Needham listed above. A convenient summary by the same author is available in his essay "Science and China's Influence on the World" published in R. Dawson, ed., *The Legacy of China* (Oxford: Clarendon, 1964). Brief popular accounts of the diffusion of Chinese ideas and technology are provided by the two pamphlets by D. Bodde, *China's Gifts to the West* (Washington: American Council on Education, 1942), and *Chinese Ideas in the West* (Washington: American Council on Education, 1948).

For the travels of Marco Polo and his precursors, see *The Travels of Marco*

Polo, trans. R. E. Latham (Baltimore: Penguin, 1958); L. Olschki, *Marco Polo's Precursors* (Baltimore: Johns Hopkins Press, 1943); and P. M. Sykes, *The Quest for Cathay* (London: A. and C. Black, 1936), the latter including extracts from Carpini and Rubruquis, as well as the Polos and various explorers.

Finally the expanding horizons of medieval times are described in full detail in the first volume of D. F. Lach, *Asia in the Making of Europe* (Chicago: Univ. of Chicago, 1965).

The burden of the desert of the sea.
As whirlwinds in the south pass through;
so it cometh from the desert,
from a terrible land.

ISAIAH 21:1

We have revealed to thee an Arabic Koran,
that thou mayest warn Mecca, the Mother
of Cities, and those who are about her;
that thou mayest give warning of the
Day of Judgement, of which is no
doubt—when part shall be in Paradise
and part in the flame.

KORAN, SURA XLII

Rise of Islam

The centuries between 600 and 1000 witnessed the emergence of Islam, a major turning point in Eurasian and world history. The spectacular conquests of the Moslem warriors united once more the entire Middle East as Alexander the Great had done almost a millennium earlier. The subsequent disruption of Alexander's empire, followed eventually by the imposition of Roman rule in Asia Minor and Syria, led to the division of the Middle East into two parts with the Euphrates River as the dividing line. The eastern part was the center of Persian civilization and consisted of Iran and Iraq, while the western part, the abode of Byzantine civilization, encompassed the Balkans, Asia Minor, Syria, Egypt, and North Africa. The Islamic conquests of the seventh and eighth centuries ended this division by uniting under the star and crescent all the territories from the Pyrenees to the Sind and from Morocco to Central Asia.

More remarkable than these military exploits were the cultural achievements of Islam. Although the conquered territories were the centers of the most ancient civilizations of mankind, nevertheless they were by the eleventh century linguistically Arabized and culturally Islamized. Arabic became the language of everyday use from Persia to the Atlantic, while a new Islamic civilization emerged that was an original synthesis of the preceding Judaic, Perso-Mesopotamian, and Greco-Roman civilizations. This linguistic and cultural transformation persists to the present day, so that an Iraqi and a Moroccan now have as strong linguistic and cultural ties as an Englishman and an Australian.

I. Arabia Before Islam

The Middle East on the eve of the Moslem invasions was dominated by two great empires: the Byzantine, which from Constantinople controlled the lands of the eastern Mediterranean, and the Sassanian, with its capital at Ctesiphon, ruling the Tigris-Euphrates valleys and the Iranian plateau. The hostility between these two states was chronic, one being Christian with a Greco-Roman culture, and the other Zoroastrian with Perso-Mesopotamian traditions. Between 603 and 629 they fought a series of exhausting wars that left both vulnerable to the gathering storm in the Arabian deserts.

Arabia at this time was regarded by its civilized neighbors as an obscure land of nomadic barbarians. Yet it had become economically significant in the second half of the sixth century because of a shift in the routes of trade. The traditional Red Sea-Nile Valley and Persian Gulf-Red Sea routes had become unusable because of disorders in Egypt and the Byzantine-Persian wars. The traders accordingly turned to the more difficult but tranquil route from Syria through western Arabia to the Yemen, where vessels then transported the goods back and forth across the Indian Ocean. Mecca, situated half way down the coast of Arabia, profited from this diversion, being located at the crossing of the lines of communication running north to Syria, south to the Yemen, and also east to the Persian Gulf and west to the Red Sea port of Jedda and the sea lane to Africa.

Apart from the south where agriculture and monarchical government were feasible, the rest of Arabia was pastoral and tribal. The *sheikhs,* or elective tribal leaders, were merely the first among equals, being bound by traditional custom that governed all. Their principal functions were to lead in time of war and to serve as custodians of holy places. Most of the tribes were pagan, worshipping trees, fountains and stones that were regarded as the dwelling-places of vaguely defined powers. There was also a belief in more personal gods, which were subordinate to a higher deity called Allah. Both Judaism and Christianity had penetrated Arabia from the north, winning over entire tribes in the border region as well as isolated groups in the remainder of the peninsula. Compared to these faiths, the polytheistic idolatry, tribal warfare, and political disunity of Arabia must have seemed shamefully primitive to thoughtful Arabs. Indeed we hear of several "prophets" appearing about the beginning of the seventh century, reflecting a striving towards an indigenous monotheism. Like every successful preacher, Mohammed gave voice and form to the need and longing of his time.

II. Mohammed

Mohammed, the most influential historical personage of the Medieval Age, was born in 569. He was the posthumous son of a Mecca merchant, and since his mother died when he was six, he was brought up first by his grandmother and subsequently by his uncle. Little is known of his youth, though tradition has it that at the age of twelve he was taken by his uncle on a caravan to Syria. In the course of that journey he may have picked up some Jewish and Christian lore. At the age of twenty-five he married a wealthy widow who bore him several daughters and two sons who died in infancy.

About his fortieth year Mohammed went through a period of intense spiritual tension, in the course of which he became convinced that God had chosen him to be a prophet, a successor to Abraham and Moses and Jesus. Asked to describe the process of revelation, he answered that the entire text of the Koran existed in Heaven and that one fragment at a time was communicated to him, usually by the archangel Gabriel who made him repeat every word. Others who were near Mohammed on some of these occasions neither saw nor heard the archangel. His convulsions may have been epileptic seizures, particularly since he reported hearing sounds like the ringing of bells—a frequent occurrence in epileptic fits. In any case Mohammed now believed that he had received a divine call to attest the unity and transcendence of Allah, to warn his people of the Day of Judgment, and to tell them of the rewards for the faithful in Paradise and the punishment of the wicked in Hell.

His teachings were written down soon after his death and became the sacred scripture of the new religion known as Islam, meaning "submission to God's will." Mohammed did not establish an organized priesthood nor did he prescribe specific sacraments essential for salvation. But he did call on his followers to perform certain rituals known as the Five Pillars of Islam. These are: (1) Once in his life the believer must say with full understanding and absolute acceptance, *la ilaha illa llah: muhammed rasulu'llah*—"There is no God but Allah; Mohammed is the Messenger of Allah." (2) Five times daily he must pray—at dawn, at noon, in mid afternoon, at dusk, and after it has become dark. Facing in the direction of Mecca, the worshipper prays on a carpet, with his shoes removed and his head covered. (3) The Moslem must give alms generously, as an offering to Allah and an act of piety. (4) The Moslem must fast from daybreak to sunset during the whole month of Ramadan. (5) Once in his life the Moslem, if he can, must make the pilgrimage, or Hadj, to Mecca.

These rituals provided the believers with an extraordinarily powerful social cement. They prayed and fasted together, they assumed responsibility for their less fortunate brothers, and they journeyed to Mecca together—rich and poor, yellow, white, brown, and black. Furthermore the Koran provided guidance for all phases of the life of the faithful—for manners and hygiene, marriage and divorce, commerce and politics, crime and punishment, peace and war. Thus Islam was not only a religion but also a social code and a political system. It offered to its followers not only religious commandments but also specific precepts for private and for public life. There was no cleavage between the secular life and the religious, between the temporal and the spiritual, as was the case in the Christian world. What is Caesar's, in Islam, is God's, and what is God's is also Caesar's. The *Shari'a*, or Holy Law, was until recently the law of the land throughout the Moslem world, and it is still so to a great extent in individual countries.

To these teachings Mohammed slowly won converts, the first being members of his immediate family and personal friends, who later enjoyed great prestige as "Companions of the Prophet." As the little band of converts grew, the

In front of banners proclaiming, "There is no god but Allah," mounted musicians take part in the biggest of Moslem holidays, the Great Festival. This festival marked the final days of the annual pilgrimage to Mecca. (Bibliothèque Nationale, Paris)

wealthy Meccan merchants became alarmed for fear that Mohammed's teachings would undermine the older religious beliefs and discourage pilgrims from coming to worship at the shrine of the Black Stone in their city. Because of the growing opposition, Mohammed accepted an invitation to go to Medina, an oasis town on the trade route nearly three hundred miles north of Mecca. There was a mixed population of Arab and Jewish tribes, so Mohammed was welcomed as an arbitrator. His emigration to Medina, known as the hegira, took place in 622, and the Moslem calendar is dated from the beginning of the year in which this event occurred.

Since his teachings were based largely on Judaic doctrines, tales, and themes, Mohammed expected the Medina Jews to welcome him as the successor of their own prophets. Instead they ridiculed his claims, so Mohammed turned against them, eventually driving them out of the town and dividing their property amongst his followers. The character of Islam now became more strongly Arabic, and Mecca superseded Jerusalem as the direction toward which Moslems must turn in prayer. Gradually Mohammed persuaded the Medina Arabs to accept his religion and he organized a theocratic state based on his teachings.

From his base in Medina, Mohammed organized attacks on the Mecca caravans. Such raiding was an accepted and popular economic activity amongst Arab nomads, who now flocked to the banner of the Prophet in the hope of winning booty, and incidentally salvation. By 630 the Moslems were strong enough to capture Mecca, whereupon Mohammed made the Black Stone, housed in the Ka'ba, the chief shrine of his religion. Thus he effected a compromise by which he preserved the basic tenets of his faith and yet rooted it in traditional Arab custom. By the time of his death in 632, most—though by no means all—of the Arab tribes had recognized his overlordship and paid him tribute.

Mohammed, who had found his native land a flotsam of idolatrous practices, now left it with a religion and a revealed book, and with a community and a state sufficiently well organized and armed to dominate the entire peninsula. Within a century his followers were to march on from victory to victory, building an imposing empire across the breadth of Eurasia and propagating his creed, which today boasts half a billion adherents throughout the world. If influences on the course of events be the criterion, then Mohammed surely stands out as one of the giants of history.

III. Age of Conquests

Precisely because the Moslem community was the product of Mohammed's genius, it now seemed likely with his death to break up into its component elements. The tribal sheikhs considered their submission to him as having lapsed with his death, so they stopped their tribute and resumed their freedom of action. This withdrawal, known in Islamic history as the *Ridda,* or apostasy, provoked a series of well-planned campaigns that overwhelmed the "apostate" tribes and forced them back into the community of Islam. But the subdued tribesmen, sullen and resentful, obviously would seize the first opportunity to break away again. The ideal distraction was foreign raids with the promise of booty beloved by every Bedouin. These raids, then, began not as religious crusades to propagate the faith. Mohammed did not conceive of Islam as a universal faith and did not believe that God had chosen him to preach to any other people than his own Arabs. Rather the Arab raids grew out of the need to keep the turbulent Bedouins preoccupied and loyal to Medina.

The leader of the raids was the caliph, or deputy, who was chosen in the place of the Prophet in his secular capacity. There was no question, of course, of a successor to Mohammed as Prophet, but a secular chief of the community was essential. Thus when Abu Bakr, Mohammed's father-in-law, was selected as caliph, it signified that he was the defender of the faith rather than religious leader. It was under Abu Bakr that the apostate tribes were forced back to the fold and the earliest foreign raids begun.

Under Caliph Omar, who succeeded Abu Bakr in 634, the early raids blossomed into full-fledged campaigns of conquest. They did so because the outwardly formidable Byzantine and Persian empires were soon discovered to be hollow shells. They not only had been weakened by the series of wars between them, but in addition their subjects were seriously disaffected because of heavy taxation and religious persecution. Furthermore the Moslem forces now were being transformed from raiding parties to large-scale armies as entire tribes from all Arabia migrated northward, attracted by reports of dazzling riches. Any attempt to turn them back to their barren homeland would have provoked a new and possibly fatal *Ridda,* so the Moslem leaders crossed over into Syria at the head of their Bedouin hosts. Thus the great conquests that followed represented the expansion not of Islam but of the Arab tribes, who on many occasions in earlier centuries had pushed northward into the Fertile Crescent. The unprecedented magnitude of the expansion at this time derived partly from the exceptional weakness of the two empires and partly from the unity and élan engendered by the new Islamic faith.

Once the invasions were under way the Arabs made good use of their experience in desert warfare. Being mounted on camels, in contrast to the horses of the Byzantines and Persians, they were able to attack at will, and, if necessary, to retreat back to the safety of the desert. Just as the Vikings later were to be able to ravage the coasts of Europe because of their command of the sea, so now the Arabs used their "ships of the desert" to attack the wealthy empires. It was not accidental that in the provinces they conquered the Arabs established their main bases in towns on the edge of the desert. They used existing cities like Damascus when they were suitably located, and when necessary created new ones like Kufa and Basra in Iraq, and Fustat in Egypt. These garrison towns met the same need for the emerging Arab Empire that Gibraltar, Malta, and Singapore later did for the British sea empire.

In 636 the Arabs won a decisive victory over the Byzantines in the ravines of the Yarmuk River, a tributary of the Jordan. Attacking in the midst of a blinding sandstorm they almost annihilated a mixed force of Greek, Armenian, and Syrian Christians. Emperor Heraclius fled to Constantinople, abandoning all of Syria to the victors. Caliph Omar now turned against the rich adjacent province of Iraq. Its Semitic, partly Christian, population was alienated from its Persian and Zoroastrian masters. This contributed to the great victory won by the Arabs in the summer of 637 at Qadisiya. The Persian emperor hastily evacuated his nearby capital Ctesiphon and fled eastward.

The astonishing triumphs at Yarmuk and Qadisiya left the Moslems with unheard of riches, which further swelled the flood of Bedouin tribesmen from the southern deserts. Their pressure on the frontiers was irresistible, and the Arab armies rolled onward, westward into Egypt and eastward into Persia. Within two years (639–641) they had overrun the whole of Egypt, but in Persia for the first time they encountered stiff resistance. Although the imperial leadership was incompetent and unpopular, nevertheless the nation was ready to fight for its freedom and its Zoroastrian religion against the despised Arab nomads who had always been looked down upon as "desert vermin." As the Moslems advanced, local resistance bands were organized and exacted a heavy toll of the invaders. Not until 651 was the country subdued, and long before then, in 644, Omar had been assassinated by a Persian captive.

Omar's successors in the caliphate bore the banners of Islam still further afield, driven on by the momentum of victory, of religious enthusiasm, and of nomadic cupidity. In North Africa the Arab forces, supplemented by native Berber converts, fought their way clear across to Morocco and then crossed the Straits of Gibraltar into Spain. In 711 they defeated Roderick, the last Visigothic king of Spain, and advanced to the Pyrenees and on into France. There, however, they were defeated by Charles Martel at Tours in 732. This battle is often designated as a major turning point in the history of Western Europe, though it is doubtful that the Moslems, even if successful, could have advanced much further in a region so distant from their home base. The same is true of the expansion of the Moslems to the east. In 715 they conquered the province of Sind in northwest India but were unable to push further until several centuries later when their Turkish coreligionists invaded India from the north. Likewise in 751 the Moslems defeated the Chinese at Talas in Central Asia, but again were unable to advance further towards China. Thus Talas, Sind, and the Pyrenees marked the limits for Moslem expansionism given the level of their military technology.

This points up the exceptional significance of the Arab failure to take Constantinople after a full year's siege in 717–18. Since this city was so close to the center of their empire, they presumably would have been able to overrun much of Eastern Europe had they prevailed at Constantinople. This, of course, is precisely what the Moslem Turks did in the fifteenth century, but if it had occurred nearly a millennium earlier, much of Eastern Europe would have been Arabized and Islamized, and would constitute today an integral part of the Moslem Middle East.

Despite these setbacks, the fact remains that what had started out as a simple desert religion had grown in little more than one century into a great Eurasian empire. By 750 Islam ruled over the vast territories stretching from the Pyrenees to Sind, and from Morocco to the frontiers of China. (See Map XIII, "Expansion of Islam to 1500.")

IV. ARAB KINGDOM TO ISLAMIC EMPIRE

With the first phase of expansion completed, the Arabs now settled down to enjoy the fruits of victory. They were virtually an army of occupation in their subject lands, residing mostly in the strategically located camp cities whence they controlled the surrounding countryside. Since Caliph Omar had decided at the outset that his followers should not be allotted fiefs in the conquered provinces, they now were supported by government pensions. The funds for these pensions were derived from lands confiscated by the Islamic state and from taxes which were levied at a higher rate upon non-Moslems than upon Moslems. Apart from this discriminatory taxation, the non-Moslems were left virtually undisturbed. No effort was made to convert them; indeed conversion was not at all welcomed for it involved under the circumstances a decline in revenue. Thus Islam was in effect a perquisite of the Arab warrior-aristocracy that ruled over the much more numerous subject peoples.

This arrangement was soon disturbed by the appearance in increasing numbers of the *Mawali,* or non-Arab Moslems. These converts flocked to the cities where they served the needs of the Arab aristocracy as servants, artisans, shopkeepers, and merchants. Being Moslems they claimed equality with the Arabs but this was not conceded. Although the *Mawali* fought in the armies of Islam, they were usually restricted to the infantry, which received a lower rate of pay and booty than the Arab cavalry.

As the empire expanded and wealth poured into the cities from the subject provinces, the *Mawali* increased in numbers and wealth. But they remained excluded from the ruling circles, so they became a disaffected urban element, determined to gain status commensurate with their economic power. Thus the Arab Umayyad dynasty of caliphs, which had moved the capital from Medina to Damascus in 661, came to be regarded with much justification as a parasitic clique that had outlived its usefulness once the conquests were completed. The opposition to the Arab aristocracy, therefore, was both a national and a social movement of protest.

A disputed accession to the throne precipitated a decade of civil strife culminating in the accession of the Abbasid caliphate in 750. This represented much more than a mere change of dynasty. The *Mawali,* and particularly the Persians, now replaced the old redundant aristocracy. The Arabs no longer were a privileged salaried soldiery, being replaced by a royal standing army that was at first largely Persian. The former garrison cities became great commercial centers under *Mawali* control. Some of the Arabs became absorbed into the mass of townspeople and peasants, while others reverted to nomadism.

The imperial structure also changed radically, especially with the shift of the capital from Damascus eastward to Baghdad in 762. In effect this meant that the Abbasid caliphate was turning its back on the Mediterranean and looking to Persia for traditions and support. The caliph no longer was an Arab sheikh but a divinely ordained autocrat—the "Shadow of God upon Earth." His authority rested not on tribal support but on a salaried bureaucracy and standing army. Thus the caliphate became an oriental monarchy similar to the many that had preceded it in Ctesiphon and Persepolis and Babylon. Under the order and security imposed by this monarchy, a syncretic civilization that was an amalgam of Judaic, Greco-Roman, and Perso-Mesopotamian traditions, evolved during the ensuing centuries. Islam ceased to be merely the code of a ruling warrior-aristocracy and became instead a new and distinctive civilization.

V. ISLAMIC CIVILIZATION

Caliph Mansur, who selected Baghdad as the site for the Abbasid capital, foresaw a glorious future for his choice.

This island between the Tigris in the East and the Euphrates in the West is a market place for the world. All the ships that come up the Tigris from Wasit, Basra, Uballa, Ahwaz, Fars, Uman, Yamama, Bahrain and beyond will go up and anchor here; wares brought on ships down the Tigris from Mosul, Diyar-Rabi'a, Adharbaijan and Armenia, and along the Euphrates from Diyar-Mudar, Raqqa, Syria and the border marshes, Egypt and North Africa will be brought and unloaded here. It will be the highway for the people of the Jabal, Isfahan and the districts of Khurasan. Praise be to God who preserved it for me and caused all those who came before me to neglect it. By God, I shall build it. Then I shall dwell in it as long as I live and my descendants shall dwell in it after me. It will surely be the most flourshing city in the world.[1]

Mansur's expectations were quickly realized to the full. Within a century Baghdad numbered about a million people. In the center was a citadel some two miles in diameter in which were the caliph's residence and the quarters of his officials and guards. Beyond the citadel walls a great commercial metropolis sprang up, supported by the plentiful produce of the fertile Mesopotamian valley. The main crops were wheat, barley, rice, dates, and olives. The Abbasids increased the output when they extended the area of cultivated land by draining swamps and by enlarging the irrigation works. They also were less extortionist than the previous rulers in their tax and labor levies on the peasants, though this improvement was soon nullified by the speculations of wealthy merchants and landowners and by the introduction of slave labor on the large estates.

The provinces contributed rich supplies of metals—silver from the Hindu Kush, gold from Nubia and the Sudan, copper from Isfahan, and iron from Persia, Central Asia, and Sicily. Precious stones came from many regions of the empire, while the waters of the Persian Gulf yielded pearls. Industry also flourished, textiles being the most important in the number of workers employed and the value of the output. Linen, cotton, and silk goods were produced in many parts of the empire, both for local consumption and for export. Carpets also were made almost everywhere, those of Tabaristan and Armenia being considered the best. The art of papermaking, learned from Chinese prisoners taken at Talas in 751, spread rapidly across the Islamic world, reaching Spain by 900. Other industries included pottery, metalwork, soap, and perfumes.

Such a rich economy, extended across the breadth of the far-flung Abbasid Empire, stimulated interregional trade on an unprecedented scale. Moslem merchants, as noted in the preceding chapter, traded overland through Central Asia, and overseas with India, Ceylon, Southeast Asia, and China. A flourishing trade was carried on also with Africa, whence were obtained gold, ivory, ebony, and slaves. Commerce with the northern countries is attested by the discovery in Scandinavia of large hoards of Moslem coins dating from the seventh to the eleventh centuries. In exchange for these coins the Moslems received furs, wax, amber, honey, and cattle. Such large-scale trade stimulated a highly developed banking system with branches in all leading cities, so that a check could be drawn in Baghdad and cashed in Morocco.

With this solid economic base, the Abbasid caliphs were able to indulge themselves in their dazzlingly luxurious palaces. The *Thousand and One Nights* portrays Harun al-Rashid (786–809), the best known of these caliphs, as a gay and cultured ruler, surrounded by a galaxy of poets, musicians, singers, dancers, scholars, and wits. Among the popular indoor games were chess, dice, and backgammon, while outdoor sports included hunting, falconry, hawking, polo, archery, fencing, javelin throwing, and horse racing. Harun was contemporary with Charlemagne, but their respective capitals, Baghdad and Aix-la-Chapelle, were quite incomparable—as incomparable as Baghdad and Paris today, but in the reverse sense. A Byzantine ambassador in the early tenth century, though familiar with the opulence of Constantinople, was nevertheless impressed by what he beheld in Baghdad. He reported twenty-three palaces, each with thousands of rugs and tapestries, multitudes of servants in shining uniforms, ladies in gorgeous and colorful raiment of silk and gold brocade, and a variety of tame and wild animals in the spacious parks.

The Abbasid caliphate was noted not only for its affluence and splendor but also for its relative toleration in religious matters in an age when this quality was markedly absent in the West. The explanation is to be found partly in the religious law of Islam. The sacred law recognized the Christians and Jews as being, like the Moslems, People of the Book. Both had a scripture—a written word of revelation. Their faith was accepted as true, though incomplete, since Mohammed had superseded Moses and Jesus Christ. Islam therefore tolerated the Christians and Jews. It permitted them to practice their faith, with certain restrictions and penalties.

Caliph Harun, for example, ordered that all churches built subsequent to the Moslem conquest be demolished, and that all non-Moslems, or *Dhimmis,* wear prescribed garb. His grandson decreed that Christians and Jews affix wooden images of devils to their houses and ride only on mules with wooden saddles. Islamic jurists also ruled that the testimony of a Christian or a Jew was not acceptable against a Moslem. And at all times the taxes levied on the *Dhimmis* were more onerous than those on the believers. Thus the *Dhimmis* definitely were second-class citizens, and yet their position was clearly superior to that of comparable dissenters in the West. They could practice their faith, enjoy normal property rights, and belong to craft guilds. They were often appointed to high state office, and were spared the martyrdom or exile endured, for example, by Jews and Moslems in Spain following the Christian conquest.

The Abbasid caliphate also was noteworthy for its achievements in the field of science. It is true that the tendency here was to preserve and to pass on rather than to create something new. One of their greatest scientists, al-Biruni (973–1048), stated, "We ought to confine ourselves to what the Ancients have dealt with and to perfect what can be perfected." [2] Nevertheless the sheer size of the empire, its contacts with literally all regions of Eurasia, and its almost overpoweringly rich legacy from the several great centers of civilization that it encompassed all contributed to the very real achievements of Islamic science. Baghdad, for example, boasted a "House of Wisdom" consisting of a school of translators, a library, an observatory, and an academy. The scholars associated with it translated and studied the works of Greek scientists and philosophers, as well as scientific treatises from Persia and India.

In astronomy the Moslems generally accepted the basic tenets of their Greek predecessors and made no significant advances in theory. But they did continue without interruption the astronomical observations of the ancients, so that the later Renaissance astronomers had available some nine hundred years of records which provided the basis for their crucial discoveries. Mathematics was of great interest to Moslems because it was needed both in astronomy and in commerce. Thanks to Babylonian and Indian influence they made important advances, especially in popularizing the Hindu system of numbers based on the decimal notation. (See Chapter 9, section V.) Misleadingly called Arabic numerals, this system did for arithmetic what the discovery of the alphabet had done earlier for writing. It democratized mathematics, making it available for everyday use by nonspecialists. The greatest Islamic mathematician was a Persian, Muhammad ibn Musa (780–850), called al-Khwarizmi from his birthplace Khwarizm (now Khiva), east of the Caspian Sea. He wrote on the Hindu numerals, compiled a textbook on algebra (al-Jabr) that was used in both East and West for centuries, formulated the oldest trigonometrical tables known, and collaborated with other scholars in compiling an encyclopedia of geography.

In geography, as in astronomy, the Moslems made little theoretical progress, but the extent of their empire and of their commerce enabled them to accumulate reliable and systematic data concerning the Eurasian land mass. Al-Biruni's famous book on India, for example, described not only the physical features of the country, but also the social system, religious beliefs, and scientific attainments of the Hindus in a manner that was not to be equalled until the eighteenth century. The Moslems also prepared charts and maps in which they naturally located Mecca in the center, as the contemporary Christian cartographers did for Jerusalem.

Islamic medicine also was based on that of the Greeks, but the greater geographical spread of Islam made possible a knowledge of new diseases and drugs. To the ancient pharmacopeia the Moslems added ambergris, camphor, cassia, cloves, mercury, senna, myrrh; and they also introduced new pharmaceutical preparations such as syrups, juleps, and rose water. Indeed, Arab drugs figured prominently in the cargoes that Italian captains loaded in Middle Eastern ports. Anesthesia by inhalation was practiced in some surgical operations, and hashish and other drugs were used as sedatives. Moslems established the first apothecary shops and dispensaries, founded the first medieval school of pharmacy, required state examination and certification for the practice of medicine, and operated well-equipped hospitals, of which some thirty are known. The great Islamic doctors, such as Muhammad al-Razi (844–926) and Abu Ali al-Husein ibn Sina (980–1037), famous in Europe as "Rhazes" and "Avicenna," were brilliant men of wide knowledge ranging from astronomy through botany to chemistry, and wrote texts that were used in European medical schools until the seventeenth century.

Even more significant for the general advance of science were the Moslem contributions in chemistry. To the traditions and practices of the Babylonians, Egyptians, and Greeks, they added the extensive chemical knowledge of the Indians and Chinese. They expended much talent and energy in the quest for the two ancient will-o'-the-wisps: the philosopher's stone for transforming base metals into precious ones, and the elixir for prolonging life indefinitely. Yet their treatises show that they were the first to evolve sophisticated laboratory techniques for handling drugs, salts, and precious metals. Thus they were able to develop localized chemical industries for the production of soda, alum, iron

*Fourteenth-century manuscript showing Avicenna and scholars.
This page is taken from "The Canon" of Avicenna and is in the
collection of the Bologna University Library. (Arborio Mella)*

sulphate, nitrates, and other salts for industrial purposes, especially in textiles.

The highest achievement of the Arabs in their own estimation was their poetry. In pre-Islamic times it had a public and social function, with the poet often serving as a eulogist or a satirist. The main themes were war, valor, love, praise of a patron, abuse of an enemy, and glorification of one's tribe or camel or horse. Under the Abbasids, Arabic poetry was enriched by the contributions of many non-Arabs, especially Persians. But there was no borrowing from Greco-Roman literature, which explains why Arabic literature remained strange and unknown to the West. Moslem scientists became familiar to Westerners, but not Moslem poets. Yet to the present day the Arabs find much pleasure and inspiration in their poetry with its intoxicating verbal effect and the hypnotic power of its monotonous rhyming.

In addition to their own original achievements, the Moslems made an invaluable contribution in translating and transmitting ancient works. The Umayyad caliphs had distrusted all non-Arabs and were uninterested in their civilizations. The Abbasids, by contrast, had been strongly supported by Christians, Jews, and Zoroastrian Persians, and were much more tolerant and broad-minded. The "House of Wisdom" in Baghdad included a large staff of translators, one of the outstanding ones being a Christian, Hunain ibn-Ishaq (809–873). He visited Greek-speaking lands to collect manuscripts, and with his assistants he translated a large number of them, including works of Hippocrates, Galen, Euclid, Ptolemy, Plato, and Aristotle. Another great translation center was in the city of Toledo in Moslem Spain, where the translators during the twelfth and thirteenth centuries included Jews, Spaniards, and foreign scholars from all over Europe. This activity was of utmost significance, for Western Europeans had lost direct acquaintance with Greek learning and for long were unaware even of its existence. Thus Moslem scholarship preserved the Greek works until Western Europe was ready once more to resume their study.

In conclusion it should be emphasized that two basic bonds held together the diverse peoples of the sprawling caliphate: the Arabic language and the Islamic religion. Much more remarkable than the Arab conquests was the diffusion of the Arabic language. By the eleventh century Arabic had superseded the old Greek, Latin, Coptic, and Aramaic languages and prevailed from Morocco to Persia, as it does to the present day. This common language explains the feeling of common identity prevailing in this region, even though it includes Negroid Sudanese as well as the prevailing Semites, and Christian Lebanese and Coptic Egyptians as well as the prevailing Moslems. Even beyond this vast area that was permanently Arabized, Arabic exerted a profound influence on other Moslem languages. Arabic words are as common in these other languages as Greek and Latin words in English, and some of these languages (Urdu, Malay, Swahili, and Turkish until World War I) are written in Arabic script.

The Islamic religion also is a powerful bond—much more powerful than Christianity in this respect because it is not only a religion but also a social and political system and a general way of life. (See section II of this chapter.) Religion. thus provides the basis for Islamic civilization as language does for the Arabic world. We have seen that the Islamic civilization evolved during the centuries following the conquests as a fusion of Christian, Jewish, Zoroastrian, and Arab religious elements, and Greco-Roman and Perso-Mesopo-

tamian administrative, cultural, and scientific elements. The end product was
not a mere mosaic or agglomeration of previous cultures, but rather a fusion
that represented a new and original civilization. It was diverse in its origins
and strands, yet uniquely molded by the distinctive imprint of Arabic Islam.

VI. DECLINE OF THE CALIPHATE

The Abbasid caliphate reached its height during the reign of Harun al-
Rashid, and thereafter declined under circumstances reminiscent of the collapse
of the Roman Empire. There was first the matter of sheer size—a very real
problem in an age when communications were dependent on horse and sail.
The outlying provinces were three thousand miles distant from the capital, so
that it is not surprising that they should be the first to break away: Spain in
756, Morocco in 788, and Tunisia in 800.

Also, as in the case of Rome, there was the problem of imperial expenditures that were excessive and insupportable in relation to the prevailing economy and technology. The rampant luxury of the Baghdad court and the over-
weight of the inflated bureaucracy were not counterbalanced by technological
progress. The resulting financial crisis forced the caliphs to appoint provincial
governors as tax farmers in the areas they administered. With the revenues
they collected, these governors maintained the local soldiery and officials, and
remitted an agreed sum to the central treasury. This arrangement left the
governors-farmers the real rulers of the provinces, together with the army commanders with whom they soon reached working agreements. By the mid-ninth
century the caliphs were losing both military and administrative control, and
were being appointed and deposed at will by Turkish mercenaries. The thirteenth-century Moslem historian al-Bundari describes clearly this transition
from centralized empire to feudal autonomy:

> It had been the custom to collect money from the country and pay it to
> the troops and no one had previously had a fief. Nazim al-Mulk [eleventh-
> century official] saw that the money was not coming in from the country
> on account of its disturbed state and that the yield was uncertain because
> of its disorder. Therefore he divided it among the troops in fiefs, assign-
> ing to them both the yield and the revenue. Their interest in its develop-
> ment increased greatly and it returned rapidly to a flourishing state.[3]

Imperial weakness, as usual, invited barbarian attacks. Just as the Roman
Empire had been invaded across the Rhine and the Danube, so the caliphate
now was assaulted from the north, south, and east. From the north came the
Crusaders who overran Spain, Sicily, and Syria, aided by Moslem discord in all
three areas. In Sicily the end of the local dynasty in 1040 was followed by
civil war, which facilitated the invasion of the island by the Normans from
southern Italy. By 1091 the whole of Sicily had been conquered and the mixed
Christian-Moslem population came under the rule of Norman kings.

Likewise in Spain the Umayyad dynasty was deposed in 1031 and the
country was split up into numerous petty states ruled by "parties" or factions

فاذا يزد العصير يصفه فهذا الشراب موافق لوجع الحلق والجنب والرئتين
والاستسقاء الرقيق ولمن به لغم غليظ في حلقه يصفي اللون، وكثر القيء م

وليبتدئ له غلية موافق للثانه والكلا ع ع م

::   صنعه شراب للزكام والسعال   ::

وورم البطن واستنخاء المعدة خذ مرنبح اوقيه واصول سوسن ثلث اوقيه
وفلفل ابيض نبع دمر اوقيه دقه جميعا واربطه خرقته واجعله في لته اقساط شراب
طيب واتركه تلث ايام ثم صفه وارفعه في آناء نظيف اشربته بعد العشا

reflecting diverse ethnic groups. These included the Arabs, the Berbers, the indigenous pre-Moslem Iberian stock, and the "Slavs," or European slaves. The latter, mostly from Central and Eastern Europe, had been employed as mercenary soldiers by the Umayyads as the Turks were by the Abbasids, and like them had come to dominate their masters. This fragmentation of Moslem Spain enabled the Christian states of the north to expand southward. By 1085 they captured the important city of Toledo, and by the end of the thirteenth century only Granada on the southern tip of the peninsula was left to the Moslems.

The loss of Sicily and Spain to Christendom proved permanent, but such was not the case with Syria. Here also the fratricidal warring of several Moslem states enabled the Crusaders from 1096 onward to advance rapidly down the coast of Syria into Palestine. They established four states, Edessa (1098), Antioch (1098), Jerusalem (1099), and Tripoli (1109), all organized along western feudal lines. But these states lacked roots, never assimilating their Moslem Arab subjects. Their existence depended on the sporadic arrival of recruits from Europe. Also they were all confined to the coastal areas and hence vulnerable to resistance movements organized in the interior. These states could exist only so long as the surrounding Moslem world remained divided. The disunity was ended by Salah ad-Din, better known in the West as Saladin. By uniting Moslem Syria and Egypt he surrounded the Crusader principalities and began the counterattack in 1187. By the time of his death in 1193 he had recaptured Jerusalem and expelled the westerners from all but a narrow coastal strip. During the following century this also was overrun and the Moslem reconquest was completed.

In addition to these Crusader onslaughts from the north, the caliphate was attacked by Berbers from southern Morocco and the Senegal-Niger area, and by the two Arab Bedouin tribes of Hilal and Sulaim from Upper Egypt. These tribes swept across Libya and Tunisia, wreaking havoc and devastation. It was this invasion rather than the earlier seventh-century Arab irruption that gutted civilization in North Africa. The famous fourteenth-century Arab historian Ibn Khaldun, himself a native of North Africa, noted the ruination of his homeland as follows:

> In Tunisia and the West, since the Hilal and Sulaim tribes passed that way at the beginning of the fifth century [the middle of the eleventh century A.D.] and devastated these countries, for three hundred and fifty years all the plains were ruined; whereas formerly from the Sudan to the Mediterranean all was cultivated, as is proved by the traces remaining there of monuments, buildings, farms and villages.[4]

Finally the third group of invaders were the Turks and Mongols from the East. Their incursions, persisting through several centuries and encompassing virtually the entire Eurasian land mass, constitute a major chapter of world history. The Turco-Mongol invasions are comparable to the Arab-Islamic conquests in scope and impact. Indeed the two are intimately related, for many of the Turco-Mongols were converted to Islam, and they then extended the frontiers of their faith into distant new regions. The course and significance of these Turco-Mongol invasions is the subject of the following chapter.

SUGGESTED READING

264   An excellent bibliographical guide is provided by R. H. Davison, *The Near and Middle East: An Introduction to History and Bibliography* (Washington: Service Center for Teachers of History, American Historical Association, 1959). For Mohammed and his teachings, see T. Andrae, *Mohammed* (New York: Scribner, 1936); E. Dermenghem, *The Life of Mahomet* (New York: Dial, 1930); H. A. R. Gibb, *Mohammedanism: An Historical Survey* (Home University Library, 1953); and the convenient edition of the translation of the *Koran* by M. M. Pickthall (New York: New American Library, 1953).

The Arabs and their conquests are described by P. K. Hitti, *History of the Arabs from the Earliest Times to the Present*, 5th ed. (New York: St. Martins, 1951); B. Lewis, *The Arabs in History* (Home University Library, 1950); J. B. Glubb, *The Great Arab Conquests* (Englewood Cliffs, N.J.: Prentice-Hall, 1963); and F. Gabrieli, *Muhammad and the Conquests of Islam* (World University Library, 1968). After the initial conquests, Islam continued to expand through quiet missionary work, as described by T. W. Arnold, *The Preaching of Islam: A History of the Propagation of the Muslim Faith* (London: Constable, 1913).

Various aspects of Islamic civilization are considered by G. E. von Grunebaum, *Medieval Islam*, 2nd ed. (Chicago: Univ. of Chicago, 1954); J. Stewart-Robinson, ed., *The Traditional Near East* (Englewood Cliffs, N.J.: Prentice-Hall, 1966); A. Guillaume, *Islam* (Baltimore: Penguin, 1954); T. Arnold and A. Guillaume, eds., *The Legacy of Islam* (Oxford: Clarendon, 1931); W. Montgomery Watt and P. Cachia, *A History of Islamic Spain* (Garden City, N.Y.: Doubleday, 1967), Anchor Book; and T. W. Arnold, *The Caliphate* (Oxford: Clarendon, 1924); A. G. Chejne, *The Arabic Language: Its Role in History* (Minneapolis: Univ. of Minnesota, 1969); and R. A. Nicholson, *A Literary History of the Arabs* (London: Cambridge Univ., 1969). Finally there are various editions available of the collection of stories known as the *Arabian Nights*, and of Omar Khayyam, *The Rubaiyat*.

*Nay, it is unlikely that mankind will see
the like of this calamity, until the world
comes to an end and perishes,
except the final outbreak of Gog and Magog.
For even Antichrist will spare such as
follow him, though he destroy those who
oppose him; but these [Tartars] spared none,
slaying women and men and children,
ripping open pregnant women
and killing unborn babes.*

IBN-AL-ATHIR *(Moslem historian, 1160–1233)*

Turco-Mongol Invasions

By all odds the most visible and spectacular development during the half millennium from 1000 to 1500 was the great swarming of Turco-Mongol peoples from the vast racial hive of Central Asia. These nomads overran literally the whole of Eurasia except for its distant extremities: Japan, Southeast Asia, southern India and Western Europe.

Three stages are discernible in the course of the nomadic expansion during these centuries. The first, between 1000 and 1200, marked the emergence of the Turks, first as mercenaries and then as masters of the Abbasid caliphate. They infused vigor and aggressiveness into the now moribund world of Islam, and extended its frontiers into Asia Minor at the expense of Byzantium and into northern India at the expense of Hindustan. The second stage, during the thirteenth century, witnessed the Mongol irruption which engulfed not only Central Asia, East Asia, and Russia, but also the Moslem Middle East, thereby halting abruptly the expansionism of the Moslem Turks. The final stage, between 1300 and 1500, involved the disintegration of the Mongol Empire, which cleared the way for the resurgence of the Turks and the resumption of the Turkish-Islamic advance into Christian Europe and Hindustan.

This chapter will consider each of these stages in turn, and their implications for general world history.

I. TURKISH PREDOMINANCE IN THE ISLAMIC WORLD

The Turks are a linguistic rather than an ethnic group, their common bond being that they all speak one form or another of a Turkish family of languages. Although an ethnically mixed people, they are generally Caucasoid in appearance rather than Mongoloid. By the mid-sixth century they dominated the extensive steppe lands from Mongolia to the Oxus, or Amu Darya. From the eighth century onward they came increasingly under Islamic influence as a result of the Arab conquest of Persia and defeat of the Chinese at Talas (751).

The response of the Turkish tribesmen to the brilliant Abbasid caliphate across the Oxus River was very similar to that of the Germans to the Roman Empire across the Rhine. First there was the cultural impact as the primitive Turkish pagans succumbed to the teachings of Islam and to the material allurements of a sophisticated civilization. At the same time the tribesmen were entering the military service of the caliphate, as the Germans earlier had entered that of Rome. As mounted bowmen of great mobility, they soon demonstrated their superior military qualities and increasingly replaced the Arabs and Persians in the caliph's armed forces.

As the caliphs became weaker, the Turkish mercenaries, like their German counterparts, became masters rather than servants. They made and unmade rulers in Baghdad, holding successive caliphs in tutelage. About 970 a branch of the Turkish people known as the Seljuks were crossing over unhindered into Moslem territory and soon had gathered power into their hands. This was formally recognized in 1055 when the caliph proclaimed the Seljuk leader, Tughril Beg, the "sultan," or "he who has authority." Although the caliphs remained the nominal heads of the empire, the *de facto* rulers henceforth were the Turkish sultans. Under their aggressive leadership, the frontiers of Islam now were further extended into two regions.

One was Asia Minor, which had remained for centuries a bastion of Christian Byzantine power against repeated onslaughts by Arabic Islam. But in 1071 the Seljuks won a crushing vistory at Manzikert in eastern Asia Minor, taking prisoner the Byzantine Emperor Romanus IV. This proved to be a decisive turning point in Middle Eastern history, for the battle was followed by civil war between rival Byzantine factions. In fact, this factionalism had been largely responsible for the defeat at Manzikert, and its continuation now enabled Turkish tribesmen to pour unopposed into Asia Minor. The quarreling Byzantine bureaucrats and generals, bidding against each other for the services of the Turkish tribal chieftains, handed over many towns and forts to the invaders. Furthermore the peasantry, alienated by the corruption and exploitation of Byzantine officials, accepted their new masters with passivity, if not relief. Thus between the eleventh and the thirteenth centuries the larger part of Asia Minor was transformed from a Greek and Christian to a Turkish and Moslem region, and it remains so to the present day. Furthermore Byzantium was gutted by this loss of Asia Minor, a province that hitherto had provided the bulk of the imperial revenue and army manpower. Constantinople now was like a huge head atop a shrivelled body. The roots of the fall of Constantinople in 1453 go back to 1071.

For the Seljuks, the victory at Manzikert was a giant step forward in their reconstitution of the moribund caliphate. Under Malik Shah (1073–1092) the Seljuk sultans reached their height, ruling Syria, Mesopotamia, and Iran, as well as Asia Minor. A brilliant cultural renaissance occurred under their aegis, with Persian language, literature, and art in the ascendancy. But Seljuk predominance proved short-lived. The empire disintegrated after Malik because of rivalry amongst his heirs and because of the granting of fiefs that became hereditary. (See Chapter 13, section VI.) This imperial disintegration made it possible for the Crusaders to conquer the Holy Land in the twelfth century. Another result was the emergence in western Asia Minor of the Ottoman Turks, who were destined to carry the banners of Islam to the walls of Vienna and to dominate the entire Middle East until the twentieth century.

While the Seljuks had been pushing westward in search of fame and booty, other Turks had been similarly engaged in the east, fighting their way towards the vast treasure house of India. Outstanding was a certain Mahmud (997–1030), who, from his base at Ghazni in Afghanistan, raided the Indian lands almost annually and finally annexed the Punjab, which has ever since remained Moslem. Mahmud's zeal in destroying Hindu temples and smashing their idols, a zeal that was based on the Islamic tenet that any visible representation of the deity was sinful, earned him the epithet "the image breaker." Fired by the fierce monotheism of Islam, Mahmud and his followers came to India not only in search of plunder but also to convert the infidels, or to exterminate them. There was also a social conflict involved—the clash between two different societies, one believing that all men are brothers and the other based upon caste, which presupposes inequality. It was at this time, then, that there began that struggle of two fundamentally different cultures that was to culminate after World War II in the division of the peninsula into Hindu India and Moslem Pakistan.

The successors of Mahmud were replaced in the twelfth century by another Turkish dynasty based in Ghor, also in Afghanistan. Under a certain Mohammed, the Ghori Turks advanced southward to Gujarat and eastward into the Ganges Valley. They captured Delhi in 1192 and made it the capital of the Turkish sultanate in India. During this campaign, Buddhist monasteries were destroyed and Buddhist monks were slaughtered on such a scale that Buddhism never recovered in its place of origin.

The relative ease with which the Turks ensconced themselves in a land in which they were hopelessly outnumbered is to be explained partly by the archaic Indian military tactics, which were the same as those that had proven inadequate against Alexander fifteen hundred years earlier. The infantry were usually an undisciplined rabble, while their vaunted elephants were useless against the Moslem cavalry. Equally damaging, and a more fundamental weakness, was the Hindu caste system, which left the fighting to only the Kshatriya, or warrior caste. The rest of the population was untrained and largely indifferent, particularly because class differentiation separating oppressive landlords from their peasants was added to caste fragmentation. Thus the masses either remained indifferent or else welcomed the invader and embraced his faith. This response was to be repeated frequently in the future and explains why in modern times the British Raj was able to rule from Delhi as Turkish Sultans had before.

II. Genghis Khan

268

While the Turks were becoming the masters of the Moslem world, an obscure chieftain in far-off Mongolia was beginning his career of conquest that was to culminate in the greatest empire of history. Genghis Khan (spelled also Chinggis, Chingis, Jenghiz, etc.), whose personal name was Temujin, was born about 1167, the son of a minor clan leader. When Temujin was twelve years old his father was poisoned and as a result the future Khan spent a childhood of misery. He was able to overcome these humble beginnings by mastering the complicated art of tribal politics, which called for a creative mixture of loyalty, cunning, and ruthless treachery, as well as physical prowess. After turning against his overlord and eliminating various rivals he finally was able to weld the various Mongol-speaking tribes into a single unit. At a *kuriltai,* or assembly of Mongol chieftains, held in 1206 he was proclaimed supreme head of his people with the title Genghis Khan, signifying "ruler of the universe."

He was now in a position to satisfy his natural nomadic impulse for conquest and booty. "Man's highest joy," he reportedly said, "is in victory: to conquer one's enemies, to pursue them, to deprive them of their possessions, to make their beloved weep, to ride on their horses, and to embrace their wives and daughters." In this respect Genghis Khan was no different from the long line of steppe conquerors who had gone before him. Why then was he alone destined to become the master of the greater part of Eurasia? This question is particularly intriguing because, as a Mongol, Genghis Khan did not have the manpower resources of other nomad conquerors, who were almost invariably Turks. All the Mongol tribes together numbered about one million men, women, and children, which afforded Genghis Khan a maximum of 125,000 warriors. With such limited resources, how was he able to come so close to becoming literally the "ruler of the universe"?

Genghis Khan began with the built-in advantage enjoyed by all nomad warriors—the fact that their daily life was a continuous rehearsal of campaign operations. Clad in leather and furs, leading extra horses as remounts, and capable of riding several days and nights in succession with a minimum of rest and food, these warriors introduced *blitzkrieg* into the world of the thirteenth century. During their campaigning on the plains of Hungary, they are said to have covered 270 miles in three days. They carried leather bags for water, which when empty could be inflated for use in swimming across rivers. Normally they lived off the countryside, but if necessary they drank the blood of their horses and the milk of their mares. Their skills in the hunt, acquired from boyhood, enabled them to coordinate the operations of flying horse columns over long distances. Their favorite tactic was feigned flight, during which the enemy might pursue the fleeing Mongols for days, only to be lured to ambush and destruction. Other tactical maneuvers included the tying of branches to the tails of horses to stir up dust in order to give the impression of large forces on the march, and also the mounting of dummies on spare horses for the same purpose.

The basic Mongol weapon was the compound large bow, more powerful

Fifteenth-century Chinese painting showing Genghis Khan hunting. Private collection. (Arborio Mella)

than the English longbow, and capable of killing at 600 feet with its armor-piercing arrows. This was a fearful weapon in the hands of Mongol horsemen who were able to shoot their supply of thirty arrows at full gallop. Other equipment included a steel helmet, light body armor made of hide, a saber, and sometimes a lance with a hook and a mace. The Mongol horses grazed only on the open range, with no shelter during the long bitter winter and no hay or grain for supplementary feed. This made them somewhat stunted in size but very tough and adaptable. "Even today," states one authority, "a Mongolian horse that can be lassoed on the range, saddled and with no further preparation ridden nonstop for more than a 100 miles is typical, not exceptional. But it cannot be ridden again the same way the next day; it has to be allowed several days of grazing." [1] This presented no problem for the Mongols who took large herds of remounts on their campaigns and rode a succession of horses as needed.

To these traditional nomad techniques Genghis Khan added new skills and equipment learned mostly from the Chinese. These included powerful catapults, battering-rams, and sappers who tunnelled under walls and blew them up with gunpowder. Thus Genghis Khan supplemented his incomparable mounted bowmen with the siege weapons necessary for capturing fortified cities.

The Mongols were also masters of espionage and psychological warfare. Before undertaking a campaign they collected all possible intelligence regarding the enemy's roads, rivers, fortifications, and political and economic conditions. They also used agents to spread demoralizing stories about the size of the Mongol forces and the futility of resistance. In the course of the campaigning they used ruthless terror tactics to undermine enemy morale. Prisoners of war were forced to lead the assault against their own people, and entire populations were put to the sword when any resistance was offered.

Finally Genghis Khan's grand strategy was unique in that he was careful to overcome his nomadic neighbors before assaulting the great empires. He was familiar with the traditional Chinese strategy of divide and rule, or as they put it, "Use barbarians to control barbarians." Thus many nomad chieftains in the past had been destroyed by simultaneous attacks by imperial armies and rival tribesmen. Genghis Khan's strategy, therefore, was first to unite "all the people of the felt-walled tents."

III. EARLY CONQUESTS

Even with his military genius and superb fighting machine, Genghis Khan would not have been able to become a world conqueror had he not appeared at the right historical moment. A strong and united China, such as had existed under the Han and the T'ang, could have stopped him with ease, as could also the Moslem Arabs at the height of their power. But the Eurasian balance of power was quite different in the early thirteenth century. China was divided then into three fragments, with the Chin dynasty ruling the north, the Sung the south, and the Tibetan Tanguts ensconced in the northwest with their kingdom of Hsi Hsia. To the west was the state of Kara-Khitai based on oasis cities such as Bokhara and Samarkand. Beyond that, on the Oxus River, was the Moslem kingdom of Khorezm, and still further west the Abbasid caliphate at Baghdad, both far past their prime.

Genghis Khan first subjugated the Hsi Hsia state between 1205 and 1209, and forced it to a tributary status. In 1211 he attacked North China, first overrunning the region north of the Great Wall and then in 1213 piercing the Wall and penetrating to the Yellow River plain. By 1215 he had captured and pillaged Peking and also gained the services of Chinese who knew how to besiege cities and others who knew how to administer and exploit agricultural societies. In accordance with his overall strategy, Genghis Khan now turned to the surrounding nomadic territories. Manchuria fell in 1216, Korea in 1218, and Kara-Khitai in the following year.

These conquests brought him to the frontiers of Khorezm, which he overran in 1219–1221. Rich and ancient cities such as Bokhara, Samarkand, and Balkh were pillaged and their inhabitants massacred, with the exception of skilled artisans who were sent to Mongolia. A Chinese Taoist monk who at the time journeyed through this region recorded, "We passed the great city of Balkh. Its inhabitants had recently rebelled against the Khan and had been removed; but we could still hear dogs barking in its streets." [2] Balkh had, in fact, become a ghost town, the first of many cities to suffer this fate. The stricken ruler of Khorezm perished on a small island in the Caspian Sea where he had sought refuge, while his son fled eastward to India. Relentless Mongol detachments defeated him again on the banks of the upper Indus, but he escaped to Delhi where the Turkish sultan, aghast at the carnage, granted him asylum.

Not content with these spectacular triumphs in the Middle East and India, the Mongols swung north to the Caucasus where they defeated the Georgians. Advancing on to the Ukraine they crushed a numerically far superior army of 80,000 Russians in 1223. Meanwhile Genghis Khan had returned to Mongolia to direct another victorious campaign against the Hsi Hsia kingdom, which had revolted against his rule. This proved to be his final exploit, for he died soon after in 1227. In accordance with his expressed wish he was buried in his homeland beneath a large tree he had selected. The escort that had brought the corpse to the site were all slaughtered to ensure that the location of the grave should remain secret.

IV. Mongol Empire

After a two-year interregnum, Genghis Khan's son, Ogodai, was selected as successor. During his reign from 1229 to 1241 the campaigning was resumed in the two extremities of Eurasia—China and Europe—some five thousand miles apart. In China the remnants of the Chin state in the north were liquidated by 1234 and then the Sung in the south were immediately attacked. They resisted stoutly, but the war which lasted forty-five years ended in their complete destruction. At the same time Genghis Khan's grandson, Batu, was sent with a force of 150,000 men to the European West. Crossing the middle Volga in the fall of 1237 he fell upon the principalities of central Russia. Town after town was captured, including the then comparatively unimportant Moscow. By March 1238 he was approaching Novgorod near the Baltic Sea, but he feared that the spring thaw would mire his horsemen in mud and so he withdrew suddenly to the south.

Two years later, in the summer of 1240, the Mongols attacked southern Russia again, this time from their bases in the Caucasus. By December they had captured the ancient Russian capital of Kiev. Such was Mongol frightfulness that a contemporary monk recorded that the few survivors "envied the dead." The following year the Mongols pressed on into Poland and Hungary, defeated a German army of 30,000 at Liegnitz in Silesia, crossed the frozen Danube, captured Zagreb, and reached the Adriatic coast. Thus Mongol armies now were operating across the breadth of Eurasia from the Adriatic to the Sea of Japan. In the spring of 1242 came news of the death of Ogodai Khan in Mongolia, so Batu withdrew through the Balkans to the lower Volga Valley where he laid the foundations of the khanate known as the Golden Horde, a name derived from the golden tent of its khan.

Such was the impact of these strange horsemen from the east that in far-off St. Albans, near London, the monk Matthew Paris recorded in his Chronicle:

> Swarming like locusts over the face of the earth, they have brought terrible devastation to the eastern parts of Europe laying it waste with fire and carnage. After having passed through the lands of the Saracens, they have razed cities, cut down forests, overthrown fortresses, pulled up vines, destroyed gardens, killed townspeople and peasants. If perchance they have spared any suppliants, they have forced them, reduced to the lowest condition of slavery, to fight in the foremost ranks against their own neighbours. Those who have feigned to fight, or have hidden in the hope of escaping, have been followed up by the Tartars and butchered. If any fought bravely [for them] and conquered, they have got no thanks for reward; and so they have misused their captives as they have their mares. For they are inhuman and beastly, rather monsters than men, thirsting for and drinking blood, tearing and devouring flesh of dogs and men, dressed in ox-hides, armed with plates of iron, short and stout, thickset, strong, invincible, indefatigable, their backs unprotected, their breast covered with armour; drinking with delight the pure blood of their flocks, with big, strong horses, which eat branches and even trees, and which they have to mount by the help of three steps on account of the shortness of their thighs. They are without human laws, know no comforts, are more ferocious than lions or bears, have boats made of ox-hides, which ten or twelve of them own in common; they are able to swim or manage a boat, so that they can cross the largest and swiftest rivers without let or hindrance, drinking turbid or muddy water when blood fails them [as a beverage]. They have one-edged swords and daggers, are wonderful archers, spare neither age, nor sex, nor condition. They know no other language than their own, which no one else knows; for until now there has been no access to them, nor did they go forth from their own country; so there could be no knowledge of their customs or persons through the common intercourse of men. They wander about with their flocks and their wives, who are taught to fight like men. And so they came with the

حكايت

موريقاى بزرك جنكزخان نوى سيده ند اينه نصيب نموذ ود لتبج جنكزخان رود مقدر
كث وعنايت اوحكل وبروق از آن كه نهايان ولنتن مر ذ خان هذ كدرا جون ميباركى وفرغ هارسيل كوسال بوز ما نده بوانن
مار ج بار سند اين وسنا همجرى د رآمدم د زا والمظل هارجنكز خان فنوذ مانوفى نه ا اينه سيد بباى كد نند جعيه باملت
قوريقاى نزديك ساخت ود ران بزريقاى لتبه بزرك جنكز هان رى يوي مزرك ند وساربى ند بكخ نهث

This illustration from a thirteenth-century Persian history of the Mongols shows the court of Genghis Khan. The Khan himself is seated on his throne and his three sons stand at the left. One of these sons, Ogodai, succeeded his father in 1229. (Bibliothèque Nationale, Paris)

swiftness of lightning to the confines of Christendom, ravaging and slaughtering, striking everyone with terror and incomparable horror.[3]

Whether or not this dreadful scourge would return was the great question facing Europeans. It was answered by the course of Mongol politics. After Ogodai's death, five years elapsed before the election of his son, Guyuk, as his successor. Major expeditions were impossible during this period of uncertainty, as they were also during the short two-year reign of the alcoholic Guyuk. Another interregnum of three years now ensued, ending with the accession of a capable Genghis Khan grandson, Mangu (1251–1259). That the new khan contemplated renewed invasion of Europe is indicated by the report of William of Rubruquis that he was questioned by Mangu's secretaries "about the kingdom of France, whether there were many sheep and cattle and horses there, and whether they had not better go there at once and take it all." The final decision was to complete the conquest of South China and to take over the Abbasid caliphate of Baghdad. Mangu entrusted these formidable tasks to his two brothers, Kublai, who was sent to China, and Hulagu, who was dispatched to the Middle East.

In contrast to their dashing sweeps across Central Asia, the Middle East and Eastern Europe, the Mongols were bogged down in China in decades of intermittent but large-scale fighting. Although a weak dynasty by Chinese standards, the Sung proved much more difficult for the Mongols to conquer than did the Moslem rulers of the Middle East, who were much further removed from the center of Mongol power. In their China campaigns the Mongols demonstrated once more their consummate skill in great strategic envelopment movements. In addition to pushing down the Yangtze and taking the Sung capital of Hangchow, Kublai outflanked the Sung from the west and south. In wide-ranging campaigns he overran Szechwan, Yunnan, Annam, and Tonking, thus surrounding the Sung kingdom on all sides. In 1277 he captured Canton, the great port in the south, and three years later the conquest was completed with the destruction of the Sung fleet off Hainan island.

In the meantime Mangu had died in 1259 during the Szechwan operations, and Kublai had been selected his successor. Kublai, as the Great Khan, moved the Mongol capital from Karakorum in the homeland to Peking in North China. True to the original idea of world conquest formulated by Genghis Khan, Kublai after his victory over the Sung launched new campaigns on land against Indochina and Burma, and overseas against Java and Japan. Little wonder that Marco Polo wrote that Kublai Khan, whom he served for seventeen years, was "the most puissant of men, in subjects, lands and treasure, that there is on earth or ever was, from the time of our first father Adam to this day."

Hulagu in the meantime had crossed the Oxus and rampaged through Persia, Mesopotamia, and Syria. When the Abbasid capital, Baghdad, fell in 1258, its 800,000 inhabitants are reported to have been massacred with the exception of a few artisans whose skills were prized. The hapless caliph was rolled up in a carpet and trampled to death by horses in order to avoid the shedding by the sword of royal blood, forbidden by Genghis Khan's injunctions. After the taking of Aleppo and Damascus in similar fashion, it appeared that nothing could prevent the Mongols from advancing on to Egypt and North Africa, thus completing the conquest of the entire Moslem world.

But now occurred an unexpected and fateful reversal at Ain Jalut (Goliath's Spring), Palestine, where in 1260 the Egyptian Mamelukes defeated the Mongols. One reason for the setback was that the death of Mangu Khan in 1259 had disrupted the unity of the Mongol ruling families. Hulagu supported the candidacy of his older brother Kublai for the vacant throne, but was opposed by his cousin Berke, head of the Golden Horde in Russia. In fact Berke, a convert to Islam, was so outraged by Hulagu's destruction of the caliphate that the two men were drifting towards open war. As a precautionary measure Hulagu had recrossed the Euphrates to Persia, leaving in Palestine a depleted force of mostly non-Mongol units. The defeat of this force saved Islam and marked the beginning of the end of the Mongol Empire.

V. Mongol Decline

Despite the setback in Palestine, the Mongol Empire at that time was an extraordinarily impressive edifice, encompassing Russia, the Middle East, and South China, in addition to the original conquests of Genghis Khan. Mongol armies were active from the Baltic coast to Burma, while naval units were attacking Japan and Java. And yet this gigantic empire already was beginning to fall apart, and only a few decades later was to be virtually nonexistent.

The reason, of course, was not simply the defeat by the Mamelukes. Few Mongol units had been involved in that battle, and swift retribution could be expected, as had always happened before to the few opponents who had won individual engagements. But the pattern was not repeated this time, and the reason was the process of imperial disintegration already under way.

The disintegration was in part a function of sheer overextension. After reaching the extremities of Eurasia, even the Mongols, with their extraordinary mobility, found that they were bogging down. In addition to the defeat at Goliath's Spring, Mongol raids into India between 1285 and 1303 were repelled by the Turkish sultans of Delhi, and likewise in Burma and Vietnam the Mongols discovered that jungle fighting was altogether different from cavalry raids across the steppes. Mongol naval expeditions overseas proved equally ineffective. The fleet sent in 1291 against the Liuch'iu Islands failed even to find them. An expeditionary force sent to Java two years later was withdrawn after suffering heavy losses. The greatest overseas effort was made against Japan, where large expeditions were sent in 1274 and 1281. The Japanese fought with great bravery and finally were saved by a southwest typhoon which destroyed the enemy ships and which they gratefully dubbed the "divine wind," or *Kamikaze*. Thus the sea, like the jungle, set limits to Mongol expansionism.

It was not merely a case, however, of being unable to conquer the extremities of Eurasia and the offshore islands. It was much more serious, for the Mongols found they could not retain what they already had won. The basic difficulty was that they were too few in number and too primitive in relation to their subject peoples. The Mongols, as Pushkin put it, were "Arabs without Aristotle and algebra." This left them vulnerable to assimilation as soon as they dismounted from their horses and settled down to enjoy their conquests. In this respect they differed fundamentally from the Arabs who had both a language

and a religion that their subjects were willing to adopt and that served as strong
bonds for imperial unity. The Mongols, being less advanced than the Arabs,

enjoyed no such advantage. Rather the opposite was the case with them, for
they adopted the languages, religions, and cultures of their more advanced
subjects and thereby lost their identity. This was the root reason why their
empire dissolved so soon after its creation.

Indicative of the assimilation process was Kublai Khan's decision to move
the Mongol capital from Karakorum to Peking. Inevitably he became a Chi-
nese-style emperor, ruling from a palace of Chinese design, conducting elaborate Confucian ceremonies, and building new Confucian temples. As the Grand
Khan, he was nominally the suzerain of all the Mongol khanates. Actually his
authority did not extend beyond China. His brother, Arikboga, had contested
his election as Grand Khan, and only after a four-year struggle had Kublai
Khan prevailed. Then he was challenged by his cousin, Kaidu, who controlled
Turkestan, and the ensuing forty-year civil war ended in stalemate. Thus the
Mongol Empire was shattered by dynastic rivalries as well as by cultural as-
similation.

While Kublai Khan was becoming a Chinese emperor, Hulagu was becoming
a Persian ruler. With Tabriz as his capital he established the so-called Ilkhanate.
(The term Ilkhan means "subject Khan," and was applied to the Mongol rulers
of Persia as subordinates to the Grand Khan.) His successor's adoption of
Islam in 1295 as the official religion both reflected and accelerated the Mongol's assimilation into their Iranian-Islamic milieu. Likewise the Golden Horde
across the Caucasus went its own way, influenced by the native Christian
Orthodox culture and by the official Islamic creed. Before long the only remaining pure Mongols were those in ancestral Mongolia where they came under
the influence of Buddhism and sank into impotent obscurity.

VI. MOSLEM TURKISH RESURGENCE

Since the Mongols were so few in numbers, they had incorporated an ever
increasing proportion of Turks into their armies. Then with the break-up of
the empire these Moslem Turks quickly came to the fore, as they had earlier
in the caliphate before the Mongol onslaught. A succession of military adventurers now rose and fell in the struggle for control of the Central Eurasian
steppes. The most remarkable of these was Timur, known to Europe as Tamer-
lane. He seized Samarkand in 1369, and from there struck out in all directions.
First he destroyed the Ilkhanate in Persia and Mesopotamia, then defeated
the Golden Horde in Russia and the Ottoman Turks in Asia Minor, and he
even invaded India and sacked Delhi. He was resolved to make his capital,
Samarkand, the finest city in the world, and after each campaign he sent back
caravans loaded with booty, together with craftsmen, artists, astrologers, and
men of letters. At its height, his empire extended from the Mediterranean to
China, and Timur was preparing to invade the latter country when he died in
1405. His empire then disintegrated even more rapidly than that of the
Mongols.

After Timur, the outstanding development was the extension of Moslem

Turkish power in India and in Byzantium. During the thirteenth century the Turkish sultans of Delhi, under the pressure of the Mongol threat, had confined themselves to consolidating their position in north India. In the fourteenth century, with the threat removed, they expanded two-thirds down the length of the peninsula to the Kistna River. Then in the aftermath of Timur's raid, north and central India were left a congeries of small Turkish-ruled states with none strong enough to revive the Delhi sultanate. Meanwhile the expansion of Islamic power over a large part of India had provoked a Hindu reaction in the form of the large Hindu state of Vijanagar, comprising the whole of India south of the Kistna River. Such was the fragmented state of the Indian peninsula when unity was imposed from without during the sixteenth century by another Moslem Turkish dynasty, the Mughal.

Meanwhile in the Middle East the frontiers of Islam were being extended at the expense of Byzantium by the Ottoman Turks. These newcomers from Central Asia had entered the Seljuk Empire in its decline and settled in the northwest corner of Asia Minor, less than fifty miles from the strategic straits separating Asia from Europe. In 1299 the leader of these Turks, Uthman, declared his independence from his Seljuk overlord, and from these humble beginnings grew the great Ottoman Empire, named after the obscure Uthman.

The first step was the conquest of the remaining Byzantine portion of Asia Minor. This was accomplished by 1340, thanks to the disaffection of the Christian peasantry and the plentiful supply of *ghazis*, or warriors of the faith, who flocked in from all parts of the Middle East to battle against the Christian infidels. Next the Turks crossed the straits, winning their first foothold in Europe by building a fort at Gallipoli in 1354. They hardly could have selected a more favorable moment for their advance into Europe. The Balkan Peninsula was divided by the strife of rival Christian churches and by the rivalries of the Byzantine, Serbian, and Bulgarian states, all past their prime. Also the Christian peasants of the Balkans were as disaffected as their counterparts in Asia Minor. And Western Christendom was too divided to go to the aid of the Balkans even if there was the will to do so, which was not the case because of the ancient antipathy between Catholic and Orthodox Christians. Thus the way was clear for the Ottoman Turks, and they took full advantage of the opportunity.

They surrounded Constantinople by taking Adrianople in 1362 and Sofia in 1384. Then they were diverted for some decades when their sultan was defeated and captured by Timur in 1402. But Timur was a flash in the pan, and his death, in 1405, left the Ottomans free to rebuild and to resume their advance. Finally in 1453 they took beleaguered Constantinople by assault, ending a thousand years of imperial history. Before the end of the century they were the masters of the entire Balkan Peninsula to the Danube River, with the exception of a few Venetian-held coastal fortresses. (For details, see Chapter 15, section IV.)

VII. SIGNIFICANCE OF TURCO-MONGOL INVASIONS

One result of the Turco-Mongol invasions between 1000 and 1500 was the emergence of a new Eurasian balance of power in which Islam was the central and decisive force. When the West began its overseas expansion in the late fifteenth century, Islam already was expanding overland in all directions. The Ottomans were crossing the Danube into Central Europe; Central Asia was completely won over with the exception of the eastern fringes; and the Mughals were about to begin their conquest of virtually the entire Indian peninsula. Furthermore, Islam was advancing far out onto the peripheries of the Eurasian ecumene. In Africa it was spreading steadily into the interior of the continent from two centers. From the North African coast it was carried across the Sahara to West Africa where a succession of large Negro Moslem kingdoms flourished. Likewise from the Arab colonies on the East African coast, Islam spread inward over lands that included the Christian kingdom of Nubia, which was conquered and converted. (See Chapter 17.)

Islam also was carried by Arab and Indian merchants to Southeast Asia. Here, as in Africa and other regions where the local peoples had not reached a high level of civilization, conversion was easy because of the simplicity and adaptability of the new faith. All one had to do to become a Moslem was to repeat the words, "I bear witness that there is no God but Allah and that Mohammed is the Messenger of Allah." Local practices and traditions usually were accepted and sanctified by the addition of Islamic ritual. Thus the faith was spread not by the sword, but by the unobtrusive work of traders who won over the populace by learning their language, adopting their customs, marrying their women, and converting their new relatives and business associates. The following description of the methods used by these merchant missionaries in the Philippines holds also for what was done earlier on the other islands: "The better to introduce their religion into the country, the Muhammadans adopted the language and many of the customs of the natives, married their women, purchased slaves in order to increase their personal importance, and succeeded finally in incorporating themselves among the chiefs who held the foremost rank in the state." [4]

Marco Polo found many Moslems in Ferlec (present-day Atjeh) when he visited there in 1292. "You must know that the people of Ferlec used all to be idolaters, but owing to contact with Saracen merchants, who continually resort here in their ships, they have all been converted to the law of Mahomet." [5] By the end of the fifteenth century, Islam had spread as far east as Mindanao in the Philippines. The Moslem state of Malacca played a key role in the diffusion of Islam because of its preeminence as a trade center, controlling all commerce through the straits. Not only did it draw traders from India and all Southeast Asia, but it also attracted great teachers and religious teachers by offering opportunities to instruct wealthy patrons. Malacca's greatest achievement was the conversion of Java, signalled by the success of the Javanese Moslem princes in overthrowing the old Hindu kingdom of Majapahit. Considering Southeast Asia as a whole, the main Moslem centers, as might be expected, were those areas with the most active trade contacts: the Malay Peninsula and the Indonesian archipelago.

This diffusion of Islam throughout Eurasia during these five centuries almost tripled the territory of the Moslem faith, with important repercussions on the course of world history. The initial stage of Islamic expansion in the seventh and eighth centuries had made the Mediterranean a Moslem lake; this later stage of expansion made the entire Indian Ocean a Moslem lake. This meant

The Alhambra, palace of the Moorish kings at Granada, built between 1248 and 1354. Masterpieces of Islamic architecture throughout Eurasia are indications of the vast diffusion of the Moslem faith between 1000 and 1500. (Arborio Mella)

that virtually all the goods reaching Europe from Asia now were carried along Moslem-controlled land or sea routes, especially after the Ilkhanate embraced Islam in 1295. Thus the several decades after 1240 during which the Mongol Empire permitted safe travel and trade across Eurasia proved to be but an interlude between earlier and later eras in which Arab-Turkish control of Central Asia and the Middle East constituted a barrier between China and the West. The continued expansion of the Moslem faith also served to make Islam by 1500 a world force rather than simply a Middle Eastern power. This has affected profoundly the course of world affairs to the present day. It explains why today the Indian peninsula is divided into two parts, why Moslem political parties are so influential in Southeast Asia, why Islam is a powerful and rapidly growing force in Africa, and why it is now the faith of one-seventh of the people of the world.

The Turco-Mongol invasions are significant also because of the cross-fertilization that they stimulated within Eurasia. In the technological field we have seen that *Pax-Mongolica* was responsible for the transmission of a cluster of Chinese inventions, including gunpowder, silk, machinery, printing, and the blast furnace for cast iron. (See Chapter 12, section III.) Another example of cross-fertilization is the case of Ilkhanid Persia, which, by its location, was exposed to influences from both East and West. We know of Chinese artillerymen who reached Persia in the service of the Mongol armies; also of one Fu Meng-chi who propounded the principles of Chinese astronomy, of Chinese physicians at the Ilkhan's court, and of Chinese artists who left an indelible impression on Persian miniature painting. From the opposite direction, European influence was mostly in the field of trade and diplomacy. A colony of Italian merchants flourished in the capital of Tabriz, and from their numbers the Ilkhans recruited the ambassadors and interpreters for their various missions to Europe. And then there was, of course, Marco Polo, who escorted from China to Persia a Mongol princess to be the Ilkhan's bride, and then proceeded on to Venice.

Finally, the opportunities offered by this cross-fertilization were fully exploited only by the new civilization developing in Europe—a profoundly significant fact that was to mold the course of world history to the present day. All the other Eurasian civilizations proved too set in their ways. At first it appeared that the Islamic world would have no difficulting in adapting and changing. Despite the primitive background of Arabia from which it had emerged, Islam had proven itself remarkably adept and receptive in borrowing from the great established civilizations and creating something new and impressive. But this involved an inescapable built-in tension between the dogma of the Islamic faith and the rationalist philosophy and science of the Greeks. In the early years the Caliph al-Mamun (813–833) had generously supported the translation of the ancient classics and had espoused the rationalist doctrine that the Koran was created and not eternal. But his successors were quite different and gave their support to conservative theologians who rejected all scientific and philosophical speculation as leading to heresy and atheism.

This represented the triumph of scholasticism, in the sense that seeking God was deemed more important than understanding nature. Such scholasticism had prevailed also in the early medieval West following the barbarian invasions. The Papacy had then dominated the intellectual life of the age, and theology was the accepted queen of the sciences. The same development occurred now in the Islamic world following its series of barbarian invasions—Crusaders, Berbers, Bedouins, Seljuks, and Mongols. Here, as in the West, men turned to religion for succor and consolation in the face of material disaster. But whereas in the West scholasticism eventually was challenged and superseded, in the Moslem world it remained dominant through the nineteenth century.

In his *Incoherence of Philosophy*, the outstanding theologian of Islam, al-Ghazzali (1058–1111), strongly attacked the whole secular school. He argued that the ultimate source of truth is divine revelation and that the intellect should be used to destroy trust in itself. He was challenged by the famous Moslem Aristotelian philosopher ibn Rushd of Cordova, Spain, known in the West as Averroes (1126–1198). In his *Incoherence of the Incoherence*, he asserted that knowledge should be subject to the test of reason and that philosophy was not inimical to the Faith. But he was by no means a freethinker, maintaining that the masses, whose intelligence neither desired nor was capable of philosophical reasoning, should be educated "theologically." The educated classes, which he believed could be educated "philosophically," nevertheless rejected his position, accusing him of hypocrisy and suspecting him of atheism.

The extent of orthodox reaction is reflected in the work of the great historian and father of sociology, Ibn Khaldun (1332–1406). He was the first to view history not as the conventional annalistic and episodical writing of his time, but as the science of the origin and development of civilizations. And yet this erudite and creative thinker rejected philosophy and science as useless and dangerous: "It should be known that the opinion the philosophers hold is wrong in all its aspects. . . . The problems of physics are of no importance to us in our religious affairs or our livelihoods. Therefore we must leave them alone. . . . Whoever studies it [logic] should do so only after he is saturated with the religious law and has studied the interpretation of the Koran and jurisprudence. No one who has no knowledge of the Moslem religious sciences should apply himself to it. Without that knowledge, he can hardly be safe from its pernicious aspects." [6]

Thus intellectual growth and innovation in the Moslem world ceased, and at a time when Europe's universities were in full ferment, the Islamic *madrasas* were content with rote memorization of authoritative texts. Whereas the Moslem world had been far ahead of the West between 800 and 1200, by the sixteenth century the gap had disappeared, and thereafter it was the West that boomed ahead while Islam stood still and even retrogressed. The disparity between the two worlds has been well described as follows: "Islamic medicine and science reflected the light of the Hellenic sun, when its day had fled; and shone like a moon, illuminating the darkest night of the European Middle Ages; some bright stars lent their own light; but moon and stars alike faded at the dawn of a new day—the Renaissance." [7]

A similar disparity developed between the West and the other Eurasian civilizations, for the simple reason that only the West negotiated the fateful transition to modernism. Both India and Byzantium were conquered by Islam and enveloped in its stagnancy. China, reacting against the Mongols who were expelled in 1368, manifested a strong ethnocentrism—an almost instinctive hostility and scorn for all things alien and hence barbarian. Russia also succeeded in 1480 in throwing off the Mongol yoke, but permanent scars remained. The country had been closed to fresh winds from the West for two and a half centuries, and both Mongol ideas and usages had paved the way for the absolutism of the Muscovite state and of the Orthodox church.

The West alone was the exception to this general pattern. Only there occurred the great mutation—the emergence of modern civilization with a new technological base that quickly proved its superiority and diffused not only throughout Eurasia but the entire globe. This uniqueness of the West stems, as noted earlier (Chapter 11, section VI), from the shattering impact of the barbarian invasions, which plowed under the classical civilizations and allowed new concepts and institutions to take root and flourish. The following chapters will consider first the traditional 'Byzantine and Confucian civilizations that flanked the Islamic world on each side, and then will analyze the contrasting revolutionary civilization of the West.

SUGGESTED READING

For the Turkish invasions in various regions, see T. T. Rice, *The Seljuks* (London: Thames and Hudson, 1961); C. Cahen, *Pre-Ottoman Turkey* (London: Sidgwick and Jackson, 1968); *The Cambridge History of Iran*, Vol. 5, *The Saljuk and Mongol Periods*, ed. J. A. Boyle (London: Cambridge Univ., 1931); M. Nazim, *Life and Times of Sultan Mahmud of Ghazna* (London: Cambridge Univ., 1931), for a discussion of the Turks in India; and H. Lamb, *Tamberlane the Earth Shaker* (New York: McBride, 1928). An excellent, revealing collection of readings is presented by J. J. Saunders, ed., *The Muslim World on the Eve of Europe's Expansion* (Englewood Cliffs, N.J.: Prentice-Hall, 1966).

Several biographies of Genghis Khan are available, including a popular account by H. Lamb, *Genghis Khan: The Emperor of All Men* (New York: McBride, 1927); a scholarly study by B. Y. Vladimirtsov, *The Life of Chingis-Khan* (Boston: Houghton Mifflin, 1930); and H. D. Martin, *The Rise of Chingis Khan and His Conquest of North China* (Baltimore: Johns Hopkins Press, 1950), which is strong on Mongol military organization. Broader studies of the Mongol Empire as a whole are available in M. Prawdin, *The Mongol Empire* (London: Allen and Unwin, 1940); in G. Vernadsky, *The Mongols and Russia* (New Haven: Yale Univ., 1953), which is more comprehensive than the title suggests; and in E. D. Phillips, *The Mongols* (London: Thames and Hudson, 1969), which not only deals with the Mongol Empire but which also traces the later histories of the Mongols in China, Turkestan, Iran, Russia, and Mongolia up until the nineteenth century. W. S. Ipsiroglu, *Painting and Culture of the Mongols* (London: Thames and Hudson, 1967) is a beautifully illustrated volume that provides an excellent introductory essay on Mongol culture in general. The role of the Mongols in the Middle East is analyzed in *The Cambridge History of Iran* noted above; in P. Sykes, *History of Persia*, 2 vols. (London: Macmillan, 1930); and in two chapters of Vol. 3 of S. Runciman, *A History of the Crusades*, 3 vols. (London: Cambridge Univ., 1951–54). For the dynamics of Mongol expansionism, see various essays in O. Lattimore, *Studies in Frontier History* (Paris: Mouton, 1962), and his article "Chingis Khan and the Mongol Conquests," *Scientific American*, August, 1963, pp. 55–68. For the role of the Mongols in other specific regions, see the bibliography for the following two chapters.

A thousand years of Byzantium Chapter
produced extinction; a thousand years
of medieval effort [in the West]
produced the Renaissance,
the modern state,
and ultimately the free world.

WILLIAM CARROLL BARK

15

Traditional Byzantine

Civilization

Edward Gibbon's verdict on the thousand years of Byzantium's existence as "a uniform tale of weakness and misery" has long since given way to respect and appreciation for its manifold contributions to human civilization. Yet the precise manner and context in which Byzantium's history should be presented remain somewhat of a puzzle. Should this millennium be depicted as the epilogue to Roman history, or as the background for Slavic civilization, or as the prelude to the Ottoman Empire?

Each of these approaches is valid if Byzantine history is viewed from the perspective of one region or another. But if the angle of vision is global, as is the case in this volume, then Orthodox Byzantium falls into place naturally and obviously as one of the several traditional Eurasian civilizations that survived the barbarian invasions and continued without interruption from the Classical Age to modern times. (See Chapter 11, section VI.)

This unbroken sweep of history, however, eventually meant obsolescence and extinction, especially in the political sense. Because it was the most vulnerable, the Byzantine civilization was the first to suffer this fate. China, for example, faced nomadic invasions only from the northwest and was so far out of the way on the eastern tip of Eurasia that the aggressive West was not able to break in until the mid-nineteenth century. Byzantium, by contrast, faced not only a succession of barbarian invasions from across the Danube, which were comparable to those menacing China, but also endured the onslaught of the expanding West in the form of Venetian merchants and Norman knights, as well as the assault of a resurgent East embodied first in the Sassanian Persian irruption and then in the Moslem Arab and Turkish invasions. Thus, whereas the traditional Chinese civilization endured to 1912, the Byzantine collapsed first in 1204, then was partially revived in 1261, and survived in a palsied state until the death blow in 1453. (See Map XVIII, "Decline of the Byzantine Empire.")

I. Emergence of Byzantium

No Western capital approaches the proud record of the Byzantine capital, Constantinople, in continuity and scope of imperial rule. It was already an old city when rebuilt by Constantine in A.D. 330 to be the New Rome. Its origins go back to the seventh century B.C., when it was founded as the colony Byzantion by emigrants from the Greek city-state Megara. Despite its magnificent location, Byzantium, to use the common Latin form of its name, remained a second class commercial city during the next thousand years. It was unable to rise to a rank worthy of its position as long as it was menaced and cut off from its hinterland by the barbarous Thracians. The conquests of Trajan and his successors brought the interior lands under Roman imperial control and ended this disadvantage. Thus when Byzantium became Constantinople, or the city of Constantine, it was secure by land as well as by sea, and in the following centuries it stood impregnable before the barbarian assaults to which the first Rome succumbed.

For one thousand years Constantinople played its new role as the capital of Byzantium, until it fell to the Ottoman Turks in 1453. Then it became the capital of a new empire, and as the Ottoman warriors pressed their conquests, the dominion of Constantinople spread to new frontiers, reaching from Morocco to Persia, and from Vienna to the Indian Ocean. Constantinople presided over this vast region up to modern times, when the Ottoman Empire gave way to the Turkish Republic, and Kemal Ataturk moved his capital from the shores of the Bosphorus to the safety of the Anatolian plateau.

This remarkable history of Constantinople is due in large part to its commanding position between Europe and Asia. The city stands at the southern extremity of the Bosphorus on a hilly promontory that runs out from the European side of the Straits towards the opposite Asiatic shore, as though to stem the rush of waters from the Black Sea into the Sea of Marmora. Thus Constantinople has to the south the Sea of Marmora and to the north the bay of Bosphorus, forming the magnificent harbor known as the Golden Horn. To be sure, other cities also have fine harbors and central locations. But the extraordinary feature of Constantinople is that it has both on the north and south a long, narrow, but navigable sea channel. The city is therefore protected by two marine gates that can be closed to hostile ships from either

In a miniature from the Vatican Library, the Emperor Justinian (527–565) is shown assisting in the building of St. Sophia in Constantinople. This famous church was converted into a mosque by the Turks after they had taken the city of Constantinople in 1453. (Arborio Mella)

the Aegean or Black seas. The Byzantine emperors supplemented these natural defenses with two great walls on the land side, the first 4 miles long, and the second, some 30 miles further west, 40 miles long and 20 feet wide. These double ramparts, together with the natural bulwark of the Balkan Mountains, protected the land approaches to Constantinople. Thus the city was able to hold out during the ten centuries of Byzantium, although it was a beleaguered fortress for much of this period.

The references to the Roman and Byzantine phases of Constantinople's history raise the question of when the first ended and the second began. It was not with the deposition of Romulus Augustulus in A.D. 476, for the tradition of imperial unity persisted for centuries more. The Eastern emperors continued to regard themselves as the heirs of the Caesars, even though Italy, Gaul, Britain, Spain, and North Africa had all been lost to the barbarians. The conservative, backward-looking Justinian (527–565) devoted himself to making this imperial myth a reality. Hence his conquests of North Africa, Italy, and a part of Spain, and also his codification of Roman law. (See Chapter 11, section IV.) "We are re-establishing all that existed in the past," declared Justinian, "although its value has been minimized. . . . by respecting the name of Romans we will ensure that the past will in a greater measure come back to life in our state." [1]

Justinian's efforts at imperial restoration proved ephemeral and pyrrhic. His campaigns in the western Mediterranean left the imperial treasury depleted and the Balkan and Asiatic provinces neglected and vulnerable. Within a decade after his death a new barbarian tribe, the Lombards, had overrun most of Italy. Likewise on the Danube frontier, the Avars, with their Slav and Bulgar subjects, were penetrating into the Balkans, displacing the Latinized Illyrians and weakening imperial control. In the East the Persians, who had been bribed into peace during Justinian's reign, now set out under their ambitious King of Kings, Chosroes II, to eliminate altogether the East Roman Empire. By 615 they had overrun Syria, Palestine, and Egypt, and were encamped on the shores of the Bosphorus opposite Constantinople.

With the accession of the great Emperor Heraclius (610–641), Byzantium was able to mobilize the resources and the will necessary to avert impending disaster. Even though a joint Avar-Persian force was besieging Constantinople, Heraclius took the offensive and in 627 decisively defeated the Persians in the same locality in Mesopotamia where Alexander the Great also had defeated them one thousand years earlier. The following year the Persians were forced to sign a peace returning all their conquests.

Having disposed of the danger in the East, Heraclius now discovered that the Slavs in the meantime had occupied and sunk roots in large parts of the northern Balkans. Making a virtue of necessity, he assigned to them definite areas, in return for which they acknowledged his suzerainty and agreed to pay annual tribute. Thus the Slavic new-comers changed gradually from invaders into settlers. With the passing of a few centuries these widely scattered Balkan Slavs had developed along different lines and crystallized into four major groups: the Slovenes at the head of the Adriatic, the Croatians between the Drave River and the Adriatic, the Serbs in the central Balkans between the Adriatic and the Danube, and the Slavs, who shortly were to adopt the name of their Bulgarian conquerors, in the remaining territory to the Black Sea.

The second two groups organized great though short-lived medieval kingdoms, which borrowed their culture from Byzantium. In contrast, the Slovenes and Croatians, because of their position in the western part of the peninsula, became subjects of the Holy Roman Empire and were influenced by Rome rather than Constantinople in their cultural development.

The struggle against the Avars and the Persians proved but a prelude to the greater and more fateful contest with the Moslem Arabs. As noted earlier in Chapter 13, section III, the warriors of Islam speedily overran most of the Middle East during the 630's and 640's. The long duel between Byzantium and Persia had left both empires exhausted and vulnerable. Byzantium was further weakened by the religious disaffection of the populations of the eastern provinces over the issue of Monophysitism—the belief that Christ had a single divine nature, as against the official Byzantine doctrine that Christ was both human and divine. So impassioned was the controversy that many of the Eastern Christians preferred the rule of Islam to religious dictation from Constantinople. Thus a millennium of Greco-Roman rule in Syria, Palestine, and Egypt was now ended within two decades, despite the desperate efforts of the aging Heraclius.

Later in the century the very existence of the Byzantine Empire was threatened by the combination of Moslem sea raids and Bulgar land attacks. In a remarkable feat of adaptation the Arabs developed a naval power with which they conquered Cyprus and Rhodes, and then besieged Constantinople on several occasions, beginning in 669. At the same time Byzantium was threatened from the north by the Bulgars, an Asiatic people originally used by the Byzantines against the Avars. But now the Bulgars were occupying for themselves the territory between the Danube and the Balkan Mountains, and from this base threatened Constantinople.

Once more Byzantium was saved by inspired imperial leadership, this time in the person of Leo III the Isaurian (717–741). A military commander of Syrian origin, he seized power when Constantinople was under siege by the Arabs. He not only lifted the siege but drove the Arabs back out of Asia Minor. By the end of his reign the imperial frontiers were secure, but they were drastically shrunken frontiers compared to those of Justinian. Italy had been lost to the Lombards, the northern Balkans to the Slavs and the Bulgars, and Syria, Palestine, Egypt, and North Africa to the Arabs.

This reduced empire, however, was a more homogeneous empire, for the eastern provinces had been predominantly Monophysite and non-Greek. Under the circumstances Byzantium was strengthened rather than weakened by the withdrawal to the Taurus Mountains separating Greek Asia Minor from what was now becoming the heartland of the Islamic world. This demarcation was reinforced by internal convulsions within the Moslem world culminating in the accession of the Abbasid Caliphate (750), which moved the Islamic capital from Damascus to Baghdad. The orientation of Islam now was to the east rather than towards the Mediterranean, so that the Byzantine and Moslem empires were able to coexist peacefully until the appearance of the militant Turks in the eleventh century.

A demarcation similar to that between Byzantium and Islam was developing between Byzantium and the West. With the Lombard invasion the Roman Popes had looked to Constantinople for protection, but to no avail because of Byzantine preoccupation with the Arabs. The Popes accordingly turned to the Franks, and the resulting partnership culminated in the famous Papal coronation of Charlemagne in 800. Constantinople reluctantly conceded to Charlemagne in 812 the title of *Basileus,* thereby recognizing the political entity of the West. During the following centuries Byzantium and the West drifted apart not only in politics but also in language, in ecclesiastical matters, and in general culture.

The emerging Byzantine Empire of the eighth century was much smaller than Justinian's short-lived creation, but it was also much more homogeneous. The diverse racial, cultural, and religious elements of the eastern and western provinces had been shed, and the remaining core was basically, though by no means exclusively, Greek. In this manner, then, the transition was completed from the East Roman Empire of the sixth century to the Byzantine Empire of the eighth—an empire with a culture clearly distinct from both that of Islam to the east and from that of the new Europe to the west.

II. BYZANTIUM'S GOLDEN AGE

The Byzantine Empire reached its apogee during the period between the early ninth and early eleventh centuries. Imperial administration was soundly based on the *themes,* or provinces, each headed by a *strategos,* or general, who was in charge of both civil and military affairs. This militarization of administration had been effected by Heraclius as a means of expediting action at a time of imminent foreign danger. Imperial lands in the *themes* were divided amongst the peasants in return for military service. Under strong emperors this *theme* arrangement assured effective administration, a reliable military reserve, and a well-filled treasury, since the peasants assumed much of the tax burden.

Byzantium's economy also was solidly founded on free peasant communities that functioned alongside the estates of the great landowners. In the urban centers that had survived since Greco-Roman classical times, craftsmen worked at a high level of competence. Arab writers described the quality of Byzantine handicrafts, especially the luxury products, as being equaled only by those of China. Equally important was the great volume of goods that passed through Constantinople from all regions of Eurasia—slaves and salt from the Black Sea lands, spices, perfumes, and precious stones from India, papyrus and foodstuffs from Egypt, silk and porcelain from China, and silver, wrought iron objects, and linen, cotton, and woolen fabrics from the West.

This political, economic, and military strength enabled the Byzantine emperors to launch reconquest campaigns that were more realistic if not as ambitious as those of Justinian. Crete and Cyprus were recovered, thereby curbing Arab naval raids in the Aegean waters. The imperial frontiers were extended also into northern Syria, Armenia, and Georgia. In the northern Balkans where the Bulgars were a constant threat to the empire, Basil II won such a crushing victory in 1014 that he was known thereafter as *Bulgaroktonus,* or "the Bulgar-Slayer."

In cultural matters this was a period of stability and homogeneity. The

fil; le roi daquitaine & omient il donna
abernart son neueu le roiaume de lombar
die · Et puis qment il fist assembler · v ·
concilles el roiaume defrance endiuers li
eus · pour amend lestat de sainte eglise ·
Et dela desconfiture nuchiel temp des griex
Et puis qment trumas le roi de bul grie
su desofis deuant costentinoble ·

*Fourteenth-century French illuminated manuscript depicting the
papal coronation of Charlemagne in 800. This event caused
Constantinople to recognize the political independence of the
West in 812 with the granting of the title* Basileus *to Charlemagne. (Giraudon)*

Byzantines still called themselves *Romaioi,* or Romans, but Greek, in either its literary or popular forms, was the universal language of the empire. Religious homogeneity also had been promoted with the loss of the dissident eastern provinces to Islam and with the resolution of the violent and protracted dispute between iconoclasts and iconodules—that is between breakers and worshippers of images. The compromise settlement barred religious sculpture but did allow paintings, which remain to the present day an important feature of Orthodox religious life.

The Byzantine church also demonstrated its vitality with the conversion of the Moslems on reconquered Crete, and of the Slavs in the northern Balkans. In 865 the Bulgarian Khan Boris accepted Christianity from Constantinople in return for imperial recognition of his conquests. In the following years Byzantine missionaries provided the Bulgarians with an alphabet, translated the Scriptures into their language, and prepared a Slavonic liturgy. About the same time the Serbian tribes also were converted to Orthodoxy, as were the Russians of the Kievan state. (See section VI of this chapter.) Further to the west, however, the Latin church prevailed among the Croatians and Slovenes, who followed in the wake of the neighboring Catholic Italians, Hungarians, and Germans.

Imperial stability was enhanced also by the intimate, mutually supporting relationship between emperor and patriarch. The principle of a subservient state church was traditional and accepted, the emperor calling himself not only *autokrator* but also *isapostolos,* or the equal of the apostles. The tenth-century book of ceremony for the election of the Patriarch of Constantinople explicitly defined the subservient relationship. The metropolitans of the church were to meet in Hagia Sophia on the command of the emperor and submit to him three candidates for the patriarchate. The emperor was free to select any of the three, or to reject all and to nominate his own candidate, which the metropolitans then were required to acknowledge as being worthy of the post. And in the installation ceremony the new head of the church was pronounced patriarch "by the will of God and Emperor."

In conclusion, Byzantium during these centuries was stable, powerful, wealthy, self-satisfied, and rather inward looking now that a reasonable coexistence had evolved with both the Western and Moslem worlds. These characteristics are reminiscent of China under the Ming dynasty. (See Chapter 17, section V.) Indeed Byzantium, like China, had a university whose prime purpose was to train officials for the bureaucracy. But this university in Constantinople had a precarious existence and functioned irregularly, so that it lacked the continued effectiveness of its Chinese counterpart. Reminiscent of China also is the Confucian-like commentary of the sixth-century Byzantine historian Procopius regarding the perennial religious disputes on the nature of the divinity: "I think all disputes about the nature of God are nonsensical madness; man cannot even know his own nature and therefore one should abandon all deliberations on the nature of God."

Byzantine culture never resolved its ambivalence between its classical heritage and its religious orientation. At the time when the Byzantine Empire was nearing its end, the Platonist scholar Gemistus Pletho (c. 1355–1450) was openly questioning the prospects of a state so closely bound to the Christian religion and ecclesiastical structure. He spent most of his life as a renowned teacher in Mistra, the Byzantine capital of the Peloponnesus. There he dreamed of restoring in the Peloponnesus the ancient Hellas, organized as a modified Platonic utopia and based on paganism rather than Christianity. But this classical secularist strain in Byzantine thought never prevailed. Byzantine society remained predominantly religious in its orientation. More representative of this society than Pletho was the preacher Joseph Bryennïus, whose sermons provided a religious explanation for the ills of the time.

> Our rulers are unjust, those who oversee our affairs are rapacious, the judges accept gifts, the mediators are liars, the city dwellers are deceivers, the rustics are unintelligible, and all are useless. Our virgins are more shameless than prostitutes, the widows more curious than they ought to be, the married women disdain and keep not faith, the young men are licentious and the aged drunkards. The nuns have insulted their calling, the priests have forgotten God, the monks have strayed from the straight road. . . . Many of us live in gluttony, drunkeness, fornication, adultery, foulness, licentiousness, hatred, jealousy, envy, and theft. We have become arrogant, braggarts, avaricious, selfish, ungrateful, disobedient, deserters, robbers, traitors, unholy, unjust, unrepentant, irreconcilable. . . . It is these things and other things like them which bring upon us the chastisements of God.[2]

III. BYZANTIUM'S DECLINE

When Basil, "the Bulgar-Slayer," died in 1025 the Byzantine Empire appeared unchallengeably secure in its splendid eminence. The northern frontier rested solidly on the Danube, Arabic Islam was divided and was no longer a threat, and whatever was emerging in the West was patently primitive and insignificant in comparison to the Second Rome on the Bosphorus. Yet within half a century after Basil's death the empire was in serious trouble, and less than two centuries later, in 1204, its capital had fallen to the despised barbarians of the West.

One reason for the dramatic reversal was the undermining of the imperial military system with the growing insubordination of the *strategoi,* or generals, in charge of the *themes,* or provinces. Basil II had been strong enough to keep the military in check, but his weak successors were unable to do so, especially when the *strategoi* joined forces with the great provincial landowners. Repeatedly the *strategoi* rebelled against civilian authority in Constantinople, using the peasant levies originally intended for frontier defense. In retaliation the bureaucrats disbanded the peasant levies, commuting the military service of the peasants to cash payments. The funds thus collected were used to hire mercenaries, including foreign Normans, Germans, Patzinaks, and Armenians. But in comparison with the former peasant forces, these mercenaries proved notoriously unreliable, often turning against the empire they ostensibly were defending when their pay was not forthcoming.

A closely related cause for imperial decline was the political problem of the feudalization of society. The *strategoi* and the local landowners accumulated vast estates, so that entire provinces fell under the domination of a few families. The emperors issued frequent orders against this trend, typical being the following by Constantine Porphyrogenitus in the early tenth century.

> Very often it has come to my knowledge that the wealthy men of Thrace, disregarding laws proclaimed by emperors and derived from natural human rights, and disobeying our orders, continue to infiltrate into the countryside. They expel the poor from the land which belongs to them, by tyrannizing them and by buying either gifts or wills. In consequence, having deliberated upon those cases . . . we establish a law that all those who, although forbidden by the orders of our predecessors from buying land from the poor, . . . have dared to infiltrate into the villages or to seize the land of the poor, must immediately, without any delay or explanations, vacate land obtained in such a way. They will not be entitled to claim any damages. . . .[3]

This and other similar orders proved of no avail, and for the simple reason that their implementation depended on the very class against which they were directed. After Basil II even these efforts largely ceased, and instead the emperors began to grant state properties in usufruct to those who had rendered valuable service. These grants, or *pronoia,* became associated with military service, and thus came to resemble the fiefs of the West, except for the absence of homage and subinfeudation. Indeed when the Latins conquered Byzantium in 1204 and divided it into fiefs, the Greek aristocracy recognized the fiefs as the Latin version of their own *pronoia.*

The empire was plagued also by serious economic ailments. The large private and monastic estates reduced imperial revenues, especially when Basil's successors relieved the large landowners of most taxes. At the same time imperial expenditures were rising because of court extravagances and the cost of the mercenary army. Equally serious were the mounting raids of Patzinaks and Seljuk Turks, which left certain regions devastated and unproductive. The Byzantine gold *solidus,* which had remained stable for seven centuries, now suffered successive debasements.

In Byzantium, as in many other empires, internal weakness attracted external aggression. In the West were the Norman adventurers who originally had served as Byzantine mercenaries but who now turned against the weakened empire and overran its possessions in southern Italy that had survived since the time of Justinian's conquests. Likewise in the east were the Seljuk Turks who had infiltrated from their Central Asian homeland into the Islamic Empire where they were employed as mercenaries by the Baghdad caliphs. Gradually the mercenaries became masters, and in 1055 they captured Baghdad and founded the Seljuk Empire. These Turks reanimated the moribund Islamic world, reuniting the lands between India and the Mediterranean and pressing upon the Taurus Mountain frontier that for centuries had separated the Byzantine and Islamic worlds.

This was the background of the two disasters that befell Byzantium in 1071, marking the beginning of centuries of decline. One occurred at Bari in southern Italy where the Normans conquered the sole surviving Byzantine foothold. The other, and much more decisive setback, was at Manzikert in

Asia Minor. There the Seljuks defeated the Byzantine emperor in a fateful battle that began the transformation of Asia Minor from a Greek to a Turkish stronghold. Following this battle two rival emperors fought for the Byzantine throne, employing Turkish forces against each other. Thus Turkish tribes were able to enter at will, gradually changing Asia Minor from the bedrock of Greek Byzantine power to the heartland of the Turkish nation.

The Byzantine Empire was saved from what appeared to be imminent dissolution by the astuteness and tenacity of Emperor Alexius Comnenus (1081–1118). He granted valuable commercial concessions to the Venetians in return for their support against the Normans who were threatening to attack Constantinople. He also appealed to Western Christendom for assistance against the Moslem Seljuks. Instead of a limited number of mercenaries that he had hoped for, he was confronted by hordes of undisciplined Crusaders, led in part by the Normans that Alexius had excellent reason to distrust. This contact between two societies resulted in mutual suspicion and open hostility. Greeks and Latins disliked each other's languages, religions, politics, and ways of life.

Alexius adroitly encouraged the Crusaders to cross over to Asia Minor where, together with the Byzantines, they recovered some regions from the Seljuks. But relations between Greeks and Latins became increasingly strained during the Second and Third Crusades. Also the Byzantines suffered a disastrous setback when they rashly set out to attack the Seljuk capital of Konia in central Asia Minor. On the way they were crushed by the Turks at Myriocephalon (1176), a defeat that ended whatever possibility that might have remained for a Byzantine comeback in Asia Minor. Meanwhile the Venetians were undermining the economic foundations of Byzantium with the commercial privileges they had extracted from the hard-pressed emperors. They had complete freedom from tolls or duties throughout the empire, a concession that gave them a decisive advantage over Byzantine merchants who were subject to heavy taxes. Thus not only did the Italians get a stranglehold on the empire's trade, but the treasury at Constantinople was deprived of a prime source of revenue. The contrast between Venetian affluence and Byzantine poverty provoked riots in 1183 in which many Latins were killed and their properties looted.

Such was the background of the Fourth Crusade, appropriately nicknamed the "businessmen's crusade." The economic designs of Venetian merchants, the quest for loot and lands by Western adventurers, the blandishments of a Byzantine pretender, and the long pent-up grievances harbored by Latins against what they considered to be the cunning, effeminate, grasping, and heretical Greeks, all combined to deflect the Fourth Crusade from its original goal of liberating Jerusalem to an assault upon Constantinople. A mixed force of French, Venetians, Flemings, and Germans stormed the capital in the spring of 1204 and subjected it to three days of merciless looting and slaughter. "Even the Saracens," observed a Byzantine chronicler, "would have been more merciful." Paradoxically, the end result of the Fourth Crusade was to pave the way for Islamic domination of the entire Middle East. Although the Byzantine Empire was restored in 1261, it never recovered from the traumatic shock of the Latin conquest, and remained in helpless impotence until the Ottoman capture of Constantinople in 1453.

IV. END OF BYZANTIUM

The victorious Latins set up their feudal states on the ruins of Byzantium. They established a Latin empire at Constantinople, a Latin kingdom at Thessaloniki, and several Latin states in Greece. The commercially minded Venetians occupied a whole quarter of Constantinople and annexed numerous islands and ports strategically located on their route to the Levant. These new states, however, were doomed from the outset. The native Greek Orthodox populations remained bitterly hostile to the end. Furthermore the Latin conquerors had won only a few isolated toeholds on the fringes of the Balkan Peninsula, and were surrounded on all sides by enemies. They faced not only the Serbian and Bulgarian kingdoms in the Balkan interior, but also three Greek succession states located at Arta in Epirus, at Trebizond on the southern shore of the Black Sea, and at Nicaea in western Asia Minor. The first of these Greek states was too poor to provide effective leadership, and the second was too isolated. So it was Nicaea, with its strategic location and adequate resources as well as able leadership, that organized Greek resistance to Latin rule.

By skillful diplomacy and force of arms the Nicaean rulers steadily reduced the Latin empire until only the city of Constantinople itself remained. Finally in 1261 the Latin emperor and the Venetian settlers fled from Constantinople without offering resistance. The Nicaean emperor, Michael Palaeologus, made his solemn entry into the capital and, amidst popular acclamation, took up his residence in the imperial palace.

The final phase of Byzantine history comprised the period between 1261, when Michael Palaeologus recovered Constantinople, and 1453, when his successor, Constantine Palaeologus, was killed at a gate of the capital fighting the Turks. During these two centuries the restored empire consisted merely of the cities of Constantinople and Thessaloniki, with small fluctuating areas around each, and two separate appanages: Mistra, in the Peloponnesus, and Trebizond, in northern Asia Minor.

The outlook for this pitiful remnant of empire was scarcely more promising than that of its Latin predecessors. In Asia it faced the formidable Turks, and in Europe it was surrounded by small Latin states that remained in Greece, and by the Serbians and Bulgarians to the north. To these external dangers were added internal difficulties. Economically the empire was bankrupt. The Italian stranglehold on commerce continued unbroken, so that in the mid-fourteenth century the Genoese quarter in Constantinople was collecting seven times as much as the imperial government in customs revenues. The emperors were reduced to debasing their currency and pawning their crown jewels with Venetian bankers. Increased taxes commonly were avoided by the politically influential rich. The poor rose in revolt against the aristocracy of birth and wealth, so that cities were torn by social strife.

Between 1342 and 1349 Thessaloniki was ruled by revolutionary leaders known as the Zealots. They reduced taxes on the poor, annulled their debts, confiscated and distributed monastery lands, and introduced participatory democracy with mass rallies and popularly elected officials. Their political

In the spring of 1204, Crusaders under the command of Baldwin of Flanders subjected the city of Constantinople to three days of looting and slaughter. The scene is illustrated here in a nineteenth-century painting by Eugène Delacroix. (Louvre— photo Giraudon)

program appears to have been influenced by the example of the republican city-states in Italy. But a dying Byzantine Empire could not sustain the political and social innovations then emerging naturally in the vigorous and expanding West. With Serbian and Turkish aid the emperor suppressed the Zealots and ended their republic. The episode was symptomatic, however, of the deep and widespread discord, as is evident in the following contemporary account.

> . . . the rising spread through the Empire like a terrible and cruel epidemic, attacking many who formerly were quiet and moderate. . . . And so all the cities rose against the aristocracy. . . . The whole empire was in the throes of the most cruel and desperate struggle. . . . The people were ready to rise in arms under the slightest provocation, and committed the most violent deeds because they hated the rich. . . .[1]

In addition to this socio-economic fragility, the empire was weakened by religious dissension. Hoping to obtain Western aid against the approaching Turks, the emperors on three separate occasions had agreed to the submission of the Orthodox Church to the Papacy (Unions of Lyons, 1274; Rome, 1369; and Florence, 1439). These agreements proved meaningless, for the West gave insignificant aid, while Byzantium was further torn by the bitter popular opposition to any concessions to the hated Latins. "Better Islam than the Pope" was the defiant popular response to the barbarities of the Fourth Crusade and to the exploitation by Italian merchants.

The cry of preference for the Turks had been heard frequently in the past, but in the mid-fifteenth century the situation was unique because the Turks then were in a position to accept the invitation. As noted in Chapter 14, section VI, the Ottoman Turks had taken over from the Seljuks, conquered the remaining Byzantine enclaves in Asia Minor, crossed the Straits to Europe, defeated the Bulgars and Serbs, and finally by 1453 were ready to close in on the beleaguered Byzantine capital.

Constantinople's population by this time had shrunk to between fifty and seventy thousand. The total force available for the defense of the city, including a small number from the West, amounted to no more than nine thousand. This was totally inadequate to man the extensive series of walls and to repair the breaches pounded by the enemy cannon. The Ottoman army, led by the capable Sultan Mohammed II, numbered at least eighty thousand. Yet the defenders, under the courageous leadership of Emperor Constantine, repulsed the attackers from April 2 when the siege began to May 29 when the final assault prevailed. The city was then given over to the soldiery for the promised three-day sack. The contemporary Byzantine historian Ducas describes as follows this ending of a thousand years of Byzantium.

> Three days after the fall of the city he [Muhammed] released the ships so that each might sail off to its own province and city, each carrying such a load that it seemed each would sink. And what sort of a cargo? Luxurious cloths and textiles, objects and vessels of gold, silver, bronze and brass, books beyond all counting and number, prisoners including priests and lay persons, nuns and monks. All the ships were full of cargos, and the tents of the army camps were full of captives and of the above enumerated

items and goods. And there was to be seen among the barbarian host one wearing the sakkon of an archbishop, another wearing the gold epitrahelion of a priest, leading their dogs clothed instead of with the usual collars with gold brocaded amnous (ecclesiastical vestments). Others were to be seen seated at banquets, with the holy discs before them containing fruit and other foods, which they were eating, and with the holy chalices from which they drank their wine. And having loaded all the books, reaching unto a number beyond numbering, upon carts, they scattered them throughout the east and west. For one nomisma ten books could be bought (and what kind of books), Aristotelian, Platonic, theological, and every other kind. There were gospels which had every type of embellishment, beyond number, they smashed the gold and silver from them and some they sold, others they threw away. And all the icons were thrown into the flame, from which flame they broiled their meat.[5]

V. BYZANTIUM'S LEGACY

In the light of retrospect Byzantium obviously made significant contributions in various fields. One was in its role as a protective shield behind which the West was left free to develop its own civilization. The full meaning of this became clear when, after the fall of Constantinople in 1453, the Turks within barely half a century reached the heart of Europe and besieged Vienna. Equally important was Byzantium's stimulus to trade and general economic development. For centuries Byzantium was the economic dynamo for the entire Mediterranean basin, while its currency served as the standard international medium of exchange. Its merchants and its commodities did much to lift Western Europe out of its feudalized self-sufficiency and to start the Italian city-states on the road to commercial domination of the Mediterranean.

In the realm of culture, Byzantium salvaged the intellectual and artistic treasures of antiquity and transmitted them to posterity along with her own legacy. From Byzantium came Roman law codified by Justinian, a religious art that only recently has been properly understood and appreciated, and the literary and scholarly masterpieces of classical and Hellenistic times as compiled, annotated, and preserved by conscientious scholars. Finally, as will be noted in the following section, Byzantium was for the eastern Slavs what Rome had been for the Germans—the great educator, the great initiator, the source both of religion and of civilization.

These achievements belie Gibbon's well known verdict concerning the historical significance of Byzantium. Yet at the same time it is apparent that Byzantium lacked the freshness and luster of classical Athens, even though the latter was territorially and chronologically insignificant by comparison. The reason is that the role of Byzantium was conservative in the proper sense of the word. This is not to say that Byzantium was static. From beginning to end it was adjusting itself to changing times and circumstances. But the fact remains that its destiny was to conserve rather than to create. It was born an aged state and lived in the shadow of past power and glory which it sought to maintain or recover. It produced a remarkable succession of outstanding leaders—administrators, generals, scholars, and theologians—but because of the context in which they worked very few of them were genuinely creative.

The fact that the East Roman Empire survived that of the West by a full millennium constituted a great advantage at the outset. Between the fifth and the eleventh centuries the West was primitive and insignificant in comparison to the Second Rome on the Bosphorus. But these were centuries when the West, precisely because it had to start afresh, was laying the foundations for a new civilization, while Byzantium was living on its splendid but overpowering patrimony. This is why from the eleventh century onward the West was able to forge ahead with its booming economy, rising national monarchies, new intellectual horizons, and a dynamic expansionism that manifested itself first in local crusades and then in an overseas thrust that was to lead within a few centuries to global hegemony. And, in pitiful contrast, during these later centuries Byzantium proved incapable of breaking the bonds to the past and thus became an obsolete anachronism that fought a gallant but foredoomed holding action until the ignominious but inevitable end in 1453.

VI. Byzantium and the Slavs

Although Byzantium had passed off the historical stage, Byzantine institutions and culture lived on amongst the Slavs to the north, as indeed they did in large part amongst the Balkan Christians who had passed under Turkish rule. Originating in the swampy borderland between present-day Russia and Poland, the Slavs fanned out in a great arc, the surrounding plains beckoning them in all directions.

Those who migrated westward comprise the Czechs, Slovaks, and Poles of today, and are known as the Western Slavs. Because of their location they fell under Western influence, so that their religion is Catholic and their alphabets Latin. Those who migrated across the Danube to the Balkan Peninsula are known today as the Slovenes, Croats, Serbs, and Bulgars. As noted in section I of this chapter, the first two of these South Slavic peoples adopted Western cultural forms, in contrast to the Serbs and Bulgars who were influenced by Constantinople rather than Rome in their cultural development. Finally to the east migrated the ancestors of the present-day Slavic peoples of the Soviet Union. These Eastern Slavs are known today as the Great Russians of the northern part of the country, the Little Russians, or Ukrainians, of the southern regions, and the White, or Byelo, Russians of the western borderlands where the earliest Slavs apparently originated.

The Eastern Slavs settled on the broad plains stretching from the Arctic shores in the north, to the Black Sea in the south, and to the Urals in the east. In the northern plains the colonists remained within the shelter of the forests, where they encountered little opposition from scattered and loosely organized Finnish and Lithuanian tribes with whom they intermarried or easily pushed aside. In the southern plains, by contrast, where the forests gradually gave way to the open steppes, the settlers were always vulnerable to the attacks of the peoples who ranged the great nomad route from Central Asia across the Ukraine to the Danube Valley.

These Eastern Slavs, or Russians as they are called today, engaged in trapping, fishing, and primitive slash-and-burn agriculture. Consequently, scattered homesteads and small hamlets were the general rule, rather than compact villages or towns. The few towns that did appear grew up as trade centers along main river routes. This was the case with Kiev on the Dnieper River carrying the north-south traffic, and with Novgorod on Lake Ilmen commanding the east-west commerce.

It was this long-distance trade that provided the basis for the first Russian state. According to legend, quarreling Slavic factions invited Rurik, the great Norse chieftain, to become their ruler. "Our whole land is great and rich, but there is no order in it. Come to rule and reign over us." Thus Rurik became the first prince of Novgorod in 862, and his followers soon moved southward to Kiev. The precise role of these Norsemen, or Varangians as they were called in Eastern Europe, remains a matter of dispute to the present day. The former assumption that they singlehandedly created the first Russian state and culture is now generally discounted. In fact the Varangians had little, if anything, to contribute in the realm of culture, and the degree to which they were responsible for the political organization of the early Russians is not clear.

Whatever the precise circumstances, Kiev emerged as the center of a loose confederation of Russian principalities strung out along the river routes. Kiev's preeminence was based on the flourishing trade carried on with the old centers of civilization to the south—Byzantium, Armenia, Georgia, and the Moslem world. Through Kiev were funneled raw materials gathered from the Russian countryside—furs, hides, grains, timber, and slaves—and in return were received a variety of luxury goods, including fine cloths, glassware, spices, jewelry, and wine.

The early Russians not only traded with the civilizations to the south but they also borrowed certain basic culture traits, especially Christianity from Byzantium. Hitherto the pagan Russians had worshipped forces of nature personified in certain deities such as Dazhbog, god of heat and light, Perun, god of thunder and lightning, and Striborg, god of wind. Neither temples nor priests existed, and religious ritual was limited to sacrifices offered to crude images of the deities erected in open spaces. Prince Vladimir of Kiev deemed this native Slavic pantheon inadequate and, according to the Chronicle compiled by monks at Kiev in the late eleventh and twelfth centuries, he pondered the arguments of representatives of various faiths who told him of their beliefs, and he even sent envoys to the countries where these faiths were practiced to report back to him. In this manner Vladimir rejected Catholicism because "we beheld no glory there," and Judaism because the God of the Jews had not been strong enough to enable them to remain in Jerusalem, and also Islam because it forbade pork and wine, and as he observed, "drinking is the joy of the Russes. We cannot exist without that pleasure." Thus Vladimir decided in favor of Orthodox Christianity, his envoys having been overwhelmed by the services they had beheld in the Hagia Sophia of Constantinople: ". . . we knew not whether we were in heaven or on earth. For on earth there is no such splendor or such beauty, and we are at a loss how to describe it." [6]

With his conversion about 988, Vladimir ordered all pagan statues destroyed, the idol of Perun being bound to a horse's tail and dragged to the

Dnieper. The entire population of Kiev also made its way to the river for mass baptism, and, as the Chronicle related, ". . . there was much rejoicing in heaven and on earth at the sight of so many people saved." As with Roman Christianity in northwestern Europe several centuries earlier, conversion was the decision of the ruler and his advisers, with the populace following as ordered. The absence of a priestly class amongst the pagan Slavs precluded organized resistance, but the masses clung to their traditional beliefs in witch-craft and omens. Thus a church council found it necessary to rule in 1274 that no one should be ordained a priest who had previously practiced sorcery.

Vladimir's adoption of Orthodox Christianity involved much more than a mere change of religion; the repercussions affected profoundly and pervasively the institutions and future history of the Russian people. An ecclesiastical hierarchy based on the Byzantine model was now organized. The head was the Metropolitan of Kiev, appointed by, and subject to, the jurisdiction of the Patriarch of Constantinople. For two centuries the Metropolitans were all Greeks, though the bishops appointed by the Metropolitans were mostly Russians after the first few generations. Christianity also brought with it a new religious and legal literature, including translations of the Bible, By-zantine collections of the writings of the church fathers, lives of saints, and law books. Byzantine art also was now introduced in the form of stone churches, mosaics, frescoes, paintings, and particularly icons, in which the Russians excelled and developed their distinctive Russo-Byzantine style. The Orthodox Church also brought with it Byzantine ecclesiastical law and estab-lished ecclesiastical courts. As in Western Europe, these courts had very wide jurisdiction, including all cases involving morals, beliefs, inheritance, and matrimonial matters.

In the realm of politics the new church served to strengthen the authority of the prince. Just as in Western Europe the Papacy had transformed the Frankish kings from tribal chieftains to the Lord's anointed, so now Russian Orthodoxy transformed the heads of the principalities from mere leaders of bands of personal followers to "servants of the lord" and hence rulers by divine right. Furthermore the Russian church, in accordance with Byzantine tradition, accepted secular authority and control. There was no counterpart in Moscow, as there had been none in Constantinople, of Gregory VII or Innocent III in Rome, demanding and exacting obedience from emperors and kings alike. In 1389, for example, Patriarch Antonius of Constantinople wrote to the Muscovite Grand Prince Vasilii complaining of the prince's lack of respect for him and his master, the Byzantine emperor.

> With sorrow . . . have I heard that thou dost not permit the Metropolitan to mention in the liturgy the godly name of the Emperor, saying for-sooth, "We have the Church, but the Emperor we do not have, and do not wish to know." This is not well. The holy Emperor holds a high place in the Church. He is not like other rulers—the local princes and potentates. The Emperor in the beginning established and confirmed the true faith for all the world. The Emperors called the Ecumenical Council. They also confirmed by their laws the observance of what the godly and holy canons declare to be the true dogmas and the orthodoxy of Church life. . . . It is not possible for a Christian to have the Church and not the Emperor.

For the Church and the Empire are in close union, . . . and it is not possible to separate the one from the other.[7]

After the disappearance of Byzantium and of its emperor, this submissiveness of Eastern Orthodoxy manifested itself in the subservience of the Russian church to the Russian emperor, which persisted with fateful consequences until the Tsarist empire followed the Byzantine to extinction.

It is apparent from the above that Byzantine influence in Russia constituted a great stimulus, yet at the same time it also proved to be an anesthetic. What the Russians borrowed was already fully evolved and relatively static, whether it was doctrine, ritual, music, or architecture. In this sense Byzantium had a rather stultifying effect on an awakening people, discouraging rather than encouraging creativity and originality. Furthermore, in adopting the Byzantine form of Christianity, the Russians inherited and sustained the Catholic-Orthodox feud, thereby erecting a barrier between themselves and the West. This was a distinct setback, for the Russians heretofore had developed numerous ties—commercial, dynastic and diplomatic—with the rest of Europe. Prince Yaroslav in the eleventh century, for example, had marriage connections with the leading dynasties of Europe, his sister being married to Casimir I of Poland, his son to a princess of Byzantium, and his two daughters to Henry I of France and to Harald III of Norway.

These associations between Russia and the West were dissolved not only by religious issues, but even more by the Mongol invasion and occupation. Kiev always had been extremely vulnerable to invasion, being located at the point where the forest zone gives way to the steppe. The threat of attack by the nomads hung over the city like the sword of Damocles. The sword descended in 1237 when the Mongols swept over the Russian lands as they did over most of Eurasia. Kiev and other Russian cities were razed, Novgorod being the only one of any size that escaped conquest because of its location in the far north. In the words of a chronicler, "No eye remained open to weep for the dead."

VII. THIRD ROME

Whereas the Mongols voluntarily withdrew from Central Europe, in Russia by contrast they chose to remain, establishing the kingdom, or khanate, of the Golden Horde. Its capital was Sarai, located strategically on the Volga, where the river bends furthest to the west. The ensuing two centuries of Mongol rule inevitably left a deep imprint on the Russian people. They were forced to abandon their small settlements on the steppe and to withdraw into the secure fastnesses of the forests. There they were left to their own devices so long as they recognized the suzerainty of the Mongol khan and paid him annual tribute. Indeed the khans issued certain charters, or yarlyks, granting the Russian church freedom from taxation and recognizing the Metropolitans' jurisdiction over Orthodox Christians. In return the Russian clergy offered prayers for the khans and their kin who, though they were Moslems rather than Christians, naturally welcomed such affirmations that lessened the likelihood of revolt.

Gradually the Russians recovered their strength and developed a new national center—the principality of Moscow, located deep in the forest zone away from the dangerous steppe. (See Map XIX, "The Growth of Muscovy.") Moscow had advantages other than its relative inaccessibility to the nomads. It was located at the crossroads of two important highways leading from the Dnieper to the northeastern regions. A number of rivers flowing in various directions came closest to each other in the Moscow region, enabling Moscow to profit by an inland water system. And the principality enjoyed the advantage of a line of rulers who were peaceful, frugal, and calculating. These rulers added to their possessions patiently and ruthlessly, until Moscow became the new national nucleus.

Ivan III (1462–1505) was particularly successful in his "gathering of the Russian lands," so that he may be regarded as the first of the national rulers of Russia. He conquered several neighboring principalities such as Yaroslav, Tver, and Rostov, which at one time had been more powerful than Moscow but which had since fallen behind. Most outstanding was his victory over mighty Novgorod, which had built up a vast trading empire of its own. By the end of his reign Ivan III had extended his frontiers from within a few miles of the Baltic to the Arctic Ocean in the north and the northern Urals in the east.

Ivan also successfully challenged the rule of the Mongols by exploiting divisions that had developed amongst them, and playing off contending factions against one another. More important was the fact that the Russians, in contrast to the Mongols, were able to import cannon and small arms from the West, and also possessed arsenals for the manufacture of these weapons. With these advantages, Ivan was able to renounce formally the suzerainty of the Golden Horde. The khan responded by sending an army north to the Oka River in 1472, but Ivan defiantly mustered his troops on the opposite bank. For three weeks he waited and then the Mongols withdrew, thereby acknowledging in effect the end of their domination over Russia.

Noteworthy also is Ivan's marriage in 1472 to Sophia, niece of the last Byzantine emperor, who had perished on the walls of Constantinople in 1453. Sophia had fled to Rome and converted to Catholicism, so that the Pope favored the match in hope that it would lead to the union of the Catholic and Russian churches. Instead Sophia promptly reverted to the Orthodox faith, and the Muscovite court became increasingly Byzantine and Orthodox in ritual and conviction.

The Russian church and court earlier had strongly opposed the agreement of the Greeks at Florence (1439) for union with Rome. Indeed the Russians interpreted the eventual fall of Constantinople to the Turks as divine retribution for unprincipled surrender to the Latins. Five years after the catastrophe, Metropolitan Jonah commented pointedly on what he considered to be its cause: "You well know, my children, the many ills that befell the ruling city of Constantine during the seven years the Bulgarians and Persians held it as in a net; yet it did not suffer as long as the Greeks observed their faith." [8]

With Constantinople fallen, the Russians now regarded Moscow as the home of the true faith, which they were divinely ordained to defend and to preserve in its original purity. This conviction was explicitly articulated at the end of the fifteenth century by the monk Philotheus who wrote to Ivan:

The church of ancient Rome fell because of Apollinarian heresy; as to the second Rome—the church of Constantinople—it has been hewn by the axes of Ishmaelites, but this third new Rome—the Holy Apostolic church—under thy mighty rule, shines throughout the entire world more brightly than the sun. All the Orthodox Christian realms have converged in thine own. Thou art the sole Autocrat of the universe, the only Tsar of the Christians. . . . Observe and hearken, O pious Tsar, two Romes have fallen, but the third stands, and no fourth can ever be.[9]

Ivan understandably welcomed this credo which so exalted his status and mission. With the encouragement of Sophia he adopted Byzantine court etiquette and chose the Byzantine double-headed eagle as his emblem. He became tsar and autocrat, in imitation of the past emperors of Constantinople, and his title was correspondingly grand and resplendent: "Ivan, by the mercy of God, Emperor of All Rus and Grand Prince of Vladimir and Moscow and Novgorod and Pskov and Tver and Perm and Ugra and Bolghar and the rest."

Thus Byzantium lived on in the Russian lands as the Third Rome. This Third Rome survived because it possessed vast resources and an impregnable base encompassing the great Eurasian plains and, before long, the limitless trans-Ural territories of Siberia. This was altogether different from the shrunken Byzantium that had dragged out a precarious existence for centuries prior to 1453. Cardinal Bessarion's call for modernization had evoked no response from this foredoomed anachronism (See Chapter 17, section III), but in Russia certain tsars were to appear who assumed themselves the role of Bessarion. And as the autocratic rulers of a vast empire, they possessed both the authority and the resources to translate, however imperfectly, their desires into reality, and thereby to assure, as the monk Philotheus had prophesied, that this Third Rome would not suffer the fate of the Second.

SUGGESTED READING

The best full-scale study is by G. Ostrogorsky, *History of the Byzantine State* (New Brunswick: Rutgers Univ., 1957), while the best short study is the comprehensive and up-to-date work by S. Vryonis, *Byzantium and Europe* (New York: Harcourt, Brace & World, 1967). One of the best sources of information on practically every aspect of Byzantium, the South Slavs, and relations with Kiev and Islam is the *Cambridge Medieval History*, Vol. IV (London: Cambridge Univ., 1966). Another standard work which considers cultural matters as well as political is by A. A. Vasiliev, *History of the Byzantine Empire*, 2 vols. (Madison: Univ. of Wisconsin, 1958). A short survey which concentrates on the state, on Christianity, and on the Byzantine mind is by D. A. Miller, *The Byzantine Tradition* (New York: Harper & Row, 1966). Other noteworthy general histories are C. Diehl, *Byzantium: Greatness and Decline* (New Brunswick: Rutgers Univ., 1957); N. H. Baynes, *Byzantine Studies and Other Essays* (New York: Oxford Univ., 1960); and E. Barker, *Social and Political Thought in Byzantium from Justinian I to the Last Palaeologus: Passages from Byzantine Writers and Documents* (New York: Oxford Univ., 1957).

On special aspects of Byzantine history there are G. Downey, *Constantinople in the Age of Justinian* (Norman: Univ. of Oklahoma, 1960); D. J. Geanakoplos, *Byzantine East and Latin West; Two Worlds of Christendom in Middle Ages and Renaissance* (Oxford: Blackwell, 1966); S. Runciman, *The Eastern Schism* (Oxford: Clarendon, 1955); D. T. Rice, *Byzantine Art* (Baltimore: Penguin, 1961); A. Grabar, *Byzantine Painting* (New York: World, 1953); and S. Runciman, *A History of the Crusades*, 3 vols. (London: Cambridge Univ., 1951–54), which is a comprehensive study of the Crusades to 1291.

Standard full-length general histories of Russia are by M. T. Florinsky, *Russia: A History and an Interpretation*, 2 vols. (New York: Macmillan, 1947); and N. V. Riasanovsky, *A History of Russia* (New York: Oxford Univ., 1963). An excellent, briefer, interpretative survey is by O. Hoetzsch, *The Evolution of Russia* (New York: Harcourt, Brace & World, 1966). Two studies that are based on topical rather than chronological organization are by B. H. Sumner, *A Short History of Russia* (New York: Reynal & Hitchcock, 1943); and A. G. Mazour, *Russia Past & Present* (Princeton: Van Nostrand, 1951).

Detailed histories of the Kievan period are provided by H. Paskiewicz, *The Making of the Russian Nation* (London: Darton, Longman, and Todd, 1963); and G. Vernadsky, *Kievan Russia* (New Haven: Yale Univ., 1948). On the Mongols, there is G. Vernadsky, *The Mongols and Russia* (New Haven: Yale Univ., 1953). For general economic development, see P. I. Liashchenko, *History of the National Economy of Russia to the 1917 Revolution* (New York: Macmillan, 1949); and J. Blum, *Lord and Peasant in Russia from the Ninth to the Nineteenth Century* (Princeton: Princeton Univ., 1961).

I am happy because I am a human Chapter
and not an animal; a male, and not a female;
a Chinese, and not a barbarian;
and because I live in Loyang,
the most wonderful city in all the world.

16

SHAO YUNG *(Neo-Confucianist, 1011–1077)*

Traditional Confucian

Civilization

The fact that the Han dynasty eventually was succeeded by the Sui and T'ang dynasties ensured that civilization in China was to continue along traditional lines, in contrast to the unique mutation that ·vas taking form in the West following Rome's collapse. (See Chapter 11, section III.) The ensuing millennium proved to be for the Chinese people a great Golden Age. During the Han period China had succeeded in catching up to the other Eurasian civilizations, but now, during the medieval period, China was able to forge ahead and to remain the richest, most populous, and, in many ways, the most culturally advanced country in the world.

The millennium between the sixth century, when the Sui dynasty restored imperial unity, and the sixteenth, when the Westerners began their intrusion by sea, was for China an era of unparalleled political, social, and cultural stability. But this stability paradoxically proved to be a curse as well as a blessing. It was a blessing because Chinese society during this millennium provided more material and psychological security for more people than any other society in the world. But the stability was also a curse because it was so successful and comfortable that China remained relatively unchanged, though by no means completely static. At the same time, however, as we shall

305

note in the following chapter, the West was being transformed by its technological precociousness, its economic vitality, and its social and political pluralism, all of which engendered a dynamism that was to culminate in global hegemony. The end result, then, was the disruption of the beautifully balanced but conservative Chinese society by the irresistible expansionism of the West. This denouement, however, should not be allowed to obscure the fact that for a full millennium the civilization of China led the world by its sheer viability and by its contributions to the human heritage.

I. Sui Restores Unity

The Sui dynasty (589–618) played the same role in Chinese history as the Ch'in dynasty some eight centuries earlier. Both dynasties reunited China after long periods of disorder, and both then proceeded to make fundamental contributions to the development of the country. But in doing so they drove their people so hard and antagonized so many vested interests that both scarcely survived their founders.

The great contribution of the Ch'in rulers was the imperial unity they forced upon China through road and canal building, construction of the Great Wall, standardization of weights, measures, and script, and extension and strengthening of the frontiers. The efforts of the Sui emperors were very similar and equally exhausting. They reconstructed the Great Wall, parts of which had fallen into disrepair. They built the main sections of the gigantic canal system that came to be known as the Grand Canal. This met a pressing need by linking the Yangtze Valley, which had become the economic center of the country, with the North, which remained the political center. But so heavy was the cost in treasure and lives that a later Chinese writer observed that the Sui emperor responsible for the undertaking "shortened the life of his dynasty by a number of years but benefited posterity to ten thousand generations. He ruled without benevolence, but his rule is to be credited with enduring accomplishments." [1]

Equally exhausting were the series of campaigns that extended the imperial frontiers to include Formosa, Annam and Champa in Indochina, and Kansu in the northwest. But the attempts to conquer the most northern of the three kingdoms into which Korea was then divided proved disastrous. Four successive invasions were repulsed by the resolute Korean defenders. The disaffected soldiers mutinied, while the overtaxed peasants rose in rebellion in various parts of the country. The emperor fled to South China where he was assassinated in 618. The victor in the ensuing struggle among several pretenders established the T'ang dynasty, regarded by many Chinese and Western historians as the most illustrious of them all.

II. T'ang Empire

The most manifest characteristic of the T'ang dynasty was its imperial expansionism. In a series of great campaigns, it extended the frontiers even

Sixth-century Chinese stoneware figure from the collection of the Victoria and Albert Museum, London. (Arborio Mella)

beyond those of the Han emperors. In Central Asia it established Chinese suzerainty over the Tarim Basin and beyond the Pamirs to the states of the Oxus Valley and even to the head waters of the Indus in modern Afghanistan. Other vast territories that now were constrained to accept Chinese suzerainty were Tibet in the south, Mongolia in the northwest, and Korea and Manchuria in the northeast. The only other comparable empire in the world at the time was that of the Moslem Arabs in the Middle East. That the triumphs of the Chinese were not due exclusively to superior physical power is evident in the following account by eastern Turks of their relations with the T'ang empire.

> The Chinese people, who give in abundance gold, silver, millet, and silk, have always used ingratiating words and have at their disposal enervating riches. While ensnaring them with their ingratiating talk and enervating riches, they have drawn the far-dwelling peoples nearer to themselves. . . . Because of want of harmony between the begs [princes] and the people, and because of the Chinese people's cunning and craft and its intrigues, and because the younger and the elder brothers chose to take counsel against one another and bring discord between begs and people, they brought the old realm of the Turkish people to dissolution, and brought destruction on its lawful kagans. The sons of the nobles became the bondsmen of the Chinese people, their unsullied daughters became its slaves.[2]

These foreign conquests were made possible by the reestablishment of strong central government at home. As noted earlier (Chapter 10, section V), the Han dynasty had been undermined by powerful local families that had accumulated huge, self-sufficient, and tax-free estates on which they built fortress-like manor houses from which they successfully defied central authority. This disintegration was furthered by the appearance of Buddhist monasteries, which, with their extensive and growing landholdings, offered another challenge to the imperial government.

An antidote to this political fragmentation gradually evolved during the centuries of the interregnum and was perfected by the Sui and T'ang bureaucrats. It consisted of the "equal field" system by which all able-bodied peasants were assigned plots of about nineteen acres by the central government. This did not deprive the powerful families of their holdings, for the land was obtained from other sources, such as reclamation projects and fields that had been abandoned during the wars. Also the free peasants alone received the land grants, and by no means all of them in actual practice. Nevertheless the "equal field" system did help somewhat to loosen the grip of the great families and to strengthen the T'ang regime. It halted for some time the growth of the large semifeudal estates. It increased government revenues, since the small peasants paid taxes whereas the politically powerful great landholders did not. Furthermore the peasants were given military training and organized into a regular militia, thereby strengthening the military position of the imperial government.

The T'ang dynasty consolidated its authority also by developing a competent bureaucracy to administer the empire. The Sui earlier had reinstated the Han system of civil service based on competitive public examinations.

The T'ang continued and expanded this system in accordance with the basic Confucian tenet that matters of state are better met by recruiting men of talent than by the legal and institutional change that is typical of the West. When fully evolved, the system consisted of a series of examinations held amidst an elaborate series of rituals. The first, in the district and prefectural cities, occurred every two or three years, and the approximately 2 percent of the candidates who passed these took the prefectural exams a few weeks later. Survivors (about half the candidates) became eligible for appointment to minor posts and for further examinations held every three years in the provincial capitals. Success here entitled one to take the imperial examinations at the capital. Only 6 percent passed this hurdle and became eligible for appointment to high office; and only a third of these normally passed the climactic palace examination in the presence of the Emperor himself and were admitted to membership in the most exalted fraternity of Chinese scholarship, the Hanlin Academy, from which were selected the historiographers and other high literary officers.

At first the examinations were fairly comprehensive, emphasizing the Confucian classics but including also subjects like law, mathematics, and political affairs. Gradually, however, they came to concentrate on literary style and Confucian orthodoxy. The net result was a system that theoretically opened offices to all men of talent, but that in practice favored the classes with sufficient wealth to afford the years of study and preparation. This did not mean that a hereditary aristocracy ruled China; rather, it was a hierarchy of the learned, a literocracy, providing China with an efficient and stable administration that won the respect and admiration of Europeans. On the other hand, it was a system that stifled originality and bred conformity. So long as China remained relatively isolated in East Asia, it provided stability and continuity. But with the intrusion of the dynamic West it served instead to prevent effective adjustment and response, until it was finally abolished altogether in 1905.

The three top government bodies in the capital were the Imperial Secretariat, which operated directly under the emperor and formulated policy, the Imperial Chancellery, which reviewed the decisions of the first body and returned them for reconsideration when deemed necessary, and the Secretariat of State Affairs, which implemented the decisions of the other two organs. Under the Secretariat of State Affairs were six Ministries, or Boards: Personnel, Revenue, War, Justice, Public Works, and Rites; the last of these was entrusted with the conduct of the civil service examinations.

The capital in which these and other government bodies met was Ch'ang-an, a magnificent city of probably over one million people. Its broad thoroughfares, crisscrossing in checkerboard fashion, often were crowded with Persians, Indians, Jews, Armenians, and assorted Central Asians. They came as merchants, missionaries, and mercenary soldiers, for China under the T'ang was more open to foreigners than at any other time with the exception of the short-lived Mongol Yüan interlude.

This openness was most apparent in matters of religion. The extension of imperial frontiers and the reopening of land and sea trade routes led to a great influx of foreign religious ideas and missionaries. This was particularly true of Buddhism, which first entered China from India (see Chapter 7, section III) during the Han dynasty and which began to seriously challenge the official

Relief from the tomb of the T'ang Emperor T'ai Tsung (597–649) showing a chestnut bay battle charger. (The University Museum, Philadelphia—photo Arborio Mella)

Confucianism during the chaotic interregnum following the Han. In that time of trouble Confucianism was increasingly questioned because its emphasis on filial piety and family loyalty appeared to weaken an already weak state. Consequently Buddhism gained rapidly during the interregnum and reached the height of its influence during the early T'ang, which is sometimes called the "Buddhist period" of Chinese history.

Although Buddhism attained great wealth and influence in China, it became in the process thoroughly Sinicized, and also contributed fundamentally to Neo-Confucianism. Since there was considerable religious toleration and freedom of thought in China, various Buddhist sects evolved, outstanding being Ch'an, which later appeared in Japan as Zen. This sect emphasized meditation and self-reliance and was the only one to continue a vigorous intellectual life after the T'ang. Another feature of Sinicization was the government's attempt to control and even subsidize the monasteries and temples in line with the typically Chinese concept that a religion should serve the interests of the state and function as its spiritual organ.

In the long run the attempts at control failed, and eventually the government resorted to outright persecution. The Buddhist emphasis on the salvation of the individual rather than on his obligation to the family was too contrary to basic Chinese traditions. So was the complete withdrawal from society of monks and nuns, which was considered unnatural and antisocial. And, above all, the government coveted the vast treasures and estates that the monasteries had accumulated through the centuries. Hence the series of persecutions that crippled Buddhism in China, though it did not disappear altogether as it did in India. (See Chapter 7, section III.) The persecution was restricted to the institutions and their clergy, and did not include the rank-and-file believers, as was the case in comparable situations in the West. The end result of this Buddhist interlude was minimal so far as the overall evolution of Chinese civilization was concerned. Buddhism did make significant contributions to Chinese philosophy, metaphysics, art, and literature, but it did not remold Chinese society as a whole, as Christianity had remolded the European.

Finally it should be noted that although Buddhism was the most influential of the foreign religions in China at this time, it was by no means the only one. The free field available to other religions as well is evident in the experiences of Ruben, a Nestorian Christian monk called O Lo Pen by the Chinese. Arriving at the T'ang court in A.D. 635, he was received by the Emperor, who ordered that his books should be translated into Chinese. Being favorably impressed by both the emissary and his faith, the emperor issued the following edict.

> The Way [the way of truth or religion in general] has more than one name. There is more than one Sage. Doctrines vary in different lands, their benefits reach all mankind. O Lo Pen, a man of great virtue from Ta Ts'in (the Roman Empire) has brought his images and books from afar to present them in our capital. After examining his doctrines we find them profound and pacific. After studying his principles we find that they stress what is good and important. His teaching is not diffuse and his reasoning is sound. This religion does good to all men. Let it be preached freely in Our Empire.[3]

During the last century and a half of their reign, the T'ang rulers were faced with the usual problems of a dynasty in decline. Imperial expenses outstripped revenues. Population growth likewise outstripped land supply, so that peasant families no longer could be provided with individual plots. The "equal field" system broke down, and the wealthy families once more enlarged their estates at the expense of the peasants. Since the revenue system was based on per capita taxes, the burden of paying for the mounting imperial expenses fell on the peasants at a time when their holdings were shrinking.

The government responded by shifting increasingly from per capita to land taxes. This produced more revenue, but it did not halt the decline in the number of free peasants. This decline meant a corresponding decline in the supply of manpower for militia and corvée duty. Imperial defense was entrusted increasingly to mercenaries and border "barbarian" tribes who were not as dependable as the former militia. Thus in 751 Chinese armies were defeated both in Yunnan in the south and at Talas in Central Asia. The latter battle was particularly decisive for it enabled the Moslem Arab victors to begin the Islamization of a vast area that had been one of the earliest strongholds of Buddhism.

The T'ang emperors managed to hang on for another century and a half, but it was a period of steady deterioration. Incompetence and provocative luxury in the capital combined with successive droughts and widespread famine to provoke rebellions in many provinces. The dynasty enlisted the support of local military leaders and assorted "barbarian" border peoples. But these soon were out of control, disregarding court orders and fighting amongst themselves for the succession to the obviously doomed dynasty. The end came in 907, when one of the rebel leaders deposed the last T'ang ruler and sacked Ch'ang-an. The empire now broke into fragments, and the ensuing half century is known as the interregnum of the "Five Dynasties." An able general finally was able to restore unity and to found a new dynasty, the Sung, which, like its predecessor, endured for about three centuries (960–1279).

It should be noted that this brief half century interlude between dynasties now became the pattern for future Chinese history. Never again was the country to experience several centuries of anarchy, as it had following the Han collapse. The reason is that from the T'ang onward, Chinese civilization was too massive and deep-rooted to remain disrupted for prolonged periods. Perhaps this civilization might have become more innovative and creative if imperial unity had been supplanted by the pluralism and diversity of the West. This is an "if" of history that must remain speculative. The only certainty is that the Chinese themselves regarded disunity and the attendant turmoil as abnormal and deplorable. "Just as there cannot be two suns in one sky," went an old saying, "so there cannot be two Chinese states or two rulers of China."

III. SUNG GOLDEN AGE

The Sung emperors were markedly passive in their external relations compared to their Han and T'ang predecessors. They did not begin with great campaigns reestablishing imperial frontiers in the heart of Eurasia. Instead the second Sung emperor modestly attempted to regain from nomad control merely the territory between Peking and the Great Wall. But he was disastrously defeated, and his successor gave up claim to this region, and even paid the nomads an annual "gift," which in fact was thinly veiled tribute. Thus the Sung never recovered the northeast territories in Manchuria, nor the northwest territories that provided access to the overland routes to the west.

This was a grave weakness for the Sung dynasty, leaving it vulnerable to nomadic incursions. The policy of paying "gifts" proved viable for a century and a half, but disaster came when a Sung emperor made a rash attempt to recover the northeastern lands. He was encouraged to do so when the ruling nomads in that region were defeated by newcomers from North Manchuria. Taking advantage of what appeared to be an opportunity, the emperor sent his armies into Manchuria. Instead of easy victory they sustained a crushing defeat that was followed by massive invasion of North China. The Sung defenses crumpled and the dynasty was left only with the Yangtze Valley in central China, and the lands to the south. Consequently the second half of the dynasty, from 1127 to 1279, is known as the Southern Sung; the first half, between 960 and 1127, is called the Northern Sung.

This dynasty was much berated by later Chinese historians for failing initially to regain the outlying provinces, and then suffering the loss of the entire northern half of the country. This criticism cannot be denied, yet it is also true that in many respects Chinese civilization reached its apogee during the centuries of the T'ang and the Sung. This was particularly so in the field of culture. During these centuries appeared the vast encyclopedias of Buddhist texts and Confucian classics; the comprehensive dynastic histories written by teams of scholars; the masterpieces of scores of great poets and artists; the art of calligraphy, depicted on scrolls prized as highly as paintings; the beautiful porcelain as thin as glass and almost as transparent; the priceless invention of printing that was utilized for the mass duplication and distribution of Buddhist scriptures; and the extraordinary advances in science and technology which are only now being adequately comprehended. (See Chapter 12, section III.)

In addition to its cultural attainments, the Sung period is noteworthy for a veritable commercial revolution that was quite significant for all Eurasia. The roots are to be found in a marked increase in the productivity of China's economy. Steady technological improvements raised the output of the traditional industries. Agriculture likewise was stimulated by the introduction of a quickly maturing strain of rice that allowed two crops to be grown each season where only one had been possible before. Also new water control projects undertaken by the Sung greatly expanded the acreage of irrigated paddy fields. Thus it is estimated that the rice crop doubled between the eleventh and twelfth centuries.

This increasing productivity made possible a corresponding increase in population, which in turn further stimulated production in interacting fashion. The volume of trade also rose with the quickening tempo of economic activity. For the first time large cities appeared in China that were primarily commercial rather than administrative centers.

Even more marked than this spurt in domestic trade was that in foreign trade. Considerable overseas commerce had been carried on since Han times, but during the T'ang, and more especially during the Sung, the volume of foreign trade far surpassed all previous records. The basis for this burgeoning trade was, of course, the unprecedented productivity of China's economy. Important also were the improvements in maritime technology, including the use of the compass, of an adjustable centerboard keel, and of cotton sails in place of bamboo slats. Finally overseas trade was quickened also by the initiative of Moslem merchants and mariners who were the great entrepreneurs in Asian seas at this period.

The end result was that for the first time the seaports rather than the old overland routes became China's principal contact with the outside world. Indicative of China's economic leadership at this time is the fact that her exports were mostly manufactured goods such as silk, porcelains, books, and paintings, while the imports were mostly raw materials such as spices, minerals, and horses. Finally it should be noted that during the Sung the Chinese themselves for the first time engaged on a large scale in overseas trade, no longer depending largely on foreign intermediaries. In conclusion, China during the Sung was well on the way to becoming a great maritime power. But the all important fact, for world history as well as for Chinese, is that this this potentiality was never realized. And, equally significant, this veritable commercial revolution of the Sung era had none of the explosive repercussions on Chinese society that a corresponding commercial revolution had on Western society. (See section V of this chapter.)

IV. Yüan Mongol Rule

The rule of the Southern Sung, though confined to only half the country, proved exceptionally peaceful and prosperous. Meanwhile North China was under the Chin, a people of Manchurian origin. About 1215 they appealed to the Southern Sung for help against the formidable Mongols who had driven them out of Peking. The Sung, not aware of the deadly power of the Mongols, supported them by sending infantry skilled in siege warfare. When the Chin were overwhelmed by 1234, the Sung emperor rashly attempted to secure North China for his own empire. The Mongols retaliated by promptly invading South China. The war dragged on for decades because the Mongols were preoccupied elsewhere, but the end came in 1279 when the last Sung pretender perished in a naval battle. A new Mongol dynasty that took the name Yüan now began its rule that was to endure to 1368.

This was the first and only time that China was ruled by full nomads who had not already been partly Sinicized by earlier contact with the empire. The immediate reaction of the rude conquerors was to level the cities and to incorporate their new subjects into the traditional Mongol tribal society. But they soon were advised that this was impossible and that a more lucrative alternative was feasible.

> Now that you have conquered everywhere under Heaven and all the riches of the four seas, you can have everything you want, but you have not yet organized it. You should set up taxation on land and merchants,

and should make profits on wine, salt, iron, and the produce of the mountains and marshes. In this way in a single year you will obtain 500,000 ounces of silver, 80,000 rolls of silk and 400,000 piculs of grain. How can you say that the Chinese people are of no use to you? [4]

The Mongols acted on this advice and established an administrative apparatus essentially similar to that of their Chinese predecessors. At the same time they were able to preserve their identity because their nomadic background separated them from their subjects as regards language, customs, and laws. They also took care to employ in their service many foreigners to counterbalance the suspect Chinese majority. Marco Polo is the best known of these foreign-born bureaucrats, though most of them were Central Asian Moslems.

Kublai Khan, who moved the Mongol capital from Karakorum to Peking and became essentially a Chinese emperor, dutifully performed the traditional Confucian imperial rites. Also he sought to appease the Confucian literati by exempting them from taxation, but they remained largely alienated. They resented the large number of foreigners in what had become virtually an international civil service, and they resented also the Mongol toleration and patronage of various foreign religions, including Islam and Nestorian Christianity. (See Chapter 14, sections IV and V.)

Because of its nature and relatively short duration, Mongol rule in China did not leave a deep imprint on the country. Perhaps the most lasting contribution was the selection of Peking as the capital. Situated in the North China plain on the routes leading westward to Central Asia and eastward to Manchuria, Peking has remained an important military, economic, and administrative center to the present day. Mongol rule also stimulated a sharp rise in overland trade since China now was part of a huge empire encompassing most of Eurasia. (See Chapter 12, section II.) Commerce was also facilitated by the widespread use of paper money, which was introduced by the Sung but developed further by the Mongols. Marco Polo repeatedly expressed his astonishment at the use of paper money, as did a fellow Italian merchant in the following words:

Whatever silver the merchants carry with them to Cathay the lord of Cathay takes from them and puts in his treasury and gives that paper money of theirs in exchange . . . . and with this money you can readily buy silk and whatever other merchandise you desire to buy, and all of the people of the country are bound to receive it, and you shall not pay a higher price for your goods because your money is of paper. [5]

The able Kublai Khan died in 1294 at the age of eighty and was succeeded by his equally able grandson, Timur. But he died young, and the following Khans were incompetent and debauched by palace life. Fratricidal conflicts broke out within the dynasty, and even worse, frequent flooding of the Yellow River produced widespread famine in North China. Rebellions broke out in most of the provinces, and only the rivalry amongst the rebel leaders enabled the Mongols to hold out as long as they did. Finally the turmoil was ended by an able commoner who, like the founder of the Han, rose through sheer native ability in a time of crisis and opportunity to become the Son of Heaven. Thus the Chinese Ming dynasty was established in 1368 and remained in power to 1644.

V. MING ETHNOCENTRISM AND WITHDRAWAL

Two dynasties, the Ming (1368–1644) and the Ch'ing (1644–1912), ruled China during the more than half millennium between the overthrow of the Mongols and the advent of the republic. These centuries comprise one of the great eras of orderly government and social stability in human history. A main reason for this unprecedented durability was the unchallenged primacy of a new Confucian metaphysics known as Neo-Confucianism. This renaissance of Confucian thought took place mostly during the time of troubles following the collapse of the T'ang dynasty, when the needs of the age patently called for something more than the mere memorization of Confucian classics. Accordingly a number of scholars undertook a searching reappraisal of the problems of man and of the universe.

A leader in this undertaking was Chu Hsi (1129–1200), who in his youth had studied both Buddhism and Taoism. Satisfied with neither, he turned to the Confucian classics, and with his remarkable talent for synthesis he evolved an interpretation that incorporated elements of Buddhism and Taoism and that was more satisfyingly relevant for his age. His approach was essentially that of the empirical rationalist. He taught that the universe is governed by natural law, which should be comprehended and respected. He also believed in the goodness of man and in his perfectability. He compared man to a mirror covered with dust which, if cleaned, will be as bright as ever. Evil, therefore, was the result of neglect and of defective education, and hence was correctable.

Chu Hsi's influence in the Confucian world was comparable to that of Thomas Aquinas in Western Christendom. Just as Aquinas soon was to weave Aristotle and St. Paul into the official scholastic philosophy, so Chu Hsi now integrated contemporary Chinese thought into the Neo-Confucian synthesis. And by his very comprehensiveness and persuasiveness Chu Hsi, like Aquinas, discouraged further philosophical development. This was particularly true during the Ming period when, as a reaction against the preceding foreign Mongol domination, there was a pronounced ethnocentrism and a looking backward to past traditions. In such an atmosphere, Chu Hsi came to be regarded as the absolute and final authority. "Ever since the time of the philosopher Chu," declared a Ming scholar, "the Truth has been made manifest to the world. No more writing is needed: what is left to us is practice." [6]

Since the Confucian classics, with Chu Hsi's commentaries, became the basis of the civil service examinations, this Neo-Confucianism constituted the official orthodoxy of the empire until the late nineteenth century. Its effect was to reinforce the growing social rigidity with an intellectual supplement and rationale. It contributed fundamentally to the unequalled continuity of Chinese civilization, but the cost was a stultifying conformism adverse to all originality or new ideas from the outside.

Chinese society owed its stability not only to Neo-Confucianism but also to the entrenched power of the so-called gentry ruling class, a power based on its combined possession of land and office in an agrarian-based bureaucratic empire. As landlords and as money lenders the gentry dominated the economic life of the villages and towns. Shortage of land and of capital enabled them to impose extortionate rents and interest rates. Frequent natural disasters forced bankrupt mortgagees to become virtual contractual serfs of the local gentry families. It was common for these families by late Ming times to have several thousand indentured peasant households of this sort.

317

The gentry also were degree holders; indeed this is what the Chinese term for "gentry" literally denotes. But landowning was virtually a prerequisite for financing the years of study necessary to become a degree holder, and hence gain eligibility for a post in the bureaucracy. Thus the association between the local gentry and the imperial bureaucracy was intimate and mutually supporting. Frequently the government official who appeared at his provincial post found the native dialect quite incomprehensible, in which case he was completely dependent on the local gentry for orientation and guidance.

Ming and Ch'ing China were ruled by the bureaucracy and the gentry together, if a meaningful distinction can be made between the two. Both the imperial establishment and the local gentry were interested in preserving the mutually beneficial *status quo,* and they cooperated to that end. Whereas earlier dynasties occasionally had attempted to force through land redistribution and other such reforms, the Ming and the Ch'ing carefully avoided any challenges to the gentry hegemony.

Revealing and significant is the contrasting initiative of the Ming government in controlling and repressing the merchant class. This was a basic and most meaningful difference between the Western and Chinese societies. In the West the bourgeoisie, because of the pluralism of the society in which it appeared, enjoyed from the outset considerable autonomy, and was able to increase it with the passage of time. (See Chapter 18, section IV.) In China there did exist a corresponding merchant class which during the Sung enjoyed a veritable commercial revolution. (See section III of this chapter.) Furthermore China originated most of the basic technological inventions of medieval times. Yet the commercial revolution and the technological advances together failed to bring about in China the revolutionary repercussions that completely transformed society in the West. The basic reason for this, as noted in Chapter 11, section VI, was the continuity of Chinese history—the fact that the Han dynasty was continued in essentials by the Sui, and the Sui in turn by the T'ang and the Sung, and so on in unbroken succession until the end of imperial history in 1912. Thus the traditional bureaucracy-gentry ruling establishment, buttressed by the intellectual props of Neo-Confucianism, was able to absorb the effects of the new technology and of economic growth. But in the West, Rome came to an end with no imperial successor. Instead, a new pluralistic civilization emerged in which gunpower, the compass, the printing press, and the oceangoing ship were not muffled but rather exploited to their full potential with explosive consequences, first for Europe, and then for the entire world, including China.

No such explosive repercussions were possible in China because the imperial establishment there was too enveloping and restricting. For example, Chinese merchants and industrialists customarily organized themselves into local guilds headed by chiefs, but these guild chiefs were certified by the government which held them responsible for the conduct of individual members. Boat traders also were organized under harbor chiefs similarly responsible to the government. More important were the government monopolies in the production and distribution of numerous commodities that the court and the administration consumed, including arms, textiles, pottery, leather goods, apparel, and wine. The government also controlled completely the production and distribution of basic commodities such as salt and iron that were necessities for the entire population. Such restraints deprived Chinese merchants of the opportunity for unrestricted entrepreneurship, and the economy of the possibility for unfettered growth. The restraints also promoted official corruption, for members of the imperial court used their privileged positions to manipulate the state monopolies for personal gain.

Another example of the restrictive, inward-looking policies of China's ruling establishment was its active opposition to overseas enterprise. Chinese emigrants had trickled down to Southeast Asia before the arrival of the Europeans. Probably at no time were there as many Spaniards as Chinese in the Philippines. In 1603, thirty-two years after the founding of Manila as a Spanish settlement, the Chinese population there was about 20,000, compared with perhaps 1,000 Spaniards. And these Chinese virtually controlled the economic life of the settlement, and were extending their control to the other islands of the archipelago. When in that year, 1603, the Manila Chinese suffered one of the massacres which they and their compatriots in Southeast Asia have periodically endured to the present day, an official of the nearby mainland province of Fukien condoned the massacre and denounced all overseas Chinese as deserters of the tombs of their ancestors and men who were unworthy of the emperor's concern. Likewise an imperial edict of 1712 forbade Chinese to trade and reside in Southeast Asia. Five years later another edict allowed those already abroad to come home without fear of punishment, and in 1729 still another edict set a date after which those overseas would not be allowed to return. How explicit and striking the contrast with the Western states, which soon were to be actively promoting overseas settlements and trading companies, and were to be ever ready to take up arms against any threats to these enterprises.

The most dramatic and fateful manifestation of this negative official Chinese attitude to overseas activities is to be found in the bizarre history of the early fifteenth-century Ming voyages with their technological preeminence and their astonishing range, which proved conclusively China's world leadership in maritime undertakings. Then came the imperial order forbidding further overseas expeditions and the unhesitating enforcement of that order. (See Chapter 12, section I.)

Although the precise motives behind this edict are unknown, the significant fact is that its issuance was possible because Chinese merchants lacked the political power and social status of their Western counterparts. It was this fundamental difference in institutional structure and outward-thrusting dynamism that deflected Chinese energies inward at this fateful turning point in world history, and left the oceans of the globe open to Western enterprise. The inconceivable yet inevitable sequel was the eclipse within a few centuries of the great "Celestial Kingdom" by the barbarians of the West.

VI. CHINESE CIVILIZATION IN JAPAN

Since the Chinese civilization and Chinese empires persisted in unbroken continuity to modern times, they have dominated East Asia in a way that no Western country has dominated the West. Consequently there did not develop in East Asia the political and cultural diversity that has prevailed in the West since the fall of Rome. The only exception has been in the steppes and deserts of the far north and west, where agriculture is climatically impossible and where the nomads accordingly developed a distinctive, non-Chinese, pastoral way of life. By contrast, in the neighboring Vietnamese, Korean, and Japanese lands, there was no climatic obstacle to the development of agriculture and hence to the diffusion of Chinese civilization. Of these three lands, Japan was able to remain the most independent of the Chinese colossus, both politically and culturally, and hence played a correspondingly more significant role in both East Asian and world history. The remainder of this chapter therefore, will concentrate on the evolution of Japan to the eve of the Western intrusion.

Japanese history has been shaped to a considerable degree by the influence of geographic location. In this respect there is a close parallel with the British Isles at the other end of the Eurasian landmass. The Japanese islands, however, are more isolated than the British Isles; 115 miles separate them from the mainland, compared with the 21-mile width of the English Channel. Thus before their defeat by the United States, the Japanese had been seriously threatened by foreign invasion only in the thirteenth century. The Japanese, therefore, have been close enough to the mainland to benefit from the great Chinese civilization, but distant enough to be able to select and reject as they wished. In fact, the Japanese have been unusually sensitive and alert to what they have imported from abroad. Although popularly regarded as a nation of borrowers, they have independently evolved, because of their isolation, a larger proportion of their own culture than have any other people of comparable numbers and level of development.

The Japanese are basically a Mongoloid people who migrated from Northeast Asia, but the hairy Caucasoid Ainu who originally inhabited the northern islands contributed to their racial composition; Malayan and Polynesian migrants from the south probably did also. Early Japan was organized into a large number of clans, each ruled by a hereditary priest-chieftain. Toward the end of the first century after Christ, the Yamato clan established a loose political and religious hegemony over the others. Its chief was the emperor, and its clan god was made the national deity.

This clan organization was undermined by the importation of Chinese civilization, which began on a large scale in the sixth century. Buddhism, introduced from Korea, was the medium for cultural change, fulfilling the same function here as Christianity did in Europe among the Germans and Slavs. Students, teachers, craftsmen, and monks crossed over from the mainland, bringing with them a new way of life as well as a new religion. More significant was the role of those Japanese who journeyed to the "Celestial Kingdom" and returned as ardent converts. The impetus for change culminated in the Taika Reform, which began in 645 and sought to transform

Japan into a centralized state on the model of T'ang dynasty China. In accordance with the Chinese model, the country was divided into provinces and districts ruled by governors and magistrates who derived their power from the emperor and his council of state. Also, all land was nationalized in the name of the emperor and allotted to peasant households. The new owner-cultivators were responsible for paying to the central government a land tax in the form of rice and a labor tax that sometimes involved military service.

These and other changes were designed to strengthen imperial authority, and they did so in comparison with the preceding clan structure. But in practice, the Japanese emperor was far from being the undisputed head of a highly centralized state. The powerful hereditary aristocracy forced certain modifications in this Chinese-type administration that ultimately brought about its downfall. Although officials supposedly were appointed, as in China, on the basis of merit through examination, actually the old aristocracy succeeded in obtaining positions of status and power. Likewise, they retained many of their large landholdings, which were usually tax exempt and became manors outside the governmental administrative system. During this period the Fujiwara family perfected the dyarchy, or dual system of government. They did the actual work of ruling, furnishing the consorts for the emperor, and filling the high civil and military posts. Meanwhile, the emperor passed his life in luxurious seclusion, not bothered by affairs of state or degraded by contacts with common men. His prime responsibility was to guarantee unbroken succession for ages eternal. This dyarchical system of government, which had no parallel in China, remained the pattern in Japan until the country was opened up by the Europeans in the nineteenth century.

In cultural matters there was the same adaptation of Chinese models. The Japanese borrowed Chinese ideographs but developed their own system of writing. They borrowed Confucianism but modified its ethics and adjusted its political doctrines to suit their social structure. They accepted Buddhism but adapted it to satisfy their own spiritual needs, while retaining their native Shintoism. They built new imperial capitals, first at Nara and then at Kyoto, that were modeled after the T'ang capital, Ch'ang-an. But there was no mistaking the Japanese quality of the temples, pavilions, shrines, and gardens. The imperial court became the center of highly developed intellectual and artistic activity. Court life is delightfully described in Lady Murasaki's famous eleventh-century novel, *The Tale of Genji*. But this novel also reflects a society grown effeminate and devoted almost exclusively to the pursuit of aesthetic and sensual pleasures. This degeneration, which worsened in the next century, contributed to the coming of the new age of feudalism, when political power shifted from the imperial court to virile rural warriors.

VII. JAPANESE FEUDALISM

The Chinese system of imperial organization introduced by the Taika Reform of 645 worked effectively for a long period. By the twelfth century, however, it had been undermined and replaced by a Japanese variety of feudalism. One reason was the tendency of provincial governors, who were too fond of the refinements of Kyoto, to delegate their powers and responsibilities to local subordinates. Another was that powerful local families and Buddhist communities were always hungry for land and often able to seize it by force. They were willing to bring new land under cultivation so long as the incentive of tax exemption was maintained. These trends reduced the amount of tax-paying land, which meant an increased tax load for the peasant owner-cultivators, who in turn either fled to the northern frontier areas where the Ainu were being pushed back by force of arms, or else commended themselves and their lands to lords of manors. This relieved them of taxes and provided them with protection, but at the cost of becoming serfs. The net result of this process was that by the end of the twelfth century, tax-paying land amounted to 10 percent or less of the total cultivated area, and local power had been taken over by the new rural aristocracy.

At the same time, this aristocracy had become the dominant military force because of the disintegration of the imperial armed forces. The Taika Reform had made all males between the ages of twenty and sixty subject to military service. But the conscripts were required to furnish their own weapons and food and were given no relief from the regular tax burden. This arrangement proved unworkable and was abandoned in 739. Government military posts became sinecures generally filled by effeminate court aristocrats. As a result, the campaigns against the Ainu were conducted by the rural aristocrats. They became mounted warriors and gradually increased their military effectiveness until they completely overshadowed the imperial forces. A feudal relationship now developed between these rural lords and their retainers, or *samurai* (literally, "one who serves"). This relationship was based on an idealized ethic that was known as *bushido*, or "way of the warrior." The *samurai* enjoyed special legal and ceremonial rights, and in return were expected to give unquestioning service to their lords.

By the twelfth century, Japan was controlled by competing groups of feudal lords. For some time the Fujiwara were able to maintain a balance of power by throwing what strength they had on one side or another. In the end, one of these lords, Minamoto Yoritomo, emerged victorious. In 1192 the emperor commissioned him *Seii-Tai-Shogun* (Barbarian-Subduing-Generalissimo), with the right to nominate his own successor. As Shogun, Yoritomo was commander-in-chief of all the military forces and was responsible for the internal and external defense of the realm. From his headquarters at Kamakura, Yoritomo controlled the country in the name of the emperor, who continued to remain in seclusion in Kyoto. It was during this Kamakura Shogunate that the Mongols made their two attempts to invade Japan, in 1274 and 1281. On both occasions the Mongols were able to land, were fiercely resisted by the Japanese, and then were scattered by great storms that destroyed the expeditionary forces. The Japanese, believing their deliverance due to the intervention of the gods, called these storms "divine winds," or *kamikaze*.

In 1333 the Kamakura Shogunate was brought to an end, largely as a result of intrigues at the imperial court as well as growing disaffection among the warrior class. The Ashikaga family now obtained the title of Shogun, but their authority never extended far beyond the environs of Kyoto. In the rest of Japan, local lords struggled to gain control of as much land as possible. The outcome was the rise of great territorial magnates known as *daimyo* ("great name"). At the beginning of the sixteenth century there were several hundred of these daimyo, each seeking to attain hegemony over all Japan.

VIII. JAPAN'S WITHDRAWAL AND ISOLATION

The period of daimyo control witnessed rapid economic growth with important repercussions for Japanese society. Important technological advances were made in agriculture as well as in handicrafts, so that production per acre apparently doubled or even tripled in some parts of the country. The increased productivity stimulated more trade and a shift from a barter to a money economy. Towns gradually developed in the fifteenth and sixteenth centuries at strategic crossroads or coastal harbors or major temples. In these towns appeared the Japanese guilds, or *za,* which, like their Western counterparts, sought to gain monopoly rights in the production or transportation of certain goods, or in the exercise of certain trades or professions. They obtained these monopoly rights by paying fees to certain local authorities, thereby gaining greater freedom and higher status for their members.

Foreign and domestic trade quickened with the rising productivity of the Japanese economy. As early as the twelfth century enterprising Japanese had ventured overseas to Korea and then to China, prepared both for trade and for piracy. Gradually they extended the range of their operations, so that by the late fourteenth century these pirate-traders were active throughout Southeast Asia. Japanese settlers and soldiers of fortune also were widely scattered, especially in Indochina, Siam, and the Philippines.

These socio-economic developments began to undermine feudalism in Japan, as they had done earlier under similar circumstances in the West. If this trend had continued without interruption, Japan presumably would have followed the West European example and developed into a modern unified nation-state with an overseas empire. But Japan did not do so; instead she withdrew into seclusion.

A prime reason for this appears to have been the intrusion of the Western powers into the waters of Southeast and East Asia. This blocked the natural course of Japanese expansionism. If the Westerners had not appeared, the Japanese probably would have secured footholds in Formosa and in various parts of Southeast Asia. But now the Japanese were alarmed by the obvious superiority of Western military technology on the seas, as well as by the surprising effectiveness of Western missionaries on the home islands. Their response was to withdraw into the almost complete seclusion adopted in the early seventeenth century by the Tokugawa Shogunate.

All missionaries were forced to leave and their converts required to renounce their faith. Eventually all foreigners had to depart, with the exception of a few Chinese and Dutch who were allowed to trade under restricted conditions on the Deshima islet in Nagasaki harbor. In addition, Japanese subjects were forbidden to go abroad on penalty of death. Thus began over two centuries of seclusion for Japan.

The end result, then, was not a modern expansionist nation-state. Rather, Japanese feudalism was preserved and shielded from outside influences by the

Tokugawa walls of seclusion. The cost for Japan, as for China, was institutional rigidity and obsolescence. Yet there was a fundamental difference between the two countries. Japan was not saddled with a monolithic, overpowering imperial structure as was the case in China. Rather the Tokugawas had merely papered over the cracks, so that when the West intruded in the nineteenth century, Japan, unlike China, was able to respond positively and creatively.

SUGGESTED READING

The basic works for China are listed in the bibliography for Chapter 10. To that list should be added the interpretative bibliographical essay published by the American Historical Association's Service Center for Teachers of History: J. K. Fairbank, *New Views of China's Tradition and Modernization* (Washington, 1968). This bibliography describes recent works on subjects such as the rise of the bureaucratic state, the role of the merchants, and class structure and mobility.

Some of the more important studies on the period from 220 to 1644 are W. Bingham, *The Founding of the T'ang Dynasty* (Baltimore: Waverly Press, 1941); E. A. Kracke, *Civil Service in Early Sung China, 960–1067* (Cambridge, Mass.: Harvard Univ., 1953); J. T. C. Liu, *Reform in Sung China* (Cambridge, Mass.: Harvard Univ., 1959); C. O. Hucker, *The Traditional Chinese State in Ming Times, 1368–1644* (Tucson: Univ. of Arizona, 1961); and E. Balazs, *Chinese Civilization and Bureaucracy: Variations on a Theme* (New Haven: Yale Univ., 1964). Intellectual trends are analyzed in the following two volumes presenting assorted symposia papers: A. F. Wright, ed., *Studies in Chinese Thought* (Chicago: Univ. of Chicago, 1953); and J. K. Fairbank, ed., *Chinese Thought and Institutions* (Chicago: Univ. of Chicago, 1957). Another useful collection is by J. M. Menzel, ed., *The Chinese Civil Service: Career Open to Talent?* (Boston: Heath, 1963).

On Japan, the American Historical Association's Service Center for Teachers of History has published a convenient general bibliography by J. W. Hall, *Japanese History: New Dimensions of Approach and Understanding*, 2nd ed. (Washington, 1961). The standard, full-scale, meticulously annotated bibliography is by B. Silberstein, *Japan and Korea: A Critical Bibliography* (Tucson: Univ. of Arizona, 1962). Invaluable source materials on Japanese political, moral, and philosophical thought are provided in R. Tsunoda, *et. al., Sources of the Japanese Tradition* (New York: Columbia Univ., 1958). Standard general histories have been written by the British scholar G. B. Sansom, *Japan: A Short Cultural History,* rev. ed. (New York: Appleton, 1944), and his definitive three-volume *A History of Japan* (Stanford: Stanford Univ., 1958–64). The best introductory survey is by E. O. Reischauer, *Japan Past and Present,* rev. ed. (New York: Knopf, 1953). Other aspects of Japanese history are treated in M. Anesaki, *History of Japanese Religion* (London: Kegan Paul, 1930); D. Keene, *Japanese Literature: An Introduction for Western Readers* (New York: Grove Press, 1955); and the same author's excellent *Anthology of Japanese Literature From the Earliest Era to the Mid-Nineteenth Century,* 2 vols. (New York: Grove Press, 1955).

Chapter

17

*The chief glory of the later Middle Ages
was not its cathedrals or its epics
or its scholasticism: it was the building
for the first time in history of a complex
civilization which rested not on the backs
of sweating slaves or coolies
but primarily on non-human power.*

LYNN WHITE, JR.

Revolutionary

Western Civilization

"We should note the force, effect, and consequences of inventions which are nowhere more conspicuous than in those three which were unknown to the ancients, namely, printing, gunpowder, and the compass. For these three have changed the appearance and state of the whole world." [1] The significance of this statement by the British philosopher-scientist Francis Bacon (1561–1626) is that all three of the inventions that he perceptively selected had originated in China, and yet they had little effect on that country in comparison with their explosive repercussions in the West. Chinese civilization was too deeply rooted and Chinese imperial organization too pervasive to allow such inventions to disrupt traditional institutions and practices. Thus printing was used to disseminate old ideas rather than new; gunpowder reinforced the position of the emperor rather than of emerging national monarchs; and the compass, despite the remarkable expeditions of Cheng Ho, was not used for worldwide exploring and trading and empire building as was done by the Westerners.

The root of this fateful difference is to be found in the unique characteristics of the new Western civilization—pluralistic, adaptable, and free of the shackles of tradition that bound all the other Eurasian civilizations. The result was a historic mutation that transformed not only the West but also, as Bacon foresaw, the entire globe as it endured the dynamic expansionism of the revolutionary new society.

I. Pluralism in the West

"In order to escape the evils which they saw coming, the people divided themselves into three parts. One was to pray God; for trading and ploughing the second; and later, to guard these two parts from wrongs and injuries, knights were created." [2] This analysis by the secretary of Philip VI of France depicts simply but essentially the division of medieval Western society into priests, workers, and warriors. Although these three classes were to be found in all Eurasian civilizations, yet their status and interrelationships were unique in the West because of the disintegration of the Roman Empire and the failure to reconstitute an imperial structure. Precisely how these classes functioned under these circumstances will be considered now within the context of the three institutions they personified: feudalism, manorialism, and the church.

Feudalism was a system of government in which those who possessed landed estates also possessed political power, so that state authority was replaced by contractual agreements between lords and vassals. Feudalism appeared when the German kings who had usurped Roman imperial authority lacked the funds to maintain a bureaucracy, a judiciary, and armed forces. The alternative was to grant estates as reward for service, but the recipients, or vassals, tended to administer them as private realms. Charlemagne was strong enough to exact and enforce oaths of loyalty from his vassals, but under his weak successors political power shifted to the vassals, whose estates or fiefs became virtually inalienable. These powerful lords in turn subdivided their holdings into lesser fiefs which they allocated to followers that were dependent on them rather than on the king. The feudal contract between these lords and vassals specified certain mutual obligations. The most important were that the lord should provide protection as well as the fief, while the vassal rendered military service for as long a time each year as local custom required—usually about forty days.

This process of feudalization proceeded apace within each of the feudal kingdoms that took form following the disintegration of Charlemagne's empire. Since the legal justification for the fiefs of the great lords derived nominally from royal authority, the lords were careful to select a king even though they had no intention of respecting his sovereignty. But as Western Europe settled down after 1000 with the cessation of foreign invasions, the rulers gradually were able to assert their feudal rights and to begin the building of strong monarchies. The ensuing struggle between kings and nobles was the essence of Western political history during the following centuries.

Just as feudalism emerged with the collapse of large-scale political organization, so manorialism emerged with the collapse of large-scale economic organization. Consequently the manor was a self-sufficient village that was worked by serfs who were not free to leave, and who with their labor supported a hierarchy of lay and clerical lords. The size of the manor varied considerably, its inhabitants numbering in the scores or hundreds. Unlike a slave, the serf had recognized rights as well as responsibilities. He was entitled to protection, he was assured a plot for the support of himself and his family, and he enjoyed numerous religious holidays and harvest festivals that provided respite from toil. In return he was required to till those strips in the cultivated fields reserved for the lord, to perform other domestic and farm chores for the lord, and to give him a portion of any income from any source.

The manor of necessity provided almost all its own needs because of the virtual disappearance of long distance trade, of centralized handicraft production, of imperial currencies, and the like. Despite, or perhaps because of, this self-sufficiency, manorial technology was not at all primitive compared to that of Roman times. With imperial economic disintegration there was a loss of luxury crafts, irrigation works, aqueducts, and road systems. But the self-sufficient villages, precisely because of their self-sufficiency, had no need for imperial organization. They functioned, and with steadily improving efficiency, on a local, village-to-village basis. The manors kept and improved the mills and smithies and used more iron than ever before, since it could be produced locally. Thus agricultural technology in the medieval West, as will be noted in section III of this chapter, advanced substantially beyond Greco-Roman standards, with far-reaching repercussions on all aspects of life.

Turning to the church, we find a similarly paradoxical development; that is, the Pope emerged more powerful precisely because of the fall of Rome. He did not have to contend against imperial domination as did the bishops of Constantinople, Alexandria, and Antioch against the dictates of the Byzantine emperor. When one of these emperors sought to control the church in the West, Pope Gelasius (492–496) sent him a famous letter in which he asserted that "bishops, not the secular power, should be responsible for the administration of the church." More important, the Pope went on to claim the superiority of spiritual over temporal authority: "Of the two the charge of the priests is heavier, in that they have to render an account in the Divine judgment for even the kings of men."

Justinian's conquest of Italy enabled him and his successors to dominate the Papacy, so that no less than eleven of the thirteen Popes between 678 and 752 were Greeks or Syrians by birth. But with the Lombard invasion of Italy and the Islamic conquest of Egypt, Syria, and North Africa, the Byzantine emperors' ability to intervene in the West was severely curtailed. (See Chapter 15, section I.) The Papacy now turned from beleaguered Constantinople to the Franks, with whom it concluded an alliance that culminated in the crowning of Charlemagne by Pope Leo III in 800. Meanwhile the Papacy was further consolidating its supremacy in the West through its missions to convert the pagan northlands. With their success, new churches were founded which accepted the pope's "Catholic," or "universal," discipline, including the English church in 597, the Lombard and Frisian in the seventh century, and the German in the eighth.

Such, then, were the components of the new pluralistic society emerging in the West: an independent church instead of dictation by the emperor; a congeries of feudal kings and lords in place of imperial authority; autonomous manors individually taming the wilderness instead of the slave plantations of Roman times; and, before long, a rising merchant class operating with unique effectiveness from its urban bases against nobles, prelates, and, ultimately, monarchs. How this society, and this alone in all Eurasia, evolved and adapted during the half millennium after 1000 and eventually developed the strength and dynamism for overseas expansion is the subject of the following sections.

II. Geographic Background

Geographic considerations comprise a significant factor in Europe's thrust forward ahead of other regions during the medieval period. One of these considerations was an advantageous location. Being on the western tip of the Eurasian landmass, Europe escaped invasions after the year 1000. The significance of this remoteness of Western Europe is evident in the light of the disastrous Mongol conquest of Russia in the thirteenth century, of the Ottoman Turkish conquest of the Balkan Peninsula in the fifteenth and sixteenth centuries, and of the repeated Berber assaults in North Africa. Being spared such ravages, Western Europe indubitably enjoyed substantial advantage over the more vulnerable regions to the east.

Equally significant was Europe's exceptionally favorable endowment of natural resources. A large part of northern Europe comprises a great plain that begins at the western end of the Pyrenees and flares out to the north and east, becoming wider as it progresses until eventually it extends uninterruptedly from the Black Sea to the Baltic. The prevailing westerly winds from the Atlantic sweep unhindered over these plains across all Europe and deep into Russia. Hence Europe north of the Mediterranean basin enjoys a relatively moderate climate and constant rainfall, which together with the fertile soils provide an ideal combination for productive agriculture. Rivers usually run ice free and full, providing convenient means of transportation and communication. This advantage is further enhanced by the deeply indented coastline, which gives inland regions relatively easy access to coastal outlets. Some plateaus and mountain ranges interrupt the sweep of the great plains, but they are not so high or massive that they interfere seriously with transportation. Rather these mountains are an asset, being rich in minerals that historically have been quite important.

These natural resources had, of course, been available for countless millennia, but they could not be effectively exploited until a certain level of technological competence had been reached. This requirement of adequate skills has operated everywhere and at all times. The United States, for example, has profited tremendously during the past century from the vast iron ore deposits in the Mesabi Range of northern Minnesota. But for thousands of years Indians had fished and hunted in that area without exploiting the ore, or even being aware of its existence. The same is true currently of the rich oil fields now being tapped in the Middle East, in northern Alaska, and on various ocean floors. And so it was in medieval Western Europe where advancing technology for the first time made local resources susceptible to effective exploitation. The resulting increase in productivity had profound repercussions, including the shift of the economic and political center of Europe northward from its traditional site in the Mediterranean basin.

III. TECHNOLOGICAL PRECOCITY

More technological progress was made in medieval Western Europe than had been made during the entire history of classical Greece and Rome. One reason for this was the absence of slavery, a practice that tended to inhibit technological innovation. Another was the prevalence of frontier conditions that placed a premium on labor-saving devices. The manorial system of the medieval West also contributed to technological progress. The social strata under this system ranged not from a "divine" emperor to a subhuman slave, but from a serf with very definite rights, as well as duties, to a manorial lord who was sufficiently in touch with his serfs to have some real knowledge of the processes of production. Accordingly manual labor acquired a status and respect that were unknown in the old slave-based civilizations.

Finally technology in the West was stimulated by the humanitarian ethic of Christianity, which itself began as a revolt against the inhumanity of the old imperial society. The monks in the monasteries insisted that manual labor was an integral part of the spiritual life. Or, as they put it, "to work is to pray"— *laborare est orare*. These monks were historically significant as the first intellectuals to get dirt under their fingernails. They were the first to combine brainpower and sweat, and in doing so, they aided technological advance. It was not accidental that it was a friar, Roger Bacon, who in the thirteenth century foresaw many of the technological achievements of the future.

> Machines may be made by which the largest ships, with only one man steering them, will move faster than if they were filled with rowers; wagons may be built which will move with unbelievable speed and without the aid of beasts; flying machines can be constructed in which a man may beat the air with mechanical wings like a bird . . . ; machines will make it possible for men to go to the bottom of the rivers. . . .[3]

Bacon's insight reflects the unique nature of Western society as well as his own genius. Such a statement would have been inconceivable in classical Greece and Rome, just as it had no counterpart anywhere else in contemporary Eurasia. And it helps to explain why so many inventions that were of Chinese origin or that had been known to the Greco-Romans, were fully developed and exploited only by the Western Europeans.

The specific technological achievements of the West included basic inventions in the primary occupation of agriculture. One was the "three-field" rotation system of farming, which was gradually adopted from the eighth century onward and which raised productivity substantially, since only a third of the land lay fallow at any one time instead of the half left by the former "two-field" system. Another was the development of a heavy wheeled plow with a sharp iron point that could cut under the sod 6 to 8 inches or even more. Behind the plowshare was the mold board, so placed that it heaved over the cut sod. This plow made possible the cultivation of rich bottom lands with heavy soils and dense vegetation. Certainly it was a very different implement from the primitive scratch-plow traditionally used in the light thin soils of the Mediterranean basin.

Late sixteenth-century drawing showing a cosmographer at work. (National Maritime Museum)

Another sixteenth-century drawing depicting new discoveries and inventions. Among the inventions displayed here are the three mentioned by Francis Bacon (1561–1626) in the quotation that opened this chapter—printing, gunpowder, and the compass. (Courtesy of the New York Public Library)

Agriculture was aided also by more effective use of horsepower. In antiquity the horse had been of little use on the farm because the yoke then in use encircled the belly and neck of the animal, who consequently strangled himself when he pulled too hard. By the tenth century, however, a harness had been developed that rested on the horse's shoulders; this allowed the horse to pull without choking, and thus increased tractive performance four to five times. Hence the horse, fast and efficient compared to the hitherto used ox, became an essential source of power in farming operations. Also significant was the invention of horseshoes, which facilitated the use of the horse for hauling as well as for plowing.

Finally, note should be made of the all-important watermill and windmill, both of which were known in Greco-Roman times but little used because of the abundance of slave labor and the scarcity of streams dependable the year around. With both these obstacles absent in the northern lands, the mill and the miller soon were to be found in almost every manor. And whereas the water wheel had been employed in the Mediterranean basin as a specialized device for grinding grain, in the course of the Middle Ages it was developed into a generalized prime mover. Thus water power came to be used for forge hammers and forge bellows, for saw-mills and lathes, and for fulling mills making cloth, pulping mills making paper, and stamping mills crushing ore. Indeed 5,000 mills were listed in England's Domesday Book of 1086. This represented one for every fifty households, certainly enough to substantially affect living standards.

This unique progress of the West is reflected in the changing relations with the traditional neighboring civilization of Byzantium. When the Western Crusaders began their siege of Constantinople in 1203, they were awestricken by the wealth and magnificence of that ancient capital.

> Those who had not seen [Constantinople] before, could not believe that there could be in all the world so rich a city. When they saw those high walls and those mighty towers with which it was surrounded, and those rich palaces and lofty churches, of which there were so many that no man could believe it unless he had seen it with his own eyes; and when they beheld the length and the breadth of the city, which of all others was the sovereign, know well that there was no man so bold that his flesh did not creep, and this was no wonder that he was aghast for never was so great an undertaking entered upon by human beings since the world was created.[4]

Two and a half centuries later, by contrast, a Greek scholar, Cardinal Bessarion, wrote a letter expressing a very different attitude. Having lived many years in Rome, the cardinal was impressed by the advanced state of handicrafts in Italy. So in 1444 he wrote to Constantine Palaeologos, then ruler of the autonomous Byzantine province of Peloponnesus (Morea), suggesting that "four or eight young men" be sent to Italy surreptitiously to learn Italian craft skills, and to learn Italian "so as to be conversant with what is said." Bessarion was particularly impressed by the water-driven saw mills which eliminated hand labor. He referred to "wood cut by automatic saws, mill wheels moved as quickly and as neatly as can be." Likewise he had in mind water-driven bellows when he wrote that "in the smelting and separation of metals they have leather bellows which are distended and relaxed untouched by any hand, and separate the metal from the useless and earthy matter that may be present." Bessarion also reported that in Italy "one may easily acquire knowledge of the making of iron, which is so useful and necessary to Man." The significance of this testimony is apparent. The technological advances made by medieval Western Europe had been of such magnitude that for the first time an Easterner was recommending that pupils should be sent to the West to learn the "practical arts." [5]

IV. Developing Economy

Technological advance was matched by corresponding economic advance. There was steady economic growth from 900 to 1300. Then came the four-teenth-century slump, brought on by a combination of factors: a series of crop failures and famines, especially during 1315 and 1316; the Black Death, which carried off between one-third and two-thirds of the urban populations when it first struck in 1349, and which recurred periodically thereafter for generations; and the Hundred Years' War between England and France, and other conflicts in Germany and Italy. Shortly after 1400, however, a revival set in, and the trend from then on was generally upward.

This overall economic progress naturally was related to the technological advances which stimulated productivity in agriculture and handicrafts. The complete relief from foreign invasion during these centuries also contributed to the economic growth. Also there was a population increase of about 50 percent between the tenth and fourteenth centuries. This rate of increase seems insignificant in the present age of global population explosion, but it was un-matched at the time in any equivalent world area. The demographic spurt stimulated improvements in agriculture to support the growth of population, and the increased food supply in turn made possible further population increase.

Europe's economic development was evident in all fields. New mining meth-ods led to rising output of salt, silver, lead, zinc, copper, tin, and iron ore in Central and Northern Europe. Likewise the rich timber and naval stores of Britain, Scandinavia, and the Baltic now were exploited more extensively than ever before. The same was true of the northern fisheries, particularly the cod of Iceland and Norway, and the herring of the Baltic. Most important, of course was the rising productivity in agriculture in which most of the popula-tion was engaged. Peasants first brought under cultivation the waste lands around their own villages. It is a startling but true fact that in the twelfth century only about half the land of France, a third of the land of Germany, and a fifth of the land of England was under cultivation. The rest was forest, swamp, waste. All around the edges of the small, tilled regions were larger, untilled areas open for colonization. Into these vacant spaces the European peasants streamed, preparing the way for the plow and hoe by clearing forests, burning brushwood, and draining swamps. By 1300 a larger area of France was being cultivated than is today.

Peasants not only cultivated unused lands in their midst, but with population growth they emigrated to the vast underpopulated frontier regions. Just as the United States had its westward movement to the Pacific Ocean, so Europe had its eastward movement to the Russian border. By 1350 in Silesia, for example, there were 1,500 new settlements farmed by 150,000 to 200,000 colonists. Not only were there German colonists moving beyond the Elbe at the expense of the Slavic and Baltic peoples of Eastern Europe, but other colonists were following the *reconquista* into Spain, and the Anglo-Saxon push into Wales, Scotland, and Ireland.

The combination of population increase and rising output in agriculture, mining, fishing, and forestry stimulated a corresponding growth of commerce and of cities. In the tenth century, merchants were to be found in Europe, but they trafficked mostly in luxuries. By the fourteenth century, however, commerce had advanced from the periphery to the center of everyday life. Goods exchanged included raw wool from England, woolen cloth from Flanders made from English wool, iron and timber from Germany, furs from Slavic areas, leather and steel from Spain, and luxury goods from the east. Although this commerce never engaged more than a small minority of the total population, nevertheless its great expansion in late medieval times had important repercussions for the whole of society. Towns slowly appeared, beginning as centers of local trade and local administration. The lead was taken in Italy where the inhabitants of such centers as Venice, Amalfi, and Naples were cut off from their hinterland by the Lombard invaders and so took to the sea for a living. Later other cities appeared along inland trade routes and along the Baltic coast. Important also for the distribution of goods were the great fairs that developed along the trade routes, outstanding being those in the county of Champagne, located strategically equidistant from Flanders, Italy, and Germany.

Western European cities were insignificant in medieval times compared to those of China, India, or the Middle East, as regards population or volume of trade. But they were quite unique because of their growing autonomy and political power. Precisely because they were starting afresh, and within the framework of a politically fragmented Europe rather than a monolithic empire, the burghers from the beginning exhibited a self-confidence and independence that had no parallel anywhere else in Eurasia.

As they acquired power and financial resources, they normally extracted from the king a royal charter licensing them to unite in a single commune, with the right to act as a corporation, to make agreements under its corporate seal, and to have its town hall, court of law, and dependent territory outside the walls. The charter also permitted merchants and craftsmen to organize into guilds, or sworn voluntary associations designed for protection and mutual aid, including the regulation of manufacturing standards, prices, and working hours. Thus towns gradually came to be recognized as a new element in society, their inhabitants being outside feudal law. This was reflected in the custom that if a serf escaped to a town and lived there for a year and a day without being apprehended, he became a free man. As a saying put it at that time, "Town air makes a man free."

In certain regions, groups of cities banded together to form leagues which became powerful political, as well as economic, entities. When the Hohen-staufen emperors attempted to force the wealthy cities of northern Italy—

Milan, Brescia, Parma, Verona, and others—to pay taxes and accept imperial administration, they organized themselves into the Lombard League which with Papal aid successfully waged war against the emperors. Likewise various Baltic towns—Bremen, Lübeck, Stettin, Danzig, and others comprising a total of ninety in 1350—organized themselves into the Hanseatic League which fought against pirates, pressed for trading privileges in foreign countries, and virtually monopolized the trade of Northern Europe.

This evolution gave the European merchant a status, as well as power, that was unique in Eurasia. In China and India, for example, the merchant was looked down upon as inferior and undesirable; in northwestern Europe he had status and, as time passed, growing wealth and political power. In China, the merchants at various times suffered restrictions concerning clothing, carrying of weapons, riding in carts, and owning land. Their function of transporting commodities from place to place was regarded as nonproductive and parasitic, and they were placed at the bottom of the social scale. Likewise in India, the merchant could have no prestige in the face of Hinduism's emphasis on the renunciation of worldly goods. The ideal man in India was not the bustling merchant who made money and built mansions, but the mystic who sat on mats, ate from plantain leaves, and remained unencumbered by material possessions. Consequently, merchants had no opportunity in any of the oriental empires to rise to positions of authority. In China, government was carried on by scholars; in Japan, by soldiers; in the Malay lands and in the Rajput states of India, by the local nobility; but nowhere by merchants.

Nowhere, that is, except in Europe, where they were steadily gaining in political as well as economic power. There they were becoming lord mayors in London, senators in the German Imperial Free Cities, and grand pensioners in Holland. Such social status and political connections meant more consideration and more consistent state support for mercantile interests and, later on, for overseas ventures.

V. RISE OF NATIONAL MONARCHIES

Western Europe by the tenth century had become a mosaic of petty feudal states that had acquired bit by bit the land and authority of the defunct Carolingian Empire. Several traditions and interests operated during the following centuries at cross purposes. There were feudal kings engaged in continual conflict with their feudal vassals who often held larger fiefs and wielded more power. There were feudal principalities, both lay and clerical, that raised the prickly investiture issue. There were also city-states that sometimes combined in powerful organizations such as the Lombard and Hanseatic leagues. And in opposition to the particularist interests of the preceding three groups, there was the striving for a united Latin Christendom headed by the pope in Rome, or by a "Roman" emperor as the successor to Charlemagne and his predecessors. This complex of conflicting interests produced an infinite variety of constantly changing alliances and alignments at all levels of political life.

In very broad terms, the political evolution of Western Europe after Charlemagne may be divided into three stages. Between the ninth and eleventh centuries, popes and emperors generally cooperated. The popes helped the emperors against the German secular lords, and in return were supported against the Byzantine opponents to papal authority. In 1073 a period of papal supremacy began with the accession of Pope Gregory VII. The investiture dispute between the papacy and the emperors—the struggle to control the investiture of German bishops—was won by Gregory, thereby undermining imperial administration and power. By the thirteenth century Pope Innocent III was involved in the affairs of virtually every European state, making and breaking kings and emperors. "Nothing in the world," he declared, "should escape the attention and control of the Sovereign Pontiff." For over two centuries, the papacy generally was recognized as the head of Latin Christendom, particularly because of a succession of pious French and English kings.

The period of papal supremacy ended suddenly and dramatically when Pope Boniface VIII issued the bull *Unam sanctam* (1302) in which he set forth uncompromisingly the doctrine of papal authority: ". . . we declare, state, define and pronounce that it is altogether necessary to salvation for every human creature to be subject to the Roman pontiff." But what had been acceptable in previous centuries was no longer so. The monarchs and their councillors now were placing the welfare of their kingdoms ahead of the wishes of popes. Boniface was subjected to threats and mistreatment by an agent of the French king, and died soon after his humiliation. In 1305 a French archbishop was elected pope as Clement V, and instead of going to Rome he took up residence at Avignon in southeastern France. During the next seventy years the Avignonese popes, as the pawns of the French monarchy, lost their predecessors' commanding position in Latin Christendom.

The new power of the European kings was derived in large part from their informal alliance with the rising merchant class. The burghers provided financial support to the monarchs, and also managerial talent in the form of chamberlains, overseers, keepers of the king's accounts, managers of the royal mint, and so forth. These originally had comprised the king's household in charge of the monarch's *private* affairs. Now strong centralized governments evolved as the king's household was employed to administer the realm as a whole. More specifically, it laid the foundations for a bureaucracy, a judiciary, and a system of taxation in collaboration with some representative assembly.

The monarchs in return provided the burghers with protection against the incessant wars and arbitrary exactions of the feudal lords and bishops. They also served merchant interests by ending the crazy-quilt pattern of autonomous local authorities, each with its own customs, laws, weights, and currencies. As late as the end of the fourteenth century there were thirty-five toll stations on the Elbe, over sixty on the Rhine, and so many on the Seine that the cost of shipping grain 200 miles down the river was half its selling price. With the removal of such encumbrances and the enforcement of royal law and order, national monarchies emerged by the fifteenth century, encompassing roughly the territories of modern England, France, Portugal, and, after the marriage of Ferdinand and Isabella, also Spain.

These large new political entities proved to be essential for the mobilization of the human and material resources needed for overseas enterprise. It was not accidental that although most of the early explorers were Italian navigators, their sponsors were the new national monarchies rather than their minuscule home city-states. The Spanish and Portuguese courts provided the backing for Columbus and da Gama, and the English and French courts quickly and eagerly followed up with backing for Cabot, Verrazano, and many others.

VI. AGE OF FAITH

The medieval West experienced cultural and intellectual developments as innovative and significant as the economic and political. The centuries from the fall of Rome to about the year 1000 constitute a "Dark Age" in the sense that there was a complete absence of cultural creativity. The weight of poverty, insecurity, and isolation was too great to permit the production of literary, artistic, or scholarly masterpieces. It is true that the monks in the monasteries did manage to preserve certain parts of classical culture, but they naturally concentrated on those parts that conformed to their own religious convictions, while ignoring what was more secular. The result was a "Christianized" or "clericized" culture that was supplementary to, and dependent upon, the church.

In the eleventh century, cathedral schools were established by the bishops for the education of the priests of their dioceses. A century later the first universities evolved out of the cathedral schools. A distinctive feature of these universities was that they were self-governing corporations with a legal identity of their own. Also they did not consist of only a liberal arts faculty, as did the cathedral schools, but in addition usually had faculties of canon law, civil law, medicine, and theology. The liberal arts curriculum comprised the *trivium* (Latin grammar, logic, and rhetoric) and the *quadrivium* (geometry, arithmetic, music, and astronomy). The first universities appeared in the twelfth century at Bologna, Paris, and Oxford. In the following century others were founded at Padua, Naples, and Salamanca; and in the fourteenth century they spread to Central Europe—to Prague, Cracow, and Vienna.

All these universities were primarily institutions for training the clergy. This emphasis was natural and proper at a time when the clergy had a monopoly of literate occupations and administrative positions. But in the twelfth century this restricted objective was challenged by the translation of Aristotle's metaphysical works and other classics from Arabic into Latin, and later from the original Greek into Latin. This caused a great upheaval in European thought as Western scholars for the first time were confronted by a thoroughly systematic and rationalistic natural philosophy. Their problem now was to reconcile this with traditional Christian assumptions and doctrines.

Essentially the same problem had been faced earlier by Moslem theologians and philosophers such as al-Ghazzali and Averroes (see Chapter 14, section VII), and their way out of the dilemma was the doctrine of the two truths—a higher spiritual and a lower rational truth. The outstanding figure in the search for a comparable reconciliation of Aristotle with Christian theology was the brilliant Dominican master of the University of Paris, Thomas Aquinas (1226–1274). In his great masterpiece, *Summa Theologica,* he stated that the truths of reason were most ably expounded by Aristotle, and the truths of revelation by the precepts of the church. The two truths, be argued on the basis of faith, must ultimately agree. The truth of Aristotelian philosophy must support and agree with the supreme truth of Christian tenets. This is what he set out to prove in his *magnum opus,* a brilliant example of the scholastic, synthesizing mind. He structured a comprehensive framework, with citations for and against every point discussed, together with an argument invariably ending in support of official dogma: ". . . man naturally desires, as his last end, to know the first cause. But God is the first cause of all. Therefore man's last end is to know God. . . ." The medieval age, then, was an age of faith. There were no agnostics, since the Day of Judgment haunted the popular mind.

This theology lay behind the hierarchical nature of the medieval world picture. Society, nature, and the universe were conceived of in similar hierarchical terms. The pope and bishops, emperor and kings, nobles and common folk, all had their counterparts in nature with the earth underneath, water above it, air above that, and fire, the noblest element, at the top. So it was in the universe, with spheres of the moon and sun, spheres of planets, the great sphere of the fixed stars, beyond which lay heaven, and, as a theologically necessary counterweight, the pits of hell. This world picture prevailed until the scientific revolution, when the earth-centered cosmos gave way in the sixteenth century to Copernicus' solar system, and in the seventeenth to Newton's world machine.

VII. WESTERN EUROPE'S EXPANSIONISM

Between the fourth and tenth centuries Europe was invaded by Germans, Huns, Magyars, Vikings and Moslems. But from the tenth to the fourteenth centuries this situation was dramatically reversed as Europe took the offensive on all fronts. (See Map XVI, "Expansionism of the Medieval West.") Assorted crusaders pushed back the Moslems in Spain, southern Italy, Sicily, and the Holy Land, and even overran the Christian Byzantine empire. Meanwhile in northeast Europe, German frontier lords were winning lands east of the Elbe. As this German expansion was continued east of the Oder against the pagan Prussians, it was conducted as a crusade by the Teutonic Knights. They built strongholds and settled around them German settlers, who provided the supplies and manpower for further expansion. German merchants soon appeared to found towns at strategic points along the coasts and along river routes. Thus by the end of the fifteenth century large areas formerly occupied by Slavic and Baltic peoples had become thoroughly German from top to bottom: lords, bishops, townsmen, and peasants.

These crusades were considered at one time to have been responsible for stimulating practically every constructive development in the later Middle Ages, including the growth of trade and towns, and the advances in culture. This interpretation no longer is accepted, and instead it is generally agreed that the crusades basically were the consequence rather than the cause of this progress. Without the preceding technological advances, commercial revival, demographic upsurge, and general exuberance of spirit, the crusades would have been quite inconceivable. This dynamism continued and picked up speed after the fourteenth century slump, and the result was the extension of the expansionist crusading drive to overseas territories.

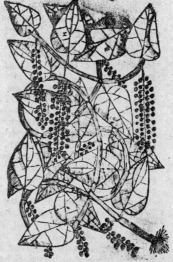

One of the causes of Western Europe's expansionism was a demand for foreign products, among them spices. Here, in three drawings by Cristobal de Acosta, are shown (from top to bottom) three of those spices—leaves and berries of wild cinnamon, a clove tree, and the leaves and berries of the pepper plant. (Courtesy of the New York Public Library)

A significant factor in the overseas drive was the Christian religion with its traditional universalism, its proselytizing zeal, and its crusading militancy. The early explorers and their backers were motivated partly by religious considerations. They wanted to reach the great countries of India and China whose existence had been known to Europeans since the thirteenth-century travels of Marco Polo. These countries were known not to be Moslem, and so it was hoped that they might join forces with the Christians. Also there was the enduring medieval legend of Prester (or Priest) John, reputed to be a powerful Christian ruler somewhere out in the vague East. For centuries, Christian leaders had dreamed of establishing contact with him and launching a great assault upon the Moslem world from both east and west. The Europeans did not find Prester John, but they did stumble upon strange new peoples in Africa and the Americas—peoples who were barbarians and heathens and, therefore, fit subjects for conquest, conversion, and redemption.

God, along with gold, was perhaps the most compelling of the many motives that led Europeans to begin their overseas enterprises. Vasco da Gama explained to the surprised Indians that he had come to their land in search of Christians and spices. Likewise, the conquistador Bernal Diaz wrote in his memoirs that he and his comrades went to the New World "to serve God and His Majesty, to give light to those who were in darkness, and to grow rich, as all men desire to do." [6]

The so-called "Renaissance ferment" with its emphasis on individualism and secularism obviously was more conducive to overseas expansion than the preceding medieval outlook. A new conception of man himself gradually emerged—a new confidence in his dignity and creativity. Man did not need to be preoccupied with forebodings of divine judgment in afterlife. He had but to develop his innate potentialities and, above all, his power to reason. Desiderius Erasmus voiced this confidence and buoyance when, at the height of his fame, he cried out, "Immortal God! What a world I see dawning! Why cannot I grow young again?" [7]

There was no counterpart to this Western intellectual ferment and exuberance in the rest of Eurasia. In China, as we have seen, Confucianism continued to dominate society. (See Chapter 16, section V.) Its esteem for age over youth, for the past over the present, for established authority over innovation, made it a deadly efficient instrument for the preservation of the *status quo* in all its aspects. Likewise in the Moslem lands the *madrasas,* or colleges, emphasized theology, jurisprudence, and rhetoric at the expense of astronomy, mathematics, and medicine. (See Chapter 14, section VII.) The graduates of these schools, like the Confucian literati, were uninformed about what was being done in the West and quite uninterested in finding out. Thus the Turks remained steeped in their religious obscurantism and, like other non-Western peoples, they paid a high price. The Christian infidels, with their new learning, eventually became the masters not only of the New World they discovered, but also of the ancient empires of Islam and of Confucianism.

The continued technological advances of the West also contributed directly to overseas expansion. Particularly significant in this respect was the progress achieved in shipbuilding, in the instruments and techniques of navigation, and in naval armaments. Between 1200 and 1500 the tonnage of the average European ship doubled or trebled. Slender galleys with a burden of 150 to 200 ns gave way to round-hulled sailing ships of 600 to 800 tons. The stern udder, adopted in the thirteenth century, rapidly displaced the older and less efficient lateral steering devices. Equally important was the adaptation by the Portuguese in the fourteenth century of the Arab lateen rig, which enabled vessels to sail more directly into the wind. These advances in the construction and rigging of ships represented a combination of features originally developed in Northern Europe, in the Mediterranean, and in the Middle East. The result was a ship that was larger, speedier, and more maneuverable. It was also more economical because the elimination of 100 to 200 oarsmen with their food and equipment greatly increased the cargo space.

Hand in hand with these advances in shipbuilding went those in the art of navigation, particularly the increasingly effective use of the compass, the astrolabe, and the new maps now being prepared with accurate compass bearings and explicit details concerning coastlines and harbors. At the same time the Europeans were attaining a decisive and obviously significant lead in naval armaments. Sea battles traditionally had consisted of boarding and hand-to-hand fighting on decks. This changed in the first two decades of the sixteenth century when Flemish and German metallurgists developed techniques for casting guns that could shoot balls capable of damaging a hull at 300 yards. Naval tactics now shifted from boarding to broadside gunfire, and Europeans were able to seize and retain control of the oceans of the world for four centuries until the epochal victory of the Japanese over the Russians at Tsushima in 1905.

Along with these advances in shipbuilding, navigation, and naval armaments came important new techniques in the conduct of business affairs. The invention in Italy of double entry bookkeeping made it possible to determine at any moment the financial state of a business. Also the growing use of money and the minting of standard coins that were generally accepted facilitated the conduct of business. So did the development of banks and of credit instruments, and the gradual abandonment of medieval Christianity's condemnation and proscription of interest charges on loans. Finally, after European overseas expansion got under way, it was greatly strengthened and accelerated by the development of joint stock companies. By providing a medium for investment with limited liability, these companies mobilized vast amounts of European capital for overseas enterprise. No Eastern merchant, limited to his own resources or those of his partners, was able to compete successfully in the long run with the several East India and Levant companies, the Muscovy Company, and the still extant Hudson's Bay Company.

In conclusion, the combination of the above factors imbued Europe with an impelling and unique dynamism. How unique it was is apparent in the variety of Eurasian responses to the expansion of the Moslem world in the fifteenth century. As noted in Chapter 14, section VI, Islam at that time was fanning out from the Middle East in all directions. The Turks, after capturing Constantinople, overran the Balkan Peninsula and then crossed the Danube and pushed through Hungary to the walls of Vienna. Likewise in the east the Turks under the colorful Babur were striking southward from Afghanistan, beginning their founding of the great Mogul Empire that was to rule India until the British takeover in the nineteenth century. In Africa also, Islam was spreading steadily into the interior from its bases on the northern and eastern coasts of the continent. Finally Moslem merchants dominated the Eurasian sea routes running from the Red Sea and the Persian Gulf across the Indian Ocean and around Southeast Asia to the China seas.

With these advances by its soldiers, merchants, and preachers, the world of Islam had become the heartland of Eurasia. It occupied the strategic center of the great landmass, and the more it expanded, the more it isolated the Chinese at the eastern end of Eurasia and the Europeans at the western. The completely different responses of the Chinese and the Europeans to this encirclement profoundly influenced the course of world history from that time to the present.

The Chinese, as noted earlier, withdrew voluntarily, even though their Cheng Ho expeditions had demonstrated conclusively that they possessed both the technology and the resources to dominate the oceans. (See Chapter 12, section I, and Chapter 16, section V.) But during this Ming period, after the interlude of Mongol domination, the Chinese were turning their backs to the outside world. And their merchant class, lacking the political power and social status of its Western counterpart, was unable to challenge imperial edicts banning overseas enterprise. Thus the Chinese turned their formidable talents and energies inward, thereby deliberately relinquishing a lead role in Eurasian, and ultimately, world, affairs.

The response of the Europeans was precisely the opposite. Their geographic horizons and commercial ambitions had been immeasurably broadened by *Pax Mongolica,* so that the sudden disintegration of the Mongol empire had left them with acute frustration and yearning. Likewise the loss of the crusaders' outposts in the Levant, the Islamization of the Il-Khanate in Persia, and the Turkish conquest of the Balkans, all served to deprive the Europeans of access to the Black Sea, to the Persian Gulf and to the Indian Ocean. Thus the Europeans were effectively fenced in on the western tip of Eurasia. It is true that the all-important spice trade still flourished, as Italian merchants continued to meet Arab traders in the ports of the Levant and to pick up cargoes for transshipment to the West. This arrangement was satisfactory for the Italians and the Arabs who reaped the golden profits of the middleman. But other Europeans were not so happy, and they sought earnestly for some means to reach the Orient to share the prize.

Their search was bound to succeed, given their technical skills, their economic strength, and their political pluralism. There was no emperor in Europe to issue restraining orders; instead there were rival national monarchies competing strenuously in overseas enterprises. Also there was in Europe a genuine need and strong demand for foreign products, and the merchants were sufficiently powerful to ensure satisfaction of the need. Thus if Columbus had not discovered America and if da Gama had not rounded the Cape, then others assuredly would have done so within the next few decades. In short, Western society had reached the take-off point. It was ready to burst out, and when it did, it found the ocean ways clear, and it spread irresistibly over the entire globe.

SUGGESTED READING

For works on the early medieval period following the invasions, see the bibliography for Chapter 11. A significant and stimulating study of medieval Europe in a global context is by R. L. Reynolds, *Europe Emerges: Transition Toward an Industrial World-Wide Society 600–1750* (Madison: Univ. of Wisconsin, 1961). Excellent recent general histories of the medieval West are R. S. Lopez, *The Birth of Europe* (Philadelphia: Lippincott, 1966); N. F. Cantor, *Medieval History: The Life and Death of a Civilization* (New York: Macmillan, 1963); and C. W. Hollister, *Medieval Europe: A Short History* (New York: Wiley, 1964). Comprehensive anthologies of medieval documents and writings are presented in N. F. Cantor, ed., *The Medieval World* (New York: Macmillan, 1968); and D. Herlihy, ed., *Medieval Culture and Society* (New York: Harper & Row, 1968).

The best introduction to feudal institutions is provided by J. R. Strayer, *Feudalism* (Princeton: Van Nostrand, 1965) and by M. Bloch, *Feudal Society,* 2 vols. (Chicago: Univ. of Chicago, 1961). On social and economic developments there is P. Boissonade, *Life and Work in Medieval Europe* (New York: Knopf, 1927); C. G. Coulton, *The Medieval Village* (New York: Harper & Row, 1926); H. Pirenne, *Economic and Social History of the Middle Ages* (London: K. Paul, Trench, and Trubner, 1936); B. H. Slicher van Bath, *The Agrarian History of Western Europe, 500–1850* (London: Arnold, 1963); and L. White, Jr., *Medieval Technology and Social Change* (Oxford: Clarendon, 1962). Various aspects of medieval culture are considered by R. W. Southern, *The Making of the Middle Ages* (New Haven: Yale Univ., 1953); C. H. Haskins, *Rise of the Universities* (Ithaca: Cornell Univ., 1957); M. W. Baldwin, *The Medieval Church* (Ithaca: Cornell Univ., 1953); and D. Knowles, *The Evolution of Medieval Thought* (Baltimore: Helicon, 1962). Finally the key question of why the West rather than some other region of Eurasia took the lead in overseas expansion is considered in the following stimulating collection of readings: J. R. Levenson, ed., *European Expansion and the Counter-Example of Asia, 1300–1600* (Englewood Cliffs, N.J.: Prentice-Hall, 1967).

NON-EURASIAN
WORLD TO 1500

In dealing thus far with the millennia to 1500, attention has been focused exclusively upon the Eurasian part of the globe. The reason, as explained in Chapter 1, section III, is the overwhelming primacy of Eurasia in world affairs during those millennia, together with the fact that human history prior to 1500 was essentially regional rather than global in scope. Once Homo sapiens dispersed to all the continents, the primitive level of his technology limited strictly the range of his operations. During the following millennia he lived and functioned in regional isolation. The peoples of Australia and of the Americas were completely isolated on their respective continents, while those of Africa were largely, though not exclusively, isolated also.

During those millennia when human history was primarily regional history, the inhabitants of the great Eurasian landmass comprised the great majority of the world's total population, and, living in proximity to each other, they interacted in varying degrees through the ages. This interaction stimulated a relatively rapid pace of development in Eurasia, and, conversely, the isolation and lack of outside stimuli retarded development in the non-Eurasian regions. This explains why, during the pre-1500 era, the overwhelming majority of the historically significant advances in human civilization were Eurasian in origin, and why, perforce, the world of today is essentially a Eurasian world. Hence the concentration thus far in this study on Eurasian peoples and civilizations.

In the fifteenth century this regional phase of world history came to an end with Europe's overseas expansion, bringing peoples of all regions into direct contact with each other. This outward thrust traditionally is viewed from the West's angle of vision. The emphasis is on Columbus and da Gama and Magellan and on their discoveries and the subsequent repercussions. This approach, however, is inadequate for global history. A global perspective requires consideration not only of the expanding West but also of the regions into which the West expanded. The peoples of these regions, after all, comprised an appreciable proportion of the human race, so that their evolution must be considered, albeit not as painstakingly as that of the historically more prominent Eurasians. Also the lands and peoples and institutions of the non-Eurasian world were as significant in determining the outcome of Western expansionism as were the Westerners themselves. For these reasons, then, the following two chapters are devoted to Africa and to the Americas and Australia.

Geographers, in Afric's maps, Chapter
With savage creatures filled the gaps;
And o'er unhabitable downs
Placed elephants for want of towns.

18

Dean Swift

Africa

If degree of accessibility to outside stimuli is a decisive factor in determining the tempo of a region's development, then a casual glance at a map suggests that Africa is tolerably well located. To the north the continent is separated from Europe by the Mediterranean, a narrow and easily crossed body of water that historically has functioned more as a highway than as a barrier. To the east the Sinai Peninsula provides a bridge to Asia, while the Red Sea is even narrower and easier to cross than the Mediterranean. Finally the great expanses of the Indian Ocean are neutralized by the monsoon winds, which facilitate communication back and forth between East Africa and South Asia.

Yet historically Africa has been much more isolated from Eurasia than these impressions would indicate, and this isolation has remained a prime and constant factor in the continent's development. This chapter will consider first the geography behind the isolation, and then the peoples involved and the nature of their historical evolution.

I. Geography

Africa, as defined in this study, refers to the part of the continent south of the Sahara Desert. The reason for this definition, as stated in Chapter 1, section III, is that the Sahara is the great barrier, the great divider, while the Mediterranean by comparison is a connecting boulevard. This explains why historically the people of North Africa have had more interaction with the other peoples around the Mediterranean basin than with those to the south of the desert barrier. Thus sub-Saharan Africa, the subject of this chapter, is in effect an island, the northern shore of which is the Sahara Desert rather than the Mediterranean.

The Sahara is by no means the only obstacle to contact with the outside world. On the east of the great desert, along the upper reaches of the Nile, are the enormous swamps of the Sudd, which historically have constituted a formidable barrier. Also contributing to Africa's inaccessibility is a coastline unbroken by bays, gulfs, or inland seas. Consequently this coastline is shorter than Europe's, though Africa has thrice the area. This lack of anything corresponding to the Mediterranean, the Baltic, or the Black Sea means that Africa's interior is relatively closed to the outside world.

Effective barriers are to be found also in the form of thousand-mile-long sandbars along the east and west coasts, and in the tremendous swells on both coasts, which make landing in a small boat quite hazardous. And if the bars and breakers are successfully negotiated, there remains still another obstacle—the rapids and waterfalls created by the rivers tumbling down a succession of escarpments from the interior plateau to the low coastlands. Africa's profile is like that of an inverted saucer, which today provides a tremendous hydroelectric potential. But historically the coastal waterfalls meant that there was no counterpart in Africa to the smooth-flowing St. Lawrence and Amazon, which provide easy access to the interior of the Americas, or to the Rhine and Danube, which do likewise for Europe. Also, the approaches to Africa are beset by the hot, humid climate of the low-lying coastal areas and by the tropical diseases accompanying such a climate. The interior uplands generally have a healthy bracing climate but the coastal regions have presented a serious health hazard to those seeking to penetrate inland.

As significant as this external inaccessibility, has been the internal—that is, the difficulty of crossing from one part of Africa to another. Viewing the continent as a whole, it begins with small fertile strips at the extreme northern and southern tips. These soon yield to the great desert expanses of the Kalahari in the south and the Sahara in the north. Next are the rolling grasslands or savannas, known in the north as the Sudan, the Arab term meaning "the country of the black people." Then come the tropical rain forests, which in their densest parts are more difficult to penetrate than the deserts.

These extremes of nature, together with the absence of nearby coastal outlets and of unencumbered river systems, have combined to inhibit interaction amongst the various regions of the continent. Inevitably this has retarded the overall development of its peoples and explains the simultaneous existence of large and complex empires in the savannas, and of hunting bands in remote desert and forest areas.

This geographic setting helps to explain also the paradoxical difference in the timing of European penetration of Africa compared to that of the Americas. Africa, in contrast to the Americas, has maintained through the millennia an unbroken, though at times tenuous, contact with Eurasia. Yet the Europeans were much slower in penetrating into neighboring Africa than into the distant Americas. Africa remained the "Dark Continent" centuries after the New World had been opened up and colonized. As late as 1865, when the Civil War was ending in the United States, only the coastal fringe of Africa was known, together with a few insignificant portions of the interior. Even by 1900 about a fourth of the continent remained unexplored. This imperviousness of Africa to Europe's dynamism was due in part to the geographic conditions that combined to make the continent unusually resistant to outside intrusion. But geography was not the only factor involved. At least as important was the African Negro's general level of social, political, and economic organization, which was high enough to effectively block the Europeans for centuries. But before considering the culture of the Negroes, we shall first examine their ethnic composition.

II. PEOPLES

In contrast to what is sometimes assumed, the African peoples are far from ethnically homogeneous. Various strains are to be found south of the Sahara, and have existed throughout history. Their origins and diffusion remain in large part a mystery, however, and authorities are far from agreement. The ethnic classification that, for the present at least, meets with the fewest objections recognizes four major peoples: (1) Bushmen, who speak the Khoïsan language, (2) Pygmies, whose original language is unknown because they adopted those of their later conquerors, (3) Negroes, who speak the Niger-Congo language, and (4) Caucasoids, known also as Capsians, Cushites and Hamites, who speak the Afroasiatic language. These four peoples seem to have originated in the region of Lake Victoria, whence the Bushmen migrated south to southern Africa, the Pygmies west to the Congo, and the coastal rain forests of West Africa, the Negroes west to West Africa and northwest to the then fertile Sahara region, and the Caucasoids northwest to Egypt and North Africa, as well as northeast to Arabia and West Asia.

These categories and migrations, it should be reemphasized, are by no means universally accepted. Indeed, one authority has summarized current knowledge, or lack of knowledge, as follows:

> . . . we can say little more than this: if one stands at Suez and looks south and southwest, people tend to get darker the further one goes. One must, even in this generalization, except the Bushmanoids. . . . The fact of the matter is that, empirically, Egyptians are more or less Mediterranean Caucasoids; that as one goes south and southwest, there is a gradual change; along the Guinea Coast or in the Congo forests, the Negro stereotype is dominant. There is not, however, an undisputed "line" that

can be drawn on a map, or distinctions that can be made between tribes (in other than statistical terms) with the claim that one is unequivocally Caucasoid and the other Negroid. In even the most dominantly Negroid tribes, there are to be found individuals with light skin and green eyes. . . .[1]

III. AGRICULTURE AND IRON

The cultures of Africa were the outcome of a much greater degree of interaction with the outside world than had been possible in the Americas or Australia. Agriculture, for example, which originated in Mesopotamia and then took root in Egypt in the fifth millennium B.C., may have spread from there to the Sudan stretching from the Ethiopian highlands to the Atlantic coast. Some authorities, it should be noted, believe that agriculture was invented independently in this zone, along the upper reaches of the Niger River. Whether or not this is so, the fact remains that the great majority of the plants that eventually were cultivated in sub-Saharan Africa were importations. The most important of these were: from Mesopotamia and Egypt via the Nile—barley, wheat, peas, and lentils; from Southeast Asia—bananas, sugar cane, the Asian yam, and new forms of rice; from the New World via the Portuguese and later slave traders—tobacco, corn, lima and string beans, pumpkins and tomatoes. Prior to the advent of iron tools, these plants were grown largely in the grasslands of the Sudan. Little agriculture was practiced in the rain forests because the edible fruits and vegetables available there provided an adequate food supply without the hard labor needed to fell trees and till soil with stone implements.

As basic for Africa as the introduction of agriculture was that of iron metallurgy. The latter was definitely an importation, with three separate sources being likely. One was Carthage, whence the art probably was spread by traders who, by 500 B.C. and perhaps earlier, had developed two regular caravan routes across the Sahara. The desert was not as wide and formidable at that time, so the traders were able to cross with carts and chariots pulled by donkeys and horses, as we know from rock engravings found along the routes. Later, when the desert passage became more difficult, the Romans solved the problem by introducing camels from Central Asia.

A second source of iron metallurgy was the kingdom of Kush located on the upper Nile, with its capital at Meroe, a little north of Khartoum. The Kushites were predominantly Negroids and known to the ancient Egyptians as Nubians. Originally they had suffered raids by the armies of the pharaohs, but gradually they built a strong enough state structure so that by 751 B.C. they conquered Egypt and ruled the country for one century. Then Assyrian armies from the east forced the Kushites to withdraw, but it was from these Assyrians that the art of ironmaking was learned.

The Kushites were able to put their knowledge to good use, for their country, unlike Egypt, had abundant resources of iron ore and fuel. Meroe soon became a great iron-producing center. The huge mounds of slag still to be seen around the ruins of the capital suggest that it had served as the Pittsburgh of Central

Iron tools were used in Africa long before the coming of the Europeans. This illustration, taken from David Livingstone's *Last Journals*, shows Africans forging hoes. (Courtesy of the Library of Congress)

Africa. Presumably the iron and other products of civilization were traded for traditional African commodities such as slaves, ivory, and ostrich feathers. After more than a thousand years' existence, the Kushan kingdom declined during the fourth century A.D., but not before ironmaking had spread far to the south and west.

A prime cause for the Kushan decline was invasion from Ethiopia, the third source of the introduction of iron metallurgy into sub-Saharan Africa. The ancestors of the Amharic people of modern Ethiopia built an empire about A.D. 50 with Axum as the capital. These Axumites were traders who exchanged their goods in the Indian Ocean lands, the Middle East, and East Africa. Although details are not yet known, they introduced both metallurgical and advanced agricultural techniques in East Africa.

The Carthaginians, the Kushites, and the Axumites together were responsible for the widespread diffusion of the art of ironmaking in sub-Saharan Africa. By about 500 B.C. the local populations had begun to make their own tools and weapons. The technique had spread westward as far as central Nigeria by 200 B.C., and southward to the Zambezi by the first century A.D. In this manner Africa entered the iron age, with repercussions as far-reaching as those noted earlier in the case of Eurasia.

Iron-tipped hoes and iron-shod axes made possible the extension of agriculture into the forests of Africa, as earlier they had into the forests of Central Europe and of the Ganges and Yangtze valleys. The resulting increase in agricultural output left a surplus available for trading purposes. As in Eurasia, this in turn led to social differentiation—to the division of peoples into rulers and ruled in place of the former simple kinship relationships. Hence the appearance about the ninth century A.D. of definite state structures with military and administrative services and with the revenue sources necessary for their support.

Another repercussion in Africa was the radical change in the ethnic composition of the continent. It was the accessible Negroes and Caucasoids of the Sudan, rather than the inaccessible Pygmies and Bushmen of the rain forests and the southern regions, who adopted and profited from agriculture and iron metallurgy. Consequently, it was they also who increased disproportionately in number and who were able, with their iron tools and weapons, to push southward at the expense of the Bushmen and Pygmies. This expansionism was particularly marked in the case of the Bantus, a predominantly Negroid linguistic group. Starting from their original center in the Cameroon Highlands, they infiltrated in the early Christian era into the Congo basin, eliminating or subjugating the sparse Pygmy hunters. From there some pushed southeast to the fertile, open Great Lakes country, between A.D. 600 and 900. They then continued southward across the savannah at the expense of the Bushmen, who suffered the same fate as the Pygmies. Meanwhile other Bantus were driving directly southward along the Atlantic coast, ultimately encountering a new people, the Hottentots. These are now believed to be simply Bushmen who had learned stockraising earlier, thus improving their diet and becoming larger than other Bushmen, whom they otherwise resemble. These migrations explain why the Negroes were the predominant ethnic group by the time the Europeans arrived, whereas a millennium earlier they had shared the continent fairly evenly with the Caucasoids, Bushmen, and Pygmies.

IV. Islam

The repercussions of agriculture and metallurgy were all accentuated by another profoundly significant historical force emanating from Eurasia, that is, Islam. Its rapid sweep across North Africa in the seventh century encountered little resistance from the Byzantine rulers but a good deal from the native Berber populations. The latter, however, were eventually won over to Islam, and they then joined the Arabs in conquering Spain and in extending the Moslem faith and culture across the Sahara to the Sudan. Berber traders converted their African counterparts that they encountered along the trans-Sahara trade routes. Tolerant Negro rulers allowed Moslems full liberty both to practice and to propagate their religion. Thus Islam first made its appearance in the markets of the western Sudan about the ninth century. By the thirteenth century it had become the state religion of the great Mali empire of the time, and spread steadily with official support.

On a much smaller local scale Islam also gained a foothold in East Africa, where Moslem Arab communities had been established from an early date. Intermarriage of the Arab settlers with Bantu women created a new people, the *Sawahila*, or "coastalists," whose language became the lingua franca of East Africa. There settlements were confined to coastal enclaves or to islands which offered more security against mainland tribes. No attempt was made to conquer the interior, so that Islam never obtained a massive base in East Africa comparable to that in North Africa and the Sudan.

The impact of Islam upon Africa was varied and profound. It was evident most obviously in the externals of life—names, dress, household equipment, architectural styles, festivals, and the like. It was evident also in the agricultural and technological progress that came with enlarged contact with the outside world. In East Africa the Arabs introduced rice and sugar cane from India. Mai Idris alooma of Bornu, roughly a contemporary of Queen Elizabeth of England, is recorded to have said that "Among the benefits which God (Most High) of his bounty and beneficence, generosity and constancy conferred upon the Sultan was the acquisition of Turkish musketeers and numerous household slaves who became skilled in firing muskets." [2]

Islam also stimulated commerce by linking the African economy to the far-flung network of Eurasian trade routes controlled by Moslem merchants. From their bases in North Africa the Moslems used the camel much more than had the Romans, and increased correspondingly the number of trans-Saharan trade routes and the volume of trade. Southward they transported cloth, jewelry, cowrie beads, and, above all, salt, which was in urgent demand throughout the Sudan. In return the Africans provided ivory, slaves, ostrich feathers, civet for perfumes, and, most important, gold from the upper Niger, Senegal, and Volta rivers. Much of this gold ultimately found its way to Europe, and in such large quantities that it became important for redressing medieval Europe's adverse balance of trade with the East. Such was the mutually stimulating interaction between the Sudanese economy and foreign trade that by 1400 the whole of West Africa was crisscrossed with trading trails and dotted with market centers.

Meanwhile a similar trading pattern had been developing in East Africa. Moslem middlemen on the coast sent agents into the interior who bought ivory, slaves, gold from Rhodesia, and copper from Katanga. These commodities then were exported through Indian Ocean trade channels, controlled at the time by Moslem merchants. In later centuries iron ore also was obtained from the interior, shipped to southern India, and made into the so-called Damascus blades. In return for these African products were received Chinese and Indian cloth, and various luxury goods, especially Chinese porcelain, remains of which still can be found along the coast. This trade was the basis for the string of thriving ports and city-states along the East African coast. By the thirteenth century two of them, Kilwa and Zanzibar, had established mints of their own, striking copper coins in considerable quantity.

Returning to the role of Islam in Africa, it served also to stimulate greatly the intellectual life of the Sudan. Literacy was spread with the establishment of Koranic schools. Scholars could pursue higher learning at various Sudanese universities, of which the University of Sankore at Timbuktu was the most outstanding. This institution was modeled after other Moslem universities at Fez, Tunis, and Cairo. It was the custom for scholars to move about freely among these universities and others in the Moslem world, to study at the feet of particular masters. The Moslem traveler Leo Africanus, who visited Timbuktu in 1513, found that the flourishing state of learning was due to the support it received from the ruler, Askia the Great. "Here [in Timbuktu] are great store of doctors, judges, priests, and other learned men, that are bountifully maintained at the king's cost and charges. And hither are brought divers manuscripts or written books out of Barbarie [North Africa], which are sold for more money than any other merchandize." [3]

The adoption of Islam also enhanced the political cohesion of the Sudanic kingdoms. Their rulers traditionally could claim the allegiance only of their own kinship units or clans, and of such other related kinship units that recognized descent from a great founding ancestor. But when the kingdoms were enlarged into great empires, this kinship relationship obviously became inadequate as the basis for imperial organization. The more widely an empire was extended, the more alien its emperor appeared to a large proportion of the subjects. Local chiefs could not be depended upon to serve as faithful vassals; they tended instead to lead their own people in resistance to imperial rule. Islam helped to meet this institutional problem by strengthening the imperial administration. Moslem schools and colleges turned out a class of educated men who could organize an effective imperial bureaucracy. These men were not dominated by their kinship alliances; their own interests were tied to imperial authority, and they normally could be counted upon to serve that authority loyally.

V. SUDAN EMPIRES

It was this combination of agricultural and metallurgical progress, corresponding growth in economic productivity, flourishing interregional trade, and the stimulus from Islam, that explains the process of state building that went on in Africa from the eighth century onward. Not surprisingly, the most complex political structures appeared in the Sudan, where long distance trade was most highly developed and where Islamic influence was the strongest. Hence the emergence in that region of three great empires: Ghana (700–1200), Mali (1200–1500), and Songhai (1350–1600). (See Map XX, "African Empires and Trade Routes.")

These empires had certain fundamental characteristics in common. They were all based primarily upon trade, so that each extended its authority northward to control the import of salt, and southward to control the purchase of gold. Each derived most of its revenues from levies on the buying and selling of these and other commodities. A contemporary scholar, al-Bikri, lists the duties levied in Ghana on "every donkey-load of salt" entering or leaving the country, as well as on donkey-loads and camel-loads of other commodities. "All pieces of gold that are found in this empire," he relates, "belong to the king of Ghana, but he leaves to his people the gold dust. . . ." [4]

The revenues from these duties made possible progressively greater sophistication in imperial administration. Thus the Songhai Empire was more complex than its two predecessors. It was divided into defined provinces, each with a governor on long-term appointment. It also boasted the beginnings of a professional army and even of a number of ministries—for finance, justice, home affairs, agriculture, and forests, as well as for "White People," that is, the Arabs and Berbers on the Saharan frontiers of the empire.

The Mali and Songhai empires owed much to Islam for furthering trade, providing a trained bureaucracy, and stimulating intellectual life. Islam also transformed the Sudan from an isolated African region to an integral part of the Moslem world. Thus the fourteenth century Arab traveller Ibn Battuta included Mali in his journeys which ranged as far east as China. Arriving at the Mali capital in June 1353 he was favorably impressed by the imperial administration and by the habits of the people.

> The negroes possess some admirable qualities. They are seldom unjust, and have a greater abhorrence of injustice than any other people. Their sultan shows no mercy to anyone who is guilty of the least act of it. There is complete security in their country. Neither traveller nor inhabitant in it has anything to fear from robbers or men of violence. They do not confiscate the property of any white man who dies in their country, even if it be uncounted wealth. On the contrary, they give it into the charge of some trustworthy person among the whites, until the rightful heir takes possession of it. They are careful to observe the hours of prayer, and assiduous in attending them in congregations, and in bringing up their children to them. On Fridays, if a man does not go early to the mosque, he cannot find a corner to pray in, on account of the crowd.[5]

Although Islam played a key role in the formation and functioning of the Sudanic empires, it should be noted that it was primarily an urban faith. It was the merchants and townspeople who became Moslems, while the country folk by and large remained loyal to their traditional pagan gods and beliefs. Thus the reliance of many of the emperors and of their imperial establishments on Islam was a source of weakness as well as of strength. Islam, as we have seen, had much to contribute, but its base was narrower than it seemed to contemporary observers who naturally visited urban centers and travelled along trade routes. Thus in times of crisis the town-centered empires proved unexpectedly fragile and quickly fell apart.

Another weakness of the Sudanic empires was their vulnerability to attack from the North by Berbers looking for the source of African gold or seeking to impose their particular version of the true faith. The fanatical Almaravids were responsible for the overthrow of Ghana in 1076, and likewise an invasion from Morocco destroyed Songhai in 1591. The latter catastrophe marked the end of the Sudanic imperial era. In the words of a seventeenth-century Timbuktu historian: "From that moment everything changed. Danger took the place of security; poverty of wealth. Peace gave way to distress, disasters, and violence. . . ." [6]

VI. KINGDOMS AND TRIBES

The three empires noted above are the best known African medieval political creations. In the rest of the continent, however, there existed a great variety of other political structures. In Southeast Africa, for example, there were certain similarities to the situation in the Sudan. Just as the Sudan was famous in the Mediterranean basin for its gold exports, so Southeast Africa was famous for the same reason in the Indian Ocean basin. And just as the Sudanic empires and North African states were nourished by the one trade pattern, so by the fifteenth century the Monomotapa empire in the interior and the Kilwa city-state on the coast were supported by the other.

Monomotapa, a word adapted by the Portuguese from the royal title *Mwenemutapa,* encompassed modern Rhodesia and Mozambique, thereby controlling the sources of the gold and the routes to the coast, after the fashion of the Sudanic empires. It was the monarchs of Monomotapa who raised the Great Temple of Zimbabwe, a massive enclosure with walls 32 feet high, constructed to provide an appropriate setting for the conduct of royal ceremonial rites. Kilwa's merchant rulers, who called themselves sultans, were middlemen who controlled the flow of goods from Monomotapa to the Moslem trading ships that ranged the Indian Ocean and even beyond to the China seas. "Kilwa is one of the most beautiful and well-constructed towns in the world. The whole of it is elegantly built," wrote Ibn Battuta—the same Battuta who later was impressed also by Mali.[7]

Just as the Sudanic kingdoms were ravaged by Berber invaders from the north, so Monomotapa and Kilwa were destroyed by Portuguese intruders from overseas. Within a decade after Vasco da Gama's rounding of the Cape of Good Hope in 1497, the Portuguese had sacked many of the coastal cities of southeast Africa and were carrying on in the Indian Ocean as though it were a Portuguese lake. Da Gama had missed Kilwa on his first voyage, but a Portuguese fleet was provided shelter there in 1500. Five years later another fleet responded to this hospitality with ruthless looting. A member of the expedition recounts that they captured this city of "many strong houses several stories high" without opposition from the surprised inhabitants. Then "the Vicar-General and some of the Franciscan fathers came ashore carrying

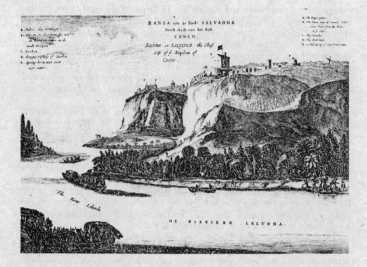

Seventeenth-century European illustration depicting the capital of the African Congo Kingdom. This kingdom predated the coming of the Europeans. (Courtesy of the Library of Congress)

In marked contrast to the illustration above, this nineteenth-century drawing shows a typical African agricultural village that is primitive in comparison to the apparent magnificence of the capital of the Congo Kingdom. (Courtesy of the Library of Congress)

two crosses in procession and singing the Te Deum. They went to the palace, and there the cross was put down and the Admiral prayed. Then everyone started to plunder the town of all its merchandise and provisions." [8]

Later the Portuguese made their way up the Zambezi river and similarly undermined the Monomotapa empire. They settled in various strategic locations along the river and extended their influence in all directions until the inevitable showdown in 1628. With their firearms the Portuguese easily defeated two Monomotapa armies, so that several petty kingdoms now arose on the ruins of the former empire.

The diversity of the African scene is manifest if one turns from southeast to northeast Africa, where Christian kingdoms existed in obscure isolation amongst the Ethiopians and the Nubians. Until the fourth century A.D. the Axumites of Ethiopia had been pagans, whose gods were those of south Arabia. In A.D. 333 Christianity was introduced by a Syrian, Frumentius, who converted the king. Since that time Christianity has remained the official religion and has permeated all phases of Ethiopian life. The Moslem conquests of the seventh century cut off Ethiopia from the Mediterranean, and the loss of the Red Sea ports to the Moslems between the eighth and tenth centuries left the country completely cut off from the outside world. But Ethiopia possessed a sufficiently large interior of mountains and plateaus to survive in substantial isolation to modern times. Under these conditions a distinctive society took form and endured—a Christian feudal society with a court comprised of priests, officials, and army commanders, and with a king who, like his early medieval European counterparts, was forced by economic necessity and political pressures to move his court continually from region to region.

The Kush kingdom in Nubia, as noted in section III of this chapter, had been destroyed by Axum in 325. The succession states that followed were converted to Byzantine or Coptic Christianity in the sixth century by a mission from Alexandria. The hold of the new faith is reflected in the large number of churches, some with superb murals still glowing in their original colors, having been preserved by covering sand. These were discovered only a few years ago by a Polish archaeological mission which rescued them from the rising waters of Egypt's new Aswan Dam and cut them out for preservation in Khartoum and Warsaw museums.

Like Ethiopia, these Christian Nubian kingdoms were isolated by the seventh-century Islamic conquest of Egypt. Despite border warfare with the Moslems, Nubian Christianity survived for another six centuries, unknown to the outside world. But in the thirteenth century Egypt came under the rule of the militant Saracens who, being at war with the Western Crusaders in the Holy Land, were unwilling to tolerate other Christians nearer to home. Thus they overran most of Nubia in the late thirteenth century, though isolated areas held out for another two centuries.

In this sampling of diverse African societies—and it is a mere sampling rather than a comprehensive survey—the most primitive should not be overlooked, for their continued existence reflected the extreme physical compartmentalization of the continent. The Pygmies and Bushmen, constricted and isolated in inaccessible deserts and rain forests, remained at the food gathering stage of development. The world passed them by as they continued with man's original mode of livelihood as hunters and food collectors. But this does not mean that their cultures are of no significance or interest. Those few who have closely observed the Pygmies report highly developed talents in dancing, choral song, acting, mimicry, and storytelling. Likewise the Bushmen are famous for their rock-paintings and engravings, executed with natural and easy rhythmical lines, and depicting animals, hunting and battle scenes, and dancing ceremonial activities.

VII. Conclusion

Allowing for the difference between the Moslem and the Christian intellectual climates, a citizen of fourteenth-century Timbuktu would have found himself reasonably at home in fourteenth-century Oxford. In the sixteenth century he would still have found many points in common between the two university cities. By the nineteenth century the gulf had grown very deep.[9]

This point made by the British Africanist, Thomas Hodgkin, describes a process that is certainly not unique to Africa. It is clear from the preceding chapters that this is a worldwide process, and for the simple reason that the West pioneered in modernization and consequently pulled ahead of all other societies. Yet the fact remains that the gap between the West and Africa opened much wider than those between the West and other Eurasian regions. Constantinople, Delhi, and Peking did decline in relation to London, Paris, and Berlin, but they did not decline to virtual extinction as did Timbuktu. The problem as to why the West took the lead in modernization and forged ahead of other regions has been considered in Chapter 17. But we face here another problem—namely, why did Africa fall behind not only the West but also Eurasia in general?

This question has scarcely been posed, let alone answered. The preceding chapters analyzing the evolution of various Eurasian civilizations suggest certain factors that may be relevant and that are here presented tentatively for consideration. Their relative significance, if indeed they are significant, cannot be assessed without much more research and reflection.

One distinctive feature of Africa's development that quickly comes to mind is that the general stimulus generated by agriculture, metallurgy and long-distance trade soon reached a plateau and failed to develop further. There was no counterpart in Africa to the chain-reaction upsurge that occurred in northern Europe and in the Ganges and Yangtze valleys, when they were opened up and exploited with iron tools. Perhaps one reason was the absence in Africa of regions of corresponding fertility and potential productivity. The combination of poor soils, climatic extremes and the tsetse fly made it impossible for the African agriculturists and craftsmen to be as productive as their Eurasian counterparts. Even the favored Sudan was excessively dependent on the export of gold and slaves, which could not provide a broad enough base for continued economic growth.

Africa's development appears to have been stunted also by the external and internal isolation, described in the first section. For example, Africa did not have anything comparable to Europe's rivers and coastal outlets, nor did it enjoy the advantages of being near the advanced Byzantine and Islamic civilizations as Europe did. Instead there were deserts and rain forests within, and oceanic expanses without. This prevented effective exploitation of even the limited output that the natural resources allowed. It is true that Africa, unlike the Americas, was close enough to Eurasia to benefit from the diffusion of basic technology such as agriculture and metallurgy. But Africa was too remote to receive, for example, the long series of inventions that were exchanged in the course of millennia amongst the Eurasian regions, to their mutual advantage.

Finally Africa suffered from vulnerability to outside attack, for retarded development means weakness, and weakness everywhere invites aggression. The disastrous effects of Berber invasions of the Sudan, and of the Portuguese onslaught on southeast Africa have been described above. They are particularly relevant in view of the fact that Western Europe, by contrast, suffered no invasions whatsoever during the critical five centuries prior to 1500 when she rose to global prominence. This vulnerability factor was to manifest itself in particularly virulent form with the later infliction of the slave trade, which not only depopulated vast areas but also caused economic and political chaos.

These various factors may explain why Africa's development stopped far short of the levels reached by the Eurasian societies. This retardation is reflected in the continued collective ownership of land and in the failure of urban centers to dominate the economies of any African regions. On the other hand this, in turn, made possible the preservation of the appealing egalitarianism and leisurely pace of life that prevail where kinship ties and communal land ownership remain in force. (See Chapter 3, section IV.) The British Africanist Basil Davidson has concluded that ". . . comparison between Africa and Europe is likely to be in Africa's favor. . . . So far as the comparison has any value, daily life in medieval Europe was likely to be far more hazardous or disagreeable for the common man and his wife." [10]

This positive judgment doubtless is justified, but from the perspective of world history the noteworthy point is that the appealing features of African society had survived precisely because it lacked the dynamism and continued growth of Eurasian societies. So long as the Africans remained relatively isolated from the outside world, they could preserve and enjoy a way of life that had long since been lost in the Eurasian civilizations. But when Western expansionism reached the African shores, a heavy price had to be paid. For the greater the underdevelopment, the greater the vulnerability and the resulting disruption. This was true when Bantu agriculturists expanded throughout Africa at the expense of "underdeveloped" hunting peoples, and it was to be equally true in modern times when the representatives of the industrialized West burst out over the globe at the expense of "underdeveloped" agriculturists, and especially of those who had remained at a Neolithic level of organization.

Finally, it should be noted that although the Africans had not kept up with the Eurasians, they surpassed the more isolated American Indians and Australian aborigines. This explains to a large degree why the Europeans were so much slower in penetrating into the interior of Africa than into the Americas or Australia. Geographic factors also were involved here, as noted in section I, but more basic was the higher level of development reached by the Africans, particularly those with whom the Europeans had dealings. These naturally were the most advanced, because that meant they were also the most productive, and hence offered the most opportunity for profitable trade.

The commerce that developed with the coming of the Europeans was novel for the advanced Africans only in its scale. Mercantile activity was not, in itself, something strange, since they for a long time had maintained trade ties with areas as far removed as Morocco and Egypt. It follows that the Africans reacted to the Portuguese very differently from the manner in which the American Indians were reacting to the Spaniards at the same time. It is true that the forest dwellers, who had not had direct contact with the Arabs, were astonished by the white skin of the Europeans, by the loud noise of their firearms, and by the fact that these newcomers came from the sea, which was much revered by the coastal peoples. Yet the fact remains that the arrival of the Portuguese did not produce the demoralization and distintegration in Africa that the Spaniards did in the Americas. Accordingly, the Africans traded with the Europeans on terms that they themselves dictated. For centuries the coastal chieftains refused to allow the Europeans to penetrate inland because they wished to maintain their profitable position as middlemen between the European buyers and the producers in the interior. A British official wrote in 1793 that Africa remained an unknown continent "rather from the jealousy of the inhabitants of the sea coasts, in permitting white men to travel through their country, than from the danger or difficulty attending the penetration." This jealousy he attributed to the middlemen's fear "that the advantages of their trade with Europe should be lessened and transferred from them to their neighbours; or that the inland kingdoms by obtaining European arms" would become dangerous rivals.[11]

Adam Smith, writing in 1776, was aware of this difference between the American Indians and the African Negroes in their capability for resisting European penetration.

> Though the Europeans possess many considerable settlements both upon the coast of Africa and in the East Indies, they have not yet established in either of those countries such numerous and thriving colonies as those in the islands and continent of America. Africa, however, as well as several of the countries comprehended under the general name of the East Indies, are inhabited by barbarous nations. But those nations were by no means so weak and defenceless as the miserable and helpless Americans; and . . . they were besides much more populous. . . . In Africa and the East Indies, therefore, it was more difficult to displace the natives, and to extend the European plantations over the greater part of the lands of the original inhabitants.[12]

SUGGESTED READING

On Africa, there is a useful bibliographical essay by R. I. Rotberg, "The Teaching of African History," *American Historical Review,* LXIX (October, 1963), 47–63. An indispensable guide to current knowledge and research is provided by

R. A. Lystad, *The African World: A Survey of Social Research* (New York: Praeger, 1965). Equally indispensable is J. D. Fage, *An Atlas of African History* (London: Edward Arnold, 1965). There are three standard works on African geography: L. Dudley Stamp, *Africa: A Study in Tropical Development* (New York: Wiley, 1953); W. Fitzgerald, *Africa: A Social, Economic, and Political Geography of Its Major Regions*, 8th ed. (New York: Dutton, 1957); and Vol. 1 of G. H. T. Kimble, *Tropical Africa* (New York: Twentieth Century Fund, 1960). The most thorough study of African ethnography is by G. P. Murdock, *Africa: Its Peoples and Their Culture History* (New York: McGraw-Hill, 1959). A useful collection of source materials is provided by B. Davidson, *The African Past: Chronicles from Antiquity to Modern Times* (Boston: Little, Brown, 1964). Also noteworthy is the convenient collection of significant secondary sources by P. J. M. McEwan, ed., *Africa from Early Times to 1800* (London: Oxford Univ., 1968). The pre-Western history of Africa is presented, as authoritatively as current knowledge permits, by R. Oliver and J. D. Fage, *A Short History of Africa* (Baltimore: Penguin, 1962); and by B. Davidson, *Africa in History, Themes and Outlines* (New York: Macmillan, 1968). The study by D. L. Wiedner, *A History of Africa South of the Sahara* (New York: Knopf, 1962), concentrates on the period following the appearance of the Europeans. Much valuable data and interpretation of various aspects of Africa's past and present appear in the paperback by P. Bohannan, *Africa and Africans* (New York: American Museum of Science, 1964). A number of traditional rural cultures are described by the anthropologist Colin Turnbull in *The Peoples of Africa* (Cleveland and New York: World, 1962) and *Tradition and Change in African Tribal Life* (Cleveland and New York: World, 1966). For African arts, see S. Glubok, *The Art of Africa* (New York: Harper and Row, 1965); the more detailed study by E. Leuzinger, *Africa: The Art of the Negro Peoples* (New York: Crown, 1960); and B. W. Dietz and M. B. Olatunji, *Musical Instruments of Africa* (New York: John Day, 1965). On the role of Islam in African history, there are the following studies by J. S. Trimingham: *A History of Islam in West Africa* (London: Oxford Univ., 1962); *Islam in East Africa* (Oxford: Clarendon, 1964); and *The Influence of Islam upon Africa* (New York: Praeger, 1968).

To the nations, however, both of the East *Chapter*
and West Indies, all the commercial benefits
which can have resulted from these
events [the expansion of Europe] have been
sunk and lost in the dreadful
misfortunes which they have occasioned.

ADAM SMITH

19

Americas and Australia

The Vikings had stumbled upon North America in the eleventh century, and for about one hundred years they tried to maintain settlements there, but without success. In the fifteenth century Columbus likewise stumbled upon the New World, but this time the sequel was altogether different. Instead of failure and withdrawal, discovery now was followed by massive and overwhelming penetration of both North and South America. The contrast reflected the extent of the increase in European power and dynamism during the intervening half millennium.

Equally striking was the contrast between the rapid European penetration and exploitation of the Americas, and the centuries that elapsed before the same could be done in Africa. One reason was geography; the New World was physically more accessible and inviting. The other reason, as noted by Adam Smith, was "the miserable and helpless" plight of the Indians. Although they were far from all being at the same level of development, yet the overall nature of the Indian cultures was such that effective resistance was impossible. And if this was true of the American Indians, it was much more so of the Australian aborigines who were still at the food-gathering stage. In this chapter we shall consider the physical setting and the cultural background of the fateful developments that followed the landings of Columbus in the West Indies and of Captain James Cook in New South Wales.

362

I. Land and People

The Americas, in contrast to Africa, were exceptionally open to newcomers from Europe. No sandbars obstructed the approaches to the coasts. Harbors were much more frequently available along the indented coastline of the Americas than along the unbroken coastline of Africa. Also the Americas had a well-developed pattern of interior waterways that were relatively free of impediments and offered easy access to the interior. There was no counterpart in Africa to the majestic and smooth-flowing Amazon, Plata, Mississippi, or St. Lawrence. The explorers soon learned the use of the native birchbark canoe, and they discovered that with comparatively few portages they could paddle from the Atlantic up the St. Lawrence, along the Great Lakes, and thence south down the Mississippi to the Gulf of Mexico, or north down the Mackenzie to the Arctic Ocean, or west down the Columbia or the Fraser to the Pacific Ocean.

The climate of the Americas, too, is generally more attractive than that of Africa. The Amazon basin, it is true, is hot and humid, and the polar extremities of both continents are bitterly cold, but the British and the French settlers flourished in the lands they colonized north of the Rio Grande, and the Spaniards likewise felt at home in Mexico and Peru, which became their two principal centers. The climate there is not much different from that of Spain, and certainly a welcome contrast to the sweltering and pestiferous Gold and Ivory coasts.

Almost all the native peoples were descendants of immigrants who crossed the Bering Sea from northeastern Siberia. This statement must be qualified by the word "almost," because small numbers of peoples from the islands of the South Pacific reached the west coast of South America after the arrival of the Bering Sea migrants. It is not known how many times these argonauts of the South Seas "discovered" South America, but the evidence from domesticated plants alone is sufficient to establish the fact of their transoceanic expeditions. When the same plants, so highly domesticated that they cannot survive without the aid of man, are found on both sides of the Pacific, their distribution can be explained only in terms of man's migrations.

It remains true, however, that at least 99 percent of the Indians whom the Europeans found in the Americas were descended from the stock that had crossed the Bering Sea. Until recently it was believed that the Indians first began crossing over to the Americas about 10,000 years ago. New archaeological findings, together with the use of carbon-14 dating, have forced drastic revision of this estimate. It is now generally agreed that man certainly was in the New World 20,000 years ago, and probably 20,000 years or more before that. The last major migration of Indians took place about 3,000 years ago. Then came the Eskimos, who continued to travel back and forth across the Straits until modern political conditions forced them to remain on one side or the other. In any case, the parts of America closest to Asia were by this time sufficiently densely populated to discourage further migration.

The actual crossing to the New World presented little difficulty to these early newcomers. The last of the Ice Ages had locked up vast quantities of sea water, lowering the ocean level by 460 feet and thus exposing a 1,300-mile-wide land bridge connecting Siberia and Alaska. A "bridge" of such proportions was, in effect, a vast new subcontinent, that allowed ample scope for the vast diffusion of plants and animals that now took place. Furthermore this area, because of low precipitation, was covered not with ice but with lakes, mosses, grasses and assorted shrubs typical of the tundra. This vegetation offered pasturage for the large mammals of the time: mastadon, mammoth, musk oxen, bison, moose, elk, mountain sheep and goats, camels, foxes, bears, wolves, and horses. As these herds of game crossed over to the New World they were followed by the hunters that subsisted on them.

Even after rising temperatures lifted the sea level and submerged the connecting lands, the resulting narrow straits easily could have been crossed in crude boats without even losing sight of shore. Later and more advanced migrants may have travelled by boat from Asia to America and then continued along the northwest coast until they finally landed and settled in what is now British Columbia.

Most of those who crossed to Alaska moved on into the heart of North America through a gap in the ice sheet in the central Yukon plateau. They were impelled to press forward by the same forces that led them to migrate to America—the search for new hunting grounds and the continual pressure of tribes from the rear. In this manner both the continents were soon peopled by scattered tribes of hunters. Definite evidence has been found that indicates that the migrants from Asia reached the southern tip of South America by 11,000 years ago.

As regards racial traits, all Indians may be classified as Mongoloids. They have the characteristic straight black hair, sparse on the face and body; high cheekbones; and the Mongolian spot that appears at the base of the spine in young children. Considerable variation exists, however, among the different tribes: the earliest varieties of American Indian are much less Mongoloid than the later ones, because they left Asia before the Mongoloids, as we know them today, had fully evolved. That the immigrants at once spread out and settled in small, inbred groups in a variety of climates also explains the presence of individual physical types.

II. CULTURES

The migrants to the New World brought little cultural baggage with them since they came from northeast Siberia, one of the least advanced regions of Eurasia. They were, of course, all hunters, organized in small bands, possessing only crude stone tools, no pottery, and no domesticated animals, except perhaps the dog. Since they were entering an uninhabited continent they were completely free to evolve their own institutions without the influences from native populations that the Aryans had been subject to when they migrated to the Indus Valley, or the Achaeans and Dorians when they reached Greece.

During the ensuing millennia the American Indians did develop an extraordinarily rich variety of cultures, adapted to one another as well as to the wide range of physical environments they encountered. Some remained at the hunting band stage while others developed kingdoms and empires. Their religions encompassed all known categories, including monotheism. They spoke some 2,000 distinct languages, some as different from one another as Chinese and English. This represents as much variation in speech as in the entire Old World, where about 3,000 languages are known to have existed in A.D. 1500. Nor were these languages primitive, either in vocabulary or in any other respect. Whereas Shakespeare used about 24,000 words, and the King James Bible about 7,000, the Nahuatl of Mexico used 27,000 words, while the Yahgans of Tierra del Fuego, considered to be one of the world's most retarded peoples, possess a vocabulary of at least 30,000 words.[1]

Taking all types of institutions and practices into account, anthropologists have defined some twenty-two culture areas in the New World—the Great Plains area, the Eastern Woodlands, the Northwest Coast area, and so forth. A simpler classification, on the basis of how food was obtained, involves three categories: hunting, gathering, and fishing cultures; intermediate farming cultures; and advanced farming cultures. This scheme is not only simpler but is also meaningful from the viewpoint of world history, for it helps to explain the varied responses of the Indians to the European intrusion.

The advanced farming cultures were located in Mesoamerica (central and southern Mexico, Guatemala, and Honduras) and the Andean highland area (Ecuador, Peru, Bolivia, and northern Chile). The intermediate farming cultures were generally in the adjacent regions, while the food-gathering cultures were in the more remote regions—the southern part of South America, and the western and northern part of North America.

This geographic distribution of culture points up the fact that, in contrast to Africa, the most advanced regions in the Americas were not located closest to Eurasia. One reason is that northeast Siberia was not a great center of civilization, as was the Middle East and the Mediterranean basin that contributed so much to the Africans. Also, climatic conditions in Alaska and the Canadian Arctic obviously were not conducive to rapid cultural development as was the case in the Sudan savannah zone. Thus the tempo of advance in the Americas depended not on proximity to Eurasia but rather on suitability for the development of agriculture. It is significant, then, that agriculture was first developed in the Americas in regions that were strikingly similar to the Middle East where agriculture originated in Eurasia—that is, highland regions not requiring extensive clearing of forests to prepare the fields for crops, with enough rainfall to allow the crops to mature, and with a supply of potentially high-yielding native plants available for domestication.

Chapter 3, section I describes the origins of agriculture in Mesoamerica about 7000 B.C. and the long stage of "incipient agriculture" to 1500 B.C. before food growing finally became the determining factor in society. The Indians domesticated over one hundred plants, or as many as were domesticated in all Eurasia, a truly extraordinary achievement. More than 50 percent of the farm products of the United States today are derived from crops grown by the Indians.

Maize, which was the staple in almost all regions, was originally a weed with ears no larger than a man's thumbnail. The Indians bred it into a plant with rows of seeds on long cobs. So completely did they domesticate maize that it became completely dependent on man for survival; it would become extinct if man stopped planting it, for in its domesticated form it cannot disperse its seeds, the kernels. Also impressive was the skill of the Indians in utilizing large numbers of poisonous plants. One of these is manioc, known in the United States as tapioca, from which they removed a deadly poison, leaving the starch. Other important plants grown by the Indians were squashes, potatoes, tomatoes, peanuts, chocolate, tobacco, and beans, a major source of protein. Among the medicinal plants bequeathed by the Indians were cascara, cocaine, arnica, inpecac, and quinine. That none of the plants grown in America was cultivated in the Old World before the discoveries proves conclusively the independent origins of agriculture in the two hemispheres.

The regions where the Indians originated agriculture were also the regions where they first developed it further and gradually evolved "advanced farming cultures." This is turn profoundly changed the Indians' way of life. In general, the result was, as in Eurasia, a greatly increased sedentary population and the elaboration of those cultural activities not directly connected with bare subsistence. In other words, it was in these advanced farming cultures that it was possible to develop large empires and sophisticated civilizations comparable in certain respects to those of West Africa. Unfortunately, these indigenous American civilizations were suddenly overwhelmed by the Spaniards and thus left little behind them other than their precious domesticated plants.

III. CIVILIZATIONS

The three major Amerindian civilizations were the Mayan, in present-day Yucatan, Guatemala, and British Honduras; the Aztec, in present-day Mexico; and the Inca, stretching for 3,000 miles from mid-Ecuador to mid-Chile. (See Map XXI, "Amerindian Empires.") The Mayans were outstanding for their remarkable development of the arts and sciences. They alone evolved an ideographic form of writing in which characters or signs were used as conventional symbols for ideas. They also studied the movements of the heavenly bodies in order to measure time, predict the future, and set propitious dates for sacrifices and major undertakings. So extensive was the astronomical knowledge compiled by highly trained priests that it is believed to have been at least equal to that of Europe at that time. The intricate sacred calendar of the Mayans was based on concurrent cycles merging into greater cycles as their multiples coincided in time. Some of their calendrical computations spanned millions of years, a particularly impressive concept of the dimension of time if it be recalled how recently in Europe the creation of the world was fixed at 4004 B.C.

Maya cities, if they may be so called, were ceremonial centers rather than fortresses or dwelling places or administrative capitals. This was so because the Mayans practiced slash and burn agriculture, which exhausted the soil within two or three years, requiring constant moving of the village settlements. To balance this transitory mode of life, the Maya cultivators expressed their social unity by erecting large stone buildings in centers that were devoted primarily to religious ceremonies. These buildings were large temple pyramids and also community houses in which the priests and novices probably lived.

This architecture, produced entirely with stone tools, was decorated with sculpture that was unsurpassed in the Americas and that ranks as one of the great world arts.

The Maya civilization flourished between the fourth and tenth centuries, but then declined for reasons that remain obscure. It may have been soil exhaustion, or epidemic disease, or, more plausibly, peasant revolutions against the burden of supporting the religious centers with their priestly hierarchies. In any case the great stone structures were abandoned to decay and were swallowed by the surrounding forest, to be unearthed only in recent decades with archaeological excavations.

The Aztecs were brusque and warlike compared to the artistic and intellectual Mayas—a contrast reminiscent of that between the Romans and the Greeks in the Old World. The Aztecs actually were latecomers to Mexico, where a series of highly developed societies had through the centuries succeeded one another. These had been vulnerable to attacks by barbarians from the arid north who naturally gravitated down in response to the lure of fertile lands. The last of these invaders were the Aztecs, who had settled on some islands on Lake Texcoco, then filling much of the floor of the valley of Anáhuac. As their numbers grew and the islands became overcrowded, the Aztecs increased their arable land by making *chinampas,* floating islands of matted weeds, covered with mud dredged from the lake floor, and anchored to the bottom by growing weeds. To the present day, this mode of cultivation is carried on in certain regions. Before each planting the farmers scoop up fresh mud and spread it over the *chinampa,* whose level steadily rises with the succession of crops. The farmers then excavate the top layers of mud, which they use to build a new *chinampa,* thus beginning a new cycle.

The *chinampas* enabled the Aztecs to boom in numbers and wealth. Early in the fifteenth century they made alliances with towns on the lake shore, and from that foothold they quickly extended their influence in all directions. Raiding expeditions went out regularly, forcing other peoples to pay tribute in kind and in services. By the time the Spaniards appeared on the scene, Aztec domination extended to the Pacific on the west, to the Gulf of Mexico on the east, almost to Yucatan on the south, and to the Rio Grande on the north. The capital, Tenochtitlán, was by then a magnificent city of 200,000 to 300,000 people, linked to the shore by causeways. The conqueror Cortes compared the capital to Venice and judged it to be "the most beautiful city in the world." His lieutenant, Bernal Diaz del Castillo, also was awed by the splendor of the capital as he viewed it from the summit of the main temple:

> Before we mounted the steps of the great temple, Motecusuma, who was sacrificing on the top to his idols, sent six papas and two of his principal officers to conduct Cortes up the steps. There were 114 steps to the summit. . . . Indeed, this infernal temple, from its great height, commanded a view of the whole surrounding neighbourhood. From this place we could likewise see the three causeways which led into Mexico. . . . We also observed the aqueduct which ran from Chapultepec, and provided the whole town with sweet water. We could also distinctly see the bridges across the openings, by which these causeways were intersected, and through which the waters of the lake ebbed and flowed. The lake itself

Nineteenth-century drawing of ruins of a Mayan temple in Yucatan. Buildings such as this were produced with stone tools and were highly ornamented as is evident from this drawing.

was crowded with canoes, which were bringing provisions, manufactures, and other merchandize to the city. From here we also discovered that the only communication of the houses in this city, and of all the other towns built in the lake, was by means of drawbridges or canoes. In all these towns the beautiful white plastered temples rose above the smaller ones, like so many towers and castles in our Spanish towns, and this, it may be imagined, was a splendid sight.

After we had sufficiently gazed upon this magnificent picture, we again turned our eyes toward the great market, and beheld the vast numbers of buyers and sellers who thronged there. The bustle and noise occasioned by this multitude of human beings was so great that it could be heard at a distance of more than four miles. Some of our men, who had been at Constantinople and Rome, and travelled through the whole of Italy, said that they never had seen a marketplace of such large dimensions, or which was so well regulated, or so crowded with people as this one at Mexico.[2]

Aztec power was based on constant war preparedness. All men were expected to bear arms, and state arsenals were always stocked and ready for immediate use. With their efficient military machine the Aztecs were able to extract a staggering amount of tribute from their subjects. According to their own extant records, they collected in one year fourteen million pounds of maize, eight million pounds each of beans and amaranth, and two million cotton cloaks in addition to assorted other items such as war costumes, shields, and precious stones.[3]

The splendor of the capital and the volume of tribute pouring into it naturally led the Spaniards to conclude that Moctezuma was the ruler of a great empire. Actually this was not so. The vassal states remained functionally quite separate, practicing full self-government. Their only tie to Tenochtitlán was the tribute, which they paid out of fear of the Aztec expeditions. None of the Amerindian states, except for that of the Incas in Peru, was organized on any concept wider than that of the city-state. The Aztecs, in contrast to the Incas, made no attempt to acculturate their subjects to the Aztec way of life in preparation for full citizenship.

The Spaniards were not only dazzled by the wealth and magnificence of the Aztec state, but also horrified by the wholesale ritual massacre of a continual procession of human victims. These were slaughtered at the top of the ceremonial pyramids that abounded everywhere and that the Spaniards soon realized functioned as altars for human sacrifice. Sacrificial cults were common in Mesoamerica but nowhere did they lead to the obsessive slaughtering practiced by the Aztecs. Indeed, their motives for aggression were to take captives for sacrifice as well as to exact tribute for their capital.

The first objective they considered even more important than the second, for their priests taught that the world was in constant danger of cataclysm, especially the extinguishing of the sun. Hence the need for offering human victims to propitiate the heavenly deities. But this practice trapped the Aztecs in a truly vicious circle: sacrificial victims were needed to forestall universal disaster; these could be obtained only through war; successful war could be waged only by sacrificing victims, but these in turn could be secured only. through war. Bernal Diaz was an eyewitness of the end result:

> One certain spot in this township [Xocotlan] I shall never forget, situated near the temple. Here a vast number of human skulls were piled up in the best order imaginable,—there must have been more than 100,000; I repeat, more than 100,000. In like manner you saw the remaining human bones piled up in order in another corner of the square; these it would have been impossible to count. Besides these, there were human heads hanging suspended from beams on both sides. . . . Similar horrible sights we saw towards the interior of the country in every townshop. . . .[4]

Turning finally to the Incas of Peru, it should be noted that "Inca" was the title of their king of kings, so that it is technically incorrect, though common usage, to refer to them as the Inca Indians. Actually they were one of the numerous tribes of Quechua stock and language that raised llamas and grew potatoes. In the twelfth century they established themselves in the Cuzco valley which they soon dominated. At this early stage they evolved a dynasty from their war chiefs, while their tribesmen constituted an aristocracy amongst the other tribal peoples. The combination of a hereditary dynasty and aristocracy, which was unique in the New World, constituted an effective empire-building instrument. This was particularly true because of the outstanding ability of the Incas, or heads of state, for generation after generation. The Inca's only legitimate wife was his own full sister, so that each Inca was the son of a sister and a brother. This full inbreeding had continued for some eight generations, and the original stock must have been exceptionally sound because the royal princes, as the Spaniards observed, were all handsome and vigorous men.

From their imperial city of Cuzco in the Peruvian highlands, the Incas sent forth armies and ambassadors, west to the coastal lands, and north and south along the great mountain valleys. By the time of the Spanish intrusion they had extended their frontiers some 2,500 miles from Ecuador to central Chile. Thus they ruled much more territory than did the Aztecs, and furthermore they ruled it as a genuine empire.

This empire was held together physically by a road system which still can be traced for hundreds of miles and which included cable bridges of plaited aloe fibre and floating bridges on pontoons of buoyant reeds. Equally important was an extensive irrigation system, parts of which are still in use, and which made the Inca empire a flourishing agricultural unit. Communications were maintained by a comprehensive system of post-stations and relays of runners who conveyed messages swiftly to all parts of the empire.

Imperial unity was furthered also by elaborate court ritual and by a state religion based on worship of the sun, of which the Inca was held to be a descendant, and in whose ceremonial worship he played an essential role. Other techniques of imperial rule included state ownership of land, mineral wealth, and herds, careful census compilations for tax and military purposes, deposition of local hereditary chieftains, forced population resettlement for the assimilation of conquered peoples, and mass marriages under state auspices. Not surprisingly, the Inca empire is considered to be one of the most successful totalitarian states the world has ever seen.

370

IV. CONCLUSION

Impressive as were these attainments of the American Indians, the fact remains that a handful of Spanish adventurers was able to easily overthrow and completely uproot all three of the great New World civilizations. And this despite the fact that Mexico and the Aztec empire each had a population of at least three million, and some estimates are as much as five times that number, this being an unresolved and much disputed question at present. The explanation for the one-sided Spanish triumph is to be found ultimately in the isolation of the Americas. This isolation, it should be noted, was, as in the case of Africa, internal as well as external. That is to say, not only were the American Indian civilizations cut off from stimulating interaction with civilizations on other continents, but also they were largely isolated from each other.

"With respect to interrelations between Peru and Mesoamerica," reports an archaeologist, "it is sufficient to state that not a single object or record of influence or contact between these areas has been accepted as authentic from the long time span between the Formative period [about 1000 B.C.] and the coming of the Spaniards. . . ." [5] In other words, there is no reliable evidence of interaction between the Mesoamerican and Peruvian civilizations over a span of 2,500 years. And during those millennia, as we have seen, the various regions of Eurasia, and to a lesser extent sub-Saharan Africa, were in continual fructifying contact. The end result was that the American Indians—even those of the Andes and Mesoamerica—lagged far behind the Eurasians and especially behind the technologically precocious Europeans. By A.D. 1500 the New World had reached the stage of civilization that Egypt and Mesopotamia had attained about 2500 B.C.

Precisely what did this mean when the confrontation occurred with the arrival of the Spaniards? It meant, in the first place, that the Indians found themselves economically and technologically far behind the civilization represented by the invaders. The highly developed art, science, and religion of the Indians should not be allowed to obscure the fact that they lagged seriously in more material fields. The disparity was most extreme in Mesoamerica, but it also prevailed in the Andean area. In agriculture, the Indians were brilliantly successful in domesticating plants but much less effective in actual production. Their cultivation techniques never advanced beyond the bare minimum necessary for feeding populations that rarely reached the density of those of the Old World. Their tools were made only of stone, wood, or bone. They were incapable of smelting ores, and though they did work with metal, it was almost exclusively for ornamental purposes. The only ships they constructed were canoes and seagoing rafts. For land transportation they made no use of the wheel, which they knew but used only as a toy. Only the human back was available for transportation, with the exception of the llama and the alpaca, which were used in the Andes but which could not carry heavy loads.

The immediate significance of this technological lag should not be exag-

The execution of Atahuallpa, the Inca king, by the conquistadores. (Courtesy of the New York Public Library)

Quauhtemoc, the last king of the Aztecs, surrenders to Cortes. (Courtesy of the New York Public Library)

gerated. The Indians obviously were at a grave disadvantage with their spears and arrows against the Spaniards' horses and guns. But after the initial shock, the Indians became accustomed to firearms and cavalry. Furthermore, the Spaniards soon discovered that the Indian weapons were sharp and durable, and they came to prefer the Indian armor of quilted cotton to their own. One of the conquistadores relates that the Aztecs had

> . . . two arsenals filled with arms of every description, of which many were ornamented with gold and precious stones. These arms consisted in shields of different sizes, sabres, and a species of broadsword, which is wielded with both hands, the edge furnished with flint stones, so extremely sharp that they cut much better than our Spanish swords: further, lances of greater length than ours, with spikes at their end, full one fathom in length, likewise furnished with several sharp flint stones. The pikes are so very sharp and hard that they will pierce the strongest shield, and cut like a razor; so that the Mexicans even shave themselves with these stones. Then there were excellent bows and arrows, pikes with single and double points, and the proper thongs to throw them with; slings with round stones purposely made for them; also a species of large shield, so ingeniously constructed that it could be rolled up when not wanted; they are only unrolled on the field of battle, and completely cover the whole body from the head to the feet.[6]

This suggests that factors in addition to technological disparity lay behind the Spanish victories. One was the lack of unity amongst the Indian peoples. In both Mexico and Peru the Spaniards were able to use disaffected subject tribes that had been alienated by the oppressive rule of Cuzco and Tenochtitlán. The Indians were also weakened by over regimentation. They had been so indoctrinated and accustomed to carrying out orders without question that when their leaders were overthrown they were incapable of organizing resistance on their own.

This passivity was compounded by religious inhibitions. Both Cortes in Mexico and Pizzaro in Peru were at first believed by the natives to be gods returning in fulfillment of ancient prophecies. This explains the suicidal vacillations of Atahuallpa in Cuzco and of Moctezuma in Tenochtitlán. To Atahuallpa the Spaniards were the creator-god Viracocha and his followers, and, for this reason the ruler waited meekly for Pizzaro, who with his 180 men quickly seized control of the great empire. Likewise, to Moctezuma, Cortes was the god Quetzalcoatl who was returning to claim his rightful throne, so that again the ruler waited listlessly for the Spaniards to ensconce themselves in his capital.

Equally disastrous for the Aztecs was their concept of war as a short-term ritual endeavor. Their main interest in war was to capture prisoners, whose hearts they offered to their gods. Accordingly their campaigns frequently were ceremonial contests during which prisoners were taken with minimal dislocation and destruction. This type of military tradition obviously was a serious handicap. The Spaniards killed to win; the Aztecs tried to take prisoners.

If the great civilizations of the New World lacked the power and the cohesion to resist the Europeans, this was even more true of the less developed food-gathering and intermediate farming culture areas. Precisely because they were less developed, they also had smaller populations, though estimates vary greatly in range. Taking the traditional lower figures, there were, as against the three million in the Inca empire, only about one million in the rest of South America. Likewise, only another million lived north of the Rio Grande as against the three million to the south. When the Europeans appeared, the American Indians in these less developed regions simply lacked the numbers to hold their ground. Their weakness in this respect was accentuated by the diseases that the first explorers brought with them. The Indians, lacking immunity, were decimated by the epidemics, so that the early colonists often found abandoned fields and deserted village sites that they could take over.

Later, when the full flood of immigration from Europe got under way, the Indians were hopelessly overwhelmed. First came the traders who penetrated throughout the Americas with little competition or resistance, for the Americas, unlike Africa, had no rival native merchant class. Then appeared the settlers who, attracted by the combination of salubrious climate and fertile land, came in ever-increasing numbers and inundated the hapless Indians. When the latter occasionally took up arms in desperation, they were foredoomed to failure because they lacked both unity and the basic human and material resources. Thus, the unequal contest ended relatively quickly with the victorious white man in possession of the choice lands and the Indians relegated to reservations or to the less desirable regions that did not interest the new masters.

It is apparent that the balance of forces was quite different in America from what it was in Africa. Geography, relatively small population, and a comparatively low level of economic, political, and social organization all worked against the Indian to make it possible for the Europeans to take over the Americas at a time when they were still confined to a few toeholds on the coasts of Africa. Adam Smith was indeed justified in referring to the Indians as "miserable and helpless Americans" in contrast to the Negroes.

V. AUSTRALIA

Australia is the most isolated large landmass in the world, being more extreme in this respect than the southern tips of South America and of Africa. This isolation made it possible for archaic forms of life to survive to modern times, including plants such as the eucalyptus family, and mammals such as the monotremes and the marsupials. In Australia archaic human types also survived that were still in the Paleolithic stage when the first British settlers arrived in the late eighteenth century. As in the case of the American Indians, the date of the first appearance of the aborigines in Australia has not been determined. Archaeological excavations have led to the pushing of the date progressively back, the latest findings indicating an arrival date of at least 31,000 years ago. Three different ethnic groups ferried over to Australia at that time when only narrow straits separated the continent from the Indonesian archipelago. These three strains are discernible in the present-day aboriginal population. The majority are slender, long-limbed people with brown skins, little body hair, and wavy to curly head hair and beards. They have survived in substantial numbers because they live in desert areas that are of little use to the white man. In the cool and fertile southeastern corner of the continent are a few survivors of a very different native stock—thick set, with light brown skin, heavy body hair, and luxuriant beards. Along the northeastern coast, in the only part of Australia covered with dense tropical rain forest, lives the third ethnic group. Part of the Negroid family, they are small, of slight build, and with woolly hair and black skins.

The culture of these peoples was by no means uniform. The most advanced were those in the southeast, where rainfall was adequate for permanent settlements. But throughout the continent, the aborigines, thanks to their complete isolation, had remained Paleolithic food gatherers. Their retardation was particularly evident in their technology and in their political organization. They wore no clothing except for decorative purposes. Their housing consisted, in dry country, of simple, open windbreaks, and, in wet country, of low, domed huts thrown together of any available material. Their principal weapons were spears, spear throwers, and boomerangs, all made of wood. They were ignorant of pottery, their utensils consisting merely of a few twined bags and baskets and occasional bowls made of bark or wood. As food gatherers and hunters they were highly skilled and ingenious. They had a wide range of vegetable, as well as animal, foods, and an intimate knowledge of the varieties, habits, and properties of these foods. They did all in their power to keep up the rate of reproduction of the plants and animals on which they depended. But not being food producers, their method of ensuring an adequate food supply was one of ritual rather than of cultivation. A typical ceremony was the mixing of blood with earth in places where the increase of game or plants was desired.

The poverty of Australian technology was matched by an almost equal poverty of political organization. Like most food-gathering peoples, the aborigines lived in bands, groups of families who normally camped together and roamed over a well-defined territory. They had no real tribes, but only territorial divisions characterized by differences in language and culture. Consequently, they did not have chiefs, courts, or other formal agencies of government. Yet these same aborigines had an extraordinarily complex social organization and ceremonial life. The hunter who brought in game or the woman who returned from a day of root digging was required to divide his take with all his kin according to strict regulations. Among the northern Queensland natives, when a man sneezed, all those within hearing slapped themselves on their bodies, the place varying according to their precise relationship to the sneezer.

So involved were these nonmaterial aspects of Australian society that they have been a delight to students of primitive institutions. But precociousness in these matters was of little help to the aborigines when the Europeans appeared in the late eighteenth century. If the American Indians with their flowering civilizations and widespread agricultural communities were unable to stand up to the white man, the Paleolithic Australians obviously had no chance. They were few in numbers, totaling about 300,000 when the Europeans arrived. This meant one or two persons per square mile in favorable coastal or river valley environments, and only one person every 30 to 40 square miles in the arid interior. In addition to this numerical weakness, the aborigines lacked both the arms and the organization necessary for effective resistance.

And unlike the American Indians and the African Negroes, they showed little inclination to secure and use the white man's "fire stick." Thus the unfortunate aborigines were brutally decimated by the British immigrants, many of whom were lawless convicts shipped out from overcrowded jails. The combination of disease, alcoholism, outright slaughter, and wholesale land confiscation reduced the native population to 45,000 today, together with some 80,000 mixed breeds. The treatment accorded to the Australians is suggested by the following typical observation of a Victorian settler in 1853: "The Australian aboriginal race seems doomed by Providence, like the Mohican and many other well known tribes, to disappear from their native soil before the progress of civilization." [7]

Even more tragic was the fate of the approximately 2,500 Tasmanians who were separated by the Bass Strait from Australia. What the Australian aborigines lacked, the Tasmanians lacked too, and still more. They did without spear throwers, boomerangs, nets, and all other implements for fishing. The British sent their most hardened criminals to Tasmania, and when these landed in 1803 they proceeded to hunt the natives as though they were animals. Within a few decades the majority were wiped out. The last male died in 1869 and the last female in 1876. This woman—Truganini—was born in 1803, the opening year of the white invasion, so that her life spanned the entire period of the extermination of her people. She begged that her body not be dissected, but despite her pitiful request her skeleton stands in Hobart Museum—an apt memorial to the fate of a people doomed because they happened to settle in an inaccessible and unstimulating portion of the globe. A Reverend Thomas Atkins, who witnessed the extermination of the natives, was moved to deduce certain conclusions that are relevant not only for Tasmania but for all the portions of the globe where the Europeans encountered peoples retarded in their material arts:

> Indeed, from a large induction of facts, it seems to me to be a universal law in the Divine government, when savage tribes who live by hunting and fishing, and on the wild herbs, roots and fruits of the earth, come into collision with civilised races of men, whose avocations are the depasturing of flocks and herds, agricultural employment and commercial pursuits, the savage tribes disappear before the progress of civilised races. . . . [8]

SUGGESTED READING

On the American Indians the most recent study is the well-written and stimulating work by P. Farb, *Man's Rise to Civilization as Shown by the Indians of North America from Primeval Times to the Coming of the Industrial State* (New York: Dutton, 1968), which does not hesitate to point out the significance for modern man of the experiences of the Indians. The latest information on the crossing of the Indians from Siberia to Alaska is in W. G. Haag, "The Bering Strait Land Bridge," *Scientific American*, January, 1962, pp. 112–23. An excellent collection of readings is provided by H. E. Driver, ed., *The Americas on the Eve of Discovery* (Englewood Cliffs, N.J.: Prentice-Hall, 1964) and also the short survey by J. Collier, *Indians of the Americas* (New York: New American Library, 1947). A more detailed and more recent study of all American Indians is by A. M. Josephy, Jr., *The Indian Heritage of America* (New York: Knopf, 1968). The standard work on the South American Indians is by J. H. Steward and L. C. Faron, *Native Peoples of South America* (New York: McGraw-Hill, 1959), and a more readable, yet reliable, account is provided by C. Beals, *Nomads and Empire Builders: Native Peoples and Cultures of South America* (Philadelphia: Chilton, 1961). The leading comparative study of the Indians from the Arctic to Panama is by H. E. Driver, *Indians of North America* (Chicago: Univ. of Chicago, 1961). V. W. Von Hagen has readable accounts of all three of the leading American civilizations: *The Aztec: Man and Tribe* (New York: New American Library, 1958); *The Incas: People of the Sun* (Cleveland: World, 1961); and *World of the Maya* (New York: New American Library, 1960). Other important studies of these civilizations are by S. G. Morley, *The Ancient Maya* (Stanford: Stanford Univ., 1946); F. A. Peterson, *Ancient Mexico: An Introduction to the Pre-Hispanic Cultures* (New York: Putnam, 1964); L. Baudin, *A Socialist Empire: The Incas of Peru* (Princeton: Van Nostrand, 1961); and J. A. Mason, *The Ancient Civilizations of Peru* (Baltimore: Penguin, 1947). The best general book on the Eskimos is by K. Birket Smith, *The Eskimos* (London: Methuen, 1959).

For the Australian aborigines the standard works are A. P. Elkin, *The Australian Aborigines*, 3rd ed. (Sydney: Angus, 1954); W. E. Harney, *Life Among the Aborigines* (London: Hale, 1957); R. M. and C. H. Berndt, *The World of the First Australians: An Introduction to the Traditional Life of the Australian Aborigines* (Chicago: Univ. of Chicago, 1964); and A. A. Abbie, *The Original Australians* (London: Muller, 1969). There is also the classic pioneer anthropological study by Baldwin Spencer and F. J. Gillen, *The Native Tribes of Central Australia* (London: Macmillan, 1899). Clive Turnbull's *Black War: The Extermination of the Tasmanian Aborigines* (Victoria: Melbourne Univ., 1949) is a harrowing documentary account of the decimation of the Tasmanians by the zealous ministrations of well-wishers who tried to Christianize and civilize them, as well as by the greed and lust of convicts and settlers. Another good short account of this tragedy, with excellent illustrations, is by R. Travers, *The Tasmanians* (London: Cassell, 1969).

. . . a technological revolution by which
the West made its fortune, got the better
of all the other living civilizations,
and forcibly united them into a single
society of literally world-wide range.
The revolutionary Western invention
was the substitution of the Ocean
for the Steppe as the principal medium
for world communication. This use
of the Ocean, first by sailing ships
and then by steamship, enabled the West
to unify the whole inhabited
and habitable world, including the Americas.

A. J. TOYNBEE

Epilogue:

The World on the Eve

of Europe's Expansion

During the medieval millennium between 500 and 1500, profound changes occurred in the global balance of power. At the outset the West was a turbulent outpost of the Eurasian ecumene, wracked by imperial disintegration and recurring invasions. As late as the twelfth century, the English chronicler William of Malmesbury voiced a sense of isolation and insecurity:

> The world is not evenly divided. Of its three parts, our enemies hold Asia as their hereditary home—a part of the world which our forefathers rightly considered equal to the other two put together. Yet here formerly our Faith put out its branches; here all the Apostles save two met their deaths. But now the Christians of those parts, if there are any left, squeeze a bare subsistence from the soil and pay tribute to their enemies, looking to us with silent longings for the liberty they have lost. Africa too, the second part of the world, has been held by our enemies by force of arms for two hundred years and more, a danger to Christendom all the greater because it formerly sustained the highest spirits— men whose works will keep the rust of age from Holy Writ as

long as the Latin tongue survives. Thirdly, there is Europe, the remaining region of the world. Of this region we Christians inhabit only a part, for who will give the name of Christians to those barbarians who live in the remote islands and seek their living on the icy ocean as if they were whales? This little portion of the world which is ours is pressed upon by warlike Turks and Saracens: for three hundred years they have held Spain and the Balearic Islands, and they live in hope of devouring the rest.[1]

But already by that time the tide had begun to turn. The West was developing the internal resources and the dynamism that found expression first in the protracted and successful crusades against Moslems and pagans, and later in the overseas expansion to all parts of the globe. By contrast, Ming China was withdrawing into seclusion, while the Ottoman Turks, after futile efforts to expel the Portuguese from the Indian Ocean, concluded resignedly, "God has given the land to us, but the sea to the Christians." Equally revealing is the fact that in his famous *Memoirs*, Babur, the founder of the Mogul Empire, never once mentioned the Portuguese, nor did any Mogul navy ever attempt to restore Moslem primacy in the Indian Ocean. The seas of the world thus were left wide open for the Westerners, who took prompt advantage of the opportunity. The significance for world affairs is apparent in the following comment by an Ottoman observer in 1625:

> Now the Europeans have learnt to know the whole world; they send their ships everywhere and seize important ports. Formerly, the goods of India, Sind, and China used to come to Suez, and were distributed by Muslims to all the world. But now these goods are carried on Portuguese, Dutch, and English ships to Frangistan, and are spread all over the world from there. What they do not need themselves they bring to Istanbul and other Islamic lands, and sell it for five times the price, thus earning much money. For this reason gold and silver are becoming scarce in the lands of Islam. The Ottoman Empire must seize the shores of Yemen and the trade passing that way; otherwise before very long, the Europeans will rule over the lands of Islam.[2]

If this perceptive analysis is compared with that of William of Malmesbury half a millennium earlier, the basic change in the global configuration becomes evident. Indeed so basic was this change that it marked the advent of the modern age of Western predominance.

The earlier Classical and Medieval ages had been heralded by land invasions by nomads who utilized their superior mobility to break into the centers of civilization when imperial weakness presented the opportunity. The modern age, by contrast, was heralded by sea invasions by the Westerners, who functioned with equal mobility on the world's oceans and thus were free to operate on a global scale.

In addition to their unchallenged maritime superiority the Westerners possessed the more important advantage of overall technological superiority that increased steadily during the following centuries. Thus whereas the sixteenth-century Europeans with their ocean sailing ships and naval artillery enjoyed an advantage comparable to that of iron weapons over bronze, by the nineteenth century their steamships and factory industries and machine guns gave them an advantage more akin to that of the agriculturist over the hunter. Thus the Europeans established their global hegemony as inexorably as the Bantus displaced the Bushmen, or the Mongoloids the Ainus. In doing so the Europeans brought all continents for the first time into direct contact with each other, thereby ending the Eurasian phase of world history and beginning the global. (See Map XXII, "Culture Areas of the World About 1500.")

NOTES
AND INDEX

Notes

CHAPTER 1

[1] F. Boas, "Racial Purity," *Asia*, XL (May, 1940), 231.

CHAPTER 2

[1] A. R. Radcliffe-Brown, *The Andaman Islanders* (New York: The Free Press, 1948), p. 192.

[2] K. Rasmussen, *People of the Polar North* (Philadelphia: Lippincott, 1908), p. 124.

[3] Leo Frobenius and Douglas C. Fox, *Prehistoric Rock Pictures in Europe and Africa.* pp. 22–23. Copyright by The Museum of Modern Art, New York, 1937, 1965, and reprinted with permission.

[4] M. D. Sahlins and E. R. Service, eds., *Evolution and Culture* (Ann Arbor: Univ. of Michigan, 1960), pp. 75, 77.

CHAPTER 3

[1] L. R. Binford and S. R. Binford, *New Perspectives in Archeology* (Chicago: Aldine, 1968), p. 328.

[2] Lewis H. Morgan, *Houses and House-life of the American Aborigines* (New York, 1881), p. 45.

[3] John Greenway, *The Primitive Reader* (Hatboro, Pa.: Folklore Associates, 1965), pp. 34–35.
[4] P. Radin, ed., *Crashing Thunder: The Autobiography of an American Indian* (New York: Appleton-Century-Crofts, 1926), pp. 56, 73.

CHAPTER 4

[1] R. Linton, *The Study of Man* (New York: Appleton-Century-Crofts, 1936), p. 353.
[2] Cited by Nels Bailkey, "Early Mesopotamian Constitutional Development," *American Historical Review*, LXXII (July, 1967), 1225.

CHAPTER 5

[1] E. A. Speiser, "The Beginnings of Civilization in Mesopotamia," *Supplement to the Journal of the American Oriental Society*, December, 1939, p. 27.
[2] Cited by *Arab World*, November–December, 1962, p. 3.

CHAPTER 6

[1] Adapted from J. Hawkes and L. Wooley, *Prehistory and the Beginnings of Civilization*, UNESCO History of Mankind, Vol. 1 (New York: Harper & Row, 1963), p. 467; and V. Gordon Childe, *Man Makes Himself* (New York: New American Library, 1951), p. 149. Mentor Book.
[2] E. R. Service, *The Hunters* (Englewood Cliffs, N. J.: Prentice-Hall, 1966), p. 69.
[3] R. Redfield, *Peasant Society and Culture* (Chicago: Univ. of Chicago, 1956), p. 79.
[4] O. Handlin, *The Uprooted* (Boston: Little, Brown, 1951), p. 7.
[5] *The New York Times*, December 25, 1957.
[6] V. Gordon Childe, *What Happened in History* (Baltimore: Penguin, 1942), p. 130.
[7] V. Gordon Childe, *op. cit.*, p. 131.
[8] V. Gordon Childe, *What Happened in History*, p. 69.
[9] W. H. and C. V. Wiser, *Behind Mud Walls 1930–1960* (Berkeley: Univ. of California, 1964), pp. 117–18.
[10] M. Covensky, *The Ancient Near Eastern Tradition* (New York: Harper & Row, 1966), pp. 102–4. Reprinted by permission of the publishers.

CHAPTER 7

[1] Cited by R. Ghirshman, *Iran* (Baltimore: Penguin, 1954), p. 182.
[2] Cited by G. Coedès, *The Making of South East Asia* (London: Routledge and Kegan Paul, 1966), pp. 52, 61.
[3] F. Hirth, *China and the Roman Orient* (Shanghai, 1885), p. 39.
[4] *Ibid.*, p. 42.
[5] Cited by G. F. Hudson, *Europe & China* (London: Arnold, 1931), p. 77.
[6] *Ibid.*, p. 114.
[7] Cited by Ying-shih Yü, *Trade and Expansion in Han China* (Berkeley: Univ. of California, 1967), p. 214.
[8] *The Geography of Strabo*, Book I, Chap. 4, trans. H. C. Hamilton and W. Falconer (London, 1854), p. 104.
[9] H. Frankfort, "The Ancient Near East," in *Orientalism and History*, ed. D. Sinor (Cambridge, Eng.: W. Heffer & Sons, 1954), p. 12.

CHAPTER 8

1 J. Lévy, *The Economic Life of the Ancient World,* ed. J. G. Birain (Chicago: Univ. of Chicago, 1967), p. 22.

2 Plato, *Laws,* III, 692.

3 Thucydides, *The Peloponnesian War* (trans. B. Jowett), Book II, Chap. 37.

4 Plato, *Apology,* in *Dialogues of Plato* (trans. B. Jowett).

5 Cited by F. M. Cornford, *Greek Religious Thought from Homer to the Age of Alexander* (London: J. H. Dent, 1923), p. 85.

6 Cited by C. J. Singer, *A History of Biology* (New York: H. Schuman, 1950), p. 4.

7 Cited by W. R. Agard, *The Greek Mind* (Princeton: Van Nostrand, 1957), p. 123.

8 *Politics,* I, 5, 2, 1254a; I, 5, 8, 1256b.

9 Herodotus, *The Persian Wars* (trans. G. Rawlinson), Book VII, Chap. 104.

10 Thucydides, *The Peloponnesian War* (trans. B. Jowett), Book I, Chap. 22.

11 Cited by J. Lévy, *The Economic Life of the Ancient World,* ed. J. G. Birain (Chicago: Univ. of Chicago, 1967), p. 31.

12 Polybius, *The Histories* (trans. W. R. Paton), Book V, 104.

13 Cicero, *First Part of the Speech against Gaius Verres at the First Hearing* (New York, 1928), Chap. V.

14 Cited by J. Carcopino, *Daily Life in Ancient Rome* (New Haven: Yale Univ., 1940), p. 50.

15 A. Piganiol, *L'Empire Chrétien* (Paris: Presses Universitaires de France, 1947), p. 422.

16 R. S. Lopez, *The Birth of Europe* (New York: Evans, 1967), p. 23.

17 *Life of Marcellus,* from *Plutarch's Lives,* Vol. 3, trans. J. and W. Langhorne (London, 1821), pp. 119 ff.

18 Lévy, *The Economic Life of the Ancient World,* p. 99.

19 Lopez, *The Birth of Europe,* p. 20.

CHAPTER 9

1 Cited by D. D. Kosambi, *Ancient India* (New York: Pantheon, 1965), p. 154.

2 Herodotus, *The Persian Wars* (trans. G. Rawlinson), Book III, Chap. 94.

3 *Ibid.,* Book VII, Chap. 65.

4 *Kantilya's Arthashastra,* trans. R. Shamasastry (Mysore: Mysore Printing and Publishing House, 1915), p. 288.

5 N. A. Nikam and R. McKeon, *The Edicts of Asoka* (Chicago: Univ. of Chicago, 1959), pp. 27–28.

6 Fa-hien, *A Record of Buddhistic Kingdoms,* trans. J. Legge (Oxford: Clarendon, 1886), pp. 42–43.

CHAPTER 10

1 A. Waley, "The Book of Changes," *Bulletin of the Museum of Far Eastern Antiquities,* No. 5 (Stockholm, 1934), cited by C. P. Fitzgerald, *China: A Short Cultural History,* rev. ed. (New York: Praeger, 1950), p. 81.

CHAPTER 11

1 Cited by A. F. Wright, *Buddhism in Chinese History* (Stanford: Stanford Univ., 1959), pp. 19–20.

2 M. Loewe, *Everyday Life in Early Imperial China* (New York: Putnam, 1968), pp. 138–41. © 1968, B. T. Batsford, Ltd., London.

3 Wing-tsit Chan, *Religious Trends in Modern China* (New York: Columbia Univ., 1953), pp. 141–43.

4 J. Needham, *Science and Civilisation in China* (London: Cambridge Univ., 1954), I, 209–10.

5 J. M. Keynes, *Essays in Persuasion* (New York: Harcourt, 1932), pp. 360–61.

6 A. H. M. Jones, "The Decline and Fall of the Roman Empire," *History*, XL, No. 140 (October, 1955), 220.

7 Cited by F. Klemm, *A History of Western Technology* (London: George Allen and Unwin, 1959), p. 23.

8 W. W. Rostow, *The Process of Economic Growth*, 2nd ed. (New York, W. W. Norton, 1962), pp. 311–12.

9 E. O. Reischauer and J. K. Fairbank, *East Asia, The Great Tradition* (Boston: Houghton Mifflin, 1958), p. 136.

10 Cited by M. Hadas, *A History of Rome* (New York: Doubleday, 1956), pp. 204–5.

11 F. Braudel, *Civilisation materielle et capitalisme, XVe–XVIIIe siècle* (Paris: Librairie Armand Colin, 1967), I, 116.

12 R. Lopez, *The Birth of Europe* (New York: M. Evans, 1967), p. 58.

Chapter 12

1 H. Yule, ed., *Cathay and the Way Thither*, Hakluyt Society, Series 2, XXXVII (London, 1914), 152, 154.

2 Cited by J. Needham, *Science and Civilisation in China* (London: Cambridge Univ., 1954), I, 219.

3 *Novum Organum*, Book I, aphorism 129.

4 W. W. Rockhill, ed., *The Journey of William of Rubruck* (London: Hakluyt Society, 1900), pp. 236–37.

5 Cited by C. R. Beazley, *The Dawn of Modern Geography* (London: John Murray, 1901), II, 366.

6 Adapted from C. R. Beazley, ed., *The Texts and Versions of John de Plano Carpini and William de Rubruquis* (London: Hakluyt Society, 1903), ex. ser. vol. 13, pp. 109–111.

Chapter 13

1 Cited by B. Lewis, *The Arabs in History* (London: Hutchinson's University Library, 1950), p. 82.

2 Cited by A. Mieli, *La science arabe* (Leiden: Brill, 1939), p. 376.

3 Cited by B. Lewis, *op. cit.*, p. 148.

4 Cited by Lewis, *op. cit.*, p. 146.

Chapter 14

1 O. Lattimore, "Chingis Khan and the Mongol Conquests," *Scientific American*, August, 1963, p. 68.

2 Cited by J. A. Boyle, "The Mongol Invasion of Eastern Persia 1220–1223," *History Today*, September, 1963, p. 617.

3 *Matthew Paris's English History*, trans. J. A. Giles (London, 1852), I, 312–13.

4 Cited by T. W. Arnold, *The Preaching of Islam* (London: Constable, 1913), p. 365.

5 *Travels of Marco Polo*, trans. R. Latham (Baltimore: Penguin, 1958), p. 225.

6 Ibn Khaldun, *Muqaddimah*, trans. F. Rosenthal (New York: Pantheon, 1958), 250–58.

7 M. Meyerhof in *The Legacy of Islam*, ed. T. Arnold and A. Guillaume (Oxford: Clarendon, 1931), p. 354.

CHAPTER 15

[1] Cited by G. L. Seidler, *The Emergence of the Eastern World* (London: Pergamon Press, 1968), p. 97.

[2] Cited by S. Vryonis, Jr. *Byzantium and Europe* (New York: Harcourt, Brace & World, 1967), p. 183.

[3] Cited by Seidler, *op. cit.*, pp. 95–96.

[4] Cited by Seidler, *op. cit.*, pp. 116–17.

[5] Cited by Vryonis, *op. cit.*, pp. 190–92.

[6] S. H. Cross, *The Russian Primary Chronicle,* Harvard Studies and Notes in Philology and Literature, XII (1930), 199.

[7] Cited by J. S. Curtiss, *Church and State in Russia: The Last Years of the Empire, 1900–1917* (New York: Columbia Univ., 1940), p. 8.

[8] Cited by P. Miliukov, *Outlines of Russian Culture* (Philadelphia: University of Pennsylvania Press, 1942), I, 15.

[9] Cited by P. Miliukov, *op. cit.*, I, 16.

387

CHAPTER 16

[1] Cited by J. Needham, *Science and Civilization in China,* Vol. I (London: Cambridge Univ., 1954), p. 123.

[2] Adapted from E. D. Ross, "The Orkhon Inscriptions," *Bulletin, School of Oriental Studies,* London, V, 4 (1930), pp. 862, 864–65.

[3] Cited by C. P. Fitzgerald, *China: A Short Cultural History* (New York: Praeger, 1935), p. 336.

[4] L. Wieger, *Textes Historiques* (Hsienhsien: 1929), II, 1656. Cited by Needham, *op. cit.*, I, 140.

[5] Cited by H. Yule, ed., *Cathay and the Way Thither,* Hakluyt Society, Series 2, Vol. XXXVII (London, 1914), 154.

[6] Cited by L. C. Goodrich, *A Short History of the Chinese People,* rev. ed. (New York: Harper & Row, 1943), p. 200.

CHAPTER 17

[1] Francis Bacon, *Novum organum,* Aphorism 129.

[2] Cited by R. S. Lopez, *The Birth of Europe* (Philadelphia: Lippincott, 1967), p. 146.

[3] Cited by L. White, "Dynamo and Virgin Reconsidered," *American Scholar* (1958), p. 192.

[4] Mailhard de la Couture, ed., *Chroniques de Villehardouin et de Henri de Valenciennes, De la Conquête de Constantinople* (Paris, 1889), pp. 63–64.

[5] A. G. Keller, "A Byzantine Admirer of 'Western' Progress: Cardinal Bessarion," *Cambridge Historical Journal,* XI (1955), 343–48.

[6] Cited by J. H. Parry, *The Age of Reconnaissance* (Cleveland: World, 1963), p. 19.

[7] Cited by Gide Santillana, ed., *The Age of Adventure* (Mentor Book, 1956), p. 17.

CHAPTER 18

[1] P. Bohannan, *Africa and Africans* (New York: American Museum of Science, 1964), pp. 67–68.

[2] Cited by T. Hodgkin, "Islam in West Africa," *Africa South,* II (April–June, 1958), p. 93.

[3] Leo Africanus, *A History and Description of Africa,* Vol. III, ed. R. Brown (London: Hakluyt Society, 1896), p. 825.

4 Cited by B. Davidson, *Africa in History: Themes and Outlines* (New York: Macmillan, 1968), p. 76.

5 Ibn Battuta, *Travels in Asia and Africa, 1325–1354*, trans. H. A. R. Gibb (London: Routledge, 1929), pp. 329–30.

6 Cited by T. Hodgkin, "Kingdoms of the Western Sudan," in *The Dawn of African History*, ed. R. Oliver (London: Oxford Univ., 1961), p. 43.

7 Cited by Davidson, *op. cit.*, p. 63.

8 Cited *ibid.*, p. 168.

9 T. Hodgkin, "Islam in West Africa," *Africa South*, II (April–June, 1958), 98.

10 Davidson, *op. cit.*, p. 125.

11 Cited by K. O. Dike, *Trade and Politics in the Niger Delta, 1830–1885* (New York: Oxford Univ., 1956), p. 7.

12 Adam Smith, *Wealth of Nations* (Edinburgh, 1838), p. 286.

Chapter 19

1 P. Farb, *Man's Rise to Civilization as Shown by the Indians of North America from Primeval Times to the Coming of the Industrial State* (New York: Dutton, 1968), p. 231.

2 J. I. Lockhart, trans., *The Memoirs of the Conquistador Bernal Diaz del Castillo* (London: J. Hatchard, 1844), I, 238.

3 Farb, *op. cit.*, p. 179.

4 Lockhart, *op. cit.*, I, 142.

5 R. M. Adams, "Early Civilizations, Subsistence, and Environment," in *City Invincible*, ed. R. M. Adams and C. H. Kraeling (Chicago: Univ. of Chicago, 1960), p. 270.

6 Lockhart, *op. cit.*, I, 231–32.

7 Cited by A. G. Price, *White Settlers and Native Peoples* (Victoria: Melbourne Univ., 1949), p. 121.

8 Cited by C. Turnbull, *Black War: The Extermination of the Tasmanian Aborigines* (Victoria: Melbourne Univ., 1948), pp. 2–3.

Chapter 20

1 Cited by W. Clark, "New Europe and The New Nations," *Daedalus* (Winter, 1964), p. 136.

2 Cited by B. Lewis, *The Emergence of Modern Turkey* (New York: Oxford Univ., 1961), p. 28.

Index

389